CompTIA Security+ 701 Made Easy

www.Yavoz.tech

By Yavo (Kie Yavorsky)

Get Started In IT Or Advance Your IT Career!

About this Book

This book is a foundation to help you understand the concepts needed to help you pass the CompTIA security+ certification exam. I recommend you use this book in addition to the video course provided for free by Professor Messer on YouTube.

https://www.youtube.com/watch?v=KiEptGbnEBc&list=PLG49S3nxzAnl4QDVqK-hOnoqcSKEIDDuv

Pairing this book with a great video course is a great way to prepare for the exam.

The steps to follow to prepare for the CompTIA Security+ exam in my opinion are to complete the follow in this order. Step 1: read this book. Step 2: Watch and complete the free Professor Messer YouTube Course so you have heard all the material twice. And finally Step 3: Test your knowledge with practice questions using resources from great sites like TopCyberPros.com and other sites.

https://topcyberpro.com/

Then when you're ready and you're regularly scoring roughly 90% on practice questions don't wait, go take your exam.

About the Exam

DOMAIN	PERCENTAGE OF EXAMINATION
General Security Concepts	12%
Threats, Vulnerabilities, and Mitigations	22%
Security Architecture	18%
Security Operations	28%
Security Program Management and Oversight	20%

Test Details	What You Need to know
Required exam	SY0-701
Number of questions	Maximum of 90
Types of questions	There are mostly multiple-choice questions and a handful of performance-based questions otherwise referred to as lab-questions. You need to correctly answer at least one performance-based question to pass.
Length of test	90 minutes

This link provides information on the policies and procedures related to CompTIA certification exams.

https://comptia.org/testing/testing-policies-procedures

The page includes several sections that describe different policies and procedures, including:

Test Policies: This section includes information on the CompTIA Candidate Code of Ethics Policy, Candidate Testing Policies, CompTIA Voucher Terms & Conditions, Candidate ID Policy, Certification Retake Policy, Exam Delivery Policies, Continuing Education Policies, Exam Development, Sharing Your Exam Results, Unauthorized Training Materials, Candidate Appeals Process, CompTIA Exam Security Hotline, and CompTIA Data Forensics.

CompTIA Candidate Agreement: This section describes the agreement that all certification candidates must agree to before taking a CompTIA exam. It includes information on modifications to exams and certification requirements, compliance with certification exam policies and the code of ethics, and the consequences of violating the agreement.

Exam Delivery Policies: This section provides information on the policies related to the delivery of CompTIA certification exams. It includes information on delivery exclusions, beta testing, and testing center suspensions.

- Certification Exam Policies: This section describes the policies related to CompTIA certification exams, including the tester's consent before taking the exam.
- Candidate Testing Policies: This section includes information on accommodations during an exam, exam scoring, exam content, international testing policies, candidate retesting, and candidate photographs.
- CompTIA Certification Retake Policy: This section provides information on the policy related to retaking a CompTIA certification exam, including waiting periods, beta examinations, and exam price.

Where can you take the exam?

CompTIA Security+ certification exams can be taken either online or in-person at any of the thousands of Pearson VUE test centers located around the world. To find the nearest testing center, visit the CompTIA Certification page on the official Pearson VUE website, select "Find a test center," enter your home address, and click on the search button. Appointments may be made in advance or on the day you wish to test, subject to availability. Pearson VUE offers a variety of scheduling options: online scheduling, scheduling by phone, and scheduling directly through the test center. Before taking a CompTIA exam, all certification candidates will be prompted to agree with the CompTIA Candidate Agreement.

To find a Pearson VUE testing center, you can visit the CompTIA Certification page on the official Pearson VUE website

https://home.pearsonvue.com/comptia

and then selecting "Find a test center" on the right. Then, enter your home address and click on the search button. The website will list the nearest testing locations, and you can choose the one that suits you best and proceed with scheduling your exam. Alternatively, you can search for other types of testing centers by using search engines or visiting specific websites. Pearson VUE has a network of more than 5,000 testing centers in 165 countries, and you can find a Pearson VUE Authorized Test Center near you by visiting the Pearson VUE website and using its Test Center Locator. You can also take a photo tour of a Pearson Professional Center on the Pearson VUE website to get an idea of what to expect when you arrive at the testing center. Before taking a CompTIA exam, all certification candidates will be prompted to agree with the CompTIA Candidate Agreement.

DoD 8570 and DoD 8140

One of the major reasons having a CompTIA security+ is so important on your resume is because of DoD 8570 and DoD 8140. These government charts of certifications can be thought about as a bingo chart, and different IT jobs require hiring professionals at different levels.

IA Technical		
IAT Level I	**IAT Level II**	**IAT Level III**
A+ CE CCNA-Security CND Network+ CE	CCNA-Security CySA+ CND Security+ CE	CASP CE CCNP CISA CISSP (or Associate)
IA Management		
IAM Level I	**IAM Level II**	**IAM Level III**
CGRC CND Cloud+ Security+ CE	CGRC CASP CISM CISSP (or Associate) CCISO	CISM CISSP (or Associate) CCISO
IA System Architecture and Engineering		
IASAE Level I	**IASAE Level II**	**IASAE Level III**
CASP CE CISSP (or Associate) CSSLP	CASP CE CISSP (or Associate) CSSLP	CISSP-ISSAP CISSP-ISSEP

Cyber Security Service Provider				
CSSP Analyst	**CSSP Infrastructure Support**	**CSSP Incident Responder**	**CSSP Auditor**	**CSSP Manager**
CEH CFR CySA+	CEH CySA+ CND CHFI Cloud+	CEH CFR CHFI Cloud+	CEH CySA+ CISA Cloud+ CHFI	CISM CCISO

The CompTIA Security+ certification appears multiple times on this bingo chart and allows you to qualify for a wide range of IT roles. If you want to better IT job you need the certifications to qualify for that IT job. The CompTIA Security+ allows you to qualify for a large range of IT jobs and is one of the best places to start your IT journey.

A video explanation can be found at
https://www.YouTube.com/watch?v=i0bL0w2mXY4

DoD 8570 is a directive that governs the information assurance functions of Department of Defense systems and those with access to them. It establishes the policies and responsibilities of Department of Defense information assurance, including training, certification, and workforce management. DoD 8570 is a baseline requirement for access to DoD IT systems, and compliance is required of all authorized users of a DoD Information System, including contractors as well as government employees. DoD 8570 compliance can be achieved by obtaining a number of different certifications, and there is no single certification called '8570.' The certifications required depend on the job category and level of access to DoD information systems. The Defense Information Systems Agency provides a list of DoD-approved baseline certifications. DoD 8570 is not a certification itself, but a policy that outlines cybersecurity certification requirements for specific job categories. DoD 8570 has been replaced by DoD 8140, but didn't change it much, which expands on 8570 to leverage the Defense Cybersecurity Workforce Framework (DCWF), which draws from the original National Initiative for Cybersecurity Education (NICE) Cybersecurity Workforce Framework (NCWF) and the DoD Joint Cyberspace Training and Certification Standards (JCT&CS). The 8140 Directive canceled and replaced DoD 8570.01, but it is taking a few years for the Department of Defense to develop a new manual; therefore, the 8570 manual is still current for the time being until it is formally canceled. DoD 8570 was established in 2005 to assess and manage the cybersecurity workforce of the Department of Defense. It was replaced by DoD 8140 in 2015, which expands upon it. DoD 8570 compliance is required of all authorized users of a DoD Information System, including contractors as well as government employees. Compliance can be achieved by obtaining a number of different certifications, and there is no single certification called '8570.' The certifications required depend on the job category and level of access to DoD information systems.

Acronyms You'll Encounter

Acronym	Meaning
AAA	Authentication, Authorization, and Accounting
ACL	Access Control List
AES	Advanced Encryption Standard
AES-256	Advanced Encryption Standards 256-bit
AH	Authentication Header
AI	Artificial Intelligence
AIS	Automated Indicator Sharing
ALE	Annualized Loss Expectancy
AP	Access Point
API	Application Programming Interface
APT	Advanced Persistent Threat
ARO	Annualized Rate of Occurrence
ARP	Address Resolution Protocol
ASLR	Address Space Layout Randomization
ATT&CK	Adversarial Tactics, Techniques, and Common Knowledge
AUP	Acceptable Use Policy
AV	Antivirus
BASH	Bourne Again Shell
BCP	Business Continuity Planning
BGP	Border Gateway Protocol
BIA	Business Impact Analysis
BIOS	Basic Input/Output System
BPA	Business Partners Agreement
BPDU	Bridge Protocol Data Unit
BYOD	Bring Your Own Device
CA	Certificate Authority
CAPTCHA	Completely Automated Public Turing Test to Tell

	Computers and Humans Apart
CAR	Corrective Action Report
CASB	Cloud Access Security Broker
CBC	Cipher Block Chaining
CCMP	Counter Mode/CBC-MAC Protocol
CCTV	Closed-circuit Television
CERT	Computer Emergency Response Team
CFB	Cipher Feedback
CHAP	Challenge Handshake Authentication Protocol
CIA	Confidentiality, Integrity, Availability
CIO	Chief Information Officer
CIRT	Computer Incident Response Team
CMS	Content Management System
COOP	Continuity of Operation Planning
COPE	Corporate Owned, Personally Enabled
CP	Contingency Planning
CRC	Cyclical Redundancy Check
CRL	Certificate Revocation List
CSO	Chief Security Officer
CSP	Cloud Service Provider
CSR	Certificate Signing Request
CSRF	Cross-site Request Forgery
CSU	Channel Service Unit
CTM	Counter Mode
CTO	Chief Technology Officer
CVE	Common Vulnerability Enumeration
CVSS	Common Vulnerability Scoring System
CYOD	Choose Your Own Device
DAC	Discretionary Access Control
DBA	Database Administrator
DDoS	Distributed Denial of

	Service
DEP	Data Execution Prevention
DES	Digital Encryption Standard
DHCP	Dynamic Host Configuration Protocol
DHE	Diffie-Hellman Ephemeral
DKIM	DomainKeys Identified Mail
DLL	Dynamic Link Library
DLP	Data Loss Prevention
DMARC	Domain Message Authentication Reportingand Conformance
DNAT	Destination Network Address Translation
DNS	Domain Name System
DoS	Denial of Service
DPO	Data Privacy Officer
DRP	Disaster Recovery Plan
DSA	Digital Signature Algorithm
DSL	Digital Subscriber Line
EAP	Extensible Authentication Protocol
ECB	Electronic Code Book
ECC	Elliptic Curve Cryptography
ECDHE	Elliptic Curve Diffie-Hellman Ephemeral
ECDSA	Elliptic Curve Digital Signature Algorithm
EDR	Endpoint Detection and Response
EFS	Encrypted File System
ERP	Enterprise Resource Planning
ESN	Electronic Serial Number
ESP	Encapsulated Security Payload
FACL	File System Access Control List
FDE	Full Disk Encryption
FIM	File Integrity Management
FPGA	Field Programmable Gate

	Array
FRR	False Rejection Rate
FTP	File Transfer Protocol
FTPS	Secured File Transfer Protocol
GCM	Galois Counter Mode
GDPR	General Data Protection Regulation
GPG	Gnu Privacy Guard
GPO	Group Policy Object
GPS	Global Positioning System
GPU	Graphics Processing Unit
GRE	Generic Routing Encapsulation
HA	High Availability
HDD	Hard Disk Drive
HIDS	Host-based Intrusion Detection System
HIPS	Host-based Intrusion Prevention System
HMAC	Hashed Message Authentication Code
HOTP	HMAC-based One-time Password
HSM	Hardware Security Module
HTML	Hypertext Markup Language
HTTP	Hypertext Transfer Protocol
HTTPS	Hypertext Transfer Protocol Secure
HVAC	Heating, Ventilation Air Conditioning
IaaS	Infrastructure as a Service
IaC	Infrastructure as Code
IAM	Identity and Access Management
ICMP	Internet Control Message Protocol
ICS	Industrial Control Systems
IDEA	International Data Encryption Algorithm
IDF	Intermediate Distribution Frame
IdP	Identity Provider
IDS	Intrusion Detection

	System
IEEE	Institute of Electrical and Electronics Engineers
IKE	Internet Key Exchange
IM	Instant Messaging
IMAP	Internet Message Access Protocol
IoC	Indicators of Compromise
IoT	Internet of Things
IP	Internet Protocol
IPS	Intrusion Prevention System
IPSec	Internet Protocol Security
IR	Incident Response
IRC	Internet Relay Chat
IRP	Incident Response Plan
ISO	International Standards Organization
ISP	Internet Service Provider
ISSO	Information Systems Security Officer
IV	Initialization Vector
KDC	Key Distribution Center
KEK	Key Encryption Key
L2TP	Layer 2 Tunneling Protocol
LAN	Local Area Network
LDAP	Lightweight Directory Access Protocol
LEAP	Lightweight Extensible Authentication Protocol
MaaS	Monitoring as a Service
MAC	Mandatory Access Control
MAC	Media Access Control
MAC	Message Authentication Code
MAN	Metropolitan Area Network
MBR	Master Boot Record
MD5	Message Digest 5
MDF	Main Distribution Frame
MDM	Mobile Device Management
MFA	Multifactor Authentication
MFD	Multifunction Device

MFP	Multifunction Printer
ML	Machine Learning
MMS	Multimedia Message Service
MOA	Memorandum of Agreement
MOU	Memorandum of Understanding
MPLS	Multi-protocol Label Switching
MSA	Master Service Agreement
MSCHAP	Microsoft Challenge Handshake Authentication Protocol
MSP	Managed Service Provider
MSSP	Managed Security Service Provider
MTBF	Mean Time Between Failures
MTTF	Mean Time to Failure
MTTR	Mean Time to Recover
MTU	Maximum Transmission Unit
NAC	Network Access Control
NAT	Network Address Translation
NDA	Non-disclosure Agreement
NFC	Near Field Communication
NGFW	Next-generation Firewall
NIDS	Network-based Intrusion Detection System
NIPS	Network-based Intrusion Prevention System
NIST	National Institute of Standards & Technology
NTFS	New Technology File System
NTLM	New Technology LAN Manager
NTP	Network Time Protocol
OAUTH	Open Authorization
OCSP	Online Certificate Status Protocol
OID	Object Identifier

OS	Operating System
OSINT	Open-source Intelligence
OSPF	Open Shortest Path First
OT	Operational Technology
OTA	Over the Air
OVAL	Open Vulnerability Assessment Language
P12	PKCS #12
P2P	Peer to Peer
PaaS	Platform as a Service
PAC	Proxy Auto Configuration
PAM	Privileged Access Management
PAM	Pluggable Authentication Modules
PAP	Password Authentication Protocol
PAT	Port Address Translation
PBKDF2	Password-based Key Derivation Function 2
PBX	Private Branch Exchange
PCAP	Packet Capture
PCI DSS	Payment Card Industry Data Security Standard
PDU	Power Distribution Unit
PEAP	Protected Extensible Authentication Protocol
PED	Personal Electronic Device
PEM	Privacy Enhanced Mail
PFS	Perfect Forward Secrecy
PGP	Pretty Good Privacy
PHI	Personal Health Information
PII	Personally Identifiable Information
PIV	Personal Identity Verification
PKCS	Public Key Cryptography Standards
PKI	Public Key Infrastructure
POP	Post Office Protocol
POTS	Plain Old Telephone Service
PPP	Point-to-Point Protocol
PPTP	Point-to-Point Tunneling Protocol

PSK	Pre-shared Key
PTZ	Pan-tilt-zoom
PUP	Potentially Unwanted Program
RA	Recovery Agent
RA	Registration Authority
RACE	Research and Development in Advanced Communications Technologies in Europe
RAD	Rapid Application Development
RADIUS	Remote Authentication Dial-in User Service
RAID	Redundant Array of Inexpensive Disks
RAS	Remote Access Server
RAT	Remote Access Trojan
RBAC	Role-based Access Control
RBAC	Rule-based Access Control
RC4	Rivest Cipher version 4
RDP	Remote Desktop Protocol
RFID	Radio Frequency Identifier
RIPEMD	RACE Integrity Primitives Evaluation Message Digest
ROI	Return on Investment
RPO	Recovery Point Objective
RSA	Rivest, Shamir, & Adleman
RTBH	Remotely Triggered Black Hole
RTO	Recovery Time Objective
RTOS	Real-time Operating System
RTP	Real-time Transport Protocol
S/MIME	Secure/Multipurpose Internet Mail Extensions
SaaS	Software as a Service
SAE	Simultaneous Authentication of Equals
SAML	Security Assertions Markup Language

SAN	Storage Area Network
SAN	Subject Alternative Name
SASE	Secure Access Service Edge
SCADA	Supervisory Control and Data Acquisition
SCAP	Security Content Automation Protocol
SCEP	Simple Certificate Enrollment Protocol
SDK	Software Development Kit
SDLC	Software Development Lifecycle
SDLM	Software Development Lifecycle Methodology
SDN	Software-defined Networking
SD-WAN	Software-defined Wide Area Network
SE Linux	Security-enhanced Linux
SED	Self-encrypting Drives
SEH	Structured Exception Handler
SFTP	Secured File Transfer Protocol
SHA	Secure Hashing Algorithm
SHTTP	Secure Hypertext Transfer Protocol
SIEM	Security Information and Event Management
SIM	Subscriber Identity Module
SLA	Service-level Agreement
SLE	Single Loss Expectancy
SMS	Short Message Service
SMTP	Simple Mail Transfer Protocol
SMTPS	Simple Mail Transfer Protocol Secure
SNMP	Simple Network Management Protocol
SOAP	Simple Object Access Protocol
SOAR	Security Orchestration, Automation, Response
SoC	System on Chip
SOC	Security Operations Center

SOW	Statement of Work
SPF	Sender Policy Framework
SPIM	Spam over Internet Messaging
SQL	Structured Query Language
SQLi	SQL Injection
SRTP	Secure Real-Time Protocol
SSD	Solid State Drive
SSH	Secure Shell
SSL	Secure Sockets Layer
SSO	Single Sign-on
STIX	Structured Threat Information eXchange
SWG	Secure Web Gateway
TACACS+	Terminal Access Controller Access Control System
TAXII	Trusted Automated eXchange of Indicator Information
TCP/IP	Transmission Control Protocol/Internet Protocol
TGT	Ticket Granting Ticket
TKIP	Temporal Key Integrity Protocol
TLS	Transport Layer Security
TOC	Time-of-check
TOTP	Time-based One-time Password
TOU	Time-of-use
TPM	Trusted Platform Module
TSIG	Transaction Signature
TTP	Tactics, Techniques, and Procedures
UAT	User Acceptance Testing
UAV	Unmanned Aerial Vehicle
UDP	User Datagram Protocol
UEFI	Unified Extensible Firmware Interface
UEM	Unified Endpoint Management
UPS	Uninterruptable Power Supply
URI	Uniform Resource Identifier

URL	Universal Resource Locator
USB	Universal Serial Bus
USB OTG	USB On the Go
UTM	Unified Threat Management
UTP	Unshielded Twisted Pair
VBA	Visual Basic
VDE	Virtual Desktop Environment
VDI	Virtual Desktop Infrastructure
VLAN	Virtual Local Area Network
VLSM	Variable Length Subnet Masking
VM	Virtual Machine
VoIP	Voice over IP
VPC	Virtual Private Cloud
VPN	Virtual Private Network
VTC	Video Teleconferencing
WAF	Web Application Firewall
WAP	Wireless Access Point
WEP	Wired Equivalent Privacy
WIDS	Wireless Intrusion Detection System
WIPS	Wireless Intrusion Prevention System
WO	Work Order
WPA	Wi-Fi Protected Access
WPS	Wi-Fi Protected Setup
WTLS	Wireless TLS
XDR	Extended Detection and Response
XML	Extensible Markup Language
XOR	Exclusive Or
XSRF	Cross-site Request Forgery
XSS	Cross-site Scripting

Basic Hardware And Concepts You'll encounter

Basic hardware	Explanation
Tablets	A tablet is a wireless, portable personal computer with a touchscreen interface. It is a mobile device that is smaller than a notebook but larger than a smartphone. Tablets can access the internet and act in many ways like a computer. They are typically controlled by means of a touch screen and are used for accessing the internet, watching videos, playing games, reading electronic books, and other applications. Tablets can be loosely grouped into several categories by physical size, kind of operating system installed, input and output technology, and uses. The most common type of tablet is the slate style, like Apple's iPad, Microsoft's Surface or Amazon's Kindle Fire. Other styles of tablets include convertible tablets, hybrid tablets, and rugged tablets.
Laptops	A laptop is a portable personal computer that integrates all the components of a desktop computer into a single unit. It is designed to be more portable than traditional desktop computers, with many of the same functionalities. A laptop can be easily transported and used in temporary spaces such as on airplanes, in libraries, temporary offices, and at meetings. It is like having a desktop computer that you can take with you wherever you go, making it ideal for people who need to work or study on the go. A laptop has an all-in-one design, with a built-in monitor,

	keyboard, touchpad, and speakers. It can be turned into a desktop computer with a docking station, which is a hardware frame that supplies connections for peripheral input/output devices such as a monitor, keyboard, and printer.
Web servers	A web server is a computer program that stores, processes, and delivers web pages to users over the internet. It is like a restaurant that stores, prepares, and serves food to customers. The web server software controls how users access hosted files, and it comprises several components, including an HTTP server that understands URLs and HTTP. The hardware side of a web server is a computer that stores web server software and files, such as HTML documents, images, and JavaScript files. The web server hardware is connected to the internet and allows data to be exchanged with other connected devices. When a user requests a web page, the web server responds by sending the requested page through HTTP. Multiple domains can be hosted on one web server. Web servers are used in web hosting, or the hosting of data for websites and web-based applications.
Firewalls	A firewall is a security device that monitors network traffic and decides whether to allow or block specific traffic based on a set of security rules. It acts as a barrier between a private internal network and the public Internet, filtering traffic within a private network. Think of the firewall like a gatekeeper at your computer's entry point

	which only allows trusted sources, or IP addresses, to enter your network. Firewalls can be hardware, software, software-as-a-service (SaaS), public cloud, or private cloud (virtual). Firewalls establish a barrier between secured and controlled internal networks that can be trusted and untrusted outside networks, such as the Internet. Firewalls filter out the good from the bad, or the trusted from the untrusted, and block traffic coming from suspicious sources to prevent cyberattacks. Firewalls can be used to create an audit trail of attempted attacks and are intended to secure the private networks and the endpoint devices within, known as network hosts.
Routers	A router is a device that connects multiple networks and directs network data using packets that contain various kinds of data such as files, communications, and simple transmissions like web interactions. It is like a traffic cop that directs the flow of traffic on a busy road, ensuring that each vehicle reaches its destination efficiently and quickly. Routers guide and direct network data, using packets that contain various kinds of data—such as files, communications, and simple transmissions like web interactions. They are essential components in any small business network and allow devices to connect and share data over the Internet or an intranet. Routers can also provide security by using embedded firewall and content

	filtering software to protect against unwanted content and malicious websites without affecting your online experience.
Switchs	A switch is a device that connects devices in a network to each other, enabling them to communicate by exchanging data packets. It operates on the data-link layer, or Layer 2, of the Open Systems Interconnection (OSI) model. A switch can be thought of as a traffic cop at an intersection, directing data packets to their intended destination. It determines where to send each incoming message frame by looking at the media access control (MAC) address. Switches maintain tables that match each MAC address to the port receiving the MAC address. There are different types of switches, including hardware devices that manage physical networks and software-based virtual devices. Switches offer full-duplex communication, connect network segments, boost network performance, and make effective use of available bandwidth. They provide the wired connections to desktop computers, wireless access points, printers, industrial machinery, and some internet of things (IoT) devices.
IDSs	An Intrusion Detection System (IDS) is a tool or software that monitors network traffic for suspicious activity and alerts when such activity is discovered. It is like a security guard that watches over a building and sounds an alarm if it detects any suspicious activity. IDSs come in different

	types and use different methods to detect suspicious activities, including signature-based and anomaly-based detection. Signature-based IDSs detect attacks based on specific patterns, while anomaly-based IDSs detect attacks based on deviations from normal network behavior. IDSs are passive monitoring devices that detect potential threats and generate alerts, enabling security operations center (SOC) analysts or incident responders to investigate and respond to the potential incident. IDSs provide no actual protection to the endpoint or network, but they are a valuable component of any organization's cybersecurity deployment.
IPSs	An Intrusion Prevention System (IPS) is a security technology that monitors network traffic for signs of malicious activity and takes action to prevent it. IPSs are like security guards at a museum who watch for suspicious behavior and intervene to prevent theft or damage. IPSs can be configured to detect and block specific types of attacks, such as malware, phishing, or denial-of-service attacks. They can also be configured to send alerts to security personnel when an attack is detected, allowing them to investigate and respond to the threat. IPSs can be configured with various options, such as enabling/disabling a fail-open scenario, configuring IPS buffer size, and including a time trend in the model that describes the process by which the series is generated.

Wireless access points	A wireless access point (WAP) is a device that creates a wireless local area network (WLAN) by connecting to a wired router, switch, or hub via an Ethernet cable, and projecting a WiFi signal to a designated area. Conceptually, a WAP is like an Ethernet hub, but instead of relaying LAN frames only to other 802.3 stations, a WAP relays 802.11 frames to all other 802.11 or 802.3 stations in the same subnet. An analogy for a WAP is a radio station that broadcasts music to a specific area. The WAP broadcasts a WiFi signal to a specific area, allowing wireless-capable devices to connect to a wired network. WAPs are used in larger businesses and venues where many WAPs are required to provide an internet connection to support thousands of users.
Virtual machines	A virtual machine (VM) is a software-based computer system that behaves like a physical computer. It is a virtualized instance of a computer that can perform almost all of the same functions as a computer, including running applications and operating systems. A VM runs on a physical machine and accesses computing resources from software called a hypervisor. The hypervisor abstracts the physical machine's resources into a pool that can be provisioned and distributed as needed, enabling multiple VMs to run on a single physical machine. VMs are used to run different operating systems on different virtual machines at the same

	time, to test applications in a safe, sandboxed environment, or to accommodate different levels of processing power needs. The end user experience emulated within the VM is nearly identical to a real-time operating system experience running on a physical machine. An analogy for a VM is a virtual apartment within a building. Each apartment is self-contained and has its own resources, but they all share the same building infrastructure.
Email systems	Email is a widely used method of exchanging messages between users over the internet. It is a fast, convenient, and cost-effective way to communicate with individuals or groups of people. An email system consists of several components, including a user agent (UA), message transfer agent (MTA), mailboxes, and spool files. The UA is a program used to send and receive mail, while the MTA is responsible for forwarding and storing messages. Email servers accept, forward, deliver, and store messages. Email clients, such as Outlook and Gmail, enable users to send, receive, and store emails. An email address is a unique identifier for each user, typically in the format of name@domain.com. To send an email, a user composes a new message in their email client and sends it to the recipient's email address. An analogy for email is that it is like sending a letter through the postal service, but instead of a physical letter, it is a digital message that is sent and

	received through the internet.
Internet accesses	Internet access is the ability to connect to the internet using computers or other devices and to access services such as email and the World Wide Web. It is often provided in schools, public places, homes, workplaces, libraries, internet cafes, etc. Internet access can be compared to a highway system. Just as highways connect cities and towns, the internet connects computers and devices around the world. Internet Service Providers (ISPs) are like the on-ramps and off-ramps of the highway system, providing access to the internet for individuals and organizations. The type of internet connection, region, and internet service provider can affect the cost, availability, speed, and reliability of internet access.
DNS servers	The Domain Name System (DNS) is like a phonebook for the internet. Just as a phonebook matches individuals to a phone number, the DNS matches a website name to its corresponding IP address. When we try to access a website, we generally type in its domain name, like google.com, into the web browser. However, web browsers need to know the exact IP address to load content for the website. The DNS is what translates the domain names to the IP addresses so that the resources can be loaded from

	the website's server. A DNS server is a device or program dedicated to providing services to other programs, referred to as clients. DNS clients, which are built into most modern operating systems, send requests to DNS servers to resolve domain names into IP addresses. DNS servers contain a database of public IP addresses and their associated hostnames and, in most cases, can resolve requests for domain names that are not in their database by forwarding the request to another DNS server.
IoT devices	IoT devices are physical objects that contain embedded technology to sense or interact with their environment and communicate with the internet. They are pieces of hardware, such as sensors, gadgets, appliances, or machines, that are programmed for certain applications and can transmit data over the internet or other networks. IoT devices can be categorized into three main groups: consumer, enterprise, and industrial. They are typically embedded with technology such as sensors and software and can include mechanical and digital machines and consumer objects. An analogy for IoT devices is that they are like the organs in a body, each with a specific function, but all working together to keep the body functioning properly. Similarly, IoT devices work together to collect and exchange data with other devices and systems over the internet, making daily activities faster, easier, or more

	convenient for consumers while also providing real-time data for industrial or enterprise use cases.
Hardware tokens	A hardware token is a small physical device that provides an extra layer of security to authenticate a user's identity when accessing a network or service. It is like an electronic key that acts as a second factor of authentication, in addition to a password. The token can be in the form of a credit card or keychain fob, and it displays a unique code that the user inputs as an added security measure. The code is usually a six-digit number that changes every 30 seconds, and it is generated by a time-based or cryptographic algorithm. The hardware token is tamper-resistant and isolated from the user's device, making it more secure than other authentication methods. It is like a physical key that only the user has access to, and it provides an additional layer of protection against unauthorized access to sensitive information.
Smartphones	A smartphone is a mobile phone that has advanced computing capabilities and features not originally associated with telephones, such as an operating system, web browsing, and the ability to run software applications. It is like having a small computer in your pocket that can make phone calls, send text messages, and access the internet. Smartphones have more advanced features than regular cell phones, including more RAM, a powerful CPU,

	high storage space, larger screens, and greater connectivity options. They also support accessories such as Bluetooth headphones, power charging cables, and extra speakers. Smartphones are used by consumers and as part of a person's business or work, providing access to many mobile applications and computing functions, and have become integral to everyday modern life.
NICs	A Network Interface Card (NIC) is a hardware component that enables a computer to connect to a network. It is like a passport that allows a computer to enter a network and communicate with other devices on that network. A NIC is typically a circuit board or chip that is installed on a computer's motherboard. It provides a dedicated, full-time connection to a network and implements the physical layer circuitry necessary for communicating with a data link layer standard, such as Ethernet or Wi-Fi. Each NIC represents a device and can prepare, transmit, and control the flow of data on the network. The NIC uses the OSI model to send signals at the physical layer, transmit data packets at the network layer, and operate as an interface at the TCP/IP layer. The NIC card acts as a middleman between a computer and a data network, converting data into electrical impulses.

Power supplies	A power supply is an electrical device that supplies electric power to an electrical load, such as a computer, server, or other electronic devices. It is like a water pump that takes water from a source and pumps it to a destination. The main function of a power supply is to convert electric current from a source to the correct voltage, current, and frequency to power the load. Power supplies may need to change voltage up or down, convert power to direct current, or regulate power for smoother outcoming voltage. They can be classified as regulated power supplies, unregulated power supplies, adjustable power supplies, adjustable regulated power supplies, isolated power supplies, or non-isolated power supplies. Power supplies are packaged in different ways and classified accordingly. A bench power supply is a stand-alone desktop unit used in applications such as circuit test and development. Open frame power supplies have only a partial mechanical enclosure, sometimes consisting of only a mounting base; these are typically built into machinery or other equipment. Rack mount power supplies are designed to be secured into standard electronic equipment racks.
GBICs	GBIC stands for Gigabit Interface Converter, which is a type of transceiver used in networking to convert electrical signals into optical signals and vice versa. It is like a translator between two people who speak different languages. The GBIC is inserted into a switch, router,

	or other network device and allows it to communicate with other devices over a fiber optic or copper network. It is a hot-swappable device, which means it can be replaced without shutting down the network. GBICs are used to connect switches, routers, and other network devices to each other, and they are available in different types to support different network speeds and distances.
SFPs	Sender Policy Framework (SPF) is an email authentication protocol designed to prevent email spoofing, a common technique used in phishing attacks and email spam. It works by allowing domain owners to create a list of approved email senders, which is represented in an SPF record published in DNS records. When an authorized user sends an email with an SPF record enabled, the recipient's mail server performs a DNS lookup to spot the TXT entry and determine whether the sender's IP address is authorized. SPF can be compared to a bouncer at a club who checks the ID of every person entering the club to ensure that only authorized individuals are allowed in. Similarly, SPF checks the IP address of every incoming email to ensure that only authorized senders are allowed to send emails from a particular domain.
Managed Switch	A managed switch is a type of network switch that provides greater control over how data travels over the network and who can access it. In contrast, an unmanaged switch is

	designed to just plug in and run, with no settings to configure. An analogy for this would be a managed switch is like a traffic cop who can direct traffic and prioritize certain vehicles, while an unmanaged switch is like a roundabout where vehicles can enter and exit freely without any direction. Managed switches are more suitable for larger networks and networks supporting critical activities, while unmanaged switches are fine to use in small networks with only basic needs. Managed switches are fully configurable, customizable, and provide a range of data on performance, while unmanaged switches offer a separate, per-port collision domain.
Wireless access point	A wireless access point (WAP) is a device that allows wireless-capable devices to connect to a wired network. It is like a bridge between the wired network and the wireless devices. Conceptually, it is like a radio station that broadcasts a signal that can be picked up by wireless devices within its range. When a wireless device moves beyond the range of one WAP, it is handed over to the next WAP. An analogy for a WAP is a lighthouse that emits a beam of light that can be seen by ships within its range. When a ship moves beyond the range of one lighthouse, it is handed over to the next lighthouse. WAPs are used in larger businesses and venues where many WAPs are required to provide an internet connection to support thousands of users.

UPS

An uninterruptible power supply (UPS) is a device that provides backup power when the regular power source fails or voltage drops to an unacceptable level. It is like a backup generator for electronic devices, but instead of using fuel, it uses batteries to provide power for a short period of time, usually a few minutes. The UPS is typically used to protect hardware such as computers, data centers, telecommunication equipment, or other electrical equipment where an unexpected power disruption could cause injuries, fatalities, serious business disruption, or data loss. The UPS works by drawing current from the AC outlet and switches to battery within a few milliseconds after detecting a power failure. The battery takes over and provides a continuous power source for the length of the battery, which varies by system for periods of time ranging from minutes to hours. The UPS also acts as a filter to shield devices against variances in the power supply, which can cause damage to sensitive equipment like computers and network gear.

Basic software	Explanation
Windows OS	Windows is an operating system developed by Microsoft that allows users to interact with a computer. It is like a conductor of an orchestra, coordinating all the different parts of the computer to work together harmoniously. Windows comes pre-installed on most new personal computers and is the most popular operating system in the world. It provides a graphical user interface (GUI) that allows users to perform various tasks such as browsing the internet, checking email, editing digital photos, listening to music, playing games, and much more. Windows also provides access to productivity tools such as calendars, word processors, and spreadsheets. There have been many versions of Windows since its first release in the mid-1980s, with the most recent ones being Windows 10, Windows 8, Windows 7, Windows Vista, and Windows XP.
Linux OS	Linux is an open-source operating system that manages all of the hardware resources associated with your computer. It is like a conductor of an orchestra, managing all the instruments and ensuring they play in harmony. The Linux kernel is the core of the system and manages the CPU, memory, and peripheral devices. The kernel communicates with the hardware and relays requests from software programs to the computer's hardware. Linux is similar to other operating systems like Windows and macOS, but it is incredibly customizable, allowing users to choose core components and swap out applications. Linux is used in many different settings, supporting many different use cases, from running databases to

	scientific computing tasks that require huge compute clusters.
Kali Linux	Kali Linux is a Debian-based open-source operating system designed for advanced penetration testing and security auditing. It is like a Swiss Army knife for cybersecurity professionals, providing them with a wide range of tools to perform various security-related tasks. Kali Linux is not a general-purpose operating system, but rather a specialized one that is used by professionals who work in the field of cybersecurity. It is like a toolbox that contains all the necessary tools for a carpenter to build a house. Kali Linux is developed and maintained by Offensive Security, and it is freely available to information security professionals and hobbyists. It is a cross-platform solution that is easily accessible and can run on a wide variety of hardware. Kali Linux is not designed for beginners, but rather for professionals who know how to operate Linux/Kali.
Packet capture software	Packet capture software is a tool used to intercept and record data packets that are traveling over a network. It is like a surveillance camera that captures everything that is happening on the network. The captured packets can be stored for further analysis, and the information obtained can be used to identify network issues, troubleshoot problems, and detect security threats. The software can capture the entire packet or specific portions of it, including the payload and header. The header contains metadata such as the packet's source and destination address, while the payload contains the actual data being transferred.

	Packet capture software is a valuable tool for network administrators and security professionals as it provides a detailed view of network traffic that is not available through other monitoring solutions.
Pen testing software	Penetration testing software is a cybersecurity tool that simulates a cyber attack on a computer system to identify vulnerabilities and weaknesses in the system's security. It is like a security audit where a professional hacker, known as an ethical hacker, attempts to hack into a system to identify possible entry points into the infrastructure. The ethical hacker uses different methodologies, tools, and approaches to perform simulated cyber attacks to test the strengths and weaknesses of the existing security systems. The goal of penetration testing is to identify and mitigate cybersecurity risks before they are exploited by malicious actors. Penetration testing software is unique from other cybersecurity evaluation methods because it can be adapted to any industry or organization, and it can be customized based on the IT personnel and their company standards.
Static and dynamic analysis tools	Static and dynamic analysis are two methods of analyzing code to identify issues and improve the development process. Static analysis is like a spell-checker for code, where the code is examined without executing the program. It can detect syntax errors, coding standards violations, potential bugs, security flaws, and other quality issues. Static analysis is performed early in development, before software testing begins, and it helps developers identify and fix issues early, improve code quality,

	enhance security, ensure compliance, and increase efficiency. Dynamic analysis, on the other hand, is like a test drive for code, where the code is analyzed while it is running. It can measure the performance, behavior, and functionality of the code, and identify runtime errors, memory leaks, resource consumption, and other issues that may affect the user experience. Dynamic analysis tools can monitor the code execution, simulate user inputs, or generate test cases, and provide insights or suggestions on how to improve the code. Static and dynamic analysis are complementary techniques that work together to create better code. Static analysis is best paired with code review, while dynamic analysis is suited to some form of automated testing and test data generation.
Vulnerability scanner	A vulnerability scanner is an automated tool that identifies and creates an inventory of all IT assets connected to a network, such as servers, desktops, laptops, virtual machines, containers, firewalls, switches, and printers. It attempts to identify operational details such as the operating system it runs and the software installed on it, along with other attributes such as open ports and user accounts. The scanner then compares the target network's details with a database of known vulnerabilities, which is regularly updated to include newly discovered issues. It identifies potential security weaknesses and flaws in systems and software running on them, and generates a report for the user to fix it. Vulnerability scanning is like a security guard who patrols a building, looking for any unlocked doors or windows that could be

	exploited by intruders. The guard then reports these vulnerabilities to the building owner, who can take action to secure the building and prevent break-ins. Similarly, a vulnerability scanner identifies potential security weaknesses in a network, and reports them to the security team, who can take action to patch vulnerabilities and prevent cyberattacks.
Network emulators	Network emulators are tools used to test the performance of real applications over a virtual network. They are different from network simulators, which use virtual models of traffic, network models, channels, and protocols to predict the performance of a computer network or a wireless communication network. An analogy to understand the difference between network emulation and network simulation is that network emulation is like a flight simulator where pilots can train in a simulated environment that mirrors the real-world conditions, while network simulation is like a video game where players can simulate flying a plane but without the real-world conditions. Network emulation allows users to connect the devices, applications, products, and/or services being tested to validate their performance, stability, or functionality against real-world network scenarios. Once tested in a controlled environment against actual network conditions, users can have confidence that the item being tested will perform as expected.
Sample code	Sample code is a concise and clear representation of a programming task or scenario that demonstrates a particular program architecture. It is like a recipe that shows how to cook a dish. Good sample code is

correct, concise, and easy to understand, and it should compile without errors. It should also be reusable, meaning that readers can easily reuse it with minimal side effects. Sample code should be accompanied by all the necessary information to run it, including any dependencies and setup. It should also be extendable or customizable in useful ways. The text leading up to the sample code should have a clear description of what the code accomplishes, any assumptions it makes, and prerequisites. Writing concise code is important because it is more readable, easier to understand, and less prone to bugs. It also improves productivity and enhances code comprehension.

Code editor	A code editor is a tool that programmers use to write and edit code. It is like a specialized text editor that is designed to make writing code easier and more efficient. A code editor can be compared to a chef's knife. Just as a chef's knife is designed to make cutting and chopping ingredients easier and more efficient, a code editor is designed to make writing and editing code easier and more efficient. A code editor has features like syntax highlighting, automatic indentation, error-checking, and code snippets that help programmers write code more quickly and accurately. It can be a standalone program or part of an integrated development environment (IDE).
SIEM	SIEM is a software solution that helps organizations detect, analyze, and respond to security threats before they harm business operations. It combines both Security Information Management (SIM) and Security Event Management (SEM) into one

	security management system. SIM retrieves and analyzes log data and generates a report, while SEM carries out analysis of event and log data in real-time to provide event correlation, threat monitoring, and incident response. SIEM gathers immense amounts of data from an organization's entire IT infrastructure, consolidates and makes that data human accessible, and applies analytics to that data to discover trends, detect threats, and enable organizations to investigate any alerts. An analogy for SIEM is a security camera system that records and analyzes all the activity in a building, and alerts security personnel when it detects any suspicious activity.
Keyloggers	A keylogger is a type of software or hardware that records every keystroke made on a keyboard, including passwords, credit card numbers, and other sensitive information. It is like a spy that watches everything you do on your computer. Keyloggers can be used for legitimate purposes, such as monitoring employee activity or troubleshooting technical problems, but they can also be used maliciously by hackers to steal personal information. Hardware-based keyloggers are small devices that are connected between the keyboard and the computer, while software-based keyloggers are programs that can be installed on a computer either intentionally or through malware. Keyloggers can be difficult to detect, especially hardware-based ones, and can be used for surveillance, espionage, or fraud purposes.

MDM software	Mobile Device Management (MDM) is a process of managing mobile devices, largely in terms of usage and security. It is like a traffic cop that manages the flow of traffic on the road, ensuring that all vehicles are moving in the right direction and following the rules. Similarly, MDM software allows IT administrators to control, secure, and enforce policies on smartphones, tablets, and other endpoints. It helps organizations manage all endpoint devices with a single console, including mobile application management (MAM) tools, identity and access management, and enterprise file sync and share. The goal of MDM is to optimize the functionality and security of mobile devices within the enterprise while protecting the corporate network. MDM software can remotely administer devices, correct malfunctions, lock and wipe the device of critical data, monitor and audit devices for usage patterns and security vulnerabilities, and perform detailed analytics.
VPN	A VPN, or virtual private network, is a service that creates a secure and encrypted connection between a device and the internet. It works by routing internet traffic through a remote server owned by a VPN provider, which creates a point-to-point tunnel that encrypts personal data, masks the user's IP address, and lets them bypass website blocks and firewalls on the internet. A VPN is like a secret tunnel between the user's device and the internet, where the data is scrambled into code and rendered illegible by anyone who does not have access to the encryption key. It is like a motorcycle rider using a tunnel to avoid traffic on a busy highway. The VPN service opens a "tunnel" between the user and the

	targeted server, and the user's data travels through this tunnel so that no one else on the network can eavesdrop and hijack the data. A VPN is an essential tool for staying secure online, preventing cybercriminals from hacking into the user's network, and avoiding encroachments on privacy by internet service providers or attackers.
DHCP service	Dynamic Host Configuration Protocol (DHCP) is a network protocol that automatically assigns IP addresses, default gateways, and other network parameters to client devices. It is like a waiter in a restaurant who assigns tables to customers and provides them with menus, utensils, and other necessary items. Without DHCP, network administrators would have to manually set up every client that joins the network, which can be cumbersome, especially in large networks. DHCP servers usually assign each client with a unique dynamic IP address, which changes when the client's lease for that IP address has expired. DHCP allows hosts to obtain required TCP/IP configuration information from a DHCP server. DHCP servers provide logging and management interfaces that aid administrators in managing their IP address scopes. DHCP servers can provide redundancy and high availability. If one DHCP server were to fail, the clients would preserve their current IP addresses and not cause an interruption in network communication.
DNS service	The Domain Name System (DNS) is like a phonebook for the internet. Just as a phonebook matches individuals to a phone number, the DNS matches a website name to its corresponding IP address. When a user types a website name into

their browser, the DNS server translates the name into a machine-readable IP address that computers can understand and use to find the website. DNS servers are responsible for translating domain names to numeric IP addresses, leading users to the correct website. DNS mapping is distributed throughout the internet in a hierarchy of authority. Access providers and enterprises, as well as governments, universities, and other organizations, typically have their own assigned ranges of IP addresses and an assigned domain name. They also typically run DNS servers to manage the mapping of those names to those addresses. DNS servers convert URLs and domain names into IP addresses that computers can understand and use. They translate what a user types into a browser into something the machine can use to find a webpage. This process of translation and lookup is called DNS resolution.

Basic tools	Explanation
Wi-Fi analyzer	A Wi-Fi analyzer is a tool that helps to optimize the performance of Wi-Fi networks by analyzing the connection, collecting data, and identifying problems responsible for a weak Wi-Fi signal. It is like a doctor who examines a patient, collects data, and identifies the problems responsible for the patient's illness. Wi-Fi analyzers collect information from different access points and channels within a network and provide a clear overview with visual reports and dashboards. They help administrators locate areas where the Wi-Fi signal is weak and identify the best places for the router to avoid disturbances. Wi-Fi analyzers can also provide several statistics about networks, such as SSID, signal strength, and last seen, which can be used by administrators to fine-tune the existing settings and increase the level of performance the network can deliver.
Network mapper	A network mapper is a tool used to discover and visualize the physical and virtual connectivity of a network. It is like a map of a city that shows the roads, buildings, and other landmarks. Similarly, a network mapper shows the devices on the network, their interconnections, and the transport layers that provide network services. It is used to locate network bottlenecks, troubleshoot connection errors, and collect information that enables root cause analysis in case of a network issue. Network mapping can be done manually using simple tools like Microsoft Visio, or it can be automated using tools that integrate auto network discovery with network mapping. The automated approach is preferred because modern networks are dynamic and complex, with devices frequently entering and leaving the network, and network devices are frequently split into various VLANs to

	enable data flow separation or security.
NetFlow analyzer	A NetFlow analyzer is a tool used to monitor and analyze network traffic flow. It is like a traffic monitoring system on a busy highway that tracks the number of vehicles, their speed, and their destinations. Similarly, a NetFlow analyzer tracks the volume and types of traffic traversing a network device, and it captures measurements for each flow and exports them to another system for analysis. NetFlow analyzers provide comprehensive insights into the data flows within a network infrastructure, enabling administrators to monitor and understand the flow of data across the infrastructure. This visibility is crucial for capacity planning, troubleshooting network issues, and identifying potential security threats. NetFlow analyzers work by generating flow data, conducting flow analysis, and processing and analyzing stored flow data to extract useful information. They can calculate metrics like bandwidth utilization, top talkers, top applications, protocols, and identify sources of congestion or network anomalies

The type of security control category called Technical

The Technical security control category refers to the use of technology to protect information and systems. This includes the use of firewalls, intrusion detection systems, encryption, and other technical measures to prevent unauthorized access or damage to systems. An analogy for Technical controls could be a security camera system in a building. Just as a security camera system monitors and records activity in a building to prevent unauthorized access or damage, Technical controls use technology to monitor and protect information and systems from unauthorized access or damage.

The type of security control category called Managerial

The Managerial security control category, as described in the CompTIA Security+ SY0-701 Exam Objectives, refers to policies, procedures, and guidelines that are put in place to manage and oversee security controls. This category can be compared to the role of a coach in a sports team. Just as a coach sets the rules and guidelines for the team, the Managerial security controls establish the policies and procedures that govern the overall security posture of an organization. These controls include activities such as risk management, security awareness training, and incident response planning, which are all critical to ensuring the security of an organization's assets

The type of security control category called Operational

Operational security controls are a type of security control category that focuses on the processes and procedures used to protect an organization's assets. These controls are like the rules of the road that drivers follow to ensure safe and efficient travel. Just as drivers must obey traffic signals, speed limits, and other rules to prevent accidents and maintain order on the road, organizations must establish and enforce policies and procedures to prevent security incidents and maintain order in their operations. Examples of operational security controls include access controls, security awareness training, and incident response procedures.

The type of security control category called Physical

The Physical security control category refers to measures that are put in place to protect physical assets, such as buildings, equipment, and people. These controls are like the locks on the doors of a house, which prevent unauthorized access and protect the people and possessions inside. Physical security controls can include things like security cameras, access control systems, and security guards. They are designed to prevent physical threats, such as theft, vandalism, and unauthorized access, and to ensure that only authorized individuals have access to sensitive areas and information.

The type of security control type called Preventive

Preventive security controls are measures that are put in place to prevent security incidents from happening. These controls are like the seatbelts in a car, which are designed to prevent accidents and protect the passengers in case of a collision. Preventive security controls can include things like firewalls, access control systems, and security awareness training. They are designed to prevent security incidents, such as unauthorized access, data breaches, and malware infections, and to ensure that the organization's assets are protected. Preventive security controls are one of the three primary categories of security controls, along with detective and corrective controls.

The type of security control type called Deterrent

A Deterrent security control is a type of control that is designed to discourage or prevent unauthorized access to a system or facility. It is similar to a fence around a house that is designed to deter burglars from attempting to break in. The idea is to make it difficult or unattractive for an attacker to try to gain access, so they will move on to an easier target. Examples of deterrent controls include security cameras, warning signs, and security guards.

The type of security control type called Detective

Detective controls are a type of security control that aim to detect and identify security incidents or events that have already occurred. They are similar to a smoke detector in a house, which is designed to detect smoke and alert the occupants of a potential fire. In the same way, Detective controls are designed to detect and alert security personnel of potential security breaches or incidents, allowing them to take appropriate action to mitigate the damage and prevent future incidents. Examples of Detective controls include security cameras, intrusion detection systems, and log analysis tools.

The type of security control type called Corrective

Corrective security controls are a type of security control that are implemented after a security incident has occurred. They are designed to correct or mitigate the damage caused by the incident and prevent similar incidents from happening in the future. An analogy for corrective security controls would be a fire extinguisher. Just as a fire extinguisher is used to put out a fire after it has started, corrective security controls are used to address a security incident after it has occurred. The goal is to minimize the damage caused by the incident and prevent it from happening again in the future.

The type of security control type called Compensating

Compensating security controls are a type of security control that are put in place to address a weakness or deficiency in another control. They are like a spare tire in a car. Just as a spare tire is not the primary means of transportation, compensating controls are not the primary means of security. However, they are there to provide additional support in case the primary control fails or is not sufficient. Compensating controls are often used when it is not feasible or practical to implement the primary control, or when the primary control is not effective enough on its own.

The type of security control type called Directive

According to the reference provided, Directive security controls are policies and procedures that are put in place to guide the behavior of people within an organization. These controls are similar to traffic signs on a road that direct drivers on how to behave. Just as traffic signs tell drivers when to stop, go, or yield, Directive controls tell employees what actions are allowed or prohibited. They are designed to ensure that employees follow the rules and regulations set by the organization, and they include policies, procedures, standards, and guidelines.

The fundamental security concept called Confidentiality, Integrity, and Availability (CIA)

The CIA triad is a fundamental security concept that consists of three core principles: Confidentiality, Integrity, and Availability. Confidentiality refers to the protection of sensitive information from unauthorized access or disclosure. Integrity refers to the assurance that data is accurate, complete, and trustworthy. Availability refers to the ability to access data and resources when needed. An analogy to understand the CIA triad is to think of a bank vault. The vault protects the contents inside (confidentiality), ensures that the contents are not tampered with (integrity), and allows authorized individuals to access the contents when needed (availability).

The fundamental security concept called Non-repudiation

Non-repudiation is a fundamental security concept that ensures that a party cannot deny the authenticity of a message or transaction that they have sent or received. It is like a signed contract, where both parties have agreed to the terms and cannot later deny that they signed it. In the context of digital security, non-repudiation is achieved through the use of digital signatures, which provide a way to verify the authenticity of a message or transaction and ensure that it cannot be altered or repudiated by either party. This is important for maintaining the integrity and trustworthiness of digital communications and transactions.

The fundamental security concept called Authentication, Authorization, and Accounting (AAA)

Authentication, Authorization, and Accounting (AAA) is a fundamental security concept that is used to control access to resources in a network. AAA is a framework that consists of three components: authentication, authorization, and accounting. Authentication is the process of verifying the identity of a user or device that is attempting to access a network resource. Authorization is the process of determining what actions a user or device is allowed to perform on a network resource. Accounting is the process of tracking the actions of a user or device on a network resource. An analogy for AAA is a bouncer at a nightclub. The bouncer checks the ID of the person trying to enter the club (authentication), determines if the person is on the guest list (authorization), and keeps track of who enters and exits the club (accounting).

The fundamental security concept called AAAAuthenticating people

Authentication is a fundamental security concept that is used to verify the identity of a user or device that is attempting to access a network resource. Authentication is the first component of the AAA framework, which also includes authorization and accounting. An analogy for authentication is a bouncer at a nightclub who checks the ID of the person trying to enter the club. The bouncer verifies that the person is who they claim to be before allowing them to enter the club. Similarly, in a network, authentication verifies the identity of a user or device before granting access to network resources.

The fundamental security concept called AAAAuthenticating systems

The fundamental security concept called AAA stands for Authentication, Authorization, and Accounting. This concept is used to ensure that only authorized individuals have access to a system or network. Authentication is like a bouncer at a club who checks IDs to make sure only those who are authorized to enter are allowed in. Authorization is like a VIP list that specifies what each person is allowed to do once they are inside the club. Accounting is like a record of who entered the club and what they did while they were there. This concept is essential for maintaining the confidentiality, integrity, and availability of information and systems

The fundamental security concept called AAAAuthorization models

AAA (Authentication, Authorization, and Accounting) is a fundamental security concept that is used to control access to resources. It is like a bouncer at a club who checks your ID (authentication) to make sure you are who you say you are, checks if you are on the guest list (authorization) to see if you are allowed to enter, and keeps track of how many drinks you have had (accounting) to ensure you are not over-served. In the context of computer security, AAA is used to ensure that only authorized users have access to resources and to keep track of their activities. Authentication verifies the identity of the user, authorization determines what resources the user can access, and accounting tracks the user's activities for auditing purposes.

The fundamental security concept called Gap analysis

Gap analysis is a fundamental security concept that involves identifying the difference between the current state of security and the desired state of security. It is similar to a road trip where the destination is the desired state of security, and the current location is the current state of security. The gap between the two represents the areas that need to be addressed to reach the desired state. By conducting a gap analysis, organizations can identify vulnerabilities and risks, prioritize security measures, and develop a plan to close the gap and improve their security posture.

The fundamental security concept called Zero Trust

Zero Trust is a security concept that assumes that all users, devices, and applications are untrusted and must be verified before being granted access to a network or resource. It is based on the principle of "never trust, always verify." This means that even if a user or device is inside the network perimeter, they are not automatically trusted and must be continuously authenticated and authorized. An analogy for Zero Trust is a bouncer at a nightclub who checks everyone's ID before allowing them to enter. The bouncer does not assume that everyone is of legal age and must verify each person's identity before granting access to the club. Similarly, Zero Trust assumes that all users and devices are potentially malicious and must be verified before being granted access to the network.

The fundamental security concept called Zero TrustControl Plane

The Zero Trust Control Plane is a fundamental security concept that assumes that all network traffic is untrusted, regardless of its source or destination. It requires that all users and devices be authenticated and authorized before they are granted access to network resources. This is similar to a bouncer at a nightclub who checks everyone's ID before allowing them to enter. The bouncer doesn't assume that anyone is trustworthy just because they look like they belong there; instead, they verify everyone's identity before granting access. Similarly, the Zero Trust Control Plane assumes that all network traffic is potentially malicious and requires authentication and authorization before granting access to network resources.

The fundamental security concept called Zero Trust Control PlaneAdaptive identity

Zero Trust is a security concept that assumes that no device, user, or resource is trusted and must always be verified before access is granted and frequently evaluated for further sessions and activities. The Zero Trust Control Plane is the foundation of this model, and it is based on extremely granular and distributed trust based on users, computing session scenarios, systems, and data. Adaptive identity is a fundamental security concept in Zero Trust, and it is based on the idea that identities must be authenticated and authorized before any access to resources is granted. In other words, Zero Trust assumes that there is no implicit trust granted to assets or user accounts based solely on their physical or network location or based on asset ownership. An analogy for Zero Trust is a bouncer at a nightclub who checks everyone's ID before allowing them to enter. Similarly, Zero Trust requires that every user, device, and application must be verified before being granted access to resources.

The fundamental security concept called Zero Trust Control PlaneThreat scope reduction

Zero Trust Control Plane is a fundamental security concept that assumes that no implicit trust is granted to assets or user accounts based solely on their physical or network location or based on asset ownership. It eliminates the traditional idea of perimeters, trusted networks, devices, personas, or processes and shifts to multi-attribute-based levels of confidence that enable authentication and authorization policies founded on the concept of least privileged access. In other words, Zero Trust Control Plane reduces the threat scope by assuming that all devices, users, and resources are not trusted and must always be verified before access is granted and frequently evaluated for further sessions and activities. An analogy for Zero Trust Control Plane is a bouncer at a nightclub who checks everyone's ID before allowing them to enter, regardless of their appearance or reputation. The bouncer assumes that everyone is underage until they can prove otherwise, just as Zero Trust Control Plane assumes that every device, user, or resource is not trusted until they can be verified

The fundamental security concept called Zero Trust Control PlanePolicy-driven access control

Zero Trust Control Plane is a fundamental security concept that is used to control access to resources in a network. It is a policy-driven access control mechanism that assumes that no device or user should be trusted by default, regardless of their location or network segment. The Zero Trust Control Plane is responsible for authenticating and authorizing requests for access to protected resources. It applies fine-grained policy based on factors such as the user's role in the organization, time of day, or type of device. The Control Plane is separate from the Data Plane, which is responsible for transmitting data between devices. The Control Plane coordinates and configures the Data Plane, and interactions between the two are the most critical points requiring automation. An analogy for the Zero Trust Control Plane could be a bouncer at a nightclub who checks the ID of every person who wants to enter the club, regardless of whether they have been there before or not. The bouncer applies a policy of only allowing people who meet certain criteria, such as age or dress code, to enter the club. Similarly, the Zero Trust Control Plane applies a policy of only allowing authenticated and authorized users and devices to access protected resources.

The fundamental security concept called Zero Trust Control PlanePolicy Administrator

The Zero Trust Control Plane Policy Administrator is a fundamental security concept that is part of the Zero Trust Architecture. The Zero Trust Architecture is a cybersecurity paradigm that moves defenses from static, network-based perimeters to focus on users, assets, and resources. The Zero Trust Control Plane Policy Administrator is a supporting system that coordinates and configures most everything else, which is referred to as the data plane. Requests for access to protected resources are first made through the control plane, where both the device and user must be authenticated and authorized. Fine-grained policy can be applied at this layer, perhaps based on role in the organization, time of day, or type of device. The Zero Trust Control Plane Policy Administrator is like a bouncer at a club who checks IDs and only allows authorized individuals to enter.

The fundamental security concept called Zero Trust Control PlanePolicy Engine

The Zero Trust Control Plane Policy Engine is a fundamental security concept that is part of the Zero Trust Architecture (ZTA). The Policy Engine is an essential component of the ZTA, which is a security model that trusts no user or device by default. The Policy Engine works hand in hand with Zero-Trust policy management (ZTPM) to enforce policy and grant access to enterprise resources. In other words, the Policy Engine is responsible for making authorization decisions by comparing the request coming from the enforcement component against policy. An analogy for the Policy Engine could be a bouncer at a nightclub who checks IDs and only allows people who meet the criteria to enter. Similarly, the Policy Engine checks the request and only allows access to resources for authorized users and devices based on the policies defined.

The fundamental security concept called Zero Trust Data Plane

The Zero Trust Data Plane is a fundamental security concept that is part of the Zero Trust security framework. The Zero Trust model assumes that no user, device, or application is trusted, and access to resources is granted based on continuous authentication, authorization, and validation of security posture. The Data Plane is responsible for enforcing security policies and controls, and it is designed to prevent unauthorized access to resources by default. In other words, the Data Plane denies access to digital resources by default and grants access only to authenticated users and devices based on their identities and roles. An analogy for the Zero Trust Data Plane is a bouncer at a nightclub who checks the ID of every person who wants to enter and only allows those who are authorized to come in. Similarly, the Zero Trust Data Plane checks the identity and security posture of every user and device that wants to access a resource and only grants access to those who are authorized and meet the security requirements.

The fundamental security concept called Zero Trust Data PlaneImplicit trust zones

The Zero Trust Data Plane is a security concept that assumes that no user, device, or application is trusted in a network. It replaces the default trust granted by traditional network boundary security models such as firewalls, NAT, and VPNs. The Zero Trust Data Plane is based on the principle of least privilege, which means that users and devices are granted access to only the resources they need to perform their tasks and nothing more. This is similar to how a bouncer at a nightclub only allows people with the right credentials to enter the VIP section, while everyone else is kept in the general area. In the same way, the Zero Trust Data Plane creates implicit trust zones that do not include links, which means that users and devices are only granted access to the resources they need to perform their tasks, and nothing more.

The fundamental security concept called Zero Trust Data PlaneSubject/System

The Zero Trust Data Plane/System is a security concept that is based on the Zero Trust security model. This model is a cybersecurity approach that denies access to an enterprise's digital resources by default and grants authenticated users and devices tailored, siloed access to only the applications, data, services, and systems they need to do their jobs. The Zero Trust Data Plane/System is the part of the network that enforces access policies based on context, including the user's role and location, their device, and the data they are requesting, to block inappropriate access and lateral movement throughout an environment. An analogy for the Zero Trust Data Plane/System could be a bouncer at a nightclub who checks everyone's ID and only allows those who meet the criteria to enter. Similarly, the Zero Trust Data Plane/System checks the context of each user and device and only allows access to the resources they need to do their job, minimizing the risk of data breaches and unauthorized access.

The fundamental security concept called Zero Trust Data PlanePolicy Enforcement Point

Zero Trust Data Plane Policy Enforcement Point is a fundamental security concept that is part of the Zero Trust Architecture (ZTA). The Policy Enforcement Point (PEP) is responsible for enabling, monitoring, and terminating connections between a subject and an enterprise resource. In other words, the PEP acts as a guard for trust zones that host one or more enterprise resources. It handles enabling, monitoring, and eventually terminating connections between subjects and resources. An analogy for the PEP could be a bouncer at a nightclub who checks IDs and decides who is allowed to enter the club and who is not. Similarly, the PEP checks the identity of the subject and decides whether to allow access to enterprise resources or not based on the Zero Trust security policy.

The fundamental security concept called Physical security

Physical security is a fundamental security concept that refers to the protection of physical assets, such as buildings, equipment, and people, from unauthorized access, theft, damage, or destruction. It involves the implementation of various measures, such as access controls, surveillance systems, and environmental controls, to safeguard these assets. Physical security can be compared to the locks on the doors and windows of a house, which prevent unauthorized entry and protect the occupants and their belongings from harm. Just as a homeowner would take steps to secure their property, organizations must also take steps to secure their physical assets to ensure the safety and security of their employees, customers, and other stakeholders.

The fundamental security concept called Physical security Bollards

physical security bollards are a fundamental security concept that involves the use of physical barriers to protect assets or people from harm. Bollards are typically used to prevent unauthorized vehicles from entering a restricted area, such as a government building or a pedestrian walkway. They act as a barrier to stop vehicles from penetrating the area, much like a goalie in soccer stops the ball from entering the goal. By using physical security bollards, organizations can create a secure perimeter around their assets and reduce the risk of unauthorized access or damage.

The fundamental security concept called Physical security Access control vestibule

Access control vestibule is a physical security measure that involves a small room or enclosure at the entrance of a building that serves as a buffer zone between the outside and inside of the building. It is like a double-door airlock that prevents unauthorized access by requiring individuals to pass through two sets of doors, one at a time, before gaining access to the building. This helps to prevent unauthorized access, tailgating, and piggybacking, and enhances the security of the building by controlling who enters and exits.

The fundamental security concept called Physical security Fencing

Physical security fencing is a fundamental security concept that involves the use of barriers to prevent unauthorized access to a physical location. It is similar to the way a fence is used to keep people out of a private property. Physical security fencing can include walls, gates, locks, and other physical barriers that are designed to prevent unauthorized access to a facility or area. The goal of physical security fencing is to create a secure perimeter that is difficult to breach, and to provide a visible deterrent to potential intruders.

The fundamental security concept called Physical security Video surveillance

Video surveillance is a key component of physical security that involves using cameras to monitor and record activity in and around a facility. An analogy for physical security and video surveillance is a castle with a moat and watchtowers. Just as a castle is protected by a moat and watchtowers to prevent unauthorized access and monitor activity, physical security and video surveillance work together to protect assets and monitor activity in and around a facility.

The fundamental security concept called Physical security Security guard

It is like having a security guard at the entrance of a building who checks the identity of people entering and ensures that only authorized individuals are allowed in. Physical security measures can include access controls, surveillance systems, alarms, and security personnel, among others. These measures are designed to prevent or deter unauthorized access, detect and respond to security incidents, and minimize the impact of security breaches.

The fundamental security concept called Physical security Access badge

Access badges are a common physical security measure used to control access to secure areas. Access badges are like a key to a locked door. Just as a key can be used to unlock a door and grant access to a room, an access badge can be used to grant access to a secure area. However, just as a key can be lost or stolen, an access badge can be lost or stolen, which is why it is important to have procedures in place to report lost or stolen badges and to deactivate them to prevent unauthorized access.

The fundamental security concept called Physical security Lighting

One aspect of physical security is lighting, which can be compared to a moat around a castle. Just as a moat provides a physical barrier that makes it difficult for intruders to approach a castle, lighting can make it difficult for intruders to approach a building unnoticed. By illuminating the perimeter of a building, security personnel can detect and deter potential threats, making it easier to identify and respond to security incidents.

The fundamental security concept called Physical security Sensors

Security sensors can be compared to motion detectors in a home security system. Just as a motion detector senses movement and triggers an alarm, physical security sensors detect unauthorized access or other security breaches and alert security personnel to take action. Examples of physical security sensors include cameras, motion detectors, and door sensors. By using physical security sensors, organizations can help protect their physical assets and prevent unauthorized access to sensitive areas.

The fundamental security concept of the Physical security Sensor type Infrared

The fundamental security concept of physical security is to protect the physical assets of an organization from unauthorized access, theft, damage, or destruction. One type of physical security sensor is the infrared sensor, which detects heat signatures and can be used to monitor movement in a specific area. An analogy for this would be a motion sensor light that turns on when it detects movement. Similarly, an infrared sensor can detect the presence of a person or object in a specific area and trigger an alarm or other security response.

The fundamental security concept of the Physical security Sensors type Pressure

One type of physical security sensor is a pressure sensor, which can detect changes in pressure and trigger an alarm if someone tries to enter a secured area. An analogy for this would be a scale that measures the weight of an object. Just as a scale can detect changes in weight and alert you if something is added or removed, a pressure sensor can detect changes in pressure and alert security personnel if someone tries to enter a secured area.

The fundamental security concept of the Physical security Sensors type Microwave

Microwave sensors work by emitting a beam of microwave radiation and then measuring the reflection of that beam off of nearby objects. This allows them to detect movement and changes in the environment. An analogy for this could be a bat using echolocation to navigate in the dark. The bat emits a sound wave and then listens for the echo to determine the location of objects around it. Similarly, microwave sensors emit a beam of radiation and then measure the reflection to detect movement and changes in the environment.

The fundamental security concept of the Physical security Sensors type Ultrasonic

Physical security is a fundamental security concept that involves protecting physical assets, such as buildings, equipment, and people, from unauthorized access, theft, damage, or destruction. One type of physical security sensor is the ultrasonic sensor, which uses sound waves to detect movement and proximity. An analogy for this type of sensor could be a bat using echolocation to navigate in the dark. Just as a bat emits sound waves and listens for the echoes to determine the location of objects, an ultrasonic sensor emits sound waves and listens for the echoes to detect movement and proximity.

The fundamental security concept of Deception and disruption technology called a Honeypot

A honeypot is a fundamental security concept of deception and disruption technology. It is a decoy system designed to lure attackers away from the real system and gather information about their methods and motives. It is like a trap that is set up to catch burglars. Just as a burglar may be tempted to break into a house that appears to be unguarded, an attacker may be tempted to target a honeypot that appears to be vulnerable. However, the honeypot is designed to be easily compromised, and any activity on it is monitored and analyzed to improve the security of the real system.

The fundamental security concept of Deception and disruption technology called a Honeynet

A honeynet is a network of honeybot computers that are designed to look like a legitimate network, but are actually a trap for attackers. It is similar to a spider's web, where the spider creates a trap to catch its prey. Similarly, a honeynet is designed to lure attackers into a trap, where their activities can be monitored and analyzed. The honeynet can be used to gather information about the attacker's methods and motives, and to develop countermeasures to prevent future attacks.

The fundamental security concept of Deception and disruption technology called a Honeyfile

One such technique is the use of a Honeyfile, which is a decoy file that appears to be a valuable target to an attacker but is actually designed to alert security personnel to the attacker's presence. An analogy for a Honeyfile could be a fake safe that is placed in a home to deceive burglars. The safe may look real and contain items that appear valuable, but in reality, it is a decoy designed to alert the homeowner to the presence of a burglar. Similarly, a Honeyfile is designed to deceive attackers and alert security personnel to their presence.

The fundamental security concept of Deception and disruption technology called a Honeytoken

A Honeytoken is a type of deception and disruption technology that involves creating a fake target or resource to lure attackers into revealing their presence or intentions. It is similar to a "honey trap" used in espionage, where a person is lured into a compromising situation. In the case of a Honeytoken, the attacker is lured into interacting with a fake system or data, which triggers an alert or provides valuable information to security personnel. This technique can be used to detect and prevent attacks, as well as to gather intelligence on attackers and their methods.

The importance of the Business processes impacting security operation, specifically the Approval process

Business processes play a crucial role in ensuring the security of an organization. The approval process is one such process that impacts security operations. It involves reviewing and approving requests for access to sensitive information, systems, or resources. This process ensures that only authorized personnel have access to sensitive data, which helps prevent data breaches and other security incidents. To put it in an analogy, the approval process is like a bouncer at a nightclub who checks IDs to ensure that only authorized individuals are allowed inside. Similarly, the approval process checks access requests to ensure that only authorized personnel have access to sensitive information. By integrating security into core business processes like the approval process, organizations can ensure that security is not an afterthought but a central pillar of their operations.

The importance of the Business processes impacting security operation, specifically Ownership

Ownership refers to the responsibility for maintaining and securing assets, such as data and systems. In an analogy, ownership can be compared to a homeowner who is responsible for securing their property and possessions. Similarly, in a business context, ownership involves identifying who is responsible for securing the organization's assets and ensuring that they are protected from threats. This includes implementing security controls, monitoring for potential risks, and responding to security incidents. Failure to establish clear ownership can result in security gaps and vulnerabilities that can be exploited by attackers. Therefore, it is essential for organizations to define ownership roles and responsibilities as part of their security operations.

Business processes impacting security operation, specifically Stakeholders

Business processes can have a significant impact on security operations, and it is important to identify and involve all stakeholders in the process. Just as a sports team needs all of its players to work together to achieve a common goal, a business needs all of its stakeholders to work together to ensure the security of its operations. This includes everyone from employees to customers to vendors. Each stakeholder has a unique role to play, and it is important to ensure that everyone is aware of their responsibilities and is working towards the same goal. Failure to involve all stakeholders can result in gaps in security that can be exploited by attackers, just as a sports team with missing players would be at a disadvantage.

The importance of the Business processes impacting security operation, specifically Impact analysis

The Business Impact Analysis (BIA) is an essential component of the business continuity planning process. It helps organizations identify and prioritize critical business functions and processes, and assess the potential impact of disruptions to those functions. In other words, it's like a doctor performing a diagnosis on a patient to identify the most critical organs and systems that need to be protected in case of an emergency. Just as a doctor would prioritize the most critical organs to save a patient's life, a BIA helps organizations prioritize the most critical business functions to ensure continuity of operations in the event of a disruption. By conducting a BIA, organizations can develop effective business continuity plans that minimize the impact of disruptions and ensure the survival of the business.

The importance of the Business processes impacting security operation, specifically Test results

Test results are an example of a business process that can impact security operations. By conducting regular security risk assessments, organizations can identify vulnerabilities in their IT ecosystem and understand the financial threat they pose to the organization, from downtime and related profit loss to legal fees and compliance penalties to customer churn and lost business. By prioritizing mitigation efforts based on the potential impact on business processes, organizations can avoid costly business disruptions, data breaches, compliance penalties, and other damage. In other words, just as a doctor would prioritize treating a life-threatening condition over a minor one, organizations should prioritize mitigating security risks that could have a significant impact on their business processes over those that are less critical.

The importance of the Business processes impacting security operation, specifically Backout plans

Business processes impacting security operations are critical to the success of any organization. One such process is the backout plan, which is a contingency plan that outlines the steps to be taken in case a change or update to a system or application fails. A backout plan is essential because it ensures that the system can be restored to its previous state quickly and efficiently, minimizing downtime and reducing the risk of data loss. To understand the importance of a backout plan, consider the analogy of a tightrope walker. Just as a tightrope walker needs a safety net to catch them in case they fall, a backout plan provides a safety net for an organization's systems and applications. Without a backout plan, a failed change or update could have disastrous consequences, leading to lost revenue, damaged reputation, and even legal penalties. Therefore, it is crucial for organizations to have a well-defined backout plan as part of their overall business continuity plan.

The importance of the Business processes impacting security operation, specifically Maintenance windows

One of these processes is maintenance windows, which are periods of time during which a service is made unavailable to allow for maintenance operations. Maintenance windows are essential because they allow organizations to perform necessary maintenance and be more comfortable with normal operations. The alternative is to live in a perpetual state of lack of confidence, with obsolete and non-optimized systems. An analogy to understand the importance of maintenance windows is to think of a car that needs regular maintenance to keep it running smoothly. If the car is not maintained, it will eventually break down, and the cost of repairs will be much higher than the cost of regular maintenance. Similarly, if an organization does not perform regular maintenance on its systems, it will eventually lead to system failures, which can be costly to repair and can cause significant damage to the organization's reputation. Therefore, it is essential to schedule maintenance windows during off-peak hours and inform users in advance to avoid any inconvenience.

The importance of the Business processes impacting security operation, specifically Standard operating procedures (SOP)

Standard operating procedures (SOPs) are crucial for any business as they provide consistency, reduce errors, support communication, and help standardize processes. SOPs are like a recipe for a dish, where each step is clearly defined, and the ingredients are measured precisely. Just as a recipe ensures that the dish is prepared consistently every time, SOPs ensure that tasks are completed consistently every time. SOPs are also useful for employee training, investigating accidents and incidents, identifying trends, and implementing corrective action plans. By developing and implementing SOPs, businesses can improve their efficiency, reduce costs, and set themselves up for success.

The importance and security impact of change management Technical implications

Technical implications of change management include the need to ensure that changes are properly tested and validated before they are implemented, and that they do not negatively impact the organization's security posture. An analogy for change management could be a pilot flying a plane. Just as a pilot must carefully plan and execute each step of a flight to ensure a safe arrival at the destination, an organization must carefully plan and execute each change to its IT infrastructure to ensure that it does not compromise the security of the organization.

The importance and security impact of the change management Technical implication called Allow lists/deny lists

Allow lists/deny lists are a technical implication of change management. An analogy to explain this concept is a bouncer at a nightclub who checks the IDs of people trying to enter. The bouncer has a list of allowed IDs and will only allow people with those IDs to enter the club. Similarly, in the context of change management, an allow list is a list of approved changes that are allowed to be made, while a deny list is a list of changes that are not allowed. These lists help ensure that only authorized changes are made to a system, reducing the risk of unauthorized access or other security issues.

The importance and security impact of the change management Technical implication called Restricted activities

Restricted activities are certain activities that are restricted or prohibited during the change management process to ensure that changes are made in a controlled and secure manner. An analogy for this would be a construction site where certain areas are restricted to authorized personnel only. Just as unauthorized personnel can cause damage or accidents on a construction site, unauthorized activities during change management can cause security breaches or system failures. Therefore, restricted activities are put in place to ensure that only authorized personnel make changes to the system, reducing the risk of security incidents.

The importance and security impact of the change management Technical implication called Downtime

The change management technical implication called Downtime refers to the period of time when a system or service is unavailable due to maintenance or upgrades. This can be compared to a car being taken to the mechanic for repairs. While the car is being worked on, it cannot be driven and is therefore unavailable for use. Downtime can have a significant impact on the security of a system, as it can create opportunities for attackers to exploit vulnerabilities or gain unauthorized access. It is important to carefully plan and schedule downtime to minimize its impact on system availability and security. Additionally, it is crucial to ensure that all necessary security measures are in place before and after downtime to prevent potential security breaches.

The importance and security impact of the change management Technical implication called Service restart

One of the technical implications of change management is the service restart. A service restart is like a car engine that needs to be turned off and on again to fix a problem. Similarly, a service restart is a process of stopping and starting a service to fix an issue or implement a change. This technical implication is important because it can impact the availability and performance of the service. Without proper change management, a service restart can be done without proper testing, which can lead to unintended consequences such as service downtime or data loss. Therefore, it is crucial to follow change management procedures to ensure that service restarts are done correctly and with minimal risk to the organization.

The importance and security impact of the change management Technical implication called Application restart

This is important because it ensures that the application is functioning properly and that any changes made have been implemented correctly. It is similar to restarting a computer after installing new software or updates to ensure that the changes take effect and the system is running smoothly. From a security perspective, Application Restart can help prevent vulnerabilities and ensure that any security-related changes have been properly implemented and are functioning as intended.

The importance and security impact of the change management Technical implication called Legacy applications

The change management technical implication called Legacy applications refers to the use of outdated software or hardware that is no longer supported by the vendor. This can pose a significant security risk as these legacy applications may contain vulnerabilities that can be exploited by attackers. It is similar to using an old lock on a door that is no longer secure and can be easily picked by a burglar. Therefore, it is important to ensure that legacy applications are either updated or replaced with newer, more secure alternatives to prevent potential security breaches.

The importance and security impact of the change management Technical implication called Dependencies

The Dependencies technical implication in change management refers to the relationships between different components of a system and how changes to one component can impact others. This is similar to how a game of Jenga works, where each block represents a component of the system and removing or changing one block can cause the entire structure to collapse. It is important to understand these dependencies and their potential impact on the system before making any changes, as failure to do so can result in unintended consequences and security vulnerabilities. By properly managing dependencies, organizations can ensure that changes are made in a controlled and secure manner, minimizing the risk of system failures and security breaches.

The importance and security impact of Documentation

Documentation is a crucial aspect of security, as it helps organizations protect their information and property. Documentation security involves the maintenance of all essential documents stored, filed, backed up, processed, delivered, and eventually discarded when they are no longer needed. Documentation includes everything from building occupant rosters to cybersecurity penetration test reports. It is essential for all types of cybersecurity, but it is particularly critical for companies that deal with high-risk activities like financial transactions or electronic health records. Documentation plays a central role in preparing for potential security incidents, and automating as much of it as possible makes a huge difference. Documentation can help reduce potential confusion and simplify the process as much as possible to ensure a successful outcome. An analogy for documentation is that it is like a blueprint for a building. Just as a blueprint provides a detailed plan for constructing a building, documentation provides a detailed plan for protecting an organization's information and property.

The importance and security impact of Documentation and Version control Version control

Documentation and version control are essential for ensuring the accuracy, completeness, and security of documents. Version control is the process of tracking and managing a document's journey from draft to final copy. It helps ensure that the most up-to-date and accurate documents are being used and that employees and decision-makers are not acting on information that is out-of-date, incomplete, or missing across individuals and departments. Version control allows multiple parties to work on the same document simultaneously and tracks changes made by each person, improving collaboration and communication among team members. It also helps identify and resolve conflicts more quickly, enhances quality, and provides a record of the changes made to a document over time, which can be useful for compliance and regulatory purposes. In an analogy, version control is like a librarian who keeps track of all the books in the library, ensuring that each book is in its proper place and that the library's collection is up-to-date and accurate. Without proper documentation and version control, organizations risk compromising the effectiveness of their operations and decision-making, leading to major financial and efficiency concerns.

The importance and security impact of Documentation and Updating policies/procedures

Documentation and updating policies/procedures are crucial for maintaining the security of an organization. They provide a clear set of guidelines and instructions for employees to follow, ensuring that everyone is on the same page and working towards the same goals. Think of it like a recipe book - if everyone follows the same recipe, the end result will be consistent and predictable. Similarly, if everyone in an organization follows the same policies and procedures, the security of the organization will be more consistent and predictable. Regularly updating these policies and procedures is also important, as it ensures that they remain relevant and effective in the face of changing threats and technologies. It's like updating a map - if you don't update it regularly, you might end up lost or taking a longer route than necessary. In the same way, if policies and procedures aren't updated regularly, they may become outdated and ineffective, leaving the organization vulnerable to security threats.

The importance and security impact of Version control

Version control is a critical aspect of software development and has a significant impact on security. It is like a time machine that allows developers to track changes made to the codebase over time and revert to previous versions if necessary. This is important because it enables developers to identify and fix security vulnerabilities that may have been introduced in the codebase. Without version control, it would be difficult to keep track of changes made to the codebase, making it harder to identify and fix security issues. Additionally, version control allows multiple developers to work on the same codebase simultaneously, reducing the risk of errors and conflicts that could lead to security vulnerabilities. Overall, version control is an essential tool for ensuring the security and integrity of software development projects.

The importance of using Public key infrastructure (PKI)

Public Key Infrastructure (PKI) is a system that uses digital certificates and public and private key pairs to secure communications over the internet. It is important to use PKI because it provides a secure way to transmit sensitive information, such as credit card numbers or personal data, over the internet. PKI works like a lock and key system, where the public key is the lock and the private key is the key. The public key is used to encrypt the data, and the private key is used to decrypt it. This ensures that only the intended recipient can read the information, and that it has not been tampered with during transmission. PKI also provides a way to verify the identity of the sender, which is important for preventing fraud and ensuring that the information is coming from a trusted source.

The importance of using Public key infrastructure (PKI) Public key

Public Key Infrastructure (PKI) is a framework that is used to create, manage, distribute, use, store, and revoke digital certificates and manage public-key encryption. It is like a passport that certifies one's identity as a citizen of a country, but in the digital world, it establishes the identity of users within the ecosystem. PKI uses asymmetric encryption methods to ensure that messages remain private and also to authenticate the device or user sending the transmission. It involves the use of a public and private key, where the public key authenticates the sender of the digital message, while the private key ensures that only the recipient can open and read it. In PKI, the public key is widely available and used by others who want to encrypt a message being sent to you. The private key is a secret key held by the user and is the only key that can decrypt messages that are sent to it. When someone wants to disseminate a public key, they go to a CA and provide sufficient proof of their identity to satisfy the Certificate Authority (CA). In turn, the CA produces a certificate that asserts that the public key is a certain key and includes sufficient information about the user's identity that we can be confident about associating the user with the public key in the certificate.

The importance of using Public key infrastructure

(PKI) Private key

Public Key Infrastructure (PKI) is a security framework that uses encryption to protect and authenticate digital communications. PKI uses a pair of keys: the public key and the private key to achieve security. The public key is available to anyone who requests it and is issued by a trusted certificate authority. This public key verifies and authenticates the sender of the encrypted message. The private key is kept private by the recipient of the encrypted message and used to decrypt the transmission. An analogy to understand PKI is to think of a locked mailbox. The mailbox is the recipient's private key, and only the recipient has the key to open it. The sender can put a message in the mailbox, but only the recipient can open it with their key. PKI certificates verify the owner of a private key and the authenticity of that relationship going forward to help maintain security. The importance of using PKI private key is that it significantly increases the security of a network and provides the foundation for securing all internet-connected things.

The importance of using Public key infrastructure (PKI) Key escrow

Key escrow is a process of storing important cryptographic keys in a secure location. It involves the creation of a third-party repository for these keys, where they can be securely stored and accessed by authorized parties. Key escrow is important in cybersecurity because it provides a way to ensure that encrypted data can be accessed in the event of an emergency or easily without the organization needing to build a way to do it themselves. It is like a safety deposit box at a bank where the bank holds the key to the box, but only the owner of the box can access its contents. Similarly, in key escrow, the trusted third party holds the key, but only the parties involved in the communication can access the encrypted data. Key escrow is often used in situations where the owner of the system has forgotten their password or has become incapacitated.

The importance of using Encryption

Encryption is a crucial aspect of information security that helps protect sensitive data from unauthorized access. It involves converting plain text into a coded message that can only be deciphered with a key or password. Encryption is like a secret code that only the intended recipient can understand. Without encryption, sensitive information such as passwords, credit card numbers, and personal data can be easily intercepted and read by attackers. Encryption ensures that even if an attacker intercepts the data, they cannot read it without the key or password. Therefore, it is essential to use encryption to safeguard sensitive information and prevent unauthorized access.

The importance of selecting the appropriate Encryption Level

Selecting the appropriate encryption level is crucial in ensuring the security of data. Encryption is like a lock on a door, and the encryption level determines the strength of the lock. Just as a weak lock can be easily picked, weak encryption can be easily broken, leaving sensitive data vulnerable to theft or misuse. On the other hand, overly strong encryption can be like a lock that is too complex to open, making it difficult or impossible to access the data when needed. Therefore, it is important to select the appropriate encryption level that provides adequate security without being overly complex or difficult to manage.

The importance of selecting the appropriate Encryption Level such as Full-disk Encryption

Encryption is a crucial aspect of information security, and selecting the appropriate encryption level is essential to protect sensitive data. Full-disk encryption is a type of encryption that encrypts an entire hard drive, making it unreadable without the correct decryption key. This is similar to locking a safe that contains valuable items. Just as a safe protects its contents from unauthorized access, full-disk encryption protects the data on a hard drive from unauthorized access. It is important to select the appropriate encryption level, such as full-disk encryption, to ensure that sensitive data is protected from unauthorized access in the event of theft or loss of the device.

The importance of selecting the appropriate Encryption Level such as Partition Encryption

Partition encryption is a type of encryption that

encrypts specific parts of a hard drive or storage device. It is similar to locking a specific drawer in a cabinet that contains sensitive information, while leaving the other drawers unlocked. Just as you would not lock the entire cabinet for a single sensitive document, it is important to use partition encryption to protect only the sensitive data, rather than encrypting the entire storage device. This helps to reduce the overhead of encryption and decryption, and ensures that only the sensitive data is protected, while the rest of the data remains easily accessible.

The importance of selecting the appropriate Encryption Level such as File Encryption

File encryption is a type of encryption that is used to protect individual files or folders. It is important to select the appropriate encryption level to ensure that the data is protected from unauthorized access. Choosing a weak encryption level is like using a simple lock to secure a valuable item, which can be easily broken into by a thief. On the other hand, choosing a strong encryption level is like using a complex lock that requires a unique key to open, making it much more difficult for a thief to break into. Therefore, selecting the appropriate encryption level is crucial to ensure the security of sensitive data.

The importance of selecting the appropriate Encryption Level such as Volume Encryption

Volume encryption is a type of encryption that encrypts an entire volume or disk, making it unreadable without the appropriate decryption key. It is like locking a safe that contains all your valuables, making it impossible for anyone to access the contents without the key. The appropriate encryption level should be selected based on the sensitivity of the data being protected, the potential risks, and the performance impact of the encryption. For example, highly sensitive data such as financial records or personal health information should be encrypted with a high level of encryption, while less sensitive data such as public information may require a lower level of encryption.

The importance of selecting the appropriate Encryption Level such as Database Encryption

Database encryption is one such encryption level that can be used to protect sensitive data stored in databases. It works by converting plain text data into a coded format that can only be read by authorized users with the decryption key. Choosing the appropriate encryption level is like choosing the right lock for a door. Just as a flimsy lock can be easily picked, weak encryption can be easily broken, leaving data vulnerable to theft or misuse. Therefore, it is important to select the appropriate encryption level, such as database encryption, to ensure that data is protected from unauthorized access.

The importance of selecting the appropriate Encryption Level such as Record Encryption

Record encryption is a type of encryption that encrypts individual records within a database, providing an additional layer of security. It is like locking individual drawers in a cabinet, where each drawer contains sensitive information. If an attacker gains access to the cabinet, they will still need to unlock each drawer to access the information, making it more difficult for them to steal the data. Therefore, selecting the appropriate encryption level, such as record encryption, is crucial to protect sensitive data from unauthorized access and maintain the confidentiality and integrity of the information.

The importance of selecting the appropriate Encryption solution such as Transport/communication

Transport/communication encryption is used to secure data in transit, such as when sending an email or accessing a website. On the other hand, disk encryption is used to secure data at rest, such as when storing data on a hard drive. Selecting the appropriate encryption solution depends on various factors, such as the type of data being protected, the level of security required, and the potential threats and risks.

The importance of selecting the appropriate Encryption solution such as Asymmetric

Asymmetric encryption is where two keys, a public key, and a private key, are used to encrypt and decrypt data. The public key is used to encrypt the data, and the private key is used to decrypt the data. This method is like a mailbox where anyone can drop a letter into the mailbox, but only the person with the key can open the mailbox and read the letter. Asymmetric encryption has enabled the exchange of symmetric keys, encryption of data, digital signatures, and other significant security features. It is essential to select the appropriate encryption solution to ensure that data is secure and protected from unauthorized access.

The importance of selecting the appropriate Encryption solution such as Symmetric

Symmetric encryption is a type of encryption that uses the same key for both encryption and decryption. It is like a lock and key system, where the same key is used to lock and unlock a door. The key must be kept secret to ensure that only authorized parties can access the encrypted data. Selecting the appropriate encryption solution, such as symmetric encryption, is important because it ensures that the data is protected from unauthorized access and that the encryption process does not introduce additional vulnerabilities.

The importance of selecting the appropriate Encryption solution such as Key exchange

Selecting the right encryption solution, such as key exchange, is important because it determines the level of security and the ability to protect data from unauthorized access. An analogy to explain this is a lock and key. Just as a lock and key protect a physical object, encryption protects digital data. However, just as a weak lock can be easily picked, a weak encryption solution can be easily broken, leaving the data vulnerable to unauthorized access. Therefore, selecting the appropriate encryption solution is essential to ensure the security and privacy of sensitive data.

The importance of selecting the appropriate Encryption Algorithms

Encryption algorithms are like locks on a door, and just as different locks provide varying levels of security, different encryption algorithms provide varying levels of protection. Choosing the right algorithm depends on the sensitivity of the data being protected and the potential threats it may face. For example, a simple lock may be sufficient to secure a garden shed, but a more complex lock would be needed to secure a bank vault. Similarly, a less complex encryption algorithm may be sufficient for less sensitive data, but more complex algorithms are needed for highly sensitive data. It is important to select the appropriate encryption algorithm to ensure that data is protected from unauthorized access and tampering.

The importance of selecting the appropriate Encryption Key length

Encryption key length is an important factor in ensuring the security of data. The longer the key length, the more difficult it is for an attacker to decrypt the data. It is like a lock on a door, where a longer key is like a more complex lock that is harder to pick. The appropriate key length depends on the level of security required and the sensitivity of the data being protected. For example, a 128-bit key is considered secure for most applications, but for highly sensitive data, a longer key length may be necessary. It is important to select the appropriate key length to ensure that the data is protected from unauthorized access.

The importance of selecting the appropriate Encryption tool named Trusted Platform Module (TPM)

The Trusted Platform Module (TPM) is an encryption tool that is used to secure sensitive data by providing a secure storage area for cryptographic keys. It is important to select the appropriate encryption tool like TPM because it can help protect against unauthorized access to data. An analogy for this would be a safe deposit box at a bank. Just as a safe deposit box provides a secure storage area for valuable items, TPM provides a secure storage area for cryptographic keys. By using TPM, sensitive data can be protected from unauthorized access, just as valuable items are protected in a safe deposit box.

The importance of selecting the appropriate Encryption tool named Hardware security module (HSM)

Hardware Security Modules (HSMs) are specialized computing devices designed to securely store and use cryptographic keys. They are tamper-resistant physical devices that perform various operations surrounding cryptography, such as encryption, decryption, authentication, and key exchange facilitation, among others. HSMs are considered the "Root of Trust" in an organization's security infrastructure because they are trusted and free of any potential breach from malware, viruses, and unauthorized access. HSMs are crucial in protecting cryptographic keys by generating and protecting keys within a secured environment. They are used to control access and limit risk to a company's sensitive private keys. An analogy to understand the importance of selecting the appropriate encryption tool named HSM is like keeping your valuables in a safe deposit box at a bank. Just as you trust the bank to keep your valuables safe, you can trust HSMs to keep your cryptographic keys safe from attackers trying to hack your systems.

The importance of selecting the appropriate Encryption tool named Key management system

Key Management System (KMS) is responsible for generating, exchanging, storing, using, destroying, and replacing encryption keys. It ensures that only authorized individuals can access the encryption keys needed to decrypt sensitive information, and it helps ensure the integrity of encrypted data by preventing unauthorized changes or tampering. The importance of selecting the appropriate KMS can be compared to choosing the right key for a lock. Just as the wrong key cannot open a lock, the wrong KMS cannot provide adequate encryption key management, which can lead to data breaches and other security incidents. Therefore, careful planning, secure systems, and well-defined policies and procedures are necessary to ensure the safety of encryption keys and the security of sensitive information.

The importance of selecting the appropriate Encryption tool named Secure enclave

The Secure Enclave is an encryption tool used in Apple devices to protect sensitive data such as fingerprints, passwords, and other personal information. It is like a safe within a house, where the most valuable possessions are kept. The Secure Enclave is a separate processor that is isolated from the main processor and has its own memory, which makes it difficult for hackers to access the data stored within it. It is designed to perform cryptographic operations such as generating and storing encryption keys, and it can also authenticate users and devices. Overall, the Secure Enclave is an important security feature that helps to protect users' sensitive data from unauthorized access.

The importance of Obfuscation

Obfuscation is the practice of making something unclear or difficult to understand. In the context of security, obfuscation is important because it can help protect sensitive information from unauthorized access. It involves hiding or disguising information in a way that makes it difficult for attackers to decipher. An analogy for obfuscation in security could be a secret code that only the intended recipient knows how to decode. Just as a code can protect a message from being understood by someone who doesn't have the key, obfuscation can protect sensitive information from being understood by unauthorized parties.

The importance of Steganography

Steganography is the practice of hiding information within other information in a way that is not apparent to the casual observer. It is an important tool for maintaining the confidentiality of sensitive information, as it allows for the transmission of information without arousing suspicion. An analogy for steganography would be a spy writing a message in invisible ink on a seemingly innocuous piece of paper. To the casual observer, the paper appears to be blank, but to those who know where to look, the hidden message can be revealed. In the same way, steganography allows for the transmission of information in a way that is hidden in plain sight. This is particularly important in situations where the transmission of sensitive information must be kept secret from prying eyes.

The importance of Tokenization
Tokenization is a process of replacing sensitive data with unique identification symbols, or tokens, that retain all the essential information about the data without compromising its security. It is an essential security measure that helps protect sensitive data such as credit card numbers, social security numbers, and other personal information from unauthorized access and theft. An analogy for tokenization is a valet key for a car. Just as a valet key allows a driver to operate a car without access to the trunk or glove compartment, a token allows authorized users to access the data they need without exposing the sensitive information to potential attackers.

The importance of Data masking
Data masking is an important security technique that involves hiding sensitive data by replacing it with fictitious data. This is similar to wearing a mask to hide one's identity. The purpose of data masking is to protect sensitive data from unauthorized access and to reduce the risk of data breaches. By masking sensitive data, organizations can ensure that only authorized personnel have access to it, while still allowing other users to work with the data in a meaningful way. This is particularly important in industries such as healthcare and finance, where sensitive data such as patient records and financial information must be protected.

The importance of Hashing
Hashing is a crucial aspect of information security that involves transforming data into a fixed-length string of characters. This process is similar to a meat grinder, where the input is the meat and the output is the ground meat. The resulting hash value is unique to the input data, and any change to the input data will result in a different hash value. Hashing is important because it allows for the verification of data integrity and authenticity. By comparing the hash value of the original data to the hash value of the received data, one can determine if the data has been tampered with or corrupted. This is similar to checking the seal on a jar of food to ensure that it

has not been opened or contaminated.

The importance of Salting
Salting is an important technique used in cryptography to protect passwords and other sensitive data. It involves adding a random string of characters to the password before it is hashed, making it more difficult for attackers to crack the password using precomputed hash tables or rainbow tables. An analogy for salting would be adding a secret ingredient to a recipe to make it more difficult for someone to replicate the dish. Just as the secret ingredient adds an extra layer of protection to the recipe, salting adds an extra layer of protection to passwords and other sensitive data.

The importance of Digital signatures
Digital signatures are a secure and efficient way to authenticate digital documents and verify the identity of the signer. They provide proof of the message origin and a method to verify the integrity of the message. Digital signatures are like a seal on a letter, ensuring that the contents of the letter have not been tampered with and that the sender is who they claim to be. They are legally binding in many countries, including the US, and have the same value as traditional handwritten document signatures. Digital signatures offer several benefits, including cost-cutting, time-saving, and improved security. They are used in various industries, including healthcare, finance, and government, to improve efficiency, reduce waste, and secure personal data. Digital signatures are an essential tool in reducing the risk of fraud and ensuring accountability within business and employment contracts.

The importance of Key stretching
Key stretching is a technique used in cryptography to make a weak key, such as a password or passphrase, stronger by increasing the time and resources required to test each possible key. Passwords or passphrases created by humans are often short or predictable enough to allow password cracking, and key stretching is intended to make such attacks more difficult by complicating a basic step of trying a single password candidate. Key

stretching algorithms depend on an algorithm which receives an input key and then expends considerable effort to generate a stretched cipher (called an enhanced key) mimicking randomness and longer key length. An analogy for key stretching is like stretching a rubber band. Just as stretching a rubber band makes it harder to break, key stretching makes it harder for attackers to crack passwords or keys. Key stretching is an important technique to improve the security of stored passwords and prevent the success of some password attacks such as brute force attacks and rainbow table attacks.

The importance of Blockchain
A Blockchain is a decentralized technology that can transform various industries, including banking, education, and democracy. It offers secure and efficient transactions, reduces compliance costs, and speeds up data transfer processing. Blockchain technology can help with contract management, audit the origin of a product, and manage titles and deeds. It can also streamline record-keeping and sharing, enhance security and improve trust, simplify the verification and traceability of multistep transactions, and lower education costs. An analogy to understand blockchain is to think of it as a digital ledger that records transactions in chronological order, making it easy to trace the data's origins and verify its authenticity. Blockchain eliminates the need for a middleman, making it a peer-to-peer payment system with the highest security and low fees. Blockchain technology has the potential to strengthen democracies by enhancing trust and better protecting information.

The importance of Open public ledger
A public ledger is a decentralized record-keeping system that tracks value as it moves around. It is accessible to anyone, anywhere in the world. The importance of a public ledger lies in its ability to maintain transparency, security, and accountability in transactions. It is like a public library where anyone can access the books, and the books cannot be altered or removed once they are in the library. Similarly, a public ledger is immutable, meaning that once a transaction is recorded, it cannot be changed or deleted. This makes it an effective tool for maintaining the integrity of financial systems and preventing fraud. The use of public ledgers has gained popularity in the world of

cryptocurrency, where it is used to maintain participants' identities anonymously, their respective cryptocurrency balances, and a record of all the genuine transactions executed between network participants.

The importance of Certificates

Certificates are digital documents that verify the identity of a person, organization, or device. They are important in cybersecurity because they help ensure secure communication between parties. Certificates work like a passport or driver's license, providing proof of identity and allowing access to certain resources. In the same way that a passport confirms a person's identity and allows them to travel internationally, a certificate confirms the identity of a device or user and allows them to access secure resources. Without certificates, it would be difficult to verify the identity of parties involved in communication, leaving them vulnerable to attacks.

The importance of Certificate authorities

A Certificate Authority (CA) is a trusted organization that issues digital certificates used to establish trust in electronic communications and transactions. A digital certificate is like a passport that verifies the identity of an individual or organization and binds their identity to a public key. The CA's role is to verify the identity of the entity and issue a certificate that binds the entity's identity to a public key. This certificate can establish a secure connection between the entity and a website or a device. In other words, a CA is like a trusted third party that vouches for the identity of an entity, just like a passport office vouches for the identity of a person. Without trusted CAs to issue digital certificates, online transactions would be less secure, and data entered into a webform could potentially be captured by a hacker who is "sniffing" the data between the browser and the server. Therefore, CAs are a reliable and critical trust anchor of the internet's public key infrastructure (PKI), and they help secure the internet for both organizations and users.

The importance of Certificate revocation lists (CRLs)

Certificate revocation lists (CRLs) are lists of digital certificates that have been revoked by the issuing certificate authority (CA) before their actual or scheduled expiration date. CRLs are an important component of a public key infrastructure (PKI) system designed to identify and authenticate users to a shared resource like a Wi-Fi network. They are used to inform clients whenever a certificate has been revoked, and they warn site visitors not to access a site that may be fraudulently impersonating a legitimate site. CRLs are like a "blacklist" of revoked certificates, and they protect visitors from man-in-the-middle attacks. CRLs are necessary because they help ensure that digital certificates are trustworthy, and they are an essential step in a PKI-based transaction. Without CRLs, users would be faced with numerous security and privacy risks. An analogy for CRLs is a "no-fly list" that prevents individuals who pose a security risk from boarding a plane.

The importance of Online Certificate Status Protocol (OCSP)

The Online Certificate Status Protocol (OCSP) is a protocol used to check the revocation status of an X.509 digital certificate. It is an alternative to certificate revocation lists (CRL), which had to be frequently downloaded to keep the list current at the client end. OCSP overcomes this limitation of CRL and enables real-time status checks on security certificates. OCSP works by sending a request for certificate status information when a user attempts to access a server. The server then sends back a response stating that the certificate is either "current," "expired," or "unknown". OCSP can be compared to a bouncer at a club who checks your ID to make sure you are allowed to enter. Similarly, OCSP checks the revocation status of a digital certificate to ensure that it is valid and has not been revoked before allowing access to a website.

The importance of Self-signed

Self-signed certificates are digital certificates that are not signed by a trusted third-party certificate authority (CA). Instead, they are signed with their own private key, which means that they are not backed by a well-known and trusted third party, and therefore may not be considered as secure as a certificate issued by a trusted authority. Self-signed certificates offer some advantages when used in internal networks and software development phases, as they are fast, free, and easy to issue. However, they can also create several risks without proper visibility and control, and they are not appropriate for commercial use. Using a self-signed certificate is like creating your own driver's license instead of getting one from the DMV. While it may be faster and easier, it is not as secure or trustworthy as a license issued by a trusted authority.

The importance of Third-party

Third-party refers to an external entity that provides services or products to an organization. Third-party vendors can pose a significant risk to an organization's security posture. This is because they may have access to sensitive data or systems, and if they are not properly vetted, they can be a potential entry point for attackers. An analogy for this would be like inviting a stranger into your home to fix your plumbing without verifying their credentials or background. You are essentially giving them access to your personal space without knowing if they can be trusted. Therefore, it is crucial for organizations to establish a robust third-party risk management program to ensure that their vendors are properly vetted and monitored to minimize the risk of a security breach.

The importance of Root of trust

A root of trust is a fundamental security concept that is critical to the security of a computing system. It is a security foundation for a computing system that is essential to secure the boot process to prevent the installation of malicious software. A hardware root of trust is the foundation on which all secure operations of a computing system depend. It contains the keys used for cryptographic functions and enables a secure boot process. A hardware root of trust is like the foundation of a building, which must be strong and secure to support the entire structure. If the foundation is weak, the building will be vulnerable to collapse. Similarly, if the root of trust is not secure, the entire computing system will be vulnerable to attacks. Therefore, it is crucial to have a hardware root of trust to ensure the security of the computing system.

The importance of Certificate signing request (CSR) generation

A Certificate Signing Request (CSR) is a crucial component in obtaining an SSL/TLS certificate, which is used to encrypt online transactions and secure web traffic. A CSR is an encoded file containing information about your website, service, organization, and domain name. It is generated on the same server where you plan to install the certificate and contains information that the Certificate Authority (CA) will use to create your certificate. The CSR also contains your public key and signature, which helps to verify your identity and secure communications to your site. In other words, a CSR is like a request form that you fill out to get a certificate, and it contains all the necessary information that the CA needs to verify your identity and issue the certificate. Without a CSR, you cannot obtain an SSL/TLS certificate, which means that your website or online service will not be secure and may be vulnerable to cyber attacks.

The importance of Wildcards

Wildcards are symbols used in computing to represent one or more characters in a string of text. They are often used in search functions to broaden the scope of a search. An analogy for wildcards would be a fishing net. Just as a fishing net catches a variety of fish, a wildcard can match a variety of characters in a search string. For example, the wildcard symbol "*" can match any number of characters in a search string, while the "?" symbol can match a single character. Wildcards are commonly used in security settings to allow or block access to a range of IP addresses or domain names. Wildcards are used in digital certificates to secure multiple subdomains of a domain with a single certificate. Wildcard certificates are a type of SSL/TLS certificate that includes a wildcard character (*) in the domain name field. They can be used to secure a primary domain and all its first-level subdomains. Wildcard certificates can provide significant time and cost savings, particularly for small businesses. However, they also have some limitations and potential security risks. For example, if the certificate's private key is compromised, an attacker can impersonate any domain under that wildcard certificate. Cybercriminals use certificates to host malicious websites for phishing campaigns. Wildcard certificates can also be difficult to track, and teams may not remember all the places they installed a wildcard certificate, making it difficult to keep track and manage effectively at scale.

Domain 2.0
Threats, Vulnerabilities, and Mitigations

Threat actors and their motivations

Threat actors are entities that are responsible for an event that has an impact on the safety of another entity. They are the bad guys who are trying to harm your network and data. Threat actors can be categorized into different types based on their motivations and objectives. For example, some threat actors are looking to implement an advanced persistent threat (APT), while others are looking to steal sensitive data or disrupt services. Threat actors can be insiders, such as employees or contractors, who have a lot of control over what they can do inside your network. They can also be external entities, such as nation-states or cybercriminals, who are trying to exploit vulnerabilities in your network. Understanding the different types of threat actors and their motivations is crucial for developing effective security strategies to protect your network and data. An analogy for threat actors could be burglars who are trying to break into your house to steal your valuables. Just as burglars can have different motivations, such as financial gain or personal vendettas, threat actors can have different motivations for attacking your network.

Nation-state Threat actors and their motivations

A nation-state threat actor is a group of individuals who are sponsored by a government to conduct cyber attacks against other countries or organizations. These groups are often well-funded and have access to advanced tools and techniques that allow them to carry out sophisticated attacks. An analogy to explain this concept could be a group of professional thieves who are hired by a wealthy individual to break into a rival's home and steal valuable information. The thieves are well-trained, have access to advanced tools and techniques, and are motivated by the promise of a large payout. Similarly, nation-state threat actors are well-funded, have access to advanced tools and techniques, and are motivated by the interests of their sponsoring government. It is important to note that nation-state threat actors are considered to be some of the most dangerous and sophisticated cyber attackers, and their attacks can have significant consequences for their targets.

Unskilled attacker Threat actors and their motivations

An unskilled attacker is someone who has little to no knowledge or experience in hacking or cyber attacks. They may use basic tools and techniques to try to gain unauthorized access to a system or network, but they lack the expertise to carry out more sophisticated attacks. An analogy for an unskilled attacker could be a burglar who tries to break into a house by using a crowbar to force open a window, but doesn't know how to bypass the security system or pick a lock. In contrast, a threat actor is a broader term that refers to anyone who poses a threat to the security of a system or network, including hackers, cybercriminals, insiders, and even natural disasters or other external events. Threat actors can range from individual attackers to organized crime groups or nation-state actors, and they may use a variety of tactics and tools to achieve their goals. An analogy for a threat actor could be a group of thieves who plan a heist, using a combination of tools, tactics, and teamwork to break into a high-security vault and steal valuable items.

Hacktivist Threat actors and their motivations

Hacktivist threat actors are individuals or groups who use hacking techniques to promote a political or social agenda. They are motivated by a desire to bring attention to a particular cause or issue, and they often use their skills to disrupt or damage the systems of organizations or individuals they perceive as being opposed to their goals. An analogy for hacktivist threat actors could be a group of activists who stage a protest or demonstration to raise awareness about a particular issue. Just as activists might block a street or disrupt a public event to draw attention to their cause, hacktivists might use hacking techniques to disrupt or damage the systems of organizations they believe are acting against their interests.

Insider threat Threat actors and their motivations

an insider threat is a security risk that comes from within an organization, such as an employee or contractor who has access to sensitive information. These individuals may intentionally or unintentionally cause harm to the organization, either by stealing data or damaging systems. An analogy for an insider threat could be a Trojan horse, where the threat appears to be harmless or even beneficial, but actually contains hidden dangers that can cause significant damage. Threat actors can have various motivations, such as financial gain, revenge, or ideology. It is important for organizations to have policies and procedures in place to detect and prevent insider threats, as well as to educate employees on the risks and consequences of their actions.

Organized crime Threat actors and their motivations

Organized crime is a type of criminal activity that is carried out by a group of individuals who work together to achieve a common goal, usually financial gain. An analogy for organized crime could be a spider web, where the criminals work together to create a complex network of illegal activities that are difficult to detect and dismantle. According to the UNODC, organized criminal groups are mainly motivated by financial profit through crime, and they respond to public demand for services. Corruption is an enabler that protects organized crime operations, and sometimes intimidation, threats, and/or force are also needed to protect those operations. Organized criminal groups can also adopt terrorist tactics of indiscriminate violence and large-scale public intimidation to further criminal objectives or fulfill special operational aims. Organized criminal groups and terrorist organizations may build alliances with each other. The nature of these alliances varies broadly and can include one-off, short-term, and long-term relationships. Career cybercriminals are the most common type of threat actor, and their attacks are intended to steal data for financial gain. Threat actors pose a risk to individuals and organizations, and they can use various techniques, such as malware, phishing scams, and ransomware, to carry out their attacks.

Shadow IT Threat actors and their motivations
Shadow IT refers to the use of unauthorized tools, applications, or devices by employees within an organization. The use of shadow IT can pose a significant threat to an organization's IT security, as it can create an entry point for cybercriminals. Threat actors who take advantage of shadow IT can be grouped by their set of goals, motivation, and capabilities. Some common motivations for threat actors include financial gain, political reasons, espionage, activism, revenge, or some other purpose. An analogy for shadow IT could be a secret door in a house that is not visible to the owner, but is known to a burglar. The burglar can use this door to enter the house undetected and steal valuable items. Similarly, cybercriminals can use shadow IT to enter an organization's network undetected and steal valuable data. It is important for organizations to be aware of the risks posed by shadow IT and to take steps to limit the use of unauthorized tools, applications, or devices.

Attributes of Threat actors
Threat actors are individuals or groups who pose a threat to an organization's security. They can be categorized based on their attributes, which include their motivation, capability, and intent. Motivation refers to the reason why a threat actor is targeting an

organization, such as financial gain or political ideology. Capability refers to the resources and skills that a threat actor possesses, such as technical expertise or access to specialized tools. Intent refers to the specific actions that a threat actor plans to take, such as stealing data or disrupting operations. An analogy for threat actors could be burglars who break into a house. The motivation could be to steal valuable items, the capability could be the tools and skills needed to bypass security measures, and the intent could be to quickly grab the items and leave undetected.

Internal/external Threat actors and their motivations
internal threat actors are individuals within an organization who have authorized access to its resources, while external threat actors are individuals outside the organization who attempt to gain unauthorized access. Internal threat actors may be motivated by a variety of factors, such as financial gain, revenge, or ideology. External threat actors may include hackers, cybercriminals, and state-sponsored actors, and their motivations may include espionage, financial gain, or disruption of services. An analogy for this could be a bank robber who is an external threat actor, and a corrupt bank employee who is an internal threat actor. Both may have different motivations, but their actions can have serious consequences for the organization.

Resources/funding Threat actors and their motivations
Resources/funding is one of the factors that can motivate threat actors to carry out attacks. Threat actors can be compared to burglars who are motivated to break into a house if they believe there are valuable items inside. Similarly, threat actors may be motivated to carry out attacks if they believe there are valuable resources or funding to be gained. These resources could include sensitive data, intellectual property, or financial information. Threat actors may also be motivated by the potential financial gain from ransomware attacks or by the desire to disrupt or damage an organization's operations. It is important for organizations to be aware of the potential motivations of threat actors and to take steps to protect their valuable resources and funding.

Level of sophistication/capability Threat actors and their motivations

Threat actors can be classified into different categories based on their motives and objectives, and their level of sophistication and capability can vary widely. Threat actors can be compared to burglars, with some using basic tools like crowbars to break into homes, while others may use more advanced techniques like lock-picking or hacking tools to gain access to more secure buildings. Similarly, some burglars may be motivated by financial gain, while others may be driven by other factors such as revenge or a desire for power. Threat actors' motivations can be complex and multifaceted, and they may evolve over time. Organizations and individuals must remain vigilant and adopt proactive cybersecurity measures to mitigate the risks posed by these different motivations. Threat actors' capabilities can vary widely depending on their motivations, expertise, and resources. Common capabilities a threat actor can use include malware development and deployment, exploitation of software vulnerabilities, phishing attacks, and social engineering.

Threat actor Motivations

Threat actor motivations can be categorized into three main groups: financial gain, political or ideological beliefs, and personal or psychological reasons. An analogy to explain this could be a bank robbery. The motivation for robbing a bank could be financial gain, as the robbers are seeking to steal money. Alternatively, the motivation could be political or ideological, such as a group robbing a bank to fund a political cause. Finally, the motivation could be personal or psychological, such as an individual robbing a bank due to personal financial difficulties or psychological issues. Similarly, threat actors may have different motivations for their actions, which can range from financial gain to personal or psychological reasons.

Threat actor Motivation of Data exfiltration

Data exfiltration is a type of cyber attack where an attacker steals sensitive data from a target organization. Threat actors may be motivated to perform data exfiltration for various reasons, such as financial gain, espionage, or sabotage. An analogy for data exfiltration could be a thief breaking into a house to steal valuable items. In this case, the thief is the threat actor, the house is the target organization, and the valuable items are the sensitive data. The thief may be motivated by financial gain, just as a threat actor may be motivated by financial gain when performing data exfiltration.

Threat actor Motivation of Espionage

Threat actors may be motivated to engage in espionage for a variety of reasons, including financial gain, political advantage, and competitive advantage. Espionage can be compared to a game of chess, where the goal is to gather information about an opponent's moves and strategies in order to gain an advantage. In the same way, threat actors engaged in espionage seek to gather sensitive information about their targets, such as trade secrets or government secrets, in order to gain an advantage over them. This information can be used to make strategic decisions or to gain a competitive edge in the marketplace.

Threat actor Motivation of Service disruption

One of the objectives of a threat actor is to cause service disruption, which means to interrupt or stop the normal functioning of a service or system. An analogy to understand this could be a traffic jam on a busy highway. Just as a traffic jam disrupts the flow of vehicles on a road, a service disruption caused by a threat actor can disrupt the normal functioning of a system or network, making it difficult or impossible for users to access the service. This can result in significant financial losses, damage to reputation, and loss of productivity.

Threat actor Motivation of Blackmail

Blackmail is a type of threat actor that involves an attacker threatening to reveal sensitive information or take harmful action unless the victim complies with their demands. It is a form of extortion where the perpetrator seeks favors other than money, such as sexual favors or other benefits to gain power over their victim. Blackmailers rely on their victim's fear to pressure them into doing things. It is important to note that the crime occurs when the threat is made – no money or property has to change hands. If someone blackmails you, they are breaking the law whether or not you comply with their demands. To constitute blackmail, the demand and threats in question must be made with an intent to cause loss to the victim, or a view to gain something specific – for example, money or property – on the part of the perpetrator. It is important for organizations to have strong security measures in place to prevent blackmail attacks and to have a plan in place for responding to such attacks if they occur.

Threat actor Motivation of Financial gain
A threat actor motivated by financial gain is someone who seeks to profit from their malicious activities. This could be compared to a thief who breaks into a bank vault to steal money. In the digital world, a threat actor motivated by financial gain might attempt to steal sensitive financial information, such as credit card numbers or bank account details, in order to sell them on the black market or use them to make fraudulent purchases. They might also use ransomware to encrypt a victim's files and demand payment in exchange for the decryption key. Overall, a threat actor motivated by financial gain is primarily interested in making money through illegal means.

Threat actor Motivation of Philosophical/political beliefs
A threat actor's motivation can be influenced by philosophical or political beliefs. This means that an attacker may be driven by a particular ideology or belief system that they wish to promote or defend. An analogy to understand this could be a political activist who is motivated by their beliefs to take action, such as protesting or lobbying for a particular cause. In the same way, a threat actor may be motivated by their philosophical or political beliefs to carry out cyber attacks against a particular target or group. It is important for security professionals to understand these motivations in order to better anticipate and defend against potential attacks.

Threat actor Motivation of Ethical
A threat actor ethical is defined as an individual who

uses their knowledge and skills to identify vulnerabilities in systems and networks, and then reports these vulnerabilities to the appropriate parties so that they can be fixed. An analogy for a threat actor ethical could be a locksmith who is hired to test the security of a building by attempting to pick the locks. If the locksmith finds a weakness in the lock, they report it to the building owner so that it can be fixed and the building can be made more secure. Similarly, a threat actor ethical uses their skills to identify weaknesses in a system or network, and then reports these vulnerabilities to the appropriate parties so that they can be fixed and the system or network can be made more secure.

Threat actor Motivation of Revenge
a threat actor seeking revenge is someone who has been wronged or harmed in some way and seeks to retaliate against the person or organization responsible. This can be compared to a person who has been cheated by a business and decides to leave a negative review or tell their friends not to use that business. In the case of a threat actor seeking revenge, they may use various methods to harm the target, such as launching a cyber attack or stealing sensitive information. It is important for organizations to be aware of the potential for revenge attacks and take steps to prevent them, such as implementing strong security measures and monitoring for suspicious activity.

Threat actor Motivation of Disruption/chaos
A threat actor is an entity that has the capability to cause harm to an organization's assets or interests. One of the objectives of a threat actor is to cause disruption or chaos. This can be compared to a burglar who breaks into a house not only to steal valuable items but also to create chaos and confusion by damaging property and leaving a mess behind. In the context of cybersecurity, a threat actor may use various techniques such as denial-of-service attacks, malware, or social engineering to disrupt an organization's operations, cause system failures, or damage data. The goal of such attacks is to create chaos and confusion, making it difficult for the organization to function normally and causing harm to its reputation and financial stability.

Threat actor Motivation of War

Threat actors who are motivated by war are those who seek to cause harm to a target for political or ideological reasons. They may be affiliated with a nation-state or a non-state actor, and their actions may be intended to disrupt or damage critical infrastructure, steal sensitive information, or cause physical harm. An analogy for this type of threat actor could be a soldier on a battlefield who is fighting for a cause they believe in, and who is willing to use any means necessary to achieve their objectives.

Message-based threat vectors and attack surfaces

Message-based threat vectors refer to the various ways in which attackers can use messages to gain unauthorized access to systems or data. This can include email phishing attacks, instant messaging, and other forms of communication that can be used to trick users into clicking on malicious links or downloading malware. Attack surfaces, on the other hand, refer to the various points of entry that attackers can use to gain access to a system or network. This can include vulnerabilities in software, hardware, or even human error. An analogy for message-based threat vectors and attack surfaces could be a burglar trying to break into a house. The message-based threat vector would be the various ways in which the burglar could try to trick the homeowner into opening the door, such as pretending to be a delivery person or a repairman. The attack surface would be the various points of entry that the burglar could use to gain access to the house, such as an unlocked window or a weak lock on the front door.

Message-based threat vectors and attack surfaces focussing on Email

email threat vectors refer to the different ways that attackers can use email to gain unauthorized access to systems or data. Attack surfaces, on the other hand, refer to the different points of vulnerability in an organization's email system that can be exploited by attackers. An analogy to explain this could be a house with multiple doors and windows. The doors and windows represent the attack surfaces, while the different ways that burglars can enter the house, such as through the front door, back door, or windows, represent the email threat vectors. Just as a homeowner would want to secure all the doors and windows to prevent burglars from entering, an organization should take steps to secure all the different points of vulnerability in their email system to prevent attackers from gaining unauthorized access.

Message-based threat vectors and attack surfaces focussing on Short Message Service (SMS)

A threat vector is a path or means by which an attacker can gain access to a system or network to deliver an attack. An attack surface is the sum of all the vulnerabilities in a system or network that can be exploited by an attacker. In the context of Short Message Service (SMS), a threat vector could be a malicious link or attachment sent via SMS that, when clicked or opened, delivers malware to the recipient's device. The attack surface for SMS could include vulnerabilities in the SMS protocol or in the recipient's device that could be exploited by an attacker to gain unauthorized access to the device or to intercept SMS messages. An analogy for this could be a burglar who uses a key (threat vector) to enter a house through an unlocked window (attack surface).

Message-based threat vectors and attack surfaces focussing on Instant messaging (IM)

Message-based threat vectors and attack surfaces refer to the potential vulnerabilities that exist in communication channels such as instant messaging (IM). Just as a virus can spread through physical contact with an infected person, malicious software can spread through communication channels like IM. In other words, just as a virus can spread through a handshake, malware can spread through an instant message. Attackers can use IM to send malicious links or attachments that can infect a user's device or network. Therefore, it is important to be cautious when using IM and to avoid clicking on links or downloading attachments from unknown sources, just as one would avoid physical contact with someone who is sick.

Threat vectors and attack surfaces

Threat vectors and attack surfaces are important concepts in cybersecurity. A threat vector is the method that an attacker uses to gain access to a computer or network. Attack surfaces refer to the different ways that an attacker can exploit vulnerabilities in a system. An analogy for this is a house with multiple entry points. The doors, windows, and garage are all potential attack surfaces, and an attacker may use a threat vector such as picking a lock or breaking a window to gain entry. Understanding the different threat vectors and attack surfaces is crucial for cybersecurity professionals to identify and mitigate potential vulnerabilities in a system. The consequences of cyber attacks can be severe, and it is important to take a proactive approach to cybersecurity to minimize risk to human life and ensure the security and stability of nations.

Image-based Threat vectors and attack surfaces

Image-based threat vectors and attack surfaces refer to the potential security risks that can arise from the use of images in various forms, such as email attachments, social media posts, or website content. These images can be used to deliver malware or other malicious code that can compromise the security of a system or network. An analogy for this could be a Trojan horse, where the image appears harmless on the surface but contains hidden threats that can cause damage once it is inside the system. Therefore, it is important to be aware of the potential risks associated with image-based threats and take appropriate measures to protect against them, such as using anti-malware software and avoiding opening suspicious image files.

File-based Threat vectors and attack surfaces

The term "file-based threat vectors and attack surfaces" refers to the different ways that attackers can use files to gain unauthorized access to a system or network. Attackers can use files to deliver malware, exploit vulnerabilities, or steal sensitive information. File-based attack surfaces can include email attachments, downloaded files, and files shared over a network. Attackers can also use social engineering techniques to trick users into opening malicious files. An analogy for file-based threat vectors and attack surfaces is a burglar using a key to enter a house. Just as a burglar can use a key to gain access to a house, attackers can use files to gain access to a system or network. It is important to implement security measures such as antivirus software, firewalls, and user education to reduce the risk of file-based attacks.

Threat vectors and attack surfaces such as Voice calls

voice call threat vectors and attack surfaces refer to the potential ways in which a voice call can be compromised or attacked. An analogy to understand this concept is to think of a voice call as a house with multiple entry points. Each entry point represents a potential attack surface, such as the network connection, the device used to make the call, or the software used to facilitate the call. Threat vectors, on the other hand, represent the specific methods or tools that an attacker might use to exploit these attack surfaces, such as eavesdropping, man-in-the-middle attacks, or malware. By understanding these threat vectors and attack surfaces, security professionals can better protect voice calls from potential attacks.

Threat vectors and attack surfaces such as Removable devices

Removable devices, such as USB drives, can be a threat vector and an attack surface because they can be used to introduce malware or other malicious code into a system. An analogy for this would be a key to a locked door. Just as a key can be used to unlock a door and gain access to a building, a removable device can be used to gain access to a computer or network and deliver a malicious payload.

Vulnerable software threat vectors and attack surfaces

vulnerable software threat vectors refer to the ways in which attackers can exploit weaknesses in software to gain unauthorized access or cause damage. Attack surfaces, on the other hand, refer to the points of entry that attackers can use to exploit these vulnerabilities. An analogy to understand this concept is to think of a house with multiple doors and windows. The doors and windows represent the attack surfaces, while the vulnerabilities in the locks or hinges represent the vulnerable software threat vectors. An attacker can exploit these vulnerabilities to gain entry through the doors or windows and cause harm. Similarly, in the context of software, attackers can exploit vulnerabilities in the software to gain entry through various attack surfaces and cause damage to the system.

Unsupported systems and applications threat vectors and attack surfaces.
Unsupported systems and applications are a threat vector and attack surface in cybersecurity. This refers to systems and applications that are no longer supported by their vendors, meaning they no longer receive security updates or patches. This is similar to a car that is no longer maintained or serviced, which becomes more vulnerable to breakdowns and accidents over time. Attackers can exploit vulnerabilities in unsupported systems and applications to gain unauthorized access to sensitive data or systems. Therefore, it is important to keep systems and applications up-to-date with the latest security patches to reduce the risk of cyber attacks.

Common threat vectors and attack surfaces in Unsecure networks
Attack vectors are methods used by cybercriminals to gain unauthorized access to a network or computer system. These vectors can take many different forms, including malware, viruses, email attachments, web pages, pop-ups, instant messages, text messages, social engineering, and more. In an analogy, we can consider a graph where the x-axis lists all the devices and apps on a network, and the y-axis lists the different breach methods such as weak and default passwords, reused passwords, phishing, social engineering, unpatched software, misconfigurations, etc., the plot is the attack surface. The most common attack vectors include compromised credentials, weak and stolen credentials, ransomware, phishing, zero-day vulnerabilities, missing or poor encryption, misconfiguration, trust relationships, brute force attacks, and distributed denial of service (DDoS). In unsecure networks, these attack vectors can be exploited by hackers to gain unauthorized access to sensitive data, jeopardizing an organization's brand, customers, and assets.

Common threat vectors and attack surfaces in Unsecure Wireless networks

The Common threat vectors and attack surfaces in Unsecure Wireless networks include rogue access points, evil twin attacks, and man-in-the-middle attacks. Rogue access points are unauthorized access points that are set up by attackers to mimic legitimate access points. Evil twin attacks are similar to rogue access points, but they are set up to look like legitimate access points to trick users into connecting to them. Man-in-the-middle attacks occur when an attacker intercepts communication between two parties and can eavesdrop on or modify the communication. An analogy for these attacks could be a thief who sets up a fake storefront to trick customers into entering and giving away their personal information, or a person who intercepts and reads someone else's mail.

Common threat vectors and attack surfaces in Unsecure Wired networks

Wired networks are computer networks that use physical cables to connect devices and transmit data. These cables can be made of copper or fiber optic material and are used to connect devices such as computers, printers, and servers. Wired networks are considered more secure than wireless networks because they require a physical connection to access the network. Attack vectors include malware, viruses, email attachments, web pages, pop-ups, instant messages, text messages, and social engineering. Attackers can exploit system vulnerabilities, including the human element, to gain access to the network. Attack vectors can be compared to entry points in a building that can be exploited by an intruder. In an unsecure wired network, the attack surface can be compared to a building with multiple entry points, such as doors and windows, that can be exploited by an intruder.

Common threat vectors and attack surfaces in Unsecure Bluetooth networks

A Bluetooth network is a type of wireless personal area network (PAN) that allows devices to communicate with each other over short distances. Bluetooth technology uses radio waves to transmit data between devices, such as smartphones, laptops, and wireless headphones. Bluetooth networks are commonly used in various devices, but they are also vulnerable to security threats. One of the most significant vulnerabilities in Bluetooth technology is its ability to be intercepted by unauthorized users. Hackers can use a "Bluejacking" technique to send unsolicited messages to Bluetooth-enabled devices. This can lead to unwanted data transfer or even malware installation on the device. Man-in-the-middle attacks are another common Bluetooth threat, where hackers intercept Bluetooth signals and manipulate them to gain unauthorized access to the device. Bluetooth technology is vulnerable to various security threats, and new threats are emerging. For example, a set of vulnerabilities affecting almost every Bluetooth-connected desktop, mobile, and smart device on the market has been revealed. These vulnerabilities are not in the Bluetooth protocol but in the Bluetooth implementations. The vulnerabilities allow an attacker to gain control of affected devices and their data, and steal sensitive business data from corporate networks. Malware exploiting the attack vector may be particularly virulent by passing peer-to-peer and jumping laterally, infecting adjacent devices when Bluetooth is switched on.

Common threat vectors and attack surfaces in Open service ports

Open service ports are one of the most common attack surfaces that can be exploited by attackers. Attackers can use open service ports to gain unauthorized access to a network or system. Open service ports are like open doors in a house. If a door is left open, anyone can enter the house without permission. Similarly, if a service port is left open, attackers can enter the network or system without permission. In computer networking, a port is a communication endpoint that identifies a specific process or service. A port number is assigned to each process or service, and it is used by the transport layer of the Internet Protocol Suite to transmit and receive data packets. An open port is a TCP or UDP port number that is actively accepting packets, meaning that there is an application or service listening on that port and processing incoming packets. On the other hand, a closed port is a port that rejects connections or ignores all packets directed at it. Closed ports are accessible, but there is no application listening on them. Closed ports can be helpful in showing that a host is up on an IP address and as part of OS detection. However, open ports can pose security risks if the services listening on them are misconfigured, unpatched, or vulnerable to attacks. Therefore, it is important to monitor and secure open ports to prevent unauthorized access and protect against cyber attacks.

Common threat vectors and attack surfaces in Default credentials

One common attack vector is default credentials, which are the pre-set usernames and passwords that come with a device or software. Attackers can use these credentials to gain access to a system or network, as many users do not change them or use weak passwords. This is similar to a burglar using a key to enter a house that was left under the doormat. To prevent this, users should change default credentials to strong, unique passwords and use two-factor authentication to add an extra layer of security. Organizations should also monitor for suspicious activity and enforce strict password policies to reduce the risk of a security breach. Attackers can also use vulnerability assessment software to scan for applications or appliances with default credentials enabled. Once attackers gain access to a system or network, they can move laterally and escalate privileges to gain more control. To prevent this, users should change default credentials to strong, unique passwords and use two-factor authentication to add an extra layer of security. Organizations should also monitor for suspicious activity and enforce strict password policies to reduce the risk of a security breach

Common threat vectors and attack surfaces in Supply chain

A supply chain attack is a type of cyber attack that targets the weakest link in a supply chain, which could be a third-party vendor or supplier. Attackers exploit vulnerabilities in the software or hardware of the supplier to gain access to the enterprise network. This is similar to how a burglar might target a house by first breaking into a less secure neighboring house. The attack surface of an enterprise is expanded when it relies on third-party vendors or suppliers, and the risks associated with a supply chain attack have never been higher due to new types of attacks, growing public awareness of the threats, and increased oversight from regulators. The most common attack vectors used by cybercriminals in supply chain attacks include malware, viruses, email attachments, web pages, pop-ups, instant messages, text messages, and social engineering. Organizations can mitigate the risk of supply chain attacks by performing cybersecurity risk assessments on vendors, measuring and mitigating third-party risks, and implementing proactive cybersecurity measures.

Common threat vectors and attack surfaces in Managed service providers (MSPs)

Managed service providers (MSPs) are businesses that provide IT services to other companies. MSPs are vulnerable to various cyber threats and attack surfaces. Attack surfaces are the sum-total of points on a network where attacks can occur, where an unauthorized user can try to manipulate or extract data using a myriad of breach methods. MSPs work with numerous clients and manage enormous amounts of information and data. Gaining access to their systems increases the likelihood of obtaining access to thousands of companies' systems. MSPs' clients often rely on them to provide a comprehensive range of IT services, including security. If MSP cybersecurity threats become real, the implications can affect their whole client base, resulting in financial loss, legal ramifications, and severe reputational damage. The most common cyber attack vectors that MSPs face include ransomware, phishing, social engineering, unpatched software, misconfigurations, and compromised credentials. MSPs can protect themselves and their clients by implementing multi-layered, in-depth security systems, extended threat detection and response solutions, and by measuring and mitigating third-party risks and fourth-party risks. An analogy for attack surfaces could be a house with multiple entry points, such as doors, windows, and vents. Attackers can use any of these entry points to gain access to the house, just as cybercriminals can use any of the attack surfaces to gain access to a network or computer system.

Common threat vectors and attack surfaces in Vendors

Attack vectors can take many different forms, ranging from malware and ransomware, to man-in-the-middle attacks, compromised credentials, and phishing. One often overlooked attack vector is third-party vendors and service providers. It doesn't matter how sophisticated your internal network security and information security policies are — if vendors have access to sensitive data, they can be a huge risk to your organization. This is similar to how a house with multiple doors and windows is more vulnerable to break-ins than a house with only one door and window. The more entry points a house has, the more vulnerable it is to burglars. Similarly, the more attack vectors a network or system has, the more vulnerable it is to cyber attackers. Therefore, it is important to measure and mitigate third-party risks and fourth-party risks, and to invest in threat intelligence tools that help automate vendor risk management and automatically monitor your vendor's security posture and notify you if it worsens.

Common threat vectors and attack surfaces in Suppliers

Suppliers can pose a significant cybersecurity risk to organizations. Attackers can exploit system vulnerabilities, including the human element, to breach or infiltrate an entire network/system. Attack vectors (or threat vectors) enable hackers to exploit system vulnerabilities, including the human element. Security breaches occur when sensitive, protected, or confidential data is accessed or stolen by an unauthorized party, jeopardizing an organization's brand, customers, and assets. The rise in outsourcing means that vendors pose a huge cybersecurity risk to customer data and proprietary data. Some of the biggest data breaches were caused by third parties. An analogy to understand this is that suppliers are like doors to a house. If the doors are not secure, then anyone can enter the house and steal valuable items. Similarly, if suppliers are not secure, then attackers can exploit their vulnerabilities to gain access to an organization's sensitive data. Therefore, it is important to measure and mitigate third-party risks and fourth-party risks. Organizations should invest in threat intelligence tools that help automate vendor risk management and automatically monitor their vendor's security posture and notify them if it worsens.

Common threat vectors and attack surfaces in Human vectors/social engineering

Social engineering is a human vector that exploits the human mind, used often in phishing, pretexting, vishing, and other manipulative techniques to mislead the human. The attack surface is the total number of attack vectors an attacker can use to manipulate a network or computer system or extract data. If you consider a graph, where the x-axis lists all of the devices and apps on your network (infrastructure, apps, endpoints, IoT, etc.) and the y-axis are the different breach methods such as weak and default passwords, reused passwords, phishing, social engineering, unpatched software, misconfigurations, etc. – the plot is your attack surface. Cybercriminals are growing increasingly sophisticated, and it is no longer enough to rely on antivirus software as the primary security system. Organizations must employ defense in depth to minimize cybersecurity risk

Common threat vectors and attack surfaces in Human vectors/social engineering such as Phishing

Phishing is a specific type of social engineering that involves sending fraudulent emails, text messages, or phone calls that appear to be from reputable companies to induce individuals to reveal personal information. Attackers use phishing to trick victims into believing that the message they receive from the phishing perpetrator contains something they want or need, such as a request from their bank or a note from someone within their company. The attacker's primary goal is to compromise systems to obtain usernames, passwords, and other account and/or financial data. To avoid falling victim to phishing attacks, individuals and organizations should be trained on how to identify and report potential cybercriminal activity. An analogy for phishing could be a fisherman who uses bait to lure fish into biting the hook. In the same way, attackers use fraudulent messages to lure individuals into revealing sensitive information.

Common threat vectors and attack surfaces in Human vectors/social engineering such as Vishing

Social engineering attacks focus on human vectors can take many forms, such as phishing, vishing, smishing, and business email compromise. Vishing, for example, is a type of social engineering attack that uses voice communication to trick victims into divulging sensitive information or performing an action that benefits the attacker. An analogy for social engineering attacks is that they are like a con artist who uses deception and manipulation to gain the trust of their victim and convince them to do something that they wouldn't normally do. In the case of vishing, the attacker might pose as a trusted authority figure, such as a bank representative, and use social engineering tactics to convince the victim to reveal their account information or transfer money. To prevent social engineering attacks, it is important to educate users about the risks and to implement security controls, such as multi-factor authentication and email filters, that can help detect and prevent these types of attacks

Common threat vectors and attack surfaces in Human vectors/social engineering such as Smishing

The human attack surface is the most vulnerable and weakest link in the security system. Cybercriminals manipulate users using social engineering tactics such as phishing, smishing, and vishing. Smishing is a type of cyber-attack that targets individuals through SMS (Short Message Service) or text messages. It is a variant of phishing, where victims are deceived into giving sensitive information to a disguised attacker. Smishing is a type of social engineering attack that relies on exploiting human trust rather than technical exploits. Cybercriminals use fraudulent messages to lure users into clicking on links or downloading attachments that contain malware or viruses. Smishing messages can be dangerous only if the targeted user acts on them by clicking the link or providing information. The goal of a smishing attack is to typically gain confidential information for identity theft or financial crimes, such as names, addresses, usernames, passwords, credit card numbers, credit card codes, and banking data. Smishing can attack any mobile device with text messaging capabilities. Smishing is like a fisherman using a fishing rod to catch fish. The attacker casts a baited hook to catch the victim's sensitive information. Smishing can be prevented by not responding to suspicious messages, not clicking on links or downloading attachments from unknown sources, and using anti-malware software.

Common threat vectors and attack surfaces in Human vectors/social engineering such as Misinformation/disinformation

Misinformation/disinformation is a type of social engineering attack that involves spreading false or misleading information to deceive people. It is a deliberate attempt to spread false information to manipulate people's beliefs or actions. Misinformation is the unintentional dissemination of incorrect information, while disinformation is intentionally disseminating false information, often to further a political agenda. Misinformation/disinformation can be spread through various channels, including social media, email, and messaging apps. It is important to be aware of these common threat vectors and attack surfaces to protect against cyber attacks. Organizations must train and re-train their employees on detecting potential disinformation and social engineering attacks, stressing the following best practices: Trust nothing, treat every email, text, article, or advert as a potential threat, and verify the information before taking any action

Common threat vectors and attack surfaces in Human vectors/social engineering such as Impersonation

Impersonation is a social engineering attack technique where an attacker pretends to be someone else to gain access to sensitive information or systems. Impersonation is the foundation of social engineering, and it is a key technique for the social engineering attacker. Attackers use impersonation to circumvent security technologies and manipulate people into divulging sensitive information or performing actions that compromise security. Impersonation can be carried out via social media platforms, phone, or even email. Attackers can impersonate a vendor, delivery person, employee, contractor, or person of authority to gain access to restricted areas of a company. Impersonation scams can be carried out by pretending to be someone with the help desk, telecommunications company, or someone higher in rank. Attackers usually start with a pretext, which is simply a lie that sets up the entire scenario for the particular attack. To prevent social engineering attacks, employees should be trained to identify and report potential cybercriminal activity.

Common threat vectors and attack surfaces in Human vectors/social engineering such as Business email compromise

Business email compromise (BEC) is a type of social engineering attack that targets businesses working with foreign suppliers and businesses that regularly perform wire transfer payments. The attackers begin by building a targeted list of emails, which they obtain by mining LinkedIn profiles, sifting through business email databases, or even going through various websites in search of contact information. They then launch their BEC attacks by sending out mass emails, which are difficult to identify as malicious since attackers will utilize tactics such as spoofing, look-alike domains, and fake email names. The emails often use spoofed and lookalike sender addresses that are easy to miss if the recipient isn't paying attention. Once the attackers gain access to the email accounts, they use them to conduct unauthorized fund transfers or to request personally-identifiable information of other employees. An effective BEC defense secures all of the channels that attackers exploit, including corporate email, personal webmail, business partners' email, cloud apps, your web domain, the web, and users' own behavior. Attack visibility, email protection, and user awareness all play key roles in an effective defense. An analogy for BEC is a thief who steals a key to a bank vault and uses it to steal money from the bank.

Common threat vectors and attack surfaces in Human vectors/social engineering such as Pretexting

Pretexting is a type of social engineering attack that involves creating a false scenario or pretext to manipulate people into giving away information that they would not otherwise reveal. It is a hyper-targeted attack that requires extensive research on the target to make the pretext as believable as possible. Hackers may use personal details about the target to make small talk before requesting information. Pretexting is like a con artist who creates a fake identity or story to gain the trust of their victim and convince them to part with their money. To prevent social engineering attacks, organizations can create a risk-aware culture to ensure employees are alert and incorporate security awareness training programs that teach employees how to identify and prevent social engineering attacks

Common threat vectors and attack surfaces in Human vectors/social engineering such as Watering hole

A watering hole attack is a type of social engineering attack that targets a specific group of users by infecting websites that members of the group are known to visit. It is similar to a predator waiting at a watering hole for its prey to come and drink. In a watering hole attack, the attacker first identifies the websites that the targeted group frequently visits and then infects one or more of those websites with malware. When a member of the targeted group visits the infected website, their computer becomes infected with the malware, which can then be used to gain access to the victim's computer and network. Watering hole attacks are difficult to detect and can be extremely destructive, as they can breach several layers of security. They are also challenging to prevent since they target highly secure organizations through their less security-conscious employees, business partners, or connected vendors

Common threat vectors and attack surfaces in Human vectors/social engineering such as Brand impersonation

One example of social engineering is brand impersonation, where the attacker pretends to be a well-known brand or individual to gain the victim's trust and obtain sensitive information. For instance, an attacker may pose as a vendor, such as a pest control or office equipment technician, to gain access to a building. The attacker may conduct open-source intelligence (OSINT) on the target company to identify its current vendors and then impersonate one of them. The most challenging element of this attack is looking the part and having the correct credentials and papers in order. With good planning, attackers can gain physical access to restricted areas of a company. Therefore, it is essential to test an organization's human network and educate employees on how to identify and avoid social engineering attacks.

Common threat vectors and attack surfaces in Human vectors/social engineering such as Typosquatting

Typosquatting is a type of social engineering attack that involves registering domain names that closely resemble popular websites or applications. These domain names are intentionally crafted to exploit common typing errors made by users when entering a web address into their browsers. Users are then redirected to malicious websites where attackers can gain unauthorized access to sensitive information. An analogy for typosquatting is a thief who sets up a fake store with a similar name to a popular store in a mall, hoping that customers will accidentally enter the fake store and provide their personal information or credit card details. To prevent typosquatting attacks, users should be cautious when entering web addresses and double-check the spelling of the domain name.

Organizations can also use domain name monitoring services to detect and prevent typosquatting attacks

Application vulnerabilities

Application vulnerabilities refer to weaknesses or flaws in software applications that can be exploited by attackers to gain unauthorized access to systems or data. These vulnerabilities can be compared to holes in a fence that allow intruders to enter a property. Just as a hole in a fence can be exploited by burglars to gain access to a house, application vulnerabilities can be exploited by attackers to gain access to sensitive information or to take control of a system. It is important for organizations to identify and address application vulnerabilities to prevent unauthorized access and protect their systems and data.

The Application vulnerability of Memory injection

Memory injection is an application vulnerability that allows an attacker to insert malicious code into a running process by exploiting a flaw in the application's memory management. It is similar to a burglar breaking into a house through an unlocked window. The attacker can use this vulnerability to execute arbitrary code, steal sensitive information, or take control of the system. This type of attack can be prevented by implementing secure coding practices, such as input validation and proper memory management, and by using security tools like firewalls and intrusion detection systems. It's like a burglar sneaking into a house through an unlocked window and leaving a bomb inside. Once the malicious code is injected into the application's memory, it can be executed and used to perform various malicious activities, such as stealing sensitive data or taking control of the system. Memory injection attacks can be prevented by implementing proper input validation and sanitization in the application code, as well as using security mechanisms such as address space layout randomization (ASLR) and data execution prevention (DEP).

The Application vulnerability of Buffer overflow
A buffer overflow is an application vulnerability that occurs when a program tries to store more data in a buffer than it can hold. It's like trying to pour too much water into a cup that's already full. The excess water spills over and can cause damage. Similarly, when a buffer overflows, the excess data can overwrite adjacent memory locations, causing the program to crash or allowing an attacker to execute malicious code. Buffer overflows are a common attack vector for hackers, and can be prevented by implementing proper input validation and buffer size checks in the application code. This can overwrite adjacent memory locations and cause the application to behave unexpectedly or crash. Attackers can exploit buffer overflow vulnerabilities to execute arbitrary code on the system or gain elevated privileges. To prevent buffer overflow attacks, input data should be properly validated, buffer sizes should be properly allocated, and programming languages with built-in memory protection mechanisms can be used. Intrusion detection and prevention systems can also be used to detect and prevent buffer overflow attacks.

The Application vulnerability of Race conditions
A race condition is an application vulnerability that occurs when two or more processes or threads access a shared resource in an unexpected order, leading to unpredictable behavior. It is like a situation where two people are trying to use the same elevator at the same time, but only one person can fit in the elevator at a time. If the two people do not coordinate their use of the elevator, they may end up blocking each other and causing delays. Similarly, in an application, if two processes or threads do not coordinate their access to a shared resource, they may end up blocking each other and causing the application to behave unpredictably or even crash. This can lead to unpredictable behavior, such as deadlocks, data corruption, and security vulnerabilities. Race conditions can be difficult to detect and fix, and can be exploited by attackers to gain unauthorized access or cause denial of service. Therefore, it is important for developers to be aware of the potential for race conditions and to implement proper synchronization mechanisms to prevent them. Race conditions can be difficult to detect and fix, and can be exploited by

attackers to gain unauthorized access or cause denial of service.

Time-of-check (TOC) vulnerabilities

Time-of-check (TOC) vulnerabilities refer to a type of security vulnerability that occurs when a system checks a resource's security state at one point in time and then uses that information to make a decision at a later point in time. This time gap between the check and the decision can be exploited by attackers to manipulate the resource's security state in the interim, leading to unauthorized access or other security breaches. An analogy for this could be a security guard who checks a door to ensure it is locked, but then leaves the area without actually locking the door. If an attacker enters the area during the guard's absence and finds the door unlocked, they can exploit this vulnerability to gain unauthorized access to the area.

Time-of-use (TOU) vulnerabilities

Time-of-use (TOU) vulnerabilities refer to the security risks that arise when access to a system or resource is granted based on the time of day or week. This type of vulnerability can be compared to a bank that only has security guards during the day, but not at night. If a thief knows that the bank is unprotected at night, they may attempt to break in during that time. Similarly, if a system is only protected during certain hours, an attacker may attempt to exploit it during the unprotected hours. TOU vulnerabilities can be mitigated by implementing security measures that are active 24/7, such as intrusion detection systems and security cameras.

Time-of-use (TOU) vulnerabilities such as Malicious update

Time-of-use (TOU) vulnerabilities are a type of vulnerability that occurs during a specific time period when a system is vulnerable. TOU vulnerabilities can be compared to a timed lock on a safe, which can be vulnerable to attack during the time window when it is open. One example of a TOU vulnerability is a malicious update, which occurs when a system is vulnerable during the time when it is being updated. Attackers can exploit this vulnerability by injecting malicious code into the update, which can then be executed when the system is restarted. This type of vulnerability can be mitigated by implementing security controls that limit access to the system during the vulnerable time period, or by using secure update mechanisms that verify the integrity of the update before it is installed. The CompTIA Security+ certification exam covers TOU vulnerabilities as part of its objective to assess the security posture of an enterprise environment and recommend and implement appropriate security solutions.

Operating system (OS)-based vulnerabilities

Operating system (OS)-based vulnerabilities are weaknesses or loopholes in an operating system that can be exploited by cyber attackers to cause damage on any device where the OS is installed. These vulnerabilities can be caused by unpatched and outdated software, exposing the system running the application and sometimes endangering the entire network. An analogy to understand this is to think of a house with a faulty lock on the front door. The lock is the operating system, and the house is the device. Just as a faulty lock can be exploited by burglars to gain access to a house, an operating system vulnerability can be exploited by cyber attackers to gain access to a device. Therefore, it is essential to keep the operating system up-to-date with the latest security patches to prevent cyber attackers from exploiting vulnerabilities and gaining unauthorized access to the device or network.

Web-based vulnerabilities

Web-based vulnerabilities refer to security weaknesses that can be exploited through web-based applications such as web browsers, web servers, and web services. These vulnerabilities can be exploited by attackers to gain unauthorized access to sensitive information or to execute malicious code on a system. Examples of web-based vulnerabilities include cross-site scripting (XSS), SQL injection, and file inclusion vulnerabilities. Web-based vulnerabilities can be compared to a house with multiple entry points such as doors and windows that can be exploited by intruders to gain unauthorized access. It is important to identify and mitigate these vulnerabilities to ensure the security of web-based applications and the data they handle.

Web-based vulnerabilities such as Structured Query Language injection (SQLi)

Web-based vulnerabilities are security weaknesses that can be exploited by attackers to gain unauthorized access to web applications. One such vulnerability is SQL injection (SQLi), which is a type of attack that targets web applications that use databases. In SQLi attacks, attackers inject malicious SQL code into web application input fields, such as search boxes or login forms, to manipulate the database and gain access to sensitive information. An analogy for SQLi is a burglar who gains access to a house by exploiting a weakness in the lock. In the same way that a burglar can use a lock picking tool to bypass a lock, an attacker can use SQLi to bypass security measures and gain access to a web application's database. It is important for web developers to implement security measures, such as input validation and parameterized queries, to prevent SQLi attacks and protect sensitive data.

Web-based vulnerabilities such as Cross-site scripting (XSS)

Cross-site scripting (XSS) is a type of web-based vulnerability that allows attackers to inject malicious code into a web page viewed by other users. This can be compared to a burglar who sneaks into a house and hides a trap in a room that is frequently used by the homeowners. When the homeowners enter the room, they trigger the trap and are exposed to danger. Similarly, an attacker can inject malicious code into a web page that is frequently accessed by users, such as a login page or a forum, and when users access the page, they inadvertently trigger the malicious code, which can steal their sensitive information or perform other harmful actions. To prevent XSS attacks, web developers need to carefully validate and sanitize user input to ensure that it does not contain any malicious code.

Hardware vulnerabilities

Hardware vulnerabilities refer to weaknesses or flaws in the physical components of a computer system that can be exploited by attackers to gain unauthorized access or cause damage. An analogy to understand hardware vulnerabilities is to think of a house with weak locks on the doors and windows. Just as a burglar can exploit these weak points to break into a house, an attacker can exploit hardware vulnerabilities to gain access to a computer system. Examples of hardware vulnerabilities include outdated firmware, unsecured ports, and weak passwords. It is important to regularly update hardware components and implement security measures to mitigate the risk of hardware vulnerabilities.

Firmware vulnerabilities

Firmware vulnerabilities refer to security weaknesses in the software that is embedded in hardware devices such as routers, printers, and cameras. Firmware is like the operating system of these devices, and just like how a computer's operating system can have vulnerabilities that can be exploited by attackers, firmware can also have vulnerabilities that can be exploited. These vulnerabilities can allow attackers to gain unauthorized access to the device, steal sensitive information, or even take control of the device. It is important to keep firmware up-to-date with the latest security patches to mitigate the risk of these vulnerabilities being exploited.

End-of-life Hardware vulnerabilities

End-of-life hardware vulnerabilities refer to security risks that arise when hardware devices reach the end of their useful life and are no longer supported by the manufacturer. Just like an old car that is no longer maintained, end-of-life hardware devices can become vulnerable to security threats because they are no longer receiving security updates or patches. Hackers can exploit these vulnerabilities to gain unauthorized access to the device or the network it is connected to. Therefore, it is important to replace end-of-life hardware devices with newer ones that are still supported by the manufacturer and receive regular security updates to ensure the security of the network.

Legacy Hardware vulnerabilities

Legacy hardware vulnerabilities refer to security weaknesses that exist in outdated hardware components that are no longer supported by the manufacturer. These vulnerabilities can be compared to a house with old locks that are easily picked by intruders. Just as old locks can be easily bypassed by burglars, legacy hardware vulnerabilities can be exploited by attackers to gain unauthorized access to a system. These vulnerabilities can include outdated firmware, unpatched software, and weak encryption protocols. It is important to identify and mitigate these vulnerabilities to prevent potential security breaches.

Virtualization vulnerabilities

Virtualization is a technology that allows multiple virtual machines to run on a single physical machine. It is like having multiple houses built on a single plot of land. However, virtualization can also introduce vulnerabilities. For example, if one virtual machine is compromised, it can potentially access the data of other virtual machines running on the same physical machine. This is like if one house on the plot of land is broken into, the thief can potentially access the contents of other houses on the same plot of land. Additionally, if the hypervisor, which is the software that manages the virtual machines, is compromised, it can potentially access all the virtual machines running on the physical machine. This is like if the property manager of the plot of land is compromised, they can potentially access all the houses on the same plot of land. Therefore, it is important to secure the hypervisor and ensure that virtual machines are isolated from each other to prevent unauthorized access and data breaches.

Virtual machine (VM) escape vulnerabilities
A virtual machine (VM) is like a sandbox where you can run programs and applications without affecting the host operating system. However, VMs can be vulnerable to "escape" attacks, where an attacker can break out of the VM and access the host operating system. This can happen when there are vulnerabilities in the VM software that allow an attacker to execute code on the host system. It's like a burglar breaking out of a house's locked room and gaining access to the rest of the house. To prevent VM escape vulnerabilities, it's important to keep the VM software up to date and apply security patches as soon as they become available.

Virtualization Resource reuse vulnerabilities
Virtualization is a technology that allows multiple virtual machines (VMs) to run on a single physical machine. This technology enables resource reuse, which means that multiple VMs can share the same physical resources, such as CPU, memory, and storage. However, this resource reuse can also lead to vulnerabilities. An analogy to this would be a shared kitchen in an apartment building. While it is convenient for all the tenants to share the same kitchen, it also means that one tenant's actions can affect the others. For example, if one tenant leaves the stove on, it can cause a fire that affects the entire building. Similarly, if one VM is compromised, it can affect the security of the other VMs that share the same physical resources. Therefore, it is important to implement proper security measures, such as access controls and isolation, to prevent these vulnerabilities.

Cloud-specific vulnerabilities
Cloud-specific vulnerabilities are unique security risks that are associated with cloud computing environments. These vulnerabilities include the lack of physical control over cloud infrastructure, shared technology vulnerabilities, data loss and leakage, and account hijacking. Cloud service providers are responsible for securing the underlying infrastructure, but customers are responsible

for securing their own data and applications. Therefore, organizations must implement appropriate security controls and best practices to mitigate these vulnerabilities.

Supply chain vulnerabilities

Supply chain vulnerabilities refer to the risks that arise from the use of third-party vendors, suppliers, and contractors in the development, production, and distribution of products and services. These vulnerabilities can be compared to a chain, where each link represents a different vendor or supplier involved in the supply chain. If one link in the chain is weak or compromised, it can weaken the entire chain and make it vulnerable to attack. For example, if a supplier of a company's hardware components is compromised, it can lead to the compromise of the entire product line, which can have serious consequences for the company and its customers. Therefore, it is important for organizations to identify and mitigate supply chain vulnerabilities to ensure the security and integrity of their products and services.

Service provider vulnerabilities

Service provider vulnerabilities refer to the weaknesses in the security of third-party providers that offer services to organizations. These vulnerabilities can be compared to a house with multiple doors and windows. If one of the doors or windows is not properly secured, it can be exploited by an intruder to gain access to the house. Similarly, if a service provider has a vulnerability, it can be exploited by an attacker to gain access to the organization's network or data. These vulnerabilities can arise due to various reasons such as inadequate security measures, errors in software, and complexity of critical systems. Organizations must ensure that their service providers have proper security measures in place to prevent such vulnerabilities.

Hardware provider vulnerabilities

Hardware provider vulnerabilities refer to the security

risks that arise from the use of hardware components that have been tampered with or compromised by the manufacturer or supplier. This can be compared to a situation where a person buys a lock for their house, but the lock manufacturer has intentionally weakened the lock's security, making it easier for an attacker to break in. Similarly, hardware provider vulnerabilities can allow attackers to exploit the compromised components to gain unauthorized access to systems, steal sensitive data, or launch other malicious activities. It is important for organizations to carefully vet their hardware providers and ensure that they are using trusted sources to minimize the risk of hardware provider vulnerabilities.

Software provider vulnerabilities

Software provider vulnerabilities refer to weaknesses or flaws present in software code or infrastructure that fail to protect against violations of data and software integrity. These vulnerabilities can be exploited by attackers to gain unauthorized access to sensitive data or systems. An analogy to understand this is a house with a weak foundation or a door with a faulty lock. Just as a weak foundation or a faulty lock can make a house vulnerable to burglars, software provider vulnerabilities can make software vulnerable to attackers. It is important to identify and prevent software vulnerabilities to reduce the overall impact of attacks. Taking a proactive approach to application security is better than reactive security measures. Being proactive enables defenders to identify and neutralize attacks earlier, sometimes before any damage is done.

Cryptographic vulnerabilities

Cryptographic vulnerabilities refer to weaknesses or flaws in the design, implementation, or use of cryptographic algorithms or protocols that can be exploited by attackers to compromise the confidentiality, integrity, or availability of sensitive information. An analogy to understand cryptographic vulnerabilities is a lock on a door. Just like a lock can be picked or bypassed if it is weak or poorly designed, cryptographic algorithms can be broken or circumvented if they have vulnerabilities. For example, if a cryptographic key is too short or predictable, an attacker can use brute force attacks to guess the key and decrypt the encrypted data. Similarly, if a cryptographic protocol does not properly authenticate or authorize users, an attacker can impersonate a legitimate user and gain unauthorized access to the system. Therefore, it is important to use strong and well-tested cryptographic algorithms and protocols, and to follow best practices for key management, encryption, and authentication to minimize the risk of cryptographic vulnerabilities.

Misconfiguration vulnerabilities

Misconfiguration vulnerabilities refer to security weaknesses that arise from incorrect or incomplete configuration of systems, applications, or network devices. It is like leaving the front door of your house unlocked or leaving the keys in your car's ignition. Just as these actions make it easier for an intruder to gain access to your property, misconfigurations make it easier for attackers to exploit vulnerabilities and gain unauthorized access to sensitive data or systems. Misconfigurations can occur due to human error, lack of knowledge, or inadequate security policies and procedures. It is important to regularly review and update configurations to ensure that systems and devices are properly secured and protected against potential threats.

Mobile device vulnerabilities

Mobile device vulnerabilities refer to weaknesses in the security of mobile devices that can be exploited by attackers. These vulnerabilities can lead to various threats, including malware, which can disrupt the operation of the device and transmit or modify user data. Mobile devices are like a house with many doors and windows, and if one of them is left open, burglars can easily enter and steal valuable items. Similarly, if there is a vulnerability in a mobile device, attackers can exploit it and gain access to sensitive information stored on the device. Therefore, it is essential to keep mobile devices up-to-date with the latest security patches and use security software to protect against threats. Mobile app development cycles are incredibly short, and vulnerabilities can arise due to the use of open-source tools, libraries, and frameworks.

Mobile device Side loading vulnerabilities

Mobile device side loading vulnerabilities refer to the

installation of an application onto a device, such as a phone or computer, from a source other than the device's official app store. This practice can expose users to various security issues, including malware infection, security vulnerabilities, and lack of updates. The key difference between side loading and a normal installation is that in side loading, the application has not been approved by the developer of the device's operating system. This means that users are exposed to threats by installing them, and such applications may not have been security tested and can be malicious in nature. Side loading can be compared to opening a side door to a house that is not secured, which can allow intruders to walk in and cause damage. Therefore, it is important to educate users on the risks involved in side loading and to have a zero-trust policy in place to prevent users from being able to install software from unauthorized locations and restrict each user's access to resources across the network to only that which is necessary for their job

Mobile device Jailbreaking vulnerabilities

Jailbreaking is the process of removing restrictions imposed by the manufacturer on a mobile device to install unauthorized software or modify the operating system. This can lead to various security issues for the device and the user. Jailbreaking is like removing the lock on a door to allow anyone to enter the house, including intruders. It can make the device more vulnerable to malware, spyware, and viruses, and can also weaken security measures and put sensitive data at risk. Jailbreaking can also lead to the loss of warranty and device protection, and the possibility of not having access to manufacturer updates. Therefore, it is not recommended to jailbreak a mobile device unless it is necessary and the user is aware of the risks involved

Zero-day vulnerabilities

A zero-day vulnerability is a security flaw in a software or system that is unknown to the vendor or developer. The term "zero-day" refers to the fact that the vendor has just learned of the flaw, which means they have "zero days" to fix it. A zero-day attack occurs when hackers exploit the vulnerability before developers have a chance to address it. Zero-day attacks are especially dangerous because the only people who know about them are the attackers themselves. Once they have infiltrated a network, criminals can either attack immediately or sit and wait for the most advantageous time to do so. Zero-day vulnerabilities can take multiple forms, such as missing data encryption, missing authorizations, broken algorithms, bugs, problems with password security, and so on. They can be challenging to detect because detailed information about zero-day exploits is available only after the exploit is identified. A firewall plays an essential role in protecting your system against zero-day threats. An analogy for zero-day vulnerabilities could be a thief who discovers a secret entrance to a house that the owner is unaware of. The thief can use this entrance to enter the house undetected and steal valuable items before the owner has a chance to discover the entrance and secure it.

Malware attacks

Malware is a type of malicious software that is designed to cause harm to a computer, server, client, or computer network. Malware attacks can take many forms, including ransomware, spyware, command and control, viruses, worms, bots, Trojan horses, keyloggers, rootkits, fileless malware, cryptojacking, wiper malware, and adware. Malware can be installed on a device without the user's consent and can cause a range of unpleasant effects, such as crippling computer performance, mining personal information, erasing or encrypting data, or hijacking device operations. Malware can be delivered via email, text, vulnerable network service, compromised website, or physical media such as USB thumb drives or CDs/DVDs. Malware attacks can be prevented by maintaining strong cybersecurity hygiene, such as patching and updating software, using firewalls and security software, following email security best practices, deploying email filters, and educating users about the risks of malware. An analogy for malware attacks could be a virus that spreads from person to person, causing illness and harm. Just as viruses can be prevented by maintaining good hygiene practices, malware attacks can be prevented by maintaining good cybersecurity hygiene practices.

Ransomware

Ransomware is a type of malware that encrypts or locks a user's files or system, preventing access to them until a ransom is paid to the attacker. It is like a kidnapper who takes a person hostage and demands a ransom in exchange for their release. Ransomware can be delivered through various means, such as email attachments, malicious websites, or software vulnerabilities. Once the ransomware infects a system, it can spread to other devices on the network, causing widespread damage. To prevent ransomware attacks, organizations can take measures such as keeping software up to date, limiting user privileges, and backing up data regularly.

Trojans

A Trojan horse is a type of malware that disguises itself as a legitimate program or file, but is actually malicious. It is like a wooden horse that the Greeks used to enter the city of Troy, which appeared to be a gift but was actually filled with soldiers who took control of the city's defense system. Similarly, a Trojan virus looks like legitimate software, but once downloaded, it can take control of the user's computer, potentially leaving it vulnerable to other attacks. Trojans can be spread through emails or files attached to emails, which are spammed to reach as many people as possible. Once the email is opened and the malicious attachment is downloaded, the Trojan server will install and automatically run every time the infected device is turned on. Trojans can perform several harmful actions like data deletion, data censorship, data modification, data copying, and causing interference in the operation of computers or computer networks. To protect against Trojans, it is essential to stay vigilant, avoid suspicious websites and software vendors, and use Trojan scanners or malware-removal software to detect and remove them.

Worms

A worm is a type of malware that replicates itself and spreads to other computers without any user intervention. It can spread through various means, such as email attachments, network shares, and software vulnerabilities. Once a worm infects a computer, it can use that computer to scan for other vulnerable computers on the network and infect them as well. This process can continue until a large number of computers are infected, causing significant damage to the network. An analogy for a worm could be a contagious disease that spreads from person to person without any intervention, such as the flu. Just as a person infected with the flu can spread the virus to others through coughing or sneezing, a computer infected with a worm can spread the malware to other computers through various means without user intervention or action.

Spyware

Spyware is a type of malware that is installed on a computing device without the user's knowledge or consent. It can gather sensitive information about the user and their online behavior and relay it to third parties, such as advertisers or data collection firms, for profit. Spyware can also interfere with a user's control of their computer by installing additional software or redirecting web browsers. An analogy for spyware could be a private investigator who secretly follows and gathers information about a person's activities without their knowledge or consent. Just as a private investigator can collect sensitive information about a person's personal life, spyware can collect sensitive information about a user's online behavior and personal data.

Bloatware

Bloatware is defined as "software that is loaded on a device that uses an excessive amount of system resources, such as memory and processing power, and provides little or no value to the user." An analogy for bloatware could be a car that has too many unnecessary accessories that take up space and add weight, but do not improve the car's performance or functionality. Just as these accessories can slow down the car and make it less efficient, bloatware can slow down a device and make it less effective. Removing bloatware can help improve the performance and security of a device.

Viruses

Viruses are malicious software programs that can replicate themselves and spread to other computers or devices. They can be compared to a biological virus that infects a host and spreads to other individuals. Once a virus infects a computer, it can cause damage to the system, steal sensitive information, or allow unauthorized access to the device. Viruses can be spread through email attachments, infected websites, or infected software downloads. To protect against viruses, it is important to use antivirus software and keep it up to date, avoid opening suspicious emails or attachments, and only download software from trusted sources.

Keyloggers

A keylogger is a type of malicious software that records every keystroke made on a computer or mobile device. It can be compared to a spy who secretly watches and records everything a person types, including passwords, credit card numbers, and other sensitive information. The recorded data is then sent to the attacker who can use it for malicious purposes such as identity theft, financial fraud, or espionage. Keyloggers can be installed on a device through various means, including phishing emails, infected software downloads, or physical access to the device. They can be difficult to detect and remove, making them a serious threat to computer security.

Logic bombs

A logic bomb is a type of malicious code that is intentionally inserted into a software program. It is designed to execute a specific action when certain conditions are met, such as a particular date or time. An analogy for a logic bomb could be a time bomb that is set to go off at a specific time or when a specific event occurs. Just as a time bomb is designed to cause destruction when it detonates, a logic bomb is designed to cause harm to a computer system or network when it is triggered.

Rootkits

A rootkit is a type of malware that is designed to hide its presence on a system by modifying the operating system or other software components. It can be compared to a burglar who has broken into a house and is hiding in the attic, making it difficult for the homeowner to detect their presence. Similarly, a rootkit can be difficult to detect and remove, as it is designed to evade detection by antivirus software and other security measures. Once installed, a rootkit can be used to gain unauthorized access to a system, steal sensitive information, or carry out other malicious activities. Therefore, it is important to have effective security measures in place to prevent rootkits from being installed on a system, and to regularly scan for and remove any that may have already been installed.

Physical attacks

Physical attacks are a type of attack that involve the use of physical devices to assist with the attack. These attacks are not done across the network, but rather involve the use of physical devices. An analogy for physical attacks is that they are like a burglar breaking into a house to steal something. The burglar uses physical tools like a crowbar or a lock pick to gain access to the house. Similarly, attackers use physical devices like malicious USB cables, malicious flash drives, skimming, and card cloning to gain access to a system. Physical security tools like surveillance cameras, access control systems, and alarms can be used to protect against physical attacks.

Brute force password attacks

A brute force password attack is a type of cyber attack where an attacker tries every possible combination of characters until they find the correct password. It is similar to trying every possible combination of numbers on a combination lock until the lock opens. Brute force attacks can be time-consuming and resource-intensive, but they can be successful if the password is weak or short. To prevent brute force attacks, it is important to use strong and complex passwords, limit the number of login attempts, and use multi-factor authentication.

Radio frequency identification (RFID) cloning

Radio Frequency Identification (RFID) cloning is the process of creating a copy of an RFID tag or card. It involves copying the data from an existing RFID tag or card and then programming the data onto a new tag or card. An analogy for RFID cloning could be making a photocopy of a key. Just as a photocopy of a key can be used to open a lock, a cloned RFID tag or card can be used to gain access to a secure area or system. This is a security concern because unauthorized individuals can use cloned RFID tags or cards to gain access to restricted areas or systems.

Network attacks

A network attack is an attempt to gain unauthorized access to a computer network with the intent to cause damage, disrupt, destroy, or control computer systems or to alter, block, delete, manipulate, or steal the data held within these systems. It is like a burglar trying to break into a house to steal valuable items or cause damage. Network attacks can happen in stages, starting with hackers surveying or scanning for vulnerabilities or access points, initiating the initial compromise, and then executing the full attack. Attackers are focused on penetrating the corporate network perimeter and gaining access to internal systems. Once inside, attackers will combine other types of attacks, such as compromising an endpoint, spreading malware, or exploiting a vulnerability in a system within the network. To prevent network attacks, organizations should use a combination of skilled security professionals, processes, and technology. Defensive actions include preventing attempted attacks from entering the organization's IT systems, detecting intrusions, and disrupting attacks already in motion.

Environmental attacks

Environmental attacks are a type of security threat that exploit physical vulnerabilities in an organization's infrastructure. These attacks can include natural disasters, power outages, and other environmental factors that can disrupt normal operations and compromise the security of an organization's data. An analogy for environmental attacks could be a burglar who takes advantage of an unlocked door or window to gain access to a house. In the same way, environmental attacks take advantage of weaknesses in an organization's physical infrastructure to gain unauthorized access to sensitive information.

Distributed denial-of-service (DDoS)

Distributed denial-of-service (DDoS) is a type of cyber attack that aims to disrupt the normal functioning of a website or network by overwhelming it with traffic from multiple sources. It is like a traffic jam on a highway where too many cars are trying to use the same road at the same time, causing the road to become congested and slow down or even come to a complete stop. In a DDoS attack, the attacker uses a network of compromised devices, known as a botnet, to flood the target with traffic, making it unavailable to legitimate users. The goal of a DDoS attack is to cause disruption, damage, or financial loss to the target organization.

Amplified Network attacks

Amplified network attacks are a type of Distributed Denial-of-Service (DDoS) attack that uses a technique called reflection to amplify the amount of traffic sent to the target. It is like a megaphone that amplifies the sound of a person's voice, making it louder and more powerful. In an amplified network attack, the attacker sends a small request to a server that is vulnerable to reflection, such as a Domain Name System (DNS) server, with a spoofed source IP address that appears to be the target's IP address. The server then responds with a much larger reply, which is sent to the target's IP address, flooding it with traffic and overwhelming its resources. Amplified network attacks are particularly effective because they can generate a high volume of traffic with a relatively small number of requests, making it difficult for the target to defend against them. To protect against amplified network attacks, organizations can implement measures such as filtering and blocking traffic from known reflection sources, limiting the use of open DNS resolvers, and using anti-DDoS solutions that can detect and mitigate these types of attacks.

Reflected Network attacks

Reflected network attacks are a type of cyber attack where the attacker sends a request to a server, which then reflects the request back to the victim's computer. This can overwhelm the victim's computer with traffic, causing it to crash or become unresponsive. An analogy for this type of attack is a boomerang. The attacker throws the boomerang (request) at the server, which then sends it back to the attacker's target (victim's computer). The attacker can then catch the boomerang and throw it again, repeating the process until the victim's computer is overwhelmed. Reflected network attacks can be prevented by implementing security measures such as firewalls and intrusion detection systems.

Domain Name System (DNS) attacks

The Domain Name System (DNS) can be compared to a phonebook for the internet. It matches domain names with their corresponding IP addresses. DNS attacks exploit vulnerabilities in the DNS protocol to redirect internet traffic to malicious websites. DNS poisoning and DNS cache poisoning are two types of DNS attacks that use security gaps in the DNS protocol to redirect internet traffic to malicious websites. DNS poisoning occurs when a malicious actor intervenes in the process of a browser asking a local DNS server to find the IP address for a website name. The malicious actor supplies the wrong answer, tricking the browser into thinking it received the right answer to its query. Once the browser is tricked, the malicious actor can divert traffic to whatever fake website it wants. To defend against DNS attacks, experts recommend implementing multifactor authentication when making changes to the organization's DNS infrastructure. Operations personnel should also monitor for any changes publicly associated with their DNS records or any digital certificates associated with their organization. Another strategy is to deploy Domain Name System Security Extensions (DNSSEC), which strengthens authentication in DNS by using digital signatures based on public key cryptography.

Wireless attacks

Wireless attacks refer to the unauthorized access or manipulation of wireless networks or devices. An analogy to understand this could be a thief breaking into a house through an unlocked window. In this case, the wireless network or device is the house, and the attacker is the thief. The attacker can exploit vulnerabilities in the wireless network or device to gain access to sensitive information or cause damage. Examples of wireless attacks include eavesdropping, man-in-the-middle attacks, and denial-of-service attacks. It is important to implement security measures such as encryption, strong passwords, and regular updates to prevent wireless attacks.

On-path attacks

On-path attacks, also known as man-in-the-middle attacks, are a type of network attack where an attacker intercepts and alters network traffic between two hosts. The attacker sits in the middle of the conversation and can access information and modify data flows. The attacker can use this technique to steal sensitive information, such as login credentials or financial data, or to launch other types of attacks, such as session hijacking, HTTPS spoofing, or eavesdropping over the Wi-Fi connection. On-path attacks can be executed automatically by malware as soon as the user starts sending communication packets to certain devices. One simple way to have an on-path attack is through the use of ARP poisoning, where the attacker takes advantage of the lack of security associated with ARP to manipulate where certain devices can send traffic. Another way to perform an on-path attack is through the use of DNS poisoning, where the attacker modifies the entries that are inside the DNS server. To prevent on-path attacks, encryption and secure communication protocols, such as HTTPS, can be used, and network security measures, such as firewalls and intrusion detection systems, can be implemented.

Credential replay attacks

A credential replay attack is a type of cyber attack where an attacker intercepts and captures a user's authentication credentials, such as a username and password, and then replays them to gain unauthorized access to a system or network. This is similar to a scenario where a thief steals a key to a house and then uses that key to enter the house without the owner's permission. In a credential replay attack, the attacker does not need to know the actual password, but can simply replay the captured credentials to gain access. To prevent credential replay attacks, security measures such as multi-factor authentication and session tokens can be used to ensure that the authentication credentials are unique and cannot be reused by an attacker.

Malicious code attacks

Malicious code attacks are a type of cyber attack that involves the use of harmful software to compromise a system or network. This can include viruses, worms, trojans, and other types of malware that are designed to infiltrate a system and cause damage or steal sensitive information. Malicious code attacks can be compared to a burglar who sneaks into a house through an unlocked window or door. Once inside, the burglar can steal valuables, damage property, or even harm the occupants. Similarly, malicious code can enter a system through vulnerabilities in software or user error, and can then cause damage, steal data, or allow unauthorized access to sensitive information. It is important to have strong security measures in place to prevent these types of attacks, such as firewalls, antivirus software, and regular software updates.

Application attacks

Application attacks refer to cyber attacks that target vulnerabilities in software applications. These attacks exploit weaknesses in the application's code or design to gain unauthorized access to sensitive data or to disrupt the application's normal operation. There are many types of application attacks, including SQL injection, cross-site scripting (XSS), buffer overflow attacks, memory vulnerabilities, directory traversal, improper error handling, API attacks, and resource exhaustion attacks. Attackers can manipulate the application programming interface of an application to gain access to data that would not normally be available to them. To prevent application attacks, secure coding practices should be implemented, regular vulnerability assessments should be performed, and software should be kept up to date with the latest security patches.

Application Injection attacks

A prompt injection attack is a type of injection attack that involves manipulating or injecting malicious content into prompts to exploit the system. This attack aims to elicit an unintended response from LLM-based tools. The issue with prompt injection lies in how LLMs process input—there is no mechanism to differentiate between essential instructions and regular input words. This fundamental challenge makes prompt injection attacks difficult to fix. The attacker can include instructions in the data fields under their control and force the engine to perform unexpected actions. An analogy for prompt injection attacks could be a person who sneaks into a building by manipulating the security system to open the door, even though they do not have the proper credentials to enter. To mitigate prompt injection attacks, developers and users should take appropriate precautions, such as input validation, prompt filtering, and monitoring the generated content for malicious activities

Application Buffer overflow attacks

A buffer overflow attack is a type of cyber attack where an attacker tries to write more data to a fixed-length block of memory, or buffer, than the buffer is allocated to hold. This can cause the extra data to overwrite adjacent memory locations, which can lead to the execution of malicious code or a system crash. An analogy to this would be a person trying to fill a glass with more water than it can hold, causing the water to overflow and spill onto the table, potentially damaging other items on the table. Attackers can exploit buffer overflow vulnerabilities to take control of a system, steal sensitive data, or cause a denial of service. To prevent buffer overflow attacks, developers can use memory-safe programming languages, perform input validation, and use runtime protections such as address space layout randomization (ASLR) and stack canaries

Application Replay attacks

A replay attack is a type of network attack where an attacker intercepts a secure communication between two parties and then fraudulently delays or resends it to misdirect the receiver into doing what the attacker wants. It is similar to a playback of a recorded message. The attacker does not need advanced skills to decrypt a message after capturing it from the network. The attack could be successful simply by resending the whole thing. To prevent this type of attack, both sender and receiver should establish a completely random session key, which is a type of code that is only valid for one transaction and can't be used again. Another preventative measure for this type of attack is using timestamps on all messages. This prevents hackers from resending messages sent longer ago than a certain length of time, thus reducing the window of opportunity for an attacker to eavesdrop, siphon off the message, and resend it. Another method to avoid becoming a victim is to have a password for each transaction that's only used once and discarded. This ensures that even if the message is intercepted, it cannot be reused. An analogy for a replay attack is a person intercepting a message between two people and then repeating the message to one of the parties, pretending to be the other party.

Application Privilege escalation attacks

Privilege escalation attacks are cyberattacks that aim to gain unauthorized access to elevated rights, permissions, entitlements, or privileges beyond what is normally granted to a user or application. It is like a person who has access to a certain area of a building, but then gains access to a higher level of the building that they are not authorized to enter. Attackers can gain entry into an environment by exploiting vulnerabilities such as missing security patches, social engineering, or other methods. Once inside, they will typically perform surveillance and wait for the right opportunity to continue their mission. Vertical privilege escalation requires the attacker to perform a number of intermediary steps to bypass or override privilege controls, or exploit flaws in software, firmware, the kernel, or obtain privileged credentials for other applications or the operating system itself. Horizontal privilege escalation requires the attacker to gain access to the account credentials as well as elevating the permissions. Privilege escalation attacks can be prevented by implementing proper security controls, such as the principle of least privilege, and by keeping software up to date with the latest security patches.

Application Forgery attacks

Application Forgery attacks are a type of cyber attack

that tricks a user into executing unwanted actions on a web application in which they are currently authenticated. This is done by an attacker who sends a link via email or chat, which tricks the user into executing actions of the attacker's choosing. The attacker can then make the target system perform a function via the victim's browser, without the victim's knowledge. This is similar to a phishing attack, where an attacker poses as a legitimate source and tricks victims into sending large financial transfers into their accounts. In both cases, the attacker uses social engineering to trick the victim into performing an action that benefits the attacker. To prevent Application Forgery attacks, developers can implement measures such as using built-in CSRF protection, adding CSRF tokens to all state-changing requests, and using proper authorization to verify the identity and authority of the requester.

Application Directory traversal attacks

Directory traversal attack, also known as path traversal attack, is an HTTP attack that allows attackers to access restricted directories and execute commands outside of the web server's root directory. It happens when an attacker manipulates variables that reference files with "dot-dot-slash" sequences (../) and its variations to move up to the parent directory and access files or directories outside of the web server's root directory. It is like a burglar who uses a secret passage to bypass the front door and enter a house through a window or a backdoor. The attacker can use directory traversal to download server configuration files, which contain sensitive information and potentially expose more server vulnerabilities. Ultimately, the attacker may access confidential information or even get full control of the server. To prevent directory traversal attacks, it is crucial to control access to web content, sanitize user input, and validate file paths to ensure that they are within the web server's root directory.

Cryptographic attacks

Cryptography is the practice of securing communication in the presence of adversarial behavior. Cryptographic attacks are methods used by attackers to target cryptographic solutions like ciphertext, encryption keys, etc. These attacks aim to retrieve the plaintext from the ciphertext or decode the encrypted data. Cryptographic attacks can be classified in any of several ways. In a ciphertext-only attack, the attacker has access only to the ciphertext. In a known-plaintext attack, the attacker has access to a ciphertext and its corresponding plaintext. In a chosen-plaintext attack, the attacker can choose the plaintext and obtain the corresponding ciphertext. In a chosen-ciphertext attack, the attacker can choose the ciphertext and obtain the corresponding plaintext. Cryptographic attacks can also be classified based on the cryptographic algorithm used. For example, a brute-force attack consists of an attacker submitting many passwords or passphrases with the hope of eventually guessing correctly. Cryptographic attacks can be prevented by discovering weaknesses and flaws in cryptography techniques, cryptographic protocol, encryption algorithms, or key management strategy. An analogy for cryptographic attacks could be a burglar trying to break into a house. The burglar may try different methods to break into the house, such as picking the lock, breaking a window, or finding a hidden key. Similarly, an attacker may try different methods to break into a cryptographic system, such as a brute-force attack, a chosen-plaintext attack, or a known-plaintext attack.

Cryptographic Downgrade attacks

A cryptographic downgrade attack is a type of attack that forces a system to use an older and less secure version of a cryptographic protocol, algorithm, or connection type. It is also known as a version rollback attack or bidding-down attack. The attacker positions themselves as a man-in-the-middle (MITM) and interferes with the communication between the client and server. The attacker then forces the system to use a lower version of the cryptographic protocol, algorithm, or connection type, which is typically provided for backward compatibility with older systems. This type of attack can be compared to a lockpick, where the attacker gains access to the system and can leave all the data vulnerable, including user account credentials, payment information, and personal medical data. To prevent a downgrade attack, the appropriate measure is to stop supporting weak ciphers or previous versions of cryptographic protocols, depending on the vulnerability's attack vector.

Cryptographic Collision attacks

A cryptographic collision attack is a type of attack on a cryptographic hash function that tries to find two different messages that produce the same hash value. It is like trying to find two different keys that can open the same lock. In a collision attack, the attacker has no control over the content of either message, but they are arbitrarily chosen by the algorithm. A collision attack is considered successful if the attacker can find two different messages that produce the same hash value. This type of attack is a significant concern in cryptography because it can undermine the security of digital signatures and other security mechanisms that rely on hash functions. There are different types of collision attacks, including classical collision attacks and chosen-prefix collision attacks. Classical collision attacks are harder to execute because the attacker has no control over the content of the messages, while chosen-prefix collision attacks are more powerful because the attacker can choose two different documents and append different calculated values that result in the whole documents having an equal hash value

Cryptographic Birthday attacks

A birthday attack is a type of cryptographic attack that exploits the birthday paradox in probability theory to find a collision in a hash function. The birthday paradox states that in a group of people, the probability of two people having the same birthday is higher than one might expect, even with a relatively small number of people. Similarly, in a hash function, the probability of two different inputs producing the same hash value is higher than one might expect, even with a relatively small number of inputs. A birthday attack takes advantage of this statistical property by trying to find two different input messages that produce the same hash value. This attack can be used to create fake messages or forge digital signatures. However, most modern cryptographic systems are designed to be resistant to birthday attacks, either by using hash functions with very large output sizes or by using other techniques to make it difficult for an attacker to find a collision. To protect against these threats, it is important to use strong cryptographic techniques and to securely store and manage private keys used for digital signatures.

Password attacks

Password attacks are a common method used by hackers to gain unauthorized access to computer systems or networks. Passwords are like keys that unlock doors, and password attacks are like trying to pick the lock or break down the door to gain entry. There are several types of password attacks, including brute force attacks, dictionary attacks, and credential stuffing attacks. Brute force attacks involve trying every possible combination of characters until the correct password is found. Dictionary attacks use a list of common words or phrases to guess the password. Credential stuffing attacks use previously stolen usernames and passwords to gain access to other accounts. To protect against password attacks, it is important to use strong passwords that are difficult to guess, avoid using the same password for multiple accounts, and enable two-factor authentication whenever possible.

Spraying Password attacks

Password spraying is a type of brute force attack where an attacker uses a single password against multiple accounts on the same application to avoid account lockouts that would normally occur when brute forcing a single account with many passwords. The attacker tries every user account in their list with the same password before resetting the list and trying the next password. This technique minimizes the risk of the attacker's detection and lockouts on a single account due to the time between attempts. Password spraying attacks often take place where the application or admin within a particular organization sets a default password for new users. It can target thousands or even millions of different users at once, rather than just one account, and can take place over time to evade detection. Once an attacker accesses an account via a password spray attack, they will be hoping that it contains information valuable enough to steal or has sufficient permissions to further weaken the organization's security measures to gain access to even more sensitive data. To defend against password spraying attacks, organizations should enforce strong, complex passwords that can't be easily guessed, set up a detection for login attempts to multiple accounts that occur from a single host over a short window of time, and implement company-wide training for all employees about password spraying, other cybersecurity issues, and the importance of strong passwords. Password spraying could be a burglar trying the same key to open multiple doors in a neighborhood instead of trying different keys for each door, to avoid getting caught by the police.

Brute force Password attacks
A brute force password attack is a type of cyber attack where an attacker tries every possible combination of characters until they find the correct password. It is similar to trying every possible combination of numbers on a combination lock until the lock opens. Brute force attacks can be time-consuming and resource-intensive, but they can be successful if the password is weak or short. To prevent brute force attacks, it is important to use strong and complex passwords, limit the number of login attempts, and use multi-factor authentication.

Malicious activity Indicators
Malicious activity refers to any unauthorized or harmful activity that occurs on a computer system. This activity can be caused by various factors, including malware, phishing attacks, and social engineering. The SY0-701 exam objectives document identifies indicators of malicious activity as events or artifacts that suggest an attack or compromise has occurred or is occurring. These indicators can include unusual network traffic, unauthorized access attempts, and unexpected system crashes. To prevent data breaches, it is essential to identify and analyze malicious activity and implement mitigation techniques to secure the enterprise. The SY0-701 exam domains cover diverse areas, including threat actors and their motivations, threat vectors, types of vulnerabilities, indicators of malicious activity, and crucial mitigation techniques.

Malicious activity Indicators such as Account lockout

Locked accounts are a security measure used by organizations to prevent brute force attacks on their live systems. When a user enters an incorrect password a certain number of times, the account is locked, and the user cannot log in until the account is unlocked by an administrator. This is a common practice for most organizations to ensure that no one is performing a brute force attack on their live systems. However, if a service account is locked, it could affect a large number of people, and services that rely on that account could be locked out. Therefore, it is generally not considered a good best practice to disable the brute force protection and account lockout policy for a service account. Instead, organizations should monitor for brute force attacks and take appropriate action when an account is locked. Malicious activity indicators are signs that an attacker has attempted to compromise a system or network. One such indicator is account lockout, which occurs when an account is locked after a certain number of failed login attempts. This is similar to a bank account that locks after multiple incorrect PIN entries, preventing unauthorized access. In the context of cybersecurity, account lockout can be a sign of a brute-force attack, where an attacker tries to guess a user's password by repeatedly attempting different combinations. By detecting and responding to account lockouts, security professionals can prevent unauthorized access and protect sensitive information.

Malicious activity Indicators such as Concurrent session usage

Concurrent session usage refers to the number of active sessions that a user can have at the same time. It is similar to a person having multiple phone lines or multiple browser tabs open at the same time. In the context of security, concurrent session usage is important because it can affect the security of a system. For example, if a user has multiple active sessions, it can increase the risk of unauthorized access to the system. Therefore, it is important to monitor and limit concurrent session usage to ensure the security of the system. The CompTIA Security+ certification exam covers concurrent session usage as part of its objectives

Malicious activity Indicators such as Blocked content

blocked content refers to the process of preventing unauthorized access to certain types of data or resources. This can be compared to a bouncer at a nightclub who checks IDs at the door to ensure that only authorized individuals are allowed to enter. In the same way, blocked content prevents unauthorized users from accessing sensitive information or resources, such as confidential documents or restricted websites. This is typically achieved through the use of firewalls, access control lists, and other security measures that restrict access to specific users or groups. Indicators of malicious activity are signs that an attacker is attempting to compromise a system or network. These indicators can be compared to a burglar trying to break into a house. Just as a burglar might try to pick a lock or break a window to gain entry, an attacker might use various techniques to gain unauthorized access to a system or network. Blocked content is one such indicator of malicious activity. It can be compared to a security system that prevents a burglar from entering a house. When content is blocked, it means that the system has detected something suspicious and has prevented it from executing. This could be a sign that an attacker is attempting to deliver malware or other malicious content to the system. By blocking the content, the system is preventing the attacker from gaining a foothold on the system or network.

Malicious activity Indicators such as Impossible travel

Impossible travel is a malicious activity indicator that refers to a user's login from two different geographic locations within an impossibly short time frame. This could indicate that an attacker has gained access to the user's credentials and is using them to log in from different locations simultaneously. An analogy for this could be a person who is physically present in two different places at the same time, which is impossible and could indicate that the person is using some kind of trickery or deception. Similarly, impossible travel in the context of cybersecurity could indicate that an attacker is using some kind of malicious technique to gain access to a user's account and is attempting to cover their tracks by logging in from different locations simultaneously. Basically "impossible travel" refers to a type of attack where an adversary appears to be in two places at the same time, which is impossible based on the laws of physics. This can occur when an attacker gains access to a user's credentials and uses them to log in from a different location, or when an attacker spoofs the user's IP address to make it appear as if they are in a different location. An analogy for this type of attack could be a person trying to be in two different places at the same time, like trying to be at home and at work simultaneously. It is impossible to be in two places at once, just as it is impossible for a user to log in from two different locations at the same time.

Malicious activity Indicators such as Resource consumption

Resource consumption refers to the amount of resources, such as CPU, memory, disk space, and network bandwidth, that a system or application uses. Just like a car that consumes fuel to run, a computer system consumes resources to perform its tasks. Resource consumption can be monitored and managed to ensure that the system or application is running efficiently and not wasting resources. In the context of security, monitoring resource consumption can also help detect and prevent denial-of-service (DoS) attacks, where an attacker tries to consume all available resources to make a system or application unavailable to legitimate users. Malicious activity indicators are signs that an attacker has compromised a system or network. One such indicator is resource consumption, which refers to the amount of system resources, such as CPU, memory, or network bandwidth, that an attacker's activity consumes. This can be compared to a thief who breaks into a house and starts using the utilities, such as electricity and water, without the owner's permission. The increased consumption of these resources can be a sign of malicious activity, and can cause the system or network to slow down or crash. Monitoring resource consumption can help detect and prevent attacks, and is an important part of security monitoring and incident response.

Malicious activity Indicators such as Resource inaccessibility

Resource inaccessibility refers to the inability of users to access or use a resource due to various reasons such as technical issues, lack of accessibility features, or poor design. Inaccessibility can be compared to a grocery list that is written as a paragraph instead of bullet points. Just as a long paragraph can make it difficult to find specific items on a grocery list, inaccessibility can make it difficult for users to find and use the information they need. To make resources more accessible, it is important to use short paragraphs, short sentences, and descriptive headings. Additionally, it is important to provide as much detail as possible about the problem encountered to help organizations understand and fix the problem

Malicious activity Indicators such as Out-of-cycle logging

Malicious activity indicators are signs that an attacker has gained unauthorized access to a system or network. One such indicator is out-of-cycle logging, which refers to logging activity that occurs outside of the normal logging schedule. This could indicate that an attacker is attempting to cover their tracks by deleting or modifying logs. An analogy for this could be a burglar who breaks into a house and tries to erase their footprints or any other evidence of their presence to avoid being caught. Similarly, an attacker may try to erase their tracks by deleting or modifying logs to avoid detection.

Malicious activity Indicators such as Published/documented

Published documents are important to identifying indicators of malicious activity because they can contain hidden threats that may not be immediately apparent. This can be compared to a seemingly harmless object that actually contains a hidden danger, such as a seemingly harmless plant that is actually poisonous. Just as a person may not realize the danger of a plant until they are informed of its poisonous nature, security professionals may not realize the danger of a published document until they analyze it for indicators of malicious activity. By analyzing published documents for indicators of malicious activity, security professionals can identify potential security threats and take appropriate action to mitigate them. Analyzing published documents for indicators of malicious activity can help security professionals identify potential security threats and take appropriate action to mitigate them. This involves analyzing various data sources such as OS-specific security logs, IPS/IDS logs, network logs, metadata, vulnerability scans, automated reports, dashboards, and packet captures to identify indicators of malicious activity. Once these indicators are identified, security professionals can take appropriate action to mitigate the threat, such as blocking the source of the threat, removing the malicious code, or updating security policies and procedures. By analyzing published documents for indicators of malicious activity, security professionals can help protect their organization from potential security threats.

Malicious activity Indicators such as Missing logs

Malicious activity indicators are signs that suggest the presence of a security breach or attack. One such indicator is missing logs, which are records of system activity that can be used to detect and investigate security incidents. Missing logs can be compared to a detective's notebook, which contains detailed notes of all the events and clues related to a case. If some pages of the notebook are missing, it becomes difficult for the detective to piece together the events and identify the culprit. Similarly, missing logs can make it challenging for security analysts to determine the scope and impact of a security incident, as well as the methods used by the attacker. Therefore, it is crucial to ensure that logs are properly configured, stored, and monitored to detect any suspicious activity. Missing logs can be an indicator of malicious activity, but how can you identify this type of activity? One way is to use log analysis techniques to detect anomalies or patterns that suggest a security breach. For example, you can monitor for high-impact changes, such as the creation or deletion of user accounts, changes to system configurations, or unusual network traffic. You can also set up tripwires or alerts that trigger when specific events occur, such as failed login attempts or access to sensitive files. Another approach is to look for anomalous changes in activity levels, which can indicate that an attacker is attempting to cover their tracks by deleting or modifying logs. To do this, you need to have a comprehensive log management solution that can collect, store, and analyze logs from multiple sources, such as servers, applications, and network devices. By using these techniques, you can identify missing logs and other indicators of malicious activity, and take appropriate action to mitigate the risk.

The mitigation technique, Segmentation

Segmentation is a mitigation technique used to improve security by dividing a network into smaller, isolated segments. This technique is similar to dividing a large office building into smaller rooms or cubicles. By doing so, if an attacker gains access to one segment, they will not be able to access other segments, which reduces the potential damage that can be caused. Segmentation can be achieved through the use of firewalls, VLANs, or other network devices that can restrict access between segments. This technique can help prevent lateral movement by attackers and limit the scope of a potential breach.

The mitigation technique, Access control

Access control is a mitigation technique used to restrict access to resources based on the principle of least privilege. It involves the implementation of policies, procedures, and technologies to ensure that only authorized individuals can access specific resources. Access control can be compared to a bouncer at a nightclub who checks IDs and only allows people who meet certain criteria to enter. Similarly, access control checks the identity and credentials of users and only grants access to resources that they are authorized to use. This technique helps to prevent unauthorized access, reduce the risk of data breaches, and protect sensitive information.

The mitigation technique, Access control list (ACL)

An Access Control List (ACL) is a mitigation technique used to control access to resources based on a set of rules. It is a list of permissions that specifies which users or systems are granted or denied access to a particular object or system resource. ACLs consist of access control entries (ACEs) that contain the name of a user or group of users, and the access privileges are stated in a string of bits called an access mask. An analogy for ACLs is a bouncer at a club who checks IDs and only allows people who meet certain criteria to enter. Similarly, ACLs check the identity and credentials of users and only grant access to resources that they are authorized to use. ACLs help to prevent unauthorized access, reduce the risk of data breaches, and protect sensitive information. ACLs can be placed on virtually any security or routing device, and having multiple ACLs in different parts of the network can be beneficial.

The mitigation technique, Permissions

Permissions is a mitigation technique that refers to the practice of granting or restricting access to resources based on the principle of least privilege. This means that users are only given the minimum level of access required to perform their tasks, and no more. Permissions can be compared to a bouncer at a nightclub who checks IDs and only allows people who are on the guest list to enter. In the same way, Permissions ensure that only authorized users are granted access to sensitive data or systems, while unauthorized users are denied access. This helps to prevent data breaches and other security incidents that can result from unauthorized access. Here are some additional mitigation techniques related to Permissions.

The mitigation technique, Application allow list

The Application Allow List is a mitigation technique used to prevent unauthorized or malicious software from running on a system. It is a list of approved applications that are allowed to run on a system, while all other applications are blocked. This technique is similar to a bouncer at a nightclub who only allows people on the guest list to enter, while denying entry to anyone not on the list. By using an Application Allow List, organizations can reduce the attack surface of their systems and prevent malware from executing.

The mitigation technique, Isolation

Isolation is a mitigation technique used in cybersecurity to prevent the spread of malware or unauthorized access to sensitive data. It involves separating a system or network from other systems or networks to limit the potential damage that can be caused by a security breach. An analogy for isolation is a quarantine zone in a hospital. Just as a quarantine zone is used to isolate patients with contagious diseases to prevent the spread of the disease to other patients, isolation in cybersecurity is used to contain a security breach and prevent it from spreading to other systems or networks.

The mitigation technique, Patching

Patching is a mitigation technique used to address vulnerabilities in software and systems. It involves applying updates or fixes to software or systems to prevent exploitation of known vulnerabilities. Patching can be compared to repairing a leaky roof. Just as a leaky roof can cause damage to a house, vulnerabilities in software and systems can be exploited by attackers to cause damage to an organization. Patching is like fixing the leaky roof to prevent further damage to the house. By applying patches, organizations can prevent attackers from exploiting known vulnerabilities and reduce the risk of a security breach.

The mitigation technique, Monitoring

monitoring is a mitigation technique that involves observing and analyzing system activities to detect and respond to security incidents. It is like a security guard who patrols a building to detect and respond to any suspicious activity. The security guard is trained to identify potential threats and take appropriate action to prevent them from causing harm. Similarly, monitoring involves using tools and techniques to detect and analyze system events, such as log files, network traffic, and user activity, to identify potential security incidents. Once a security incident is detected, appropriate action can be taken to prevent or mitigate the impact of the incident. Monitoring is an important mitigation technique that helps organizations to maintain the security and integrity of their systems and data.

The mitigation technique, Least privilege

Least privilege is a mitigation technique that limits user access rights to only the resources necessary to perform their job functions. This technique is designed to reduce the risk of unauthorized access to sensitive data and systems. An analogy for this technique is a hotel room key card. When you check into a hotel, you are given a key card that only grants you access to your assigned room. You cannot access other rooms or areas of the hotel without additional authorization. Similarly, the least privilege technique limits user access to only the resources they need to perform their job functions, reducing the risk of unauthorized access to sensitive data and systems.

The mitigation technique, Configuration enforcement

Configuration enforcement is a mitigation technique used to ensure that systems and devices are configured according to established security policies and standards. It involves monitoring and enforcing the configuration settings of systems and devices to ensure that they are secure and compliant with security policies. This technique is similar to a security guard checking the identification of people entering a building to ensure that only authorized personnel are allowed in. Just as a security guard enforces the rules and policies of a building, configuration enforcement enforces the security policies and standards of an organization to prevent unauthorized access and protect against security threats.

The mitigation technique, Decommissioning

Decommissioning is a mitigation technique used to retire systems and devices that are no longer needed or have reached the end of their useful life. It involves the safe and secure removal of all components and data from the system or device to prevent unauthorized access and protect against security threats. This technique is similar to the process of demolishing a building that is no longer needed. Just as a building is carefully dismantled to ensure that no hazardous materials are released into the environment, decommissioning involves the careful removal of all components and data to ensure that no sensitive information is leaked or lost. The process of decommissioning is highly regulated and requires specialized personnel and sophisticated techniques to ensure that it is performed safely and effectively.

The mitigation technique, Hardening techniques

Hardening techniques are a set of mitigation techniques used to secure systems and networks by reducing their attack surface. These techniques are like adding layers of armor to a castle to make it more difficult for attackers to breach its defenses. Hardening techniques include measures such as disabling unnecessary services, removing default accounts and passwords, applying security patches, and configuring firewalls and intrusion detection systems. By implementing these techniques, the system or network becomes more resilient to attacks, making it harder for attackers to gain unauthorized access or cause damage.

The mitigation technique, Encryption

Encryption is a mitigation technique used to protect sensitive data by converting it into an unreadable format that can only be deciphered with a unique key. Encryption can be compared to a secret code that only the intended recipient can understand. Just as a secret code can prevent unauthorized access to a message, encryption can prevent unauthorized access to sensitive data. Encryption can be implemented using various methods, such as Advanced Encryption Standard (AES) and Rivest-Shamir-Adleman (RSA), and can be used to protect data at rest or in transit. FIPS 140-2 is a recorce cybersecurity professinals can use to get a more detailed information on what types of encryption are recommended for various use cases. The FIPS 140-2 is a security standard developed by the National Institute of Standards and Technology (NIST) to test and report the integrity of cryptographic modules. The use of FIPS 140-2 certified modules ensures that encryption algorithms, such as Advanced Encryption Standard (AES), are implemented correctly. AES is a symmetric encryption algorithm that encrypts data blocks of 128 bits at a time and uses keys of 128, 192, and 256 bits to encrypt these data blocks. The 256-bit key is strongly recommended for use in public safety wireless systems in accordance with the published standard for Project 25 Block Encryption. In summary, FIPS 141 provides guidelines for the use of encryption in land mobile radio systems, and FIPS 140-2 provides a standard for testing and reporting the integrity of cryptographic modules, including those used for AES encryption.

The mitigation technique, Installation of endpoint protection

The installation of endpoint protection is a mitigation technique used to secure endpoints, such as laptops, desktops, and mobile devices, from various types of cyber threats. Endpoint protection software is designed to detect, prevent, and remove malware, viruses, and other malicious software that can compromise the security of an endpoint. It is similar to a security guard stationed at the entrance of a building, who checks everyone entering the building for any suspicious activity or items that could harm the occupants. The endpoint protection software acts as a security guard for the endpoint, monitoring all incoming and outgoing traffic, and blocking any malicious activity that could harm the device or the network it is connected to. By installing endpoint protection, organizations can ensure that their endpoints are protected against cyber threats, and reduce the risk of a security breach.

The mitigation technique, Host-based firewall

a host-based firewall is a mitigation technique that is used to protect a single device or host from unauthorized access. It is a software-based firewall that is installed on the host itself and is used to monitor and control incoming and outgoing network traffic. An analogy to explain the concept of a host-based firewall is to think of it as a security guard stationed at the entrance of a building. The security guard checks the identification of everyone who enters and exits the building, and only allows authorized personnel to enter. Similarly, a host-based firewall checks the incoming and outgoing network traffic of a device, and only allows authorized traffic to pass through. It acts as a barrier between the device and the network, and helps to prevent unauthorized access and attacks. In summary, a host-based firewall is a software-based firewall that is installed on a single device or host to monitor and control incoming and outgoing network traffic. It acts as a security guard for the device, checking the traffic and only allowing authorized traffic to pass through.

The mitigation technique, Host-based intrusion prevention system (HIPS)

A Host-based Intrusion Prevention System (HIPS) is a security mechanism that monitors and analyzes the behavior of applications and processes running on a host to detect and prevent unauthorized access or malicious activity. It is like a security guard stationed at the entrance of a building who checks the identity of everyone who enters and exits the building, and ensures that only authorized personnel are allowed in. Similarly, a HIPS monitors the behavior of applications and processes running on a host, and blocks any unauthorized or malicious activity, thereby preventing potential security breaches.

The mitigation technique, Disabling ports/protocols

The mitigation technique of disabling ports/protocols involves shutting down or blocking access to specific network ports or protocols that are not necessary for the operation of the system. This technique can help prevent unauthorized access to a network by limiting the number of entry points that an attacker can use to gain access. An analogy for this technique could be a house with multiple doors and windows. By disabling some of the doors and windows that are not necessary for entry and exit, the homeowner can limit the number of entry points that a burglar can use to break in. Similarly, by disabling ports and protocols that are not necessary for network operations, an organization can limit the number of entry points that an attacker can use to gain unauthorized access to the network.

The mitigation technique, Default password changes

The mitigation technique of default password changes is a security measure that involves changing the default passwords of devices and systems to prevent unauthorized access. Default passwords are often used by manufacturers to allow users to access their devices or systems for the first time. However, these passwords are often publicly available and can be easily exploited by attackers to gain access to the device or system. Changing the default password to a unique and strong password can be compared to changing the locks on a new house. Just as changing the locks on a new house prevents anyone with the old keys from entering, changing the default password prevents anyone with knowledge of the default password from accessing the device or system. This mitigation technique is an important step in securing devices and systems and should be implemented as part of a comprehensive security strategy.

The mitigation technique, Removal of unnecessary software

The mitigation technique of removing unnecessary software is a security measure that involves identifying and removing software that is not needed or used in a system. This technique is similar to decluttering a house by removing items that are no longer useful or needed. Just as decluttering a house can make it easier to find and access important items, removing unnecessary software can make it easier to identify and address security vulnerabilities. By reducing the amount of software in a system, the attack surface is also reduced, making it more difficult for attackers to exploit vulnerabilities.

The security implications of different Architecture and infrastructure concepts

Security architecture is a framework of security principles, methods, and models that are designed to align with an organization's objectives and help keep it safe from cyber threats. It is similar to a blueprint of a building that outlines the design and structure of the building, including the materials used, the layout, and the safety features. Just as a blueprint ensures that a building is constructed according to the design and meets safety standards, security architecture ensures that an organization's systems and assets are protected from cyber threats and meet security standards.

Different architecture and infrastructure concepts have different security implications. For example, network-level infrastructure security is generally considered the largest and most vulnerable of the enterprise when it comes to security risk. Therefore, it is important to have a strong security architecture framework for protecting an organization's most important information assets.

The security implications of, Cloud Architecture and infrastructure concepts

Cloud architecture and infrastructure concepts have significant security implications. Cloud computing is like renting a house, where the cloud provider is the landlord and the cloud user is the tenant. The cloud provider is responsible for the security of the cloud infrastructure, while the cloud user is responsible for the security of their data and applications. Cloud architecture and infrastructure concepts such as virtualization, multi-tenancy, and shared resources can introduce new security risks. For example, virtualization can lead to the co-mingling of data from different tenants on the same physical server, which can increase the risk of data leakage or unauthorized access. Multi-tenancy can also lead to the sharing of resources, which can increase the risk of denial-of-service attacks. Therefore, it is important for cloud users to understand the security implications of cloud architecture and infrastructure concepts and to implement appropriate security controls to mitigate these risks.

The security implications of ,Responsibility matrix

The responsibility matrix has significant security implications. The responsibility matrix is like a team sport, where each player has a specific role to play. The RACI (Responsible, Accountable, Consulted, Informed) model is a common responsibility matrix used in project management. The RACI model defines the roles and responsibilities of each team member for each task within a project. The responsible employee physically does the work, while the accountable employee oversees the work and shares part of the blame if the job is not done satisfactorily. The consulted employee offers advice or feedback to improve the work, while the informed party does not take part in the work but should be notified of the results. The responsibility matrix helps to ensure that each team member understands their role and responsibilities, which can help to improve the overall security of the project. For example, in a security team, the responsibility matrix can help to ensure that each team member understands their role and responsibilities for securing the organization's assets and data. The responsibility matrix can also help to ensure that there is no overlap or gaps in security responsibilities, which can help to improve the overall security posture of the organization.

The security implications of, Hybrid cloud considerations

Hybrid cloud is a combination of public and private cloud infrastructures that allows organizations to leverage the benefits of both. However, it also introduces security implications that need to be considered. For example, data stored in a hybrid cloud environment may be subject to different security policies and controls, which can lead to inconsistencies and vulnerabilities. An analogy for this could be a house with two different security systems, one for the front door and one for the back door. If one system is weaker than the other, it can create a vulnerability that can be exploited by an attacker. Therefore, it is important to ensure that security policies and controls are consistent across all cloud environments and that data is protected throughout its lifecycle, regardless of where it is stored.

The security implications of, Third-party vendors

Third-party cloud vendors can pose significant security implications for organizations that use them. Third-party vendors are like contractors who are hired to perform specific tasks, but they have access to the organization's data. Just like a contractor who has access to your home, third-party vendors can help organizations grow, but they also increase risk exposure and the probability of significant losses. When an organization moves to the cloud and relies increasingly on third parties, it introduces the security risks associated with these newly added third parties. A provider with security issues could allow attackers to penetrate the corporate network. The security paradigm is changing as the modern computing environment moves away from the isolated enterprise network. Larger attack surfaces, insufficient visibility into third-party environments, and overprivileged permissions are some of the security challenges associated with third-party service providers in the cloud. Organizations can improve visibility into third-party security risks by using scalable solutions and standardized risk assessments covering the entire supplier ecosystem. Assessing third-party risk often involves using vendor risk questionnaires to learn about the vendor's security practices, policies, and past failures. Just like a homeowner who would conduct due diligence on every contractor before signing a contract, organizations should conduct due diligence on every vendor before providing access to sensitive data or outsourcing critical business processes. It is like inviting a stranger into your home, where you need to ensure that they are trustworthy and do not pose a threat to your family. Similarly, companies must ensure that third-party vendors are trustworthy and do not pose a threat to their data and systems. Third-party vendors can be a gateway for intrusions, expose companies to financial and regulatory risks, and harm a company's reputation if a service malfunctions. In fact, nearly half of all data breaches involve a third party or vendor. Therefore, companies must fully vet all third-party vendors before allowing them access to their systems to ensure that they have implemented the proper security protocols. Companies should also take proactive measures to ensure that their third parties are effective data custodians.

The security implications of, Infrastructure as code (IaC)

Infrastructure as Code (IaC) is a process that allows administrators and DevOps to manage, provision, and configure their cloud infrastructure automatically by writing code. However, IaC also introduces security risks that need to be managed. Misconfigurations are a major security concern in cloud environments, including IaC tools. The lack of security awareness on the IaC pipeline could lead to the exposure of sensitive data or leave openings for attacks. An unpatched vulnerability in an IaC tool could serve as a threat entry point to the core infrastructure. Storing hard-coded secrets in IaC configuration files is a common mistake that is made by many developers. Passwords and API keys pose a risk if exposed, and even read-only access to an IaC template can provide attackers with valuable insight into the infrastructure, helping them identify potential misconfigurations. Therefore, it is important to follow secure coding practices, apply the principle of least privilege, and use testing frameworks and version control to validate and track changes to the code to handle errors quickly. An analogy for IaC could be a recipe for a cake. The recipe provides instructions for the ingredients and the steps to follow to bake the cake. Similarly, IaC provides instructions for the infrastructure and the steps to follow to set up and manage it. Just as a recipe can be modified to create a different cake, IaC can be modified to create different infrastructure configurations.

The security implications of, Serverless

Serverless architectures are cloud-native development models that allow developers to build and run applications and services without needing to manage server infrastructure. The main advantage of serverless technology is its ability to expedite the software development process by outsourcing server infrastructure management to the Cloud Service Provider (CSP), allowing developers to focus on application functions. However, the main challenge faced in serverless is that the CSP is only responsible for the security of the cloud, not security in the cloud. This means that the serverless application is still exposed to the risks and vulnerabilities that traditional applications face, but it also faces security challenges that are unique to the serverless architecture. For example, serverless computing exposes a significantly larger attack surface compared to its predecessors because it comprises dozens or hundreds of functions, each with its own policies, roles, APIs, and audit trails. Defending serverless applications requires thinking about each entry point. Effective serverless security focuses on ensuring code protection, behavioral protection, and security permissions on the client-side. An analogy for serverless architecture could be a restaurant where the chef only prepares the food, and the restaurant owner takes care of everything else, such as the kitchen, dining area, and customer service. The chef only needs to focus on cooking the food, but the restaurant owner is responsible for ensuring that the kitchen is clean, the dining area is safe, and the customers are satisfied. Similarly, in serverless architecture, the developer only needs to focus on the application functions, and the CSP takes care of the server infrastructure. However, the developer is still responsible for ensuring that the application functions are secure and protected from attacks, just as the chef is responsible for ensuring that the food is cooked properly and tastes good.

The security implications of, Microservices

Microservices are small, autonomous units that work together to help an application function. They are like a group of specialized workers in a factory, each responsible for a specific task, but working together to produce a final product. However, the use of microservices architecture brings several security implications. Microservices offer dozens or even hundreds of potential points of vulnerability, and each one needs to be effectively secured in order for an application to operate effectively. The distributed nature of microservices creates inherent complexities and security issues that development teams have no choice but to address. The proliferation of communications interfaces in a microservices-based application increases the attack surface, and additional consideration needs to be given to securing the connection from a client to each microservice and to the calls between them. It is important to build security into the design of microservices architecture and implement a series of best practices that make security an integral component to how developer teams work, without compromising productivity.

The security implications of, Network infrastructure
Network infrastructure refers to the underlying hardware and software that enables communication between devices on a network. It includes routers, switches, servers, and other networking devices. The security implications of network infrastructure are significant because whoever controls the routing infrastructure of a network essentially controls the data flowing through the network. Network infrastructure devices are often easy targets for attackers, and once installed, many network devices are not maintained at the same security level as general-purpose desktops and servers. This makes them vulnerable to attacks, and attackers can use them to gain access to other parts of the network. An analogy for network infrastructure security is the security of a castle's walls and gates. Just as a castle's walls and gates protect the castle from external threats, network infrastructure security protects a network from external and internal threats.

The security implications of, Physical isolation (IE: Air-gapped)

An air-gapped system is a security measure that involves isolating a computer or network and preventing it from establishing an external connection. It is like a house that is completely cut off from the outside world, with no doors or windows. and then placed in the middle of the ocean so no one can just drive right up to it. like the name air gapped implies, the system has no way to communicate with the outside world. No internet connection, no Wi-Fi, nothing. In an airgapped system if you want to connect to it you have to walk up to it and plug in to connect to it in most situations. This type of system is physically disconnected from other networks, making it difficult for attackers to gain access to the system. However, air-gapped systems are not completely secure, as they are still susceptible to electromagnetic leakage, which can be analyzed by hackers to attack the system. Therefore, it is important to apply additional security measures, such as encryption of data at rest, to ensure that the data is completely useless to attackers even if they gain access to the air-gapped system.

The security implications of, Logical segmentation

Logical segmentation is a network security technique that involves dividing a network into smaller subnets using virtual local area networks (VLANs) or network addressing schemes. It is like dividing a large house into smaller rooms with different purposes, such as a bedroom, a kitchen, and a living room. Each room has its own distinct function and is separated from the others by walls and doors. Similarly, logical segmentation divides a network into smaller subnets, each with its own distinct address range and traffic local to each subnet. This way, if one subnet is compromised, the others will remain secure. Logical segmentation enhances network security by limiting how far an attack can spread and by preventing unauthorized access to sensitive information. It also improves network performance and makes it easier to manage network resources.

The security implications of, Software-defined networking (SDN)

Software-defined networking (SDN) is a networking architecture that uses virtualization to simplify network management and increase capacity. SDN provides a centralized controller that manages the network, which can introduce new security challenges. The SDN architecture is exposed to various sources of security risk from its network architecture design perspective, which includes the control plane, application plane, and data plane layers. The security issues related to the traditional network architecture also apply to the SDN architecture. The benefits of SDN include increased network efficiency, simplified network management, and increased capacity. However, SDN also introduces new security challenges, such as a greatly expanded attack footprint that includes the control plane as well as the data plane. An analogy for SDN could be a centralized traffic control system for a city's transportation network. While it can simplify traffic management and increase efficiency, it also introduces new security risks that need to be addressed.

The security implications of, On-premises architecture models

On-premises architecture models refer to the traditional approach of building and hosting applications on local servers within an organization's premises. This model relies on physical safeguards and network security to protect data, and it requires multiple layers of security to be effective. An analogy for on-premises architecture is a house with a security system, where the owner has full control over the security measures and can monitor and protect their property. However, on-premises architecture can be expensive, and the effectiveness of such systems can vary enormously. In contrast, cloud architecture models involve hosting applications and data on remote servers managed by third-party providers. Cloud security has improved significantly in recent years, and cloud solutions can match or even surpass on-premises solutions in terms of security. An analogy for cloud architecture is renting a secure apartment in a building with a security guard, where the tenant has limited control over the security measures but can rely on the building's security features. However, cloud security can be compromised if not implemented properly, and organizations must ensure that their cloud providers have appropriate security frameworks in place.

The security implications of, Centralized vs. decentralized architecture models

Centralized and decentralized architecture models have different security implications. In a centralized architecture, all the security decisions, controls, and monitoring are handled by a single authority or entity, such as a security team or a dedicated server. This approach can simplify the management, enforcement, and auditing of security policies, as well as reduce the complexity and cost of security infrastructure. However, it can also create a single point of failure, a performance bottleneck, and a target for attackers. An analogy for centralized architecture is a spider with a central body and multiple legs. In contrast, a decentralized architecture has dispersed security teams that manage risks often at the local and/or regional levels. Their security operations are more self-contained, and the decision-making process is kept within particular business units, often based on geographic locations. This model is often initially adopted by smaller organizations with a narrow physical footprint and less sophisticated risk operations. Decentralized systems can be more secure than centralized systems because there is no single point of failure or vulnerability that can be exploited by attackers. Data is distributed across multiple nodes, making it more difficult to hack or compromise. However, decentralized systems can suffer from inefficient resource utilization as some nodes may have spare resources while others may be overloaded. An analogy for decentralized architecture is a starfish with multiple arms that can regenerate if one is lost. The choice between centralized and decentralized architecture depends on various factors, such as the size, complexity, and dynamics of the network, the type and level of security threats, the availability and capability of security resources, and the organizational culture and governance.

The security implications of, Containerization architecture models

Containerization architecture models are used to package software and its dependencies in an isolated unit called a container, which can run consistently in any environment. Containerization helps developers and operations teams manage and automate software development and deployment. It is especially useful for managing microservices applications, which consist of a large number of independent components. However, containerization also introduces new security implications. Containers need a continuous security strategy integrated into the entire software development lifecycle (SDLC). This means securing the build pipeline, container images, container host machines, container runtimes, container platforms and orchestrators, and application layers. Container security requires a different approach compared to security in traditional environments. Containers are vulnerable to attacks that bypass the isolation between the container and the host, allowing attackers to compromise the host and gain unauthorized access to other containers. Container security best practices include securing the full component stack used for building, distributing, and executing the container, minimizing the amount of software installed on each host, and configuring hosts according to security best practices. Additionally, container security measures should collectively protect cloud-based container environments, ensuring that containers only communicate with authorized services. An analogy for containerization architecture models could be a shipping container. Just as a shipping container is a standardized unit for transporting goods across different modes of transportation, a container in software development is a standardized unit for packaging and deploying software across different environments.

The security implications of, Virtualization architecture models

Virtualization architecture models are used to create a virtual version of a computing resource, which eliminates the need to recreate an actual version of that resource. Virtualization provides a logical view instead of the physical view of the computing resources and makes available multiple operating systems running in parallel in a single physical computing platform. Virtualization is a common strategy for improving the utilization of existing computing resources and provides several benefits, including cost savings, flexibility, and scalability. However, virtualization is still prone to security compromises by an attacker and has several significant security implications. Virtualization adds layers of technology, which can increase the security management burden by necessitating additional security controls. Combining many systems onto a single physical computer can cause a larger impact if a security compromise occurs. Virtualized environments are quite dynamic, which makes creating and maintaining the necessary security boundaries more complex. Confidentiality can be the most difficult aspect of security to ensure with virtualization because the entire security landscape can change quickly before security administrators have time to react. Virtualization and virtualization architecture are important ideas in cloud computing, and virtualization is also useful from a security standpoint. An analogy for virtualization architecture models could be a virtual house built on a real foundation. The virtual house is built on top of the foundation, but it is not a physical structure. It provides a logical view of the house, and multiple people can live in the same virtual house at the same time. However, the virtual house is still prone to security compromises, and additional security controls are necessary to ensure its security.

The security implications of, IoT architecture models

IoT architecture models have security implications that must be considered when designing and implementing IoT solutions. The lack of security patterns is a result of its youth within the domain and security not being the main priority when developing IoT systems. Understanding how an attacker might compromise a system helps ensure appropriate mitigations from the start. Threat modeling is recommended as part of the IoT solution design, and it is helpful to divide the IoT architecture into several zones as part of the threat modeling exercise. For example, industrial IoT architectures are usually structured based on the Purdue model for industrial control system (ICS) networks, which breaks the network into six layers, each with a defined purpose. In contrast, consumer IoT solutions typically operate under a four-tier architecture model. An analogy for IoT architecture models and their security implications could be a house with different rooms and doors. Each room represents a different layer of the IoT architecture, and each door represents a potential vulnerability that an attacker could exploit. Therefore, it is essential to secure each door to protect the entire house from intruders.

The security implications of, Industrial control systems (ICS)/supervisory control and data acquisition (SCADA) architecture models

Industrial control systems (ICS) and supervisory control and data acquisition (SCADA) architecture models are used to monitor and control industrial processes such as power grids, oil and gas industries, manufacturing industries, and nuclear power plants. These systems use programmable logic controllers (PLC), remote telemetric units (RTU), and SCADA to control and monitor field instruments such as sensors and actuators. The seamless integration of information technologies (IT) and operational technologies (OT) has made the management of industrial environments easier, but it has also created new security challenges. The security implications of ICS/SCADA architecture models are significant because they are often used to control critical infrastructure. Attackers can exploit vulnerabilities in these systems to cause physical damage, disrupt operations, or steal sensitive information. An analogy to understand the security implications of ICS/SCADA architecture models is to think of them as the control center of a large ship. If the control center is compromised, the ship can be steered off course, causing damage or even sinking the ship. Similarly, if ICS/SCADA systems are compromised, they can cause significant damage to critical infrastructure and disrupt operations.

The security implications of, Real-time operating system architecture models

Real-time operating system (RTOS) architecture models are designed to meet the specific requirements of real-time applications. Unlike traditional operating systems, RTOS does not use schedulers, data buffers, and fixed task priorities to manage system resource sharing. Instead, it uses rigorous time constraints to ensure that tasks or processes are completed within the expected time. RTOS emphasizes the need for real-time performance and the least possible latency. To achieve this, specialized data structures such as priority queues and circular buffers may be used to ensure first-in-first-out processing. Real-time scheduling algorithms may also be employed to ensure that data processing proceeds in a timely manner. The security implications of RTOS architecture models are significant, especially when it comes to securing data storage and transmission through this operating system. Security within the RTOS is essential to keep processes separate so that one task does not interrupt another, which can affect the stability of the system and cause a system failure. Therefore, it is important to ensure that the RTOS is secure and protected from malicious attacks. An analogy for RTOS could be a traffic control system that ensures that vehicles move in a timely and efficient manner, with priority given to emergency vehicles.

The security implications of, Embedded systems architecture models

Embedded systems are small computer systems that are integrated into everyday devices such as medical devices, smartphones, and home appliances. These systems are designed for specific purposes and have limited processing power and memory, making them less capable of handling security measures such as firewalls and antivirus software. As a result, they can be vulnerable to attacks that exploit these limitations, such as data theft, unauthorized access, and denial-of-service attacks. Specialized systems, on the other hand, are designed for specific uses and environments, such as industrial control systems, avionics systems, and military systems. These systems operate in mission-critical environments and are subject to strict regulatory and security requirements. The security implications of these systems are often tied to their specialized purpose and the unique risks associated with the environment in which they operate. Both embedded and specialized systems are at risk from a range of threats, including malware, network attacks, hardware attacks, and malicious insiders. To mitigate these risks, it is important to implement strong security measures, such as secure coding practices, access controls, and security testing, to help ensure the security of these systems. An analogy for embedded systems could be a small house with limited security measures, while specialized systems could be compared to a high-security prison with strict security measures in place to protect against potential threats.

The security implications of, High availability architecture models

High availability architecture models are designed to ensure that IT systems, components, or applications can operate continuously, even if certain components fail. High availability infrastructure is critical for any enterprise that hopes to protect their business against the risks brought about by a system outage. These risks can lead to millions of dollars in revenue loss. High availability architecture traditionally consists of redundancy, failover, and load balancing. Redundancy aims to get rid of single points of failure, while failover ensures that if critical IT infrastructure fails, the backup system or component takes over. Load balancing software is used to distribute network traffic and application workloads across servers, which is considered critical to help ensure high availability of an application. Multi-region architecture distributes multiple instances of an application and its database across both cloud provider availability zones and regions, ensuring the highest availability possible while mitigating the risks of financial loss and reputation damage that arise for a business when critical tier-0 applications experience disruption or downtime.

The security Considerations of an architecture model's Availability

Availability is one of the three key principles of the CIA triad (confidentiality, integrity, and availability) that must be considered in security architecture models. Availability aims to ensure that a system is always up and running, and that authorized users can access it without any issues. An analogy for availability in security architecture models could be a car that is always ready to be driven by its owner. Just like a car that is always available for use, a system that is designed with availability in mind is always ready to be used by authorized users. This means that the system must be designed to handle high traffic loads, be resilient to failures, and have redundancy built-in to ensure that it can continue to operate even if some components fail.

The security Considerations of an architecture model's Resilience

Resilience in security architecture refers to the ability of a system to withstand and recover from attacks or failures. An analogy to resilience in security architecture is a building that is designed to withstand natural disasters such as earthquakes or hurricanes. The building is constructed with materials and techniques that can absorb the impact of the disaster and minimize damage. Similarly, a resilient security architecture is designed with layers of security controls that can detect and respond to attacks, contain the damage, and recover quickly. The security considerations of an architecture model's resilience include maintaining visibility across the enterprise, detecting attacks early, containing and expelling attacks before attackers realize their objectives, and rapid recovery from any incidental damage.

The security Considerations of an architecture model's Cost

Security considerations of an architecture model's cost refer to the expenses associated with implementing a security architecture model. When designing an architecture model, it is important to consider security measures and their associated costs. A good analogy for this is building a house. Just as locks, alarms, and cameras are installed to protect a house from intruders, security measures should be implemented to protect an architecture model. However, the cost of these measures should also be taken into account. The most expensive security measures may not be the most cost-effective. Therefore, a cost-benefit analysis should be conducted to determine the most effective security measures that are also within budget. This will ensure that the architecture model is secure while also being cost-effective. It is important to note that security architecture is not a one-size-fits-all solution and requires careful planning, analysis, and implementation based on the specific context and requirements of each project. Standards and frameworks can guide the process of designing secure architectures, and security architecture patterns can provide best practices, templates, and examples that can be adapted to specific situations

The security Considerations of an architecture model's Responsiveness

The responsiveness of an architecture model's security is crucial to ensure that the system can quickly and effectively respond to security threats. A good analogy for this is the human body's immune system, which must be able to identify and respond to threats to the body. Similarly, a security architecture must be designed with security in mind from the beginning, and should include a combination of preventive and detective measures, as well as tools for monitoring and incident response. The architecture should also be adaptive, able to evolve and respond to changing security threats and technologies. This requires a combination of policies, technology, and education and awareness. By incorporating threat modeling early in the process, security requirements can be identified and integrated into the system's design, which helps in identifying potential threats, vulnerabilities, and security controls that should be implemented.

The security Considerations of an architecture model's Scalability

Scalability is a critical aspect of an architecture model, and it is essential to consider security when designing a scalable system. Scalability can be compared to a highway with multiple lanes that can accommodate more traffic as it grows, without causing congestion or slowing down the vehicles. To design a scalable and secure IT architecture, it is crucial to apply best practices for scalability, security, and adaptability. Techniques such as load balancing, caching, horizontal scaling, and partitioning can be used to design for scalability, while encryption, firewalls, and access controls can be implemented to ensure the system's security. When a solution scales, it can introduce added complexity to the overall architecture in terms of its manageability, performance, and security. Therefore, it is essential to architect the solution or application to scale reliably to avoid the introduction of additional complexity, degraded performance, or reduced security as a result of scaling. Design principles such as modularity, horizontal scaling, leveraging content delivery networks, going serverless where possible, designing for failure, and secure by design can be applied to achieve reliability in the context of scale.

The security Considerations of an architecture model's Ease of deployment

When considering the ease of deployment of an architecture model, it's important to keep security in mind. Think of it like building a house - while it's important to make the construction process easy, it shouldn't compromise the safety and security of the house. Similarly, in architecture models, ease of deployment should not compromise the security of the system. Security should be considered at every stage of the deployment process, from planning to implementation. This includes implementing authentication and authorization mechanisms, data protection, network availability, and context-aware data processing. The deployment process should be designed to ensure that the system is resilient, and there is near-instant failover in case of a security breach. The security architecture should be able to integrate with multiple frameworks and model development environments, giving data science teams the flexibility to choose any tools they find suitable for their model training needs. The deployment solution should allow for integration with CI pipelines that can test the entire serving pipeline, and inline automated tests should evaluate business logic in the code and verify that key model prediction metrics have not drifted out of acceptable bounds. Overcomplicating an installation can create security vulnerabilities because administrators may make mistakes due to the complexity. When a system is too complex, there's an increased likelihood of misconfigurations, flaws, or unintended access. The more complex a system is, the more difficult it is to manage, and the more likely it is that administrators will make mistakes. This can lead to security vulnerabilities that can be exploited by attackers. So it's important to keep the installation process as simple as possible while still ensuring that security is not compromised. So it's important to keep things as simple as possible to avoid these issues.

The security Considerations of an architecture model's Risk transference

Security considerations are crucial when it comes to an architecture model's risk transference. The main goal of security is to safeguard the value of an enterprise's systems and information assets. To put it in an analogy, security can be compared to a lock on a door. Just as a lock protects the valuables inside a house from theft, security protects an enterprise's valuable information and systems from unauthorized access, theft, or damage. It's important to address security considerations in all phases of architecture development, and architecture decisions related to security should be traceable to business and policy decisions and their risk management. Risk transference is a risk management and control strategy that involves the contractual shifting of a pure risk from one party to another. In the context of architecture models, risk transference can be compared to purchasing an insurance policy. Just as an insurance policy transfers the risk of loss from the policyholder to the insurer, risk transference in architecture models transfers the risk of loss from the enterprise to another party, such as a contractor or a security architect.

The security Considerations of an architecture model's Ease of recovery

The security considerations of an architecture model's ease of recovery refer to the activities that restore any capabilities or services that are impaired due to a security event. These activities support timely recovery to normal operations to reduce the impact of a security event. An analogy to understand this concept is to think of a hospital's emergency room. In the event of an emergency, the hospital staff must act quickly to restore the patient's health and bring them back to normal functioning. Similarly, in the event of a security breach, the architecture model must have a plan in place to restore the system's normal functioning and reduce the impact of the security event. This plan should include activities such as recovery planning, recovery testing, and communications.

The security Considerations of an architecture model's Patch availability

A patch availability report is a document that contains information about the vulnerable systems in a network and the patch details to fix the vulnerabilities. It is important to have a patch availability report for every software, hardware, and firmware used in a company to keep the tools of the company up to date and reduce the risk of an attack or exploitation of flaws in the system. The patch availability report informs not just the technicians but also the executives in a company about the current status of their programs. It is like a regular health check-up for the systems in a network, where the vulnerabilities are identified and fixed before they can be exploited by attackers. Just like how a regular health check-up can prevent a person from getting sick, a patch availability report can prevent a company from being attacked or exploited.

The security Considerations of an architecture model's Inability to patch

the inability of an architecture model to patch its systems can lead to security considerations. Patching is a crucial aspect of maintaining the security of a system, as it helps to correct errors and vulnerabilities in the software. If a system is unable to patch its systems, it becomes vulnerable to attacks that exploit these vulnerabilities. This is similar to a person who has a wound that is not treated properly. If the wound is not patched up, it becomes vulnerable to infections and other complications. Similarly, if a system is not patched up, it becomes vulnerable to attacks that can compromise its security. Therefore, it is important to ensure that systems are able to patch their systems in a timely manner to maintain their security. The longer a system remains unpatched, the more vulnerable it becomes to attacks that exploit these vulnerabilities so it's crucial to patch systems as soon as possible to maintain their security.

The security Considerations of an architecture model's Power

The security considerations of an architecture model's power can be compared to the security of a fortress. Just as a fortress has multiple layers of defense mechanisms to protect against intruders, an architecture model's power should have multiple layers of security mechanisms to protect against cyber threats. The security architecture should be fully integrated into the enterprise architecture and should not inhibit the value of the enterprise. The security architecture should have its own unique building blocks, collaborations, and interfaces that interface with the business systems in a balanced and cost-effective way, so as to maintain the security policies of the enterprise, yet not interfere with system operations and functions. The security architecture should have its own single-purpose components and should be experienced as a quality of systems in the architecture. The security architecture should have its own unique security-unique elements that control who can access the system and data, such as licenses, environment roles, Azure Active Directory, Data Loss Prevention policies, and admin connectors that can be used with Power Automate.

The security Considerations of an architecture model's Compute

The security considerations of an architecture model's compute are important to ensure that the system is secure and protected from potential threats. "Compute" refers to the hardware and software components that are used to process data in a computing system. This includes the central processing unit (CPU), memory, storage devices, and other components that are used to perform computations and run software applications. Security considerations for compute include ensuring that the trusted computing base is secure, implementing authentication and access control mechanisms, protecting data confidentiality and integrity, and ensuring non-repudiation. In other words, compute is the engine that powers a computing system, and it is important to ensure that it is secure and protected from potential threats.

The Infrastructure considerations of, Device placement

One important consideration is device placement, which refers to the physical location of devices within a network. This is analogous to the placement of security cameras in a building - just as cameras need to be placed strategically to capture all angles and minimize blind spots, devices need to be placed in a way that maximizes their effectiveness and minimizes vulnerabilities. Another important consideration is infrastructure, which refers to the underlying framework that supports a network. This is analogous to the foundation of a building - just as a strong foundation is necessary to support a building, a secure infrastructure is necessary to support a network and prevent security breaches. Most networking and security professionals place sensors and collectors in critical spots in their network, which may be built-in sensors that are part of existing infrastructures, integrated into switches, routers, servers, and firewalls. The placement of these devices should be strategic to maximize their effectiveness and minimize vulnerabilities. For example, just as security cameras need to be placed strategically to capture all angles and minimize blind spots, devices need to be placed in a way that maximizes their effectiveness and minimizes vulnerabilities.

The Infrastructure considerations of, Security zones

Security zones are used to separate network resources based on their security level and to control access between them. This is similar to how a bank separates its vault from the public area, allowing only authorized personnel to access the vault. The document also emphasizes the importance of implementing security controls, such as firewalls and intrusion detection systems, to protect the security zones and prevent unauthorized access. Overall, security zones are an important aspect of network security and should be carefully planned and implemented to ensure the protection of sensitive information.

The Infrastructure considerations of, Attack surface

The Infrastructure considerations of attack surface refer to the various points of entry that an attacker can use to gain unauthorized access to a system. This includes hardware, software, and network components that can be exploited by an attacker. An analogy for attack surface could be a house with multiple doors and windows. The more doors and windows a house has, the more opportunities there are for a burglar to break in. Similarly, the more components a system has, the more opportunities there are for an attacker to exploit vulnerabilities. To reduce the attack surface, it is important to identify and secure all entry points to the system.

The Infrastructure considerations of, Connectivity
Connectivity refers to the ability of devices to communicate with each other and with the network. It is important to ensure that connectivity is secure and reliable, and that devices are properly configured to prevent unauthorized access. An analogy for connectivity could be a road network, where each device is a vehicle and the network is the road system. Just as vehicles need to follow traffic rules and regulations to ensure safe and efficient travel, devices need to follow security protocols to ensure secure and reliable connectivity.

The Infrastructure considerations of, Failure modes
In the context of IT infrastructure, failure modes refer to the different ways in which a system or component can fail. Just like a car can break down due to a flat tire, engine failure, or a dead battery, IT systems can fail due to hardware malfunctions, software bugs, or cyber attacks. It is important to identify and plan for these failure modes to minimize the impact of a failure and ensure business continuity. An analogy for this would be a building's fire escape plan. Just as a building has a plan in place to evacuate people in case of a fire, IT infrastructure should have a plan in place to mitigate the impact of a failure and ensure that critical systems can be restored quickly.

The Infrastructure considerations of, Fail-open
The Infrastructure considerations of "Fail-open" refers to a security mechanism that allows network traffic to continue to flow even if a security device fails. This is similar to a car with a broken seatbelt that still allows the driver to continue driving, even though the safety mechanism has failed. On the other hand, "Fail-closed" is a security mechanism that blocks network traffic if a security device fails, similar to a car that won't start if the seatbelt is not fastened. These considerations are important in network security to ensure that the network continues to function even if a security device fails, while still maintaining a secure environment.

The Infrastructure considerations of, Fail-closed
The Infrastructure considerations of "Fail-closed" refers to a security mechanism that blocks access to a system or network when a security breach is detected. This is similar to a bank vault that automatically locks down when an intruder tries to break in. On the other hand, "Fail-open" refers to a security mechanism that allows access to a system or network even when a security breach is detected. This is similar to a door that remains unlocked even when an intruder tries to break in. It is important to consider these infrastructure considerations when designing a secure system or network to ensure that the appropriate security mechanisms are in place to protect against potential security breaches.

The Infrastructure considerations of, Device attribute such as Active vs. passive

The Infrastructure considerations of device attributes such as active vs. passive refer to the different ways in which devices interact with the network. Active devices, such as routers and switches, are able to actively participate in network communication by forwarding and processing data packets. Passive devices, such as firewalls and intrusion detection systems, are not involved in the actual communication but instead monitor network traffic for potential security threats. An analogy for this would be a traffic cop directing traffic (active device) versus a security camera monitoring the traffic (passive device). Understanding the differences between active and passive devices is important when designing a network infrastructure that is both efficient and secure.

The Infrastructure considerations of, Device attribute such as Inline vs. tap/monitor

The Infrastructure considerations of device attributes such as Inline vs. tap/monitor refer to the different ways in which security devices can be integrated into a network. An inline device is like a traffic cop standing in the middle of a busy intersection, directing traffic and inspecting vehicles as they pass by. In contrast, a tap/monitor device is like a surveillance camera that observes traffic without interfering with it. When choosing between these two options, it is important to consider factors such as network topology, bandwidth requirements, and security needs, as well as the potential impact on network performance and availability.

The Infrastructure considerations of, Network appliances

Network appliances include routers, switches, firewalls, and load balancers. These devices are responsible for directing and managing the flow of traffic on the network, ensuring that data is transmitted efficiently and securely. Network appliances are like the traffic lights on a busy road, controlling the flow of traffic and preventing accidents. They are deployed and configured in a way that optimizes network performance and security, taking into consideration network topology, access control, and monitoring.

The Infrastructure considerations of, Jump servers
infrastructure considerations for jump servers include
ensuring that they are properly secured and monitored.
Jump servers act as an intermediary between a user
and a target system, similar to a bouncer at a nightclub
who checks IDs and only allows authorized individuals
to enter. It is important to limit access to jump servers to
only those who need it, and to ensure that all activity on
the server is logged and audited to detect any
unauthorized access or activity. Additionally, jump
servers should be kept up-to-date with the latest
security patches and configurations to minimize the risk
of exploitation by attackers. A jump server, also known
as a jump host or jump box, is a secure intermediary
device that spans two or more networks, allowing users
to connect to it from one network and then "jump" to
another network. It acts as a gateway between
networks, often serving as a bridge from a less trusted
network, such as a public network, into a more trusted
network, such as an internal company network. Jump
servers are used to manage and control access
between networks, often serving as a single point
where authentication and access can be controlled,
reducing the potential attack surface. They provide an
added layer of security against outsiders wanting to
maliciously access sensitive company data. Only those
with the right credentials can log into a jump server and
obtain authorization to proceed to a different security
zone. Jump servers are often used in conjunction with a
proxy service such as SOCKS to provide access from
an administrative desktop to the managed device.

The Infrastructure considerations of, Proxy servers

A proxy server is a server application that acts as an intermediary between a client requesting a resource and the server providing that resource. Instead of connecting directly to a server that can fulfill a request for a resource, such as a file or web page, the client directs the request to the proxy server, which evaluates the request and performs the required network transactions. This serves as a method to simplify or control the complexity of the request, or provide additional benefits such as load balancing, privacy, or security. Proxies were devised to add structure and encapsulation to distributed systems. A proxy server can provide benefits such as improved privacy, security, and performance in the process. It can be thought of as a middleman between the client and the server, similar to how a receptionist at a company's front desk receives visitors and directs them to the appropriate department.

The Infrastructure considerations of, Intrusion prevention system (IPS)

An Intrusion Prevention System (IPS) is a cybersecurity tool that examines network traffic to identify potential threats and automatically takes action against them. It is a technology that keeps an eye on a network for any malicious activities attempting to exploit a known vulnerability. IPS technologies can detect or prevent network security attacks such as brute force attacks, Denial of Service (DoS) attacks, and vulnerability exploits. When an exploit is announced, there is often a window of opportunity for attackers to exploit that vulnerability before the security patch is applied. An IPS can be used in these cases to quickly block these attacks. IPS tools continually monitor and log network activity in real-time. IPS expands on the capabilities of intrusion detection systems (IDSes), which are similar but less advanced tools. Unlike an IPS, an IDS can detect but not respond to malicious activity. IPS appliances were originally built and released as stand-alone devices in the mid-2000s. This functionality has been integrated into unified threat management (UTM) solutions as well as Next-Generation Firewalls. the best place to place an Intrusion Prevention System (IPS) is directly behind the firewall. This is because the IPS is an inline security tool that monitors network traffic and scans for malicious activity. By placing the IPS behind the firewall, it can analyze traffic and take action, such as sending alerts, dropping malicious packets, blocking traffic, and resetting connections. This location also allows the firewall to filter the incoming data first, and the IPS can analyze traffic and look for patterns or signatures that denote an attack. However, it is important to note that the IPS should be configured correctly to avoid degraded network performance.

The Infrastructure considerations of, Intrusion detection system (IDS)

IDS can be compared to a security guard who monitors a building's entrances and exits, looking for any suspicious activity. IDS can be either network-based or host-based, and they use various methods to detect intrusions, such as signature-based detection, anomaly-based detection, and heuristics-based detection. IDS can also be configured to take automated actions, such as blocking traffic or alerting security personnel, when an intrusion is detected. the best places to place an Intrusion Detection System (IDS) are at the network perimeter, between internal network segments, and at critical points within the network. Placing an IDS at the network perimeter is like having a security guard at the entrance of a building, monitoring who enters and exits. Placing an IDS between internal network segments is like having a security guard monitoring the hallways of a building, looking for any suspicious activity. Placing an IDS at critical points within the network is like having a security guard stationed at important areas of a building, such as the server room or the CEO's office, to ensure that no unauthorized access occurs. By placing IDS in these locations, organizations can detect and respond to intrusions in a timely manner.

The Infrastructure considerations of, Load balancers

The best place to place a load balancer is between the client and the server. This ensures that incoming traffic is distributed evenly across multiple servers, preventing any single server from being overwhelmed with requests. Additionally, placing the load balancer in this location allows it to perform functions such as SSL offloading and content switching, which can help improve the efficiency and security of the network.

The Infrastructure considerations of, Port security Sensors

infrastructure considerations include port security sensors. Port security sensors are used to detect unauthorized access to network ports and can be compared to a security guard checking IDs at the entrance of a building. Just as a security guard checks IDs to ensure that only authorized personnel enter the building, port security sensors check network traffic to ensure that only authorized devices are connected to the network. This helps to prevent unauthorized access and protect the network from potential security threats. The best place to place a port security sensor is on ports that connect servers or fixed devices, because the likelihood of the MAC address changing on that port is low. Additionally, a common example of using basic port security is applying it to a port that is in an area of the physical premises that is publicly accessible, such as a meeting room or reception area available for public usage. It is important to note that port security is normally configured on access ports, not trunk ports between switches.

The Infrastructure considerations of, 802.1X

Infrastructure considerations of 802.1X include the need for a RADIUS server, a digital certificate infrastructure, and a public key infrastructure. In simpler terms, 802.1X is like a bouncer at a club who checks IDs before allowing people in. The RADIUS server is like the bouncer who checks the ID, the digital certificate infrastructure is like the ID itself, and the public key infrastructure is like the government agency that issues the ID. Together, these components help ensure that only authorized devices are allowed to connect to the network, just as the bouncer ensures that only authorized individuals are allowed into the club.

The Infrastructure considerations of, Extensible Authentication Protocol (EAP)

Extensible Authentication Protocol (EAP) is a framework for providing authentication and key agreement mechanisms in a flexible and extensible manner. It is used in wireless networks, VPNs, and other network access scenarios. EAP is like a key that unlocks a door, where the door represents the network resource that the user wants to access. The key can be a password, a smart card, or any other authentication factor. EAP provides a way to exchange this key securely between the user and the network, and to verify that the user is authorized to access the resource. EAP is extensible because it allows new authentication methods to be added without changing the underlying protocol. This makes it possible to support new types of authentication factors or to improve the security of existing ones.

The Infrastructure considerations of, Firewall types

There are primarliy three types of firewalls: packet-filtering firewalls, stateful inspection firewalls, and application-aware firewalls. Packet-filtering firewalls are like security guards who check the IDs of people entering a building. They examine each packet of data that passes through the firewall and compare it to a set of predefined rules. If the packet meets the criteria, it is allowed to pass through. Otherwise, it is blocked. Stateful inspection firewalls are like bouncers at a nightclub who not only check IDs but also keep track of who is coming and going. They maintain a record of the state of each connection and use this information to make decisions about whether to allow or block traffic. Application-aware firewalls are like customs agents who not only check passports but also inspect the contents of luggage. They examine the data payload of each packet and use deep packet inspection to identify the application that generated the traffic. They can then make more granular decisions about whether to allow or block traffic based on the specific application being used.

The Infrastructure considerations of, Web application firewalls (WAF)

The best place to place a Web Application Firewall (WAF) is behind the load balancing tier. This placement maximizes utilization, performance, reliability, and visibility. A WAF can be network-based, host-based, or cloud-based and is often deployed through a reverse proxy and placed in front of one or more websites or applications. By deploying a WAF in front of a web application, a shield is placed between the web application and the internet, similar to how a security guard is placed at the entrance of a building to check everyone coming in and out. It is important to note that a WAF does not replace a traditional network firewall, as network firewalls operate at the network layer, filtering traffic based on IP addresses, ports, and protocols, while WAFs focus on protecting web applications from specific application-layer attacks. A Web Application Firewall (WAF) is a security solution that is designed to protect web applications from attacks by filtering and monitoring HTTP traffic between a web application and the internet. It is like a security guard at the entrance of a building who checks everyone coming in and out to ensure that they are authorized to be there and that they are not carrying any harmful objects. Similarly, a WAF checks all incoming and outgoing traffic to a web application to ensure that it is legitimate and does not contain any malicious code or attacks. It is an important infrastructure consideration for organizations that want to secure their web applications from cyber threats.

The Infrastructure considerations of, Unified threat management (UTM)

The best place to place a Unified Threat Management (UTM) is at the network perimeter. The network perimeter is the boundary between the internal network and the external network, which is usually the internet. Placing the UTM at the network perimeter allows it to inspect all incoming and outgoing traffic, including email, web traffic, and other network traffic, for potential threats. The UTM can also block unauthorized access attempts and prevent malware from entering the network. By placing the UTM at the network perimeter, it provides a single point of protection against various threats, simplifies network security management, and reduces the cost of deploying multiple security devices. Unified Threat Management (UTM) is like a security guard at the entrance of a building who checks everyone's ID, monitors the CCTV cameras, and ensures that no unauthorized person enters the building. Similarly, UTM is a security solution that combines multiple security features such as firewall, antivirus, intrusion detection, and prevention, and content filtering into a single device to protect the network from various threats. It provides a comprehensive security solution that simplifies network security management and reduces the cost of deploying multiple security devices.

The Infrastructure considerations of, Next-generation firewalls (NGFW)

Infrastructure considerations for Next-generation firewalls (NGFW) include the ability to handle high traffic volumes, support for advanced security features such as intrusion prevention and application control, and integration with other security technologies such as Security Information and Event Management (SIEM) systems. An analogy for NGFW infrastructure considerations could be a high-performance sports car that needs to be able to handle high speeds, have advanced safety features such as anti-lock brakes and traction control, and integrate with other systems such as GPS navigation and entertainment systems. Just as a sports car needs to be able to handle a variety of conditions and integrate with other systems to provide a complete driving experience, NGFWs need to be able to handle a variety of traffic and security conditions and integrate with other security technologies to provide a complete security solution. The best place to place a Next-generation firewall (NGFW) is at the network perimeter, where it can inspect all incoming and outgoing traffic. This is supported by the search results, which state that NGFWs are designed to define network boundaries and inspect all traffic passing through them. NGFWs are capable of identifying and blocking advanced threats before they pose a risk to corporate systems, making them a robust first line of defense against these threats.

The Infrastructure considerations of the OSI Layer 4, the Transport Layer

The Transport Layer is responsible for providing reliable data transfer services to the upper layers. It controls the reliability of communications through flow control, segmentation, and error control. An analogy for the Transport Layer could be a postal service. Just as a postal service ensures that a package is delivered from one location to another, the Transport Layer ensures that data is delivered from one host to another. The Transport Layer also provides services such as connection-oriented data stream support, reliability, flow control, and multiplexing. It collects data from the Session Layer and transmits it to the Network Layer. The Transport Layer is located between the Session Layer and the Network Layer in the OSI Model.

The Infrastructure considerations of the OSI Layer 7, the Application Layer

The OSI model is a conceptual model that describes how data is transmitted over a network. It consists of seven layers, each of which performs a specific function. The Application Layer, which is the seventh and topmost layer of the OSI model, is responsible for providing services to the end-user applications. It is the layer that interacts directly with the user and displays data and images in a format that humans can recognize. An analogy for the Application Layer could be a person who is reading a book. The person is the end-user, and the book is the application. The Application Layer is responsible for displaying the content of the book in a format that the person can understand. It interacts with the Presentation Layer, which is responsible for formatting the data in a way that can be understood by the Application Layer. The Presentation Layer then interacts with the Session Layer, which establishes, manages, and terminates sessions between applications.

The Infrastructure considerations of, Secure communication/access

Infrastructure considerations for secure communication access include implementing secure protocols, using encryption, and ensuring secure remote access. These measures are like building a secure tunnel between two points, where the tunnel is protected by strong walls and only authorized individuals have the keys to enter. Secure protocols and encryption act as the walls of the tunnel, protecting the communication from unauthorized access, while secure remote access ensures that only authorized individuals can enter the tunnel. Just as a tunnel provides a secure passage between two points, implementing these infrastructure considerations provides a secure communication channel between two endpoints. access considerations include implementing access controls, using authentication mechanisms, and ensuring secure remote access. These measures are like securing a building with multiple layers of security, where each layer provides a different level of access control. Access controls act as the outermost layer, restricting access to unauthorized individuals, while authentication mechanisms act as the inner layer, verifying the identity of authorized individuals. Secure remote access ensures that only authorized individuals can access the building from remote locations. Just as a building's security measures provide access control to different areas of the building, implementing these access considerations provides access control to different areas of a system or network.

The Infrastructure considerations of, Virtual private network (VPN)

A Virtual Private Network (VPN) is a technology that allows users to securely connect to a private network over the internet. It creates a secure and encrypted connection between the user's device and the private network, which can be thought of as a tunnel. This tunnel protects the user's data from being intercepted or viewed by unauthorized parties, just like a tunnel protects a car from being seen or accessed by others on the road. The VPN can be used to access resources on the private network, such as files or applications, as if the user were physically present on the network. This is similar to how a remote control can be used to access and control a TV from a distance. When considering the infrastructure for VPNs, there are several factors to keep in mind. One important consideration is network design, including how the VPN will be integrated into the existing network architecture. This includes deciding whether to use a shared VPC or VPC network peering, as well as whether to use VPNs internally or externally. Another important consideration is security, including the use of security groups and network ACLs to control network access, as well as the use of encryption to protect data in transit. Additionally, it is important to consider scalability and redundancy, including the use of multiple VPN tunnels or AWS Direct Connect connections to ensure high availability. Finally, it is important to consider IP addressing and routing, including the need to avoid IP address conflicts and allocate private IP address ranges when necessary. Overall, careful planning and consideration of these factors can help ensure a secure and reliable VPN infrastructure.

The Infrastructure considerations of, Remote access

Infrastructure considerations for remote access include ensuring that remote access solutions are secure and that they are properly configured to prevent unauthorized access. This can be compared to a secure door with a lock and key. Just as a door needs to be secure and the lock needs to be properly configured to prevent unauthorized access, remote access solutions need to be secure and properly configured to prevent unauthorized access. Additionally, infrastructure considerations for remote access include ensuring that remote access solutions are available and reliable, and that they are properly monitored and maintained. This can be compared to a well-maintained road that is available and reliable for travel. Just as a road needs to be well-maintained and available for travel, remote access solutions need to be available and reliable for remote access.

The Infrastructure considerations of, Tunneling

Infrastructure considerations include tunneling, which is a technique used to encapsulate one protocol within another protocol. This can be compared to a Russian nesting doll, where one doll is encapsulated within another doll. Similarly, tunneling encapsulates one protocol within another protocol, allowing data to be transmitted securely over an untrusted network. It is important to consider the infrastructure when implementing tunneling, as it can impact network performance and security.

The Infrastructure considerations of, Transport Layer Security (TLS)

Transport Layer Security (TLS) is a protocol that provides secure communication over the internet. It is used to encrypt data that is transmitted between two endpoints, such as a web server and a web browser. TLS is like a secret code that is used to protect the information being sent. Just like how a secret code can only be understood by the person who knows the code, TLS can only be decrypted by the intended recipient who has the correct key. When implementing TLS, there are several infrastructure considerations that need to be taken into account, such as certificate management, key management, and protocol version support. These considerations ensure that the TLS implementation is secure and effective in protecting the data being transmitted.

The Infrastructure considerations of, Internet protocol security (IPSec)

Internet Protocol Security (IPSec) is a protocol suite used to secure Internet Protocol (IP) communications by encrypting and authenticating each IP packet of a communication session. It provides a secure communication channel between two endpoints over an insecure network, such as the internet. IPSec can be compared to a security guard who checks the identity of each person entering a building and ensures that they have the proper clearance to enter. Similarly, IPSec checks the identity of each IP packet and ensures that it has not been tampered with during transmission. It provides confidentiality, integrity, and authenticity to IP packets, making it a crucial component of secure communication over the internet.

The Infrastructure considerations of, Software-defined wide area network (SD-WAN)

Software-defined wide area network (SD-WAN) is a virtual WAN architecture that uses software-defined networking (SDN) principles to manage and optimize the performance of wide area networks (WANs). It allows enterprises to leverage any combination of transport services, including MPLS, LTE, and broadband, to connect data centers, branch offices, and cloud resources. An SD-WAN uses a centralized control function to steer traffic securely and intelligently across the WAN and directly to trusted SaaS and IaaS providers. It can adapt quickly to changing situations and offer better security and reliability than traditional WANs. An analogy for SD-WAN is a GPS system that helps drivers navigate through different routes to reach their destination. Similarly, SD-WAN helps enterprises navigate through different transport services to connect their resources.

The Infrastructure considerations of, Secure access Service edge (SASE)

Secure Access Service Edge (SASE) is a cloud-based security architecture that combines network and security services. It is a framework of solutions and methodology that attempts to converge wide area networking (WAN) and network security services into a single, cloud-delivered offering. SASE is a comprehensive solution that includes several core services, such as SD-WAN, WAN optimization, and zero-trust network access (ZTNA). The infrastructure considerations of SASE include asset management, equipment and tool reduction, and integration with existing infrastructure and tools. An analogy for SASE is a Swiss Army knife, which combines multiple tools into a single device. Similarly, SASE combines multiple network and security services into a single cloud-delivered offering.

The Infrastructure considerations of, Selection of effective controls

Infrastructure considerations include the physical and logical components of an organization's network, such as firewalls, routers, switches, and servers. Effective controls are measures put in place to protect these components from unauthorized access, modification, or destruction. An analogy for this would be a castle with a moat and drawbridge. The castle represents the organization's network, while the moat and drawbridge represent the infrastructure considerations and effective controls put in place to secure it. The moat and drawbridge prevent unauthorized access to the castle, just as firewalls and access controls prevent unauthorized access to an organization's network.

The concepts and strategies to protect different Data types

There are many concepts and strategies to protect different data types. One analogy to explain this is to think of data as a valuable asset, like a house. Just as a house has different entry points that need to be secured, such as doors and windows, data also has different entry points that need to be protected, such as networks and applications. Additionally, just as a house may have different levels of security for different rooms, data also has different levels of sensitivity that require different levels of protection. For example, personal information like social security numbers and credit card information require stronger protection than general information like news articles. Therefore, it is important to implement appropriate security measures, such as encryption and access controls, to protect different types of data from unauthorized access and theft.

The concepts and strategies to protect Regulated Data types

Regulated data types refer to sensitive information that is subject to legal or regulatory requirements, such as personal health information (PHI) or financial data. To protect regulated data types, organizations must implement appropriate security controls, such as access controls, encryption, and monitoring. An analogy for protecting regulated data types is locking up valuables in a safe. Just as a safe protects valuable items from theft or damage, security controls protect regulated data types from unauthorized access or disclosure. The types of regulated data can vary depending on the industry and the specific regulations that apply. Some common examples of regulated data types include personal health information (PHI), financial data, credit card numbers, social security numbers, employee agreements, and sensitive company information. To protect regulated data types, organizations must implement appropriate security controls, such as access controls, encryption, and monitoring. Data classification is a useful tactic that facilitates proper security responses based on the type of data being retrieved, transmitted, or copied.

The concepts and strategies to protect Trade secret Data types

Trade secrets are confidential information that gives a company a competitive advantage. To protect trade secrets, it is important to implement access controls, such as authentication and authorization, to ensure that only authorized personnel can access the data. Additionally, encryption can be used to protect the data while it is in transit or at rest. An analogy to understand this is to think of trade secrets as a valuable recipe that a chef wants to keep secret. The chef would keep the recipe in a locked cabinet, only allowing authorized personnel to access it. The recipe would also be written in code, so that even if someone were to steal it, they would not be able to understand it.

The concepts and strategies to protect Intellectual property Data types

Intellectual property refers to creations of the mind, such as inventions, literary and artistic works, and symbols, names, and images used in commerce. Protecting intellectual property is like protecting a valuable asset, such as a house or a car. Just as you would take measures to secure your house or car, such as locking doors and windows, installing an alarm system, and parking in a secure location, you should take measures to secure your intellectual property. This includes implementing access controls, encryption, and backup and recovery procedures to prevent unauthorized access, theft, or loss of data.

The concepts and strategies to protect Legal information Data types

One of the key strategies is to implement access controls, which can be compared to a lock on a door. Access controls limit who can access legal information data types, ensuring that only authorized individuals can view or modify the data. Other strategies include encryption, which can be compared to a secret code that only authorized individuals can decipher, and backup and recovery procedures, which can be compared to making copies of important documents in case the originals are lost or damaged. By implementing these strategies and others outlined in the document, organizations can better protect their legal information data types from unauthorized access or modification. Legal Information Data Types are information that is protected by law, such as personally identifiable information (PII), protected health information (PHI), and intellectual property. An analogy to understand this concept is to think of legal information data types as valuable assets that need to be protected. Just as a bank protects its assets by using security measures such as vaults and security guards, organizations must implement security measures to protect their legal information data types from unauthorized access, theft, or misuse.

The concepts and strategies to protect Financial information Data types

Financial information data types include credit card numbers, bank account numbers, and social security numbers. These types of data are sensitive and require special protection measures to prevent unauthorized access and misuse. An analogy to understand the importance of protecting financial information is to think of it as a valuable treasure that needs to be kept in a secure vault. Just as a vault has multiple layers of security to prevent theft, financial information must be protected with multiple layers of security measures to prevent unauthorized access and misuse. To protect financial information data types, one must understand the different types of data and the strategies to protect them. Financial information data types include credit card numbers, bank account numbers, and social security numbers. These types of data are highly sensitive and require strong protection measures. One analogy to understand this is to think of financial information as a valuable treasure that needs to be protected from thieves. Just as a treasure is kept in a secure vault with multiple layers of protection, financial information should be encrypted, backed up, and stored in secure locations with access controls and monitoring to prevent unauthorized access.

The concepts and strategies to protect Human and non-human readable Data types

Human-readable data types are those that can be easily understood by humans, such as text, images, and videos. Non-human readable data types are those that are not easily understood by humans, such as machine code and encrypted data. To protect these data types, security professionals use various strategies such as encryption, access controls, and data loss prevention. An analogy to understand this concept is to think of a safe. Just as a safe protects valuable items from theft, encryption and access controls protect valuable data from unauthorized access.

The concepts and strategies to protect different Data classifications

Data classification refers to the process of categorizing data based on its level of sensitivity and value. Just like how we protect our valuable possessions such as jewelry or money in a safe, data classification helps us identify which data needs to be protected and how. The document outlines different data classifications such as public, private, confidential, and sensitive, and provides strategies to protect each classification. For example, public data can be protected through access controls and encryption, while confidential data can be protected through data loss prevention techniques and secure storage. By implementing these strategies, organizations can ensure that their data is protected from unauthorized access and misuse. These categories include public data, which is unclassified data that anyone can access, private data, which is restricted and should only be shown to certain individuals, classified data, which is data that should remain private and is labeled as such, sensitive data, which includes intellectual property, personally identifiable information, and protected health information, and confidential data, which is the most sensitive data and requires the highest level of protection. The document outlines various strategies to protect sensitive data, such as encryption, access controls, and data backup and recovery. By implementing these strategies, organizations can ensure that sensitive data is kept secure and protected from potential threats.

The concepts and strategies to protect Sensitive Data classifications

Data classifications are used to identify the sensitivity of data and determine the level of protection required. One way to think about this is to imagine a bank vault. Just as a bank vault is designed to protect valuable assets, sensitive data classifications require protection to prevent unauthorized access, modification, or destruction. The document outlines various strategies to protect sensitive data, such as encryption, access controls, and data backup and recovery. By implementing these strategies, organizations can ensure that sensitive data is kept secure and protected from potential threats.

The following are the data classifications listed in the exam objectives:

Public data: This is unclassified data that is available to anyone.

Private data: This is data that should remain private and confidential. It may be restricted or only shown to certain individuals.

Classified data: This is data that is sensitive and requires a higher level of protection than private data. It may be restricted to certain individuals or groups.

Sensitive data: This is data that is highly sensitive and requires the highest level of protection. It may include intellectual property, personally identifiable information, or protected health information.

The concepts and strategies to protect Confidential Data classifications

Confidential data is information that is sensitive and should only be accessed by authorized personnel. To protect this data, it is important to implement security controls such as access controls, encryption, and data loss prevention. Access controls limit access to confidential data to only authorized personnel, while encryption ensures that the data is protected even if it is intercepted. Data loss prevention strategies help to prevent the accidental or intentional loss of confidential data. Confidential Data is a classification of data that requires the highest level of protection. This type of data is considered sensitive and should only be accessed by authorized personnel. An analogy to understand this classification is to think of a safe that contains valuable items. The safe is locked and only authorized individuals have the combination to open it. Similarly, Confidential Data is locked and only authorized personnel have access to it. This classification includes information such as financial data, personal identification information, and trade secrets.

The concepts and strategies to protect Public Data classifications

Public data is information that is available to anyone and does not require any special clearance or authorization to access. To protect public data, organizations can use security controls such as access controls, encryption, and firewalls. An analogy to understand this concept is to think of public data as a public park. Just like a park is open to everyone, public data is available to anyone. However, just like a park has security measures such as gates, fences, and security personnel to ensure the safety of visitors, public data needs security controls to protect it from unauthorized access and misuse. Public data refers to information that is available to anyone and does not require any special clearance or authorization to access. This type of data is not confidential and can be accessed by anyone who has the means to do so. To protect public data, organizations can use security controls such as access controls, encryption, and firewalls. These controls help to prevent unauthorized access and misuse of public data.

The concepts and strategies to protect Restricted Data classifications

Restricted Data is a classification of sensitive information that requires special handling and protection. To protect Restricted Data, organizations should implement a combination of physical, technical, and administrative controls. Physical controls include measures such as access controls, locks, and security cameras. Technical controls include encryption, firewalls, and intrusion detection systems. Restricted Data is a classification of sensitive information that requires special handling and protection. Restricted Data should be protected by a combination of physical, technical, and administrative controls. Physical controls include measures such as access controls, locks, and security cameras. Technical controls include encryption, firewalls, and intrusion detection systems. Administrative controls include policies, procedures, and training to ensure that employees understand the importance of protecting Restricted Data. Restricted Data is more sensitive than other types of data, such as public data or private data, and requires a higher level of protection. An analogy to understand the importance of protecting Restricted Data is to think of it as a valuable treasure that needs to be protected from thieves. Just as a treasure requires a combination of locks, guards, and other security measures to keep it safe, Restricted Data requires a combination of physical, technical, and administrative controls to keep it secure.

The concepts and strategies to protect Private Data classifications

Private data classifications refer to sensitive information that should be kept confidential and protected from unauthorized access. To protect private data, security professionals can use various strategies such as encryption, access controls, and data backup. Different types of data have different levels of sensitivity, and we often put labels on data to identify its classification. Some common data classifications include public data, unclassified data, confidential data, secret data, and top-secret data. Public data is available to anyone, while unclassified data may be restricted and only shown to certain individuals. Confidential data is sensitive information that requires approval to access, while secret data is even more restricted. Top-secret data is the highest level of classification and requires the highest level of clearance to access. To protect private data, security professionals can use various strategies such as encryption, access controls, and data backup.

The concepts and strategies to protect Critical Data classifications

critical data classification refers to the process of identifying and labeling different types of data based on their level of sensitivity. Different types of data have different levels of sensitivity, and it is important to classify them accordingly to ensure that they are protected using appropriate security measures. For example, public data or unclassified data can be accessed by anyone, while restricted data should only be shown to certain individuals. Private, classified, and internal use only are some of the classifications that show that data should remain private. Sensitive information, such as intellectual property or personally identifiable information, requires even more protection. By properly classifying critical data, organizations can ensure that they are using the appropriate security measures to protect it from unauthorized access, theft, or loss. One way to think about this is to imagine a bank vault. Just as a bank vault is designed to protect valuable assets, critical data classifications must be protected using a variety of security measures. These measures may include access controls, encryption, and monitoring to ensure that only authorized individuals can access the data. Additionally, data backups and disaster recovery plans can help ensure that critical data is not lost in the event of a security breach or other disaster.

The concepts and strategies regarding General data considerations

General data considerations refer to the principles and practices that organizations should follow to ensure the confidentiality, integrity, and availability of their data. These considerations include data classification, data retention, data destruction, and data backup. Data classification is like sorting laundry into different piles based on their color and fabric type. Data retention is like keeping important documents in a safe deposit box for a certain period of time. Data destruction is like shredding sensitive documents before disposing of them. Data backup is like making a copy of important files and storing them in a secure location in case the original files are lost or damaged. By following these data considerations, organizations can protect their data from unauthorized access, modification, or loss. Confidentiality ensures that data is only accessible to authorized individuals, integrity ensures that data is accurate and unaltered, and availability ensures that data is accessible when needed. An analogy for these principles could be a bank vault. The vault is designed to keep valuable items secure and confidential, with only authorized individuals having access. The items inside the vault are also kept in their original state, without any alterations or tampering. Finally, the vault is accessible to authorized individuals when needed, ensuring that the items inside are available when required. Similarly, data should be kept secure, accurate, and accessible to authorized individuals when needed.

The concepts and strategies to protect different Data states

data can exist in three different states: data at rest, data in transit, and data in use. Data at rest refers to data that is stored on a device or system, such as a hard drive or database, and is not actively being transmitted. Data in transit refers to data that is actively being transmitted between devices or systems, such as over a network or the internet. Data in use refers to data that is actively being processed by a device or system, such as when a user is working on a document or using an application. It is important to protect data in all three states to ensure the confidentiality, integrity, and availability of the data. Encryption is a commonly used strategy to protect data at rest and in transit, while access controls and physical security measures can help protect data in use. Data states refer to the different stages of data, including data at rest, data in transit, and data in use. Protecting data at rest involves securing data that is stored on a device or server, such as encrypting files or using access controls. Protecting data in transit involves securing data as it moves between devices or networks, such as using secure protocols like HTTPS or VPNs. Protecting data in use involves securing data as it is being processed or accessed, such as using firewalls or intrusion detection systems. An analogy for data states could be a person's physical state, where data at rest is like a person sleeping, data in transit is like a person traveling, and data in use is like a person working or exercising.

The concepts and strategies to protect Data at rest

Data at rest refers to data that is stored on a device or system, such as a hard drive or database, and is not actively being transmitted. To protect data at rest, encryption is a commonly used strategy. Encryption is like locking a valuable item in a safe, where the key to unlock the safe is only known by authorized individuals. Similarly, encryption uses a key to scramble the data so that it is unreadable without the key. This helps to prevent unauthorized access to the data, even if the device or system is stolen or compromised. Other strategies to protect data at rest include access controls, such as passwords and biometric authentication, and physical security measures, such as locks and surveillance cameras.

The concepts and strategies to protect Data in transit

Data in transit refers to data that is being transmitted over a network, such as email, instant messages, or file transfers. To protect this data, encryption is used to scramble the data so that it cannot be read by unauthorized parties. This is similar to sending a secret message in a locked box. Only the intended recipient, who has the key to the lock, can open the box and read the message. Similarly, encryption ensures that only the intended recipient, who has the decryption key, can read the data that is being transmitted over the network.

The concepts and strategies to protect Data in use

Data in use refers to data that is currently being processed or accessed by a system or application. To protect data in use, security professionals can use techniques such as encryption, access controls, and secure coding practices. Encryption can be thought of as a lock on a safe, where the data is the valuable item being protected. Access controls can be thought of as a bouncer at a club, only allowing authorized individuals to enter and access the data. Secure coding practices can be thought of as building a strong foundation for a house, ensuring that the data is protected from the ground up. By implementing these strategies, security professionals can help ensure that data in use is protected from unauthorized access or modification.

The concepts and strategies to protect Data sovereignty

Data sovereignty refers to the concept of having control over the data that is stored, processed, and transmitted within a specific geographic location or jurisdiction. This control can be achieved through various strategies such as data encryption, access control, and data backup. An analogy to understand data sovereignty is to think of it as a house. Just like how a homeowner has control over their house and can decide who enters and exits, data sovereignty gives organizations control over their data and who has access to it. By implementing security measures, organizations can ensure that their data is protected and only accessible to authorized personnel, just like how a homeowner can ensure that their house is secure and only accessible to those with permission.

The concepts and strategies to protect Geolocation

Geolocation is the process of identifying the physical location of an object or person using digital information. To protect geolocation, security professionals must implement strategies such as encryption, access controls, and secure communication protocols. Encryption is like a secret code that scrambles data so that it can only be read by authorized parties. Access controls are like a bouncer at a club who checks IDs to ensure that only authorized individuals are allowed in. Secure communication protocols are like a private conversation between two people in a soundproof room, where no one else can eavesdrop on what is being said. By implementing these strategies, security professionals can help protect geolocation information from unauthorized access and use.

The concepts, strategies, and Methods to secure data

Securing data involves protecting it from unauthorized access, use, disclosure, disruption, modification, or destruction. This can be achieved through various concepts, strategies, and methods such as encryption, access control, authentication, backup and recovery, and physical security. Encryption is like locking a message in a safe box that can only be opened with the right key. Access control is like a bouncer at a club who checks IDs to ensure only authorized people are allowed in. Authentication is like a password that only the user knows and can use to access their account. Backup and recovery is like making a copy of important documents in case the original is lost or damaged. Physical security is like locking the doors and windows of a house to prevent burglars from entering. By implementing these concepts, strategies, and methods, data can be secured from various threats and risks.

The concepts, strategies, and Methods to secure data such as, Geographic restrictions

Geographic restrictions are a method of securing data by limiting access to it based on the location of the user. This can be compared to a gated community where only residents and authorized visitors are allowed in. By implementing geographic restrictions, organizations can prevent unauthorized access to sensitive data from outside the approved geographic area. This can be achieved through various methods such as IP address filtering, geolocation, and virtual private networks (VPNs). IP address filtering is like a bouncer at a club who only allows people with the right ID to enter. Geolocation is like a GPS that tracks the location of the user and only allows access if they are within the approved area. VPNs are like a secret tunnel that allows authorized users to access the data securely from anywhere in the world. By using geographic restrictions, organizations can add an extra layer of security to their data and prevent unauthorized access from outside the approved area.

The concepts, strategies, and Methods to secure data such as, Encryption

Encryption is a method of securing data by converting it into a code that can only be read by authorized parties. It is like a secret code that only those who know the code can decipher the message. Encryption can be used to protect sensitive information such as passwords, credit card numbers, and personal data. There are different encryption methods such as symmetric encryption, where the same key is used to encrypt and decrypt the data, and asymmetric encryption, where a public key is used to encrypt the data and a private key is used to decrypt it. In addition to encryption, other strategies and methods to secure data include access control, firewalls, intrusion detection and prevention systems, and security policies and procedures. These measures work together to protect data from unauthorized access, theft, and other security threats.

The concepts, strategies, and Methods to secure data such as, Hashing

Hashing is a method of securing data by converting it into a fixed-length code that cannot be reversed to its original form. It is like a fingerprint that uniquely identifies the data, but cannot be used to recreate the original data. Hashing can be used to verify the integrity of data by comparing the hash value of the original data with the hash value of the received data. If the hash values match, it means that the data has not been tampered with during transmission. Hashing is commonly used in password storage, where the hash value of the password is stored instead of the password itself. When a user enters their password, the hash value of the entered password is compared with the stored hash value to authenticate the user. In addition to hashing, other strategies and methods to secure data include encryption, access control, firewalls, intrusion detection and prevention systems, and security policies and procedures. These measures work together to protect data from unauthorized access, theft, and other security threats.

The concepts, strategies, and Methods to secure data such as, Masking

Data masking is a security technique used to protect sensitive data from unauthorized access. It is a process of replacing sensitive data with fictitious data to hide the original data. For example, masking a social security number by replacing the first five digits with asterisks. This technique is similar to wearing a mask to hide one's identity. Data masking can be used to protect data in various scenarios, such as during data transfer, testing, or storage. It helps to ensure the confidentiality, integrity, and availability of data. One such method is data masking, which is like wearing a mask to hide your identity. Data masking is a technique that replaces sensitive data with fictitious data to protect it from unauthorized access. Another concept is to secure data by implementing access controls, which is like having a security guard at the entrance of a building. Access controls limit access to data based on the user's identity, role, or clearance level. Other strategies include encryption, which is like putting a lock on a box to protect its contents, and backup and recovery, which is like having a spare key in case the original is lost. These methods and strategies help to ensure the confidentiality, integrity, and availability of data.

The concepts, strategies, and Methods to secure data such as, Tokenization

Tokenization is a data security technique that replaces sensitive data with a unique identifier, or token, that has no meaning or value outside of the system that created it. This helps to protect sensitive data from unauthorized access or theft. Tokenization is like a ticket stub, which is a representation of a larger entity, such as a concert or a movie. For example, if you have a Social Security number that is 26-12-1112, we can store that data in a database and display it on the screen as 691-61-8539. We're able to tie back the original Social Security number with this new tokenized version of the Social Security number because we have a single database that matches those up, and that database is one that's relatively private. Tokenization is commonly used with credit card processing, especially if you're using your mobile phone or your smartwatch to be able to pay for goods at checkout. That token is then used at a store when you check out using near field communication, at which point the servers Merchant Payment Processing Server is going to send the validation to that Token Service Server. This token may change every time you perform a transaction, which means that if somebody was to find this token and use that information for future transactions, they would not be able to do so. It'ss like a ticket stub. Just as a ticket stub is a representation of a larger entity, such as a concert or a movie, a token is a representation of sensitive data. Tokenization replaces sensitive data with a unique identifier, or token, that has no meaning or value outside of the system that created it.

The concepts, strategies, and Methods to secure data such as, Obfuscation

Obfuscation is a method used in IT security to make data difficult to understand or read. It involves taking something and making it much more difficult to understand, similar to a secret code that only authorized individuals can decipher. Obfuscation can be used in unique ways such as steganography, tokenization, and data masking. Steganography is a common form of obfuscation where information is hidden inside of a picture. Another way to make data less readable is to put it through a particular cipher like Exclusive OR or XOR. With XOR, we're comparing two different types of input to be able to create a single output. If both of those inputs are different, then we mark them as true. If both of those inputs are the same, then we mark them as false. Obfuscation can be combined with other security strategies such as access control and encryption to create a layered approach to security. This can be compared to a secret code that only authorized individuals can decipher. Other strategies include access control, which limits who can access data, and encryption, which scrambles data so that it can only be read by authorized individuals with the key to unscramble it. These strategies can be combined to create a layered approach to security, similar to how a castle has multiple layers of defense to protect against invaders.

The concepts, strategies, and Methods to secure data such as, Segmentation

Segmentation is a security strategy that involves dividing a network into smaller subnetworks or segments. This can help to limit the spread of threats and reduce the impact of a security breach. There are many ways to implement segmentation, including physical, logical, and virtual separation. Physical segmentation involves physically separating devices or resources, such as having web servers in one rack and database servers in another. Logical segmentation involves creating logical separation within the same device, such as segmenting application instances into their own separate private segments. Virtual segmentation involves using virtual systems to create separate segments. Segmentation can also be used for compliance reasons, which can require segmentation between certain devices on the network. Overall, segmentation is an important security control that can help to prevent unauthorized access and limit the damage that can be caused by a security breach. To secure data, one of the strategies is to use segmentation, which involves dividing a network into smaller subnetworks or segments. This can help to limit the spread of threats and reduce the impact of a security breach. An analogy for segmentation is a building with multiple floors, where each floor represents a different segment of the network. Just as each floor has its own set of rooms and resources, each network segment has its own set of devices and resources that are isolated from other segments.

The importance of Uninterruptible power supply (UPS) in a secure architecture

Uninterruptible power supply (UPS) is an essential component of a secure architecture. It provides backup power in case of a power outage, ensuring that critical systems remain operational. In the same way that a backup generator provides power to a building during a power outage, a UPS provides power to critical systems during a power outage. This is important because power outages can occur due to a variety of reasons, including natural disasters, equipment failure, and cyber attacks. Without a UPS, critical systems may be vulnerable to data loss, corruption, or other security risks. Therefore, a UPS is an important part of a secure architecture, ensuring that critical systems remain operational even during a power outage.

The concepts, strategies, and Methods to secure data such as, Permission restrictions

Permission restrictions are a method of securing data that involves limiting access to data to only those who have been granted permission. This is done by assigning user rights and permissions to files, folders, and other objects. Different organizations may use different access control models, such as Mandatory Access Control (MAC) or Role-Based Access Control (RBAC), depending on their overall goals for access control. Under a MAC model, the operating system provides limits on how much access someone will have to a particular object based on certain clearance levels. Every object that someone may need to access needs to be assigned a label, such as confidential or top secret. Users are then provided with certain rights, and it's the administrator that determines what specific access role a particular user has. Under an RBAC model, access is based on the user's role within the organization, and users are assigned to groups that have specific access rights. Permission restrictions help to secure data by limiting access to only those who are authorized to access it, thereby reducing the risk of unauthorized access and data breaches. One such method is permission restrictions, which can be compared to a bouncer at a club who only allows authorized individuals to enter. Permission restrictions limit access to data to only those who have been granted permission, thereby reducing the risk of unauthorized access. Other methods include encryption, which can be compared to a secret code that only authorized individuals can decipher, and firewalls, which can be compared to a security checkpoint that only allows authorized traffic to pass through. These methods help to secure data by limiting access to only those who are authorized to access it, thereby reducing the risk of unauthorized access and data breaches.

The importance of High availability

High availability refers to the ability of a system or service to remain operational and accessible to users for a high percentage of time, typically 99.999% or more. This is achieved through the use of redundant components and failover mechanisms that ensure that if one component fails, another takes over seamlessly, without any disruption to the service. An analogy for high availability is a relay race, where each runner represents a component of the system. If one runner falls, another takes over the baton and continues the race, ensuring that the team reaches the finish line.

High availability is a crucial aspect of modern IT infrastructure that ensures that critical systems and applications remain available and accessible without interruption. It is like having a backup generator for your home. Just as a generator ensures that your home has power even during a power outage, high availability ensures that your applications and services remain available even during an outage or failure. High availability is important because it ensures that businesses that rely on their IT systems to conduct transactions, manage data, or communicate with customers can avoid downtime, lost revenue, and damaged reputation. High availability can be achieved through various approaches, such as load balancing, data replication, and redundancy, which provide resilience and minimize the risk of data loss in the event of a failure.

Load balancing security architecture vs. clustering security architecture.

Load balancing and clustering are two different approaches to improve the performance and availability of a system. Load balancing distributes the workload across multiple servers to avoid overloading any single device, while clustering combines multiple servers to function as a single entity. An analogy to understand the difference between load balancing and clustering is to think of a restaurant. Load balancing is like having multiple chefs in the kitchen, each preparing a different dish to avoid overloading a single chef. Clustering is like having a team of chefs working together to prepare a single dish, with each chef responsible for a different part of the dish. Both load balancing and clustering can be used together to improve the performance and availability of a system. However, load balancing is more flexible and sustainable than clustering, as it can support heterogeneous servers and provide support for longer hours. On the other hand, clustering requires identical servers within the cluster and is self-contained and managed by a controller automatically

The importance of hot sites

A hot site is a backup facility that stores data in real-time and is quickly operable in any disaster strike. It is a replica of the usual business environment that includes all the necessary equipment, but at another location. An analogy to understand the importance of a hot site is to think of a spare tire in a car. A spare tire is a backup plan in case of a flat tire, and it allows the driver to continue the journey without any significant delay. Similarly, a hot site is a backup plan for an organization that allows it to continue its business operations without any significant delay in case of a disaster strike. A hot site is equipped with all the necessary hardware, software, and network connectivity, which allows you to perform near real-time backup or replication of the critical data. This way the production workload can be failed over to a DR site in a few minutes or hours, thus ensuring minimal downtime and zero data loss. A hot site is more expensive than a cold site, but it is the most effective and efficient disaster recovery site among the three options

The importance of Cold sites

Cold sites are important for disaster recovery planning. A cold site is a backup facility that is not operational until a disaster occurs. It is like a spare tire in a car that is not used until a flat tire occurs. Cold sites are important because they provide a cost-effective solution for disaster recovery planning. Organizations can save money by not having to maintain a fully operational backup facility at all times. Instead, they can rely on a cold site to be activated only when needed. This allows organizations to have a disaster recovery plan in place without incurring the high costs of maintaining a fully operational backup facility.

The importance of Warm sites
A warm site is a type of disaster recovery facility that an organization uses to recover its technology infrastructure when its primary data center goes down. It is in between a hot site and a cold site, meaning it is not fully functional like a hot site, but it is not completely empty like a cold site. A warm site features an equipped data center but no customer data or applications until a disaster hits. It requires some setup, but not as much as a cold site, and is a good candidate for bringing up non-essential systems that don't require immediate restoration like mission-critical systems do. An analogy for a warm site could be a spare tire in a car. It is not as immediately useful as a fully functional tire, but it is better than having no tire at all. It can get you to a repair shop where you can get a new tire, just like a warm site can get an organization up and running until they can fully restore their primary data center.

The importance of Site considerations such as, Geographic dispersion
Geographic dispersion is a security strategy that involves spreading critical resources across multiple locations to reduce the risk of a single point of failure. This strategy is similar to having multiple bank accounts in different banks to reduce the risk of losing all your money if one bank fails. In the context of security, geographic dispersion can involve having multiple data centers in different regions or even different countries. This strategy can help ensure that critical systems remain available even if one location is affected by a natural disaster, cyber attack, or other disruptive event.

The importance of Platform diversity
Platform diversity is crucial in software development because it brings a variety of perspectives and experiences to the table, which can lead to better problem-solving, creativity, and innovation. A diverse software development team is more adaptable to changing market demands and user needs. Diversity in software development teams is not limited to technical skills; it also extends to understanding the diverse user base for software products. A team composed of members from various backgrounds is more likely to empathize with a broader range of users, leading to a more inclusive and user-friendly software design. An analogy for platform diversity in software development is a toolbox. A toolbox with only one type of tool may be useful for a specific task, but a toolbox with a variety of tools can handle a wider range of tasks and challenges. Similarly, a software development team with a variety of backgrounds and experiences can handle a wider range of problems and challenges.

The importance of Multi-cloud systems
Multi-cloud systems are becoming increasingly popular among businesses as they offer greater flexibility, scalability, and cost savings than hybrid clouds. A multi-cloud strategy allows organizations to deploy workloads across multiple cloud platforms, including both public clouds, such as AWS, Azure, and Google Cloud. However, the high complexity of multi-cloud deployments also increases the attack surface and the risk of cyberattacks, raising new cloud security concerns. Multi-cloud security is a comprehensive cloud security solution that protects and prevents enterprise and customer data, assets, and applications from advanced security threats and cyberattacks across multiple cloud infrastructures and environments. It involves integrating a range of security tools and services across multiple cloud platforms to improve security, visibility, speed, and resilience for complex hybrid and multi-cloud environments. In other words, multi-cloud security is like having multiple locks on different doors of a house, making it harder for intruders to break in. The right security framework will protect your business and allow it to maximize the full value of a multi-cloud environment.

The importance of Continuity of operations

Continuity of Operations (COOP) is a crucial aspect of business and government operations. It ensures that essential functions can continue during a wide range of emergencies. COOP requires planning for any event that could cause an agency to relocate its operations to an alternate or other continuity site to assure continuance of its essential functions. An analogy for COOP is having a backup generator for a home. Just as a backup generator ensures that a home can continue to function during a power outage, COOP ensures that organizations can continue their essential daily functions during an emergency. COOP is simply good business practice, and it is required for regulatory compliance for most organizations. By developing and maintaining a COOP plan, organizations can strengthen their cybersecurity posture, minimize the impact of security incidents, and ensure that they can continue to operate during a crisis.

The importance of Capacity planning

Capacity planning is an important aspect of security management that involves estimating the amount of resources required to meet future demands. It is like planning a road trip where you need to estimate the amount of fuel required to reach your destination. Without proper capacity planning, organizations may face issues such as system crashes, slow response times, and downtime. By estimating future demands and ensuring that sufficient resources are available, organizations can ensure that their systems are able to handle the expected workload and provide reliable services to their users. This is particularly important in today's digital age where organizations rely heavily on technology to conduct their business operations.

The importance of planning the capacity of People

"People" covers human-based security threats, which are threats that exploit human behavior or interaction to gain unauthorized access to systems or data. An analogy to explain this concept is that human-based security threats are like a Trojan horse. Just as the Greeks used a Trojan horse to gain access to the city of Troy, attackers can use social engineering techniques, such as phishing emails or pretexting, to trick people into revealing sensitive information or performing actions that compromise security. Therefore, it is important to educate and train people on security best practices, policies, and procedures to prevent these types of attacks. Additionally, organizations should implement security awareness training programs to help employees recognize and respond to potential security threats.

The importance of planning the capacity of Technology

Planning the capacity of technology is an important aspect of enterprise security. An analogy to explain this concept is that planning the capacity of technology is like planning a road trip. Just as you need to plan your route, estimate the time it will take to reach your destination, and ensure that your vehicle is in good condition, you need to plan the capacity of your technology infrastructure to ensure that it can handle the demands placed on it. This includes estimating the amount of data that will be processed, the number of users that will access the system, and the types of applications that will be used. By planning the capacity of technology, organizations can ensure that their systems are reliable, scalable, and secure. This can help prevent downtime, data loss, and other security incidents that can result from overloading or underutilizing technology resources.

The importance of planning the capacity of Infrastructure

Planning the capacity of infrastructure is crucial for ensuring that the system can handle the expected workload and traffic. This is similar to planning the seating capacity of a restaurant. If the restaurant owner does not plan the seating capacity based on the expected number of customers, the restaurant may not be able to accommodate all the customers, leading to long wait times and dissatisfied customers. Similarly, if the capacity of the infrastructure is not planned properly, it may not be able to handle the expected workload, leading to slow response times, system crashes, and other issues that can negatively impact the user experience. Therefore, planning the capacity of infrastructure is essential for ensuring that the system can handle the expected workload and provide a seamless user experience.

The importance of resilience and recovery Testing

Resilience and recovery testing are important aspects of cybersecurity. Resilience testing involves testing the ability of a system to withstand and recover from unexpected events, such as cyber attacks or natural disasters. Recovery testing involves testing the ability of a system to recover from such events and restore normal operations. These tests are like fire drills for cybersecurity, helping organizations to identify weaknesses and improve their ability to respond to and recover from cyber attacks. Just as fire drills help people to know what to do in the event of a fire, resilience and recovery testing help organizations to know what to do in the event of a cyber attack.

The importance of resilience and recovery Tabletop exercises

Resilience and recovery tabletop exercises are important for organizations to prepare for and respond to security incidents. These exercises simulate real-world scenarios and help organizations identify gaps in their incident response plans. Just like how athletes practice and train to prepare for a game, organizations need to practice and train to prepare for a security incident. By conducting tabletop exercises, organizations can improve their ability to respond to security incidents and minimize the impact of a breach. It's like having a fire drill in a building - it helps people know what to do in case of a real fire and can save lives.

The importance of resilience and recovery Fail over

Failover is a process of switching to a redundant or standby system or component when the primary system or component fails. It is like having a spare tire in your car. When one tire goes flat, you can replace it with the spare tire and continue driving. Similarly, in a failover scenario, when the primary system fails, the backup system takes over and continues to provide the required services. This ensures that the system remains available and operational even in the event of a failure. Failover is an important aspect of high availability and disaster recovery planning in IT systems.

The importance of resilience and recovery
Simulation

Resilience and recovery simulations are important in cybersecurity because they help organizations prepare for and respond to security incidents. Just as firefighters train for emergencies by simulating fires, organizations can simulate cyber attacks to test their incident response plans and identify areas for improvement. These simulations can help organizations build resilience by identifying weaknesses in their security posture and developing strategies to mitigate them. In the event of a real attack, a well-prepared organization will be better equipped to recover quickly and minimize damage, just as a well-trained firefighter is better equipped to put out a fire and prevent it from spreading.

The importance of resilience and recovery
Parallel processing

Parallel processing is a computing technique that involves running multiple processors or CPUs simultaneously to handle different parts of a task. It is like a group of people working together to complete a task. For example, if a group of people is assigned to paint a large wall, they can divide the wall into sections and each person can paint a section simultaneously. Similarly, in parallel processing, a complex task is divided into multiple parts using specialized software, and each part is assigned to a processor. Each processor solves its part, and the data is reassembled by the software to read the solution or execute the task. Parallel processing is commonly used to perform complex tasks and computations, and it can significantly reduce the time required to complete a task.

The importance of resilience and recovery Backups

Resilience and recovery backups are essential components of a comprehensive security strategy. They help organizations to prepare for and respond to security incidents, such as data breaches or system failures. Resilience refers to the ability of a system to withstand and recover from an attack or failure, while recovery backups are copies of data that can be used to restore systems in the event of a disaster. An analogy for this is having spare tires in your car. Just as you need a spare tire in case of a flat, organizations need resilience and recovery backups to ensure that they can continue to operate in the event of a security incident. Without these measures, organizations risk losing critical data and suffering significant downtime, which can be costly and damaging to their reputation.

The importance of Onsite/offsite Backups

Onsite and offsite backups are both important for ensuring data is protected in case of a disaster or data loss. Onsite backups are like having a fire extinguisher in your home - they are easily accessible and can quickly put out a small fire. However, if your entire home burns down, the fire extinguisher won't be of much use. This is where offsite backups come in - they are like having a backup fire extinguisher stored in a different location. If your home burns down, you can still access the backup fire extinguisher and put out the fire. Similarly, if your onsite backup is destroyed or inaccessible, you can still recover your data from the offsite backup.

The importance of Frequency Backups

Frequency backups are an essential part of any organization's data backup strategy. They involve creating regular backups of important data at set intervals, such as daily or weekly, to ensure that in the event of data loss, the organization can quickly recover the most recent version of the data. An analogy for frequency backups is like taking a snapshot of a document at regular intervals. If you only take one snapshot, you risk losing all the changes made since that snapshot was taken. However, if you take regular snapshots, you can easily recover the most recent version of the document in the event of a loss. This is why frequency backups are so important for organizations to ensure they can quickly recover from data loss and minimize the impact on their operations.

The importance of Encryption Backups

Encryption of backups is the process of converting the data in a backup file into a coded language that can only be read by authorized parties. It is similar to locking a valuable item in a safe and only giving the key to trusted individuals. In the event of a security breach or unauthorized access, the encrypted backup data will be unreadable and therefore useless to the attacker. This helps to ensure the confidentiality and integrity of the data in the backup file. The process of encryption involves using an encryption algorithm and a secret key to scramble the data in the backup file. The encrypted data can only be decrypted using the same secret key, which should be kept secure and accessible only to authorized parties.

The importance of Snapshots Backups
Snapshots are a feature of virtualization technology that allows the user to capture the state of a virtual machine at a specific point in time. It is similar to taking a picture of a moment in time, which can be used to revert back to that specific state if needed. Just like how a photograph captures a moment in time, a snapshot captures the state of a virtual machine at a specific point in time. This can be useful for testing, troubleshooting, or rolling back to a previous configuration. However, it is important to note that snapshots should not be used as a substitute for backups, as they are not a complete backup solution. Snapshots are like a Polaroid picture of a moment in time, capturing the state of a system at a specific point. They can be used to quickly restore a system to a previous state if something goes wrong. Backups, on the other hand, are like a photo album, containing multiple snapshots of a system over time. They are important for long-term data retention and can be used to recover from catastrophic events like hardware failure or ransomware attacks. In summary, snapshots and backups are like insurance policies for your data, providing protection and peace of mind in case of unexpected events.

The importance of Recovery Backups
Recovery backups are an essential part of any organization's security strategy. They allow for the restoration of data and systems in the event of a disaster or cyber attack. Without recovery backups, an organization could lose all of its data and systems, which could be catastrophic. To put it in an analogy, recovery backups are like a spare tire in a car. You may not need it every day, but when you get a flat tire, it can be a lifesaver. Similarly, recovery backups may not be used often, but when a disaster strikes, they can be the difference between a quick recovery and a complete loss of data and systems.

The importance of Replication Backups

Replication is the process of creating a copy of data and storing it in another location. This can be compared to making a photocopy of a document. The copy is identical to the original, but it is stored in a different location. Replication can be used to improve data availability and redundancy. Backups, on the other hand, are copies of data that are created for the purpose of restoring the original data in case of data loss or corruption. This can be compared to creating a backup of important documents in case the original is lost or damaged. Backups can be stored on different media, such as tapes or disks, and can be used to restore data to its original state in case of a disaster or other event that causes data loss.

The importance of Journaling Backups

Journaling backups is a technique used in data backup and recovery to ensure that data is not lost in the event of a system failure or other disaster. It involves keeping a record, or journal, of all changes made to the data since the last backup was taken. This allows for quick and efficient recovery of data by allowing the system to "replay" the changes made to the data since the last backup, similar to how a DVR can replay a recorded TV show. The journal acts as a log of all changes made to the data, allowing the system to quickly and easily restore the data to its most recent state in the event of a failure or disaster.

The importance of Power resilience and recovery in a secure architecture

Power resilience and recovery in a secure architecture refer to the ability of a system to withstand and recover from unexpected events or disruptions. This can be compared to a human body's immune system, which is designed to protect the body from harmful pathogens and recover from illnesses. Just as the immune system is strengthened by a healthy lifestyle, a secure architecture can be strengthened by implementing security measures such as firewalls, intrusion detection systems, and access controls. Additionally, a resilient architecture should have a disaster recovery plan in place to ensure that critical systems can be restored quickly in the event of a catastrophic occurrence. This plan should include data backup and storage procedures, recovery processes, and a strategy for restoring critical systems and applications. Overall, a secure and resilient architecture is essential for protecting against security threats, preventing unauthorized access, and ensuring the smooth running of a business.

The importance of Generators in a secure architecture

The importance of generators in a secure architecture is to ensure that critical systems remain operational during power outages or other disruptions. Just as a backup generator can provide electricity to a building during a power outage, a generator in a secure architecture can provide power to critical systems during a disruption. This is important because if critical systems go down during a security incident, it can lead to data loss or other negative consequences. Therefore, having a generator as part of a secure architecture can help ensure that critical systems remain operational and secure even during unexpected events.

Applying security techniques to, Secure baselines
Secure baselines are a set of security configurations
that are established to provide a secure starting point
for a system. They are like a blueprint for building a
house. Just as a blueprint provides a set of instructions
for constructing a house, secure baselines provide a set
of instructions for configuring a system to be secure.
Applying security techniques to secure baselines
involves implementing security controls to ensure that
the system is configured according to the secure
baseline. This is like adding locks, alarms, and security
cameras to a house to make it more secure. By
applying security techniques to secure baselines,
organizations can ensure that their systems are
configured securely and are less vulnerable to attacks.

Applying security techniques to, Establish Secure baselines

Establishing secure baselines is a security technique that involves defining a set of security standards and configurations that are considered secure for a particular system or environment. It is similar to setting up a foundation for a building. Just as a building's foundation provides a stable base for the rest of the structure, establishing secure baselines provides a stable and secure starting point for a system. Secure baselines can include things like password policies, network configurations, and software updates. By establishing secure baselines, organizations can ensure that their systems are configured in a secure and consistent manner, which can help to prevent security breaches and other security incidents.

Applying security techniques to, Deploy Secure baselines

"Deploy Secure Baselines" is a security technique that involves creating a standard configuration for a system or application that is secure by default. This configuration is then used as a starting point for all new installations or updates. It is similar to building a house with a strong foundation and sturdy walls to protect against external threats. By deploying secure baselines, organizations can reduce the risk of security breaches and ensure that all systems and applications are configured in a consistent and secure manner. This technique involves identifying and implementing security controls, such as firewalls, access controls, and encryption, to protect against known threats and vulnerabilities. It also involves regularly updating and patching systems to address new threats and vulnerabilities as they emerge. Overall, deploying secure baselines is an essential security technique that helps organizations establish a strong security posture and protect against a wide range of threats.

Applying security techniques to, Maintain Secure baselines

Maintaining secure baselines involves establishing a set of security standards and configurations that are considered the minimum level of security for a system. These baselines are used to ensure that all systems are configured consistently and securely. Applying security techniques to maintain secure baselines involves implementing security controls such as access controls, firewalls, and intrusion detection systems to protect against unauthorized access and attacks. An analogy for maintaining secure baselines could be a house with a strong foundation and sturdy walls. Just as a house needs a strong foundation and walls to protect against external threats such as weather and intruders, a system needs secure baselines to protect against external threats such as cyber attacks and unauthorized access.

Applying security techniques to, Hardening targets

Applying security techniques to harden targets involves taking measures to make a system or network more resistant to attacks. This can be compared to fortifying a castle to make it more difficult for invaders to breach its walls. Just as a castle might have multiple layers of defenses, such as walls, moats, and gates, a hardened system might have multiple layers of security controls, such as firewalls, intrusion detection systems, and access controls. Hardening targets can also involve removing unnecessary software or services, patching vulnerabilities, and configuring systems to reduce their attack surface. By hardening targets, organizations can reduce the likelihood of successful attacks and minimize the impact of any that do occur.

Applying security techniques to, Hardening targets such as Mobile devices

Hardening targets such as mobile devices involves taking steps to make them more secure and less vulnerable to attacks. This can be compared to adding extra layers of armor to a knight's suit to protect them from enemy attacks. Some ways to harden mobile devices include enabling encryption, using strong passwords, keeping software up to date, and disabling unnecessary features and services. By hardening mobile devices, users can reduce the risk of sensitive information being compromised and prevent unauthorized access to their devices.

Applying security techniques to, Hardening targets such as Workstations

Applying security techniques to harden targets such as workstations involves implementing measures to reduce the attack surface and make it more difficult for attackers to compromise the system. This can be compared to securing a house by installing locks on doors and windows, setting up an alarm system, and adding security cameras. Just as these measures make it harder for burglars to break into a house, hardening a workstation involves implementing security controls such as firewalls, antivirus software, and intrusion detection systems to prevent unauthorized access, detect and respond to security incidents, and minimize the impact of successful attacks. By hardening targets such as workstations, organizations can reduce the risk of data breaches, theft of sensitive information, and other security incidents.

Applying security techniques to Hardening targets such as Switches

Applying security techniques to hardening targets such as switches involves implementing measures to reduce the attack surface and increase the security posture of the switches. This can be compared to securing a house by installing locks on doors and windows, and adding security cameras and alarms. Some of the security techniques that can be applied to switches include disabling unused ports, enabling port security, configuring access control lists (ACLs), implementing VLANs, and enabling Spanning Tree Protocol (STP) to prevent network loops. These measures help to prevent unauthorized access, mitigate the risk of attacks, and ensure the availability and integrity of the network. By hardening switches, organizations can improve their overall security posture and reduce the likelihood of successful attacks.

Applying security techniques to Hardening targets such as Routers

Applying security techniques to harden targets such as routers involves implementing measures to reduce the attack surface and increase the overall security posture of the device. This can be compared to reinforcing the walls and doors of a house to make it more difficult for intruders to break in. Some of the security techniques that can be applied to routers include disabling unnecessary services, changing default passwords, implementing access control lists (ACLs), and enabling encryption. By hardening the router, an attacker would need to overcome additional barriers to gain unauthorized access, making it more difficult to compromise the network.

Applying security techniques to Hardening targets such as Cloud infrastructure

Applying security techniques to harden targets such as cloud infrastructure is like adding multiple layers of armor to a castle to protect it from invaders. Just as a castle has multiple layers of defense, such as walls, moats, and gates, cloud infrastructure can be hardened by implementing multiple layers of security measures, such as firewalls, intrusion detection systems, and access controls. These measures work together to create a strong defense against potential attackers, making it more difficult for them to penetrate the system and access sensitive data. By hardening cloud infrastructure, organizations can ensure that their data is protected from unauthorized access and that their systems are resilient against cyber threats.

Applying security techniques to Hardening targets such as Servers

Applying security techniques to harden targets such as servers is like adding layers of armor to a castle. Just as a castle has multiple layers of protection to prevent attackers from breaching its walls, servers can be hardened with multiple layers of security measures to prevent unauthorized access and protect against cyber attacks. These security measures can include implementing firewalls, intrusion detection and prevention systems, access controls, and encryption. By hardening servers with these security techniques, organizations can reduce the risk of data breaches and ensure the confidentiality, integrity, and availability of their data.

Applying security techniques to Hardening targets such as ICS/SCADA

Hardening targets such as ICS/SCADA involves applying security techniques to make them more secure and less vulnerable to cyber attacks. This can be compared to securing a house by installing locks, alarms, and security cameras to prevent burglars from breaking in. In the same way, hardening ICS/SCADA systems involves implementing security measures such as firewalls, intrusion detection systems, access controls, and encryption to protect against unauthorized access, data theft, and other cyber threats. These security techniques help to reduce the attack surface and make it more difficult for attackers to compromise the system. By hardening ICS/SCADA systems, organizations can ensure the reliability, availability, and safety of critical infrastructure and prevent potentially catastrophic consequences.

Applying security techniques to Hardening targets such as Embedded systems

Applying security techniques to hardening targets such as embedded systems involves implementing measures to reduce the attack surface and make the system more resilient to attacks. This can be compared to fortifying a castle by adding walls, gates, and other defenses to make it more difficult for attackers to breach. Some security techniques that can be used to harden embedded systems include disabling unnecessary services, using strong authentication and encryption, implementing access controls, and regularly updating software and firmware to patch vulnerabilities. By hardening embedded systems, organizations can reduce the risk of unauthorized access, data theft, and other security breaches.

Applying security techniques to Hardening targets such as RTOS

Hardening targets such as RTOS involves applying security techniques to make them more secure and less vulnerable to attacks. This can be compared to fortifying a castle to make it more difficult for attackers to breach its walls. Just as a castle can be fortified with walls, moats, and other defenses, an RTOS can be hardened by implementing security measures such as access controls, encryption, and intrusion detection systems. By hardening an RTOS, it becomes more resilient to attacks and better able to protect the systems and data it supports.

Applying security techniques to Hardening targets such as IoT devices

Hardening targets such as IoT devices involves applying security techniques to make them more resistant to attacks. This can be compared to fortifying a castle to make it more difficult for enemies to breach its walls. Just as a castle may have multiple layers of defense, such as walls, moats, and gates, IoT devices can be hardened by implementing multiple layers of security controls, such as firewalls, access controls, and encryption. Hardening IoT devices can help prevent unauthorized access, data theft, and other security breaches. It is important to regularly update and maintain these security controls to ensure that the devices remain secure over time.

Applying security techniques to Hardening targets

Applying security techniques to hardening targets involves implementing measures to make a system or network more resistant to attacks. This can be compared to fortifying a castle to make it more difficult for invaders to breach its walls. Just as a castle might have multiple layers of defenses, such as walls, moats, and gates, a hardened system might have multiple layers of security controls, such as firewalls, intrusion detection systems, and access controls. By implementing these measures, the system becomes more resilient to attacks and less vulnerable to compromise. The reference provided outlines the specific security techniques and best practices that can be used to harden targets, including network security, access control, and vulnerability management.

Applying security techniques to Hardening targets

Applying security techniques to hardening targets involves implementing measures to make a system or network more resistant to attacks. This can be compared to fortifying a castle to make it more difficult for invaders to breach its walls. Just as a castle might have multiple layers of defenses, such as walls, moats, and gates, a hardened system might have multiple layers of security controls, such as firewalls, intrusion detection systems, and access controls. By implementing these measures, the system becomes more resilient to attacks and less vulnerable to compromise. The reference provided outlines the specific security techniques and best practices that can be used to harden targets, including network security, access control, and vulnerability management.

Applying security techniques to Hardening targets

Applying security techniques to hardening targets involves implementing measures to make a system or network more resistant to attacks. This can be compared to fortifying a castle to make it more difficult for invaders to breach its walls. Just as a castle might have multiple layers of defenses, such as walls, moats, and gates, a hardened system might have multiple layers of security controls, such as firewalls, intrusion detection systems, and access controls. By implementing these measures, the system becomes more resilient to attacks and less vulnerable to compromise. The reference provided outlines the specific security techniques and best practices that can be used to harden targets, including network security, access control, and vulnerability management.

The security Installation considerations around Wireless devices

When it comes to installing wireless devices, security considerations are crucial. Just like how you would secure your home by locking doors and windows, you need to secure your wireless devices to prevent unauthorized access. This includes using strong passwords, enabling encryption, and disabling unnecessary features that could be exploited by attackers. Additionally, you should also consider the physical placement of your wireless devices. Just as you wouldn't leave your valuables in plain sight, you should avoid placing wireless devices in areas where they can be easily accessed or tampered with. By taking these security installation considerations into account, you can help ensure that your wireless devices are protected from potential threats.

The security Installation considerations around Wireless devices such as, Site surveys

When installing wireless devices, security considerations are crucial to ensure that the network is secure. One important aspect of security installation is conducting site surveys. Site surveys are like a blueprint for the wireless network, where the surveyor maps out the area to determine the best locations for access points and antennas. This process helps to identify potential sources of interference, such as other wireless networks or physical obstructions, and ensures that the wireless signal is strong and reliable throughout the coverage area. By conducting site surveys, network administrators can ensure that the wireless network is secure and that there are no weak spots that could be exploited by attackers.

The security Installation considerations around Wireless devices such as, Heat maps

Wireless devices have become an integral part of modern-day communication. However, their installation requires careful consideration of security measures. One such consideration is the use of heat maps. Heat maps are like a blueprint of a building that shows the areas with the strongest and weakest wireless signals. By analyzing these maps, security professionals can identify areas where wireless signals are weak and take steps to strengthen them. This helps to ensure that wireless devices are installed in a way that maximizes their security and minimizes the risk of unauthorized access.

Applying security techniques to Mobile solutions
Mobile solutions are becoming increasingly popular, and with that comes the need for security measures to protect sensitive information. Applying security techniques to mobile solutions involves implementing measures such as encryption, authentication, and access control to ensure that only authorized users can access the data. Encryption can be compared to locking a safe, where the data is protected by a key that only authorized users possess. Authentication is like a bouncer at a club, verifying that only those with the proper credentials are allowed in. Access control is like a security guard at a building, ensuring that only authorized personnel can enter certain areas. By implementing these security techniques, mobile solutions can be protected from unauthorized access and data breaches.

Applying security techniques such as, Mobile device management (MDM)
Mobile Device Management (MDM) is a security technique that allows organizations to manage and secure mobile devices such as smartphones and tablets. It provides a centralized platform for managing and monitoring mobile devices, enforcing security policies, and protecting sensitive data. An analogy for MDM could be a traffic cop who manages and directs the flow of traffic on a busy road. Just as a traffic cop ensures that vehicles move in an orderly and safe manner, MDM ensures that mobile devices are used in a secure and controlled way. It helps prevent unauthorized access to sensitive data, ensures that devices are updated with the latest security patches, and allows organizations to remotely wipe data from lost or stolen devices.

Mobile device management (MDM) Deployment models

Mobile device management (MDM) deployment models offer different options for organizations to manage and secure mobile devices used by employees.

The following are some common deployment models for mobile devices:

Corporate-owned: The organization purchases devices and issues them to employees, providing the highest level of security and control.

Choose Your Own Device (CYOD): Employees choose from a list of acceptable devices that the organization has approved, providing a balance between security and employee flexibility.

Bring Your Own Device (BYOD): Employees use their personal devices for work purposes, providing the most flexibility for employees but can be challenging to manage and secure.

Company-owned, Personally Enabled (COPE): The organization purchases the devices and issues them to employees, allowing employees to use the devices for personal purposes as well as work purposes, providing a balance between security and employee flexibility.

An analogy for these deployment models could be the different types of car ownership. Corporate-owned is like a company car, where the organization owns and controls the vehicle. CYOD is like a lease, where the employee has some choice in the type of car they get, but the organization still has some control. BYOD is like owning your own car, where the employee has full control and responsibility for the vehicle. COPE is like a company car that the employee is allowed to use for personal purposes as well as work purposes.

The Mobile device management (MDM) Deployment model, Bring your own device (BYOD)

Bring Your Own Device (BYOD) is a mobile device deployment model that allows employees to use their personal devices for work purposes. This model provides the most flexibility for employees, but it can be challenging to manage and secure. Organizations that implement BYOD policies need to ensure that employees keep their devices updated, and there is standardization among the devices. The organization also needs to have adequate control over the devices. A similar analogy for BYOD could be like owning your own car, where the employee has full control and responsibility for the vehicle. The organization can provide some level of support and security, but employees are responsible for maintaining their devices.

The Mobile device management (MDM) Deployment model, Corporate-owned, personally enabled (COPE)

The Corporate-owned, personally enabled (COPE) Mobile Device Management (MDM) Deployment model is an enterprise mobility program where an organization provides an employee with a mobile device primarily for business purposes, but personal use is allowed and limited. The company owns and pays for the device, its repairs, and applicable voice and data plans. COPE is similar to a company car that an employee can use for personal errands, but the company pays for the car, its maintenance, and gas. COPE programs have several benefits, including little to no cost for employees, complete control over devices for organizations facing strict regulations or heavy security requirements, and corporate discounts for enterprises since they typically select and buy devices in bulk before deploying them into their workforce. However, COPE programs have the slowest deployment timeframe of all the enterprise mobility programs, limited device variety for employees since employers provide employees with a pre-determined mobile device, and organizations are responsible for updating all devices, which can be a heavy task for IT departments.

The Mobile device management (MDM) Deployment model, Choose your own device (CYOD)

The Choose Your Own Device (CYOD) deployment model is an employee provisioning model in which an organization allows people to select the mobile devices they would like to use from a limited number of options. This model is similar to the Corporate-Owned, Personally-Enabled (COPE) model, but in this case, the corporation provides the end-user with a number of different options for a mobile device, and then the end-user can decide what type of device they would like the corporation to buy for them. An analogy for CYOD is like going to a restaurant with a pre-set menu where you can choose from a limited number of options. The restaurant has already pre-selected the dishes that they know are good and safe to eat, and you can choose from those options. This model is a good option for companies that want to maintain control over the devices used in the workplace while still giving employees some choice.

Applying security techniques to the Cellular Connection method

The cellular connection method can be secured using various security techniques. One such technique is encryption, which can be compared to a secret code that only the intended recipient can decipher. Another technique is authentication, which can be compared to a bouncer at a club checking IDs to ensure only authorized individuals are allowed in. Additionally, access control can be implemented to restrict access to sensitive information or resources, similar to a locked door that only authorized individuals can open. Finally, monitoring and logging can be used to detect and respond to security incidents, similar to a security camera that records any suspicious activity. By applying these security techniques to the cellular connection method, the confidentiality, integrity, and availability of data transmitted over the cellular network can be protected.

Applying security techniques to the Wi-Fi Connection method

Securing a Wi-Fi connection involves implementing various security techniques to protect the wireless network from unauthorized access and attacks. One analogy to understand this is to think of a Wi-Fi network as a house with a wireless router acting as the front door. Just as we secure our homes with locks, alarms, and security cameras, we need to secure our Wi-Fi networks with encryption, strong passwords, and firewalls. Encryption is like locking the front door, making it difficult for intruders to gain access to the network. Strong passwords act as an alarm system, alerting us to any unauthorized access attempts. Firewalls are like security cameras, monitoring network traffic and blocking any suspicious activity. By implementing these security techniques, we can ensure that our Wi-Fi networks are protected from potential threats and attacks.

Applying security techniques to the Bluetooth Connection method

Bluetooth is a wireless communication method that allows devices to connect and exchange data. However, it is vulnerable to security threats such as eavesdropping, unauthorized access, and data interception. To secure Bluetooth connections, security techniques such as authentication, encryption, and authorization can be applied. Authentication is like a bouncer at a club who checks IDs to ensure that only authorized individuals are allowed in. Encryption is like a secret code that scrambles the data being transmitted so that it cannot be read by unauthorized parties. Authorization is like a security guard who monitors the activities of authorized individuals to ensure that they are not doing anything suspicious. By applying these security techniques, Bluetooth connections can be made more secure and less vulnerable to attacks.

Applying security techniques to Wireless security settings

Wireless security settings can be compared to a lock on a door. Just as a lock on a door prevents unauthorized access to a building, security techniques applied to wireless settings prevent unauthorized access to a wireless network. These techniques include encryption, authentication, and access control. Encryption is like a key that unlocks the door, allowing authorized users to access the network while keeping unauthorized users out. Authentication is like a security guard who checks IDs before allowing people to enter a building, ensuring that only authorized users are allowed access to the network. Access control is like a bouncer at a club who decides who is allowed in and who is not, controlling who has access to the network and what they are allowed to do once they are connected. By applying these security techniques to wireless settings, organizations can ensure that their wireless networks are secure and that only authorized users have access to sensitive information.

Applying Wireless security settings such as, Wi-Fi Protected Access 3 (WPA3)

Wireless security settings such as Wi-Fi Protected Access 3 (WPA3) are used to protect wireless networks from unauthorized access and attacks. WPA3 is an improved version of WPA2 and provides stronger encryption and security features. An analogy to understand this concept is to think of a wireless network as a house with a lock on the front door. WPA3 is like a stronger lock that is more difficult to pick or break, making it harder for intruders to gain access to the house. By applying WPA3 security settings to a wireless network, it becomes more difficult for attackers to intercept and decrypt wireless traffic, ensuring that the network is secure and protected. Wi-Fi Protected Access 3 (WPA3) is a security protocol that provides enhanced security for Wi-Fi networks. It is an improvement over the previous WPA2 protocol and provides stronger encryption and authentication mechanisms. WPA3 uses a new encryption algorithm called Simultaneous Authentication of Equals (SAE) that is more secure than the previous Pre-Shared Key (PSK) method. An analogy for WPA3 could be a lock on a door. Just as a lock on a door provides security by preventing unauthorized access, WPA3 provides security for Wi-Fi networks by preventing unauthorized access to the network.

Applying Wireless security settings such as, AAA/Remote Authentication Dial-In User Service (RADIUS)

AAA stands for Authentication, Authorization, and Accounting. It is a security framework that provides a way to control access to resources based on user identity and other attributes. Remote Authentication Dial-In User Service (RADIUS) is a protocol that provides centralized authentication, authorization, and accounting for remote access services. Wireless security settings such as AAA/RADIUS are used to authenticate and authorize wireless clients before they are allowed to access the network. This is similar to a bouncer at a club who checks IDs to ensure that only authorized individuals are allowed inside. AAA/RADIUS provides a centralized authentication and authorization mechanism, allowing network administrators to manage user access to the wireless network from a single location. This helps to ensure that only authorized users are able to access the network, reducing the risk of unauthorized access and potential security breaches.

Applying Wireless security settings such as, Cryptographic protocols

Wireless security settings are important to protect wireless networks from unauthorized access and attacks. Cryptographic protocols are one of the key components of wireless security settings. Cryptographic protocols are like a secret code that is used to protect the wireless network. Just like a secret code, cryptographic protocols use encryption to scramble the data being transmitted over the wireless network. This makes it difficult for attackers to intercept and read the data. Cryptographic protocols also use authentication to verify the identity of the devices that are trying to connect to the wireless network. This ensures that only authorized devices are allowed to connect to the network. Overall, applying cryptographic protocols is an essential step in securing wireless networks and protecting them from potential threats. Cryptographic protocols are a set of rules that govern the secure communication between two parties. They are like a secret language that only the two parties can understand, and they use it to communicate securely. Just like two people who speak a secret language, they can communicate without anyone else understanding what they are saying. Cryptographic protocols use encryption algorithms to scramble the data being transmitted, making it unreadable to anyone who intercepts it. The data can only be decrypted by the intended recipient, who has the key to unlock the encryption. This ensures that the data remains confidential and secure during transmission.

Applying Wireless security settings such as, Authentication protocols

Wireless security settings are used to protect wireless networks from unauthorized access and attacks. Authentication protocols are one of the key components of wireless security settings. Authentication protocols are used to verify the identity of a user or device before granting access to the wireless network. This is similar to a bouncer at a nightclub checking IDs before allowing people to enter. Just as a bouncer checks IDs to ensure that only authorized individuals are allowed into the club, authentication protocols check the identity of users or devices to ensure that only authorized individuals or devices are allowed to access the wireless network.

Some common authentication protocols used in wireless networks include WPA2-PSK, WPA2-Enterprise, and 802.1X. Authentication protocols are used to verify the identity of a user or device attempting to access a system or network. They are like a bouncer at a club who checks your ID before allowing you to enter. The protocols ensure that only authorized users or devices are granted access to the system or network. There are several authentication protocols, including password-based authentication, biometric authentication, and multi-factor authentication. Password-based authentication is like a lock on a door that requires a key to open. Biometric authentication is like a fingerprint scanner that only allows access to those with authorized fingerprints. Multi-factor authentication is like a combination lock that requires both a key and a code to open. These protocols help to ensure the security of the system by preventing unauthorized access.

Applying security techniques to Application security such as, Input validation

Application security is the practice of securing software applications from external threats. One of the techniques used in application security is input validation. Input validation is like a bouncer at a club who checks IDs to ensure that only authorized individuals are allowed in. In the same way, input validation checks the data entered into an application to ensure that it is valid and authorized. This technique helps prevent malicious data from being entered into an application, which could lead to security vulnerabilities such as SQL injection attacks. By validating input, an application can ensure that it only processes data that is safe and authorized, thereby reducing the risk of security breaches. Application security is the practice of protecting software applications from threats and vulnerabilities. Input validation is a key aspect of application security that involves checking user input to ensure that it is valid and safe before it is processed by the application. This is similar to a bouncer at a nightclub checking IDs to ensure that only authorized individuals are allowed inside. Just as a bouncer checks IDs to prevent underage drinking and other illegal activities, input validation checks user input to prevent malicious activities such as SQL injection, cross-site scripting (XSS), and other attacks that can exploit vulnerabilities in the application. By implementing input validation, applications can ensure that user input as expected, and prevent attackers from exploiting vulnerabilities to gain unauthorized access to sensitive data or systems.

Applying security techniques to Application security such as, Secure cookies

Application security is the practice of securing software applications from external threats. One of the techniques used in application security is the use of secure cookies. Secure cookies are similar to a secret code that is exchanged between a website and a user's web browser. They are used to store user-specific information, such as login credentials, and are designed to prevent unauthorized access to sensitive data. Secure cookies are encrypted and can only be decrypted by the website that created them. This ensures that the information stored in the cookie is protected from unauthorized access, just like a secret code protects sensitive information from unauthorized access. Application security is the practice of protecting applications from unauthorized access, modification, or destruction. Secure cookies are a type of application security measure that helps protect user data. Cookies are small text files that are stored on a user's computer by a website. They are used to remember user preferences and login information. Secure cookies are encrypted and can only be accessed by the website that created them. This is similar to a lockbox that can only be opened by the person who has the key. By using secure cookies, websites can help prevent unauthorized access to user data and protect against attacks such as session hijacking and cross-site scripting (XSS).

Applying security techniques to Application security such as, Static code analysis

Static code analysis is a security technique used to identify vulnerabilities in software applications. It involves analyzing the source code of an application without executing it, to detect potential security flaws. This is similar to a doctor performing a thorough examination of a patient to identify any underlying health issues before they become serious. Just as a doctor uses various tools and techniques to diagnose a patient, static code analysis uses automated tools to scan the source code of an application and identify potential security weaknesses. By identifying these vulnerabilities early on, developers can take steps to address them before they can be exploited by attackers. Application security refers to the measures taken to protect applications from threats and vulnerabilities. Static code analysis is a technique used to identify security vulnerabilities in the source code of an application. It involves analyzing the code without executing it, to detect potential security flaws such as buffer overflows, SQL injection, and cross-site scripting. Static code analysis can be compared to proofreading a document before publishing it. Just as proofreading helps to identify and correct errors in a document, static code analysis helps to identify and correct security vulnerabilities in an application's source code before it is deployed. By using static code analysis, developers can ensure that their applications are secure and free from vulnerabilities that could be exploited by attackers.

Applying security techniques to Application security such as, Code signing

Code signing is a security technique used to ensure the authenticity and integrity of software applications. It involves digitally signing the code of an application with a unique digital signature that can be verified by the operating system or other software. This signature acts like a seal of approval, indicating that the code has not been tampered with and that it comes from a trusted source. It is similar to a notary public stamping a document to verify its authenticity. Code signing helps to prevent malicious actors from injecting malware or other harmful code into an application, and it also helps to protect against unauthorized modifications to the code. Code signing is a security technique used to ensure the authenticity and integrity of software applications. It involves digitally signing the code of an application with a unique digital signature that can be verified by the operating system or other software. This signature acts like a seal of approval, indicating that the code has not been tampered with and that it comes from a trusted source. It is similar to a notary public stamping a document to verify its authenticity. Code signing helps to prevent malicious actors from injecting malware or other harmful code into an application, and it also helps to protect against unauthorized modifications to the code.

Applying security techniques such as Sandboxing
Sandboxing is a security technique that isolates an application or process from the rest of the system to prevent it from causing harm. It is similar to a sandbox in a playground where children can play safely without affecting the rest of the playground. In the same way, a sandboxed application can run safely without affecting the rest of the system. Sandboxing can be used to test new software or to run untrusted code in a controlled environment. It can also be used to limit the damage caused by a compromised application or process. By isolating an application or process, sandboxing can prevent it from accessing sensitive data or resources on the system.

Applying security techniques such as Monitoring
Monitoring is a security technique that involves observing and analyzing system activities to detect and respond to security incidents. It is similar to a security guard who patrols a building to identify and prevent unauthorized access or suspicious behavior. By monitoring system activities, security personnel can identify potential security threats, such as unauthorized access attempts, malware infections, or unusual network traffic, and take appropriate actions to mitigate them. Monitoring can be performed using various tools and techniques, such as intrusion detection systems, security information and event management systems, and log analysis tools. It is an essential component of a comprehensive security strategy and helps organizations to maintain the confidentiality, integrity, and availability of their systems and data. Monitoring is the process of observing and analyzing activities to detect and respond to security incidents. It involves collecting data from various sources, such as network devices, servers, and applications, and analyzing it to identify potential security threats. Monitoring can be compared to a security guard who patrols a building to detect any suspicious activity. Just as a security guard keeps an eye on different areas of a building, monitoring tools keep an eye on different parts of a network to detect any unusual behavior. By monitoring network activity, security teams can identify and respond to security incidents in a timely manner, reducing the risk of data breaches and other security threats.

The security implications of asset management regarding the Acquisition/procurement process

Asset management is an important aspect of security that involves identifying, tracking, and managing an organization's assets. The acquisition/procurement process is a critical component of asset management that involves acquiring new assets for the organization. The security implications of asset management regarding the acquisition/procurement process can be compared to buying a new car. Just as a car buyer would research and evaluate different options before making a purchase, an organization should carefully evaluate potential vendors and suppliers to ensure that they meet the organization's security requirements. Additionally, just as a car buyer would perform regular maintenance and inspections to ensure that their car remains in good condition, an organization should regularly monitor and assess their assets to ensure that they remain secure and up-to-date. By effectively managing their assets, organizations can reduce the risk of security breaches and ensure that their operations remain secure and reliable.

The security implications of asset management regarding Assignment/accounting

Asset management is an important aspect of security management. It involves identifying, tracking, and managing assets to ensure their security. In the context of assignment/accounting, asset management helps to ensure that all assets are accounted for and assigned to the appropriate individuals. This is similar to a library where books are assigned to specific individuals and tracked to ensure they are returned on time. Proper asset management helps to prevent loss or theft of assets, and ensures that they are used only for their intended purpose. It also helps to ensure that assets are properly maintained and updated, reducing the risk of vulnerabilities and security breaches.

The security implications of asset management regarding Assignment/accounting Ownership

Asset management is an important aspect of security management. It involves identifying, tracking, and managing assets to ensure that they are properly secured and protected. One of the key security implications of asset management is assignment/accounting ownership. This refers to the process of assigning ownership of assets to specific individuals or groups and keeping track of their use and location. It is similar to assigning a car to a driver and keeping track of who is driving it and where it is being driven. By assigning ownership of assets, organizations can ensure that they are being used appropriately and that any misuse or theft can be quickly identified and addressed. This helps to prevent security breaches and protect sensitive information.

The security implications of asset management regarding Assignment/accounting Classification

Asset management is an important aspect of security management. It involves identifying, tracking, and managing assets to ensure their security. Assignment/accounting classification is a key component of asset management that involves assigning a value to assets based on their importance to the organization. This helps in prioritizing the security measures that need to be implemented to protect these assets. An analogy to understand this concept is to think of a bank vault where different items are stored. The bank assigns different levels of security to each item based on its value. Similarly, organizations assign different levels of security to their assets based on their importance. This helps in ensuring that the most valuable assets are protected with the highest level of security measures.

The security implications of asset management, Monitoring/asset tracking

Asset management involves identifying, tracking, and managing assets to ensure their security. Monitoring/asset tracking is a crucial component of asset management that involves keeping track of the assets and their activities to detect any suspicious behavior. An analogy to understand this concept is to think of a security guard who monitors the activities of people entering and leaving a building. The security guard keeps track of who enters and leaves the building, what they are carrying, and their purpose for being there. Similarly, organizations monitor their assets to detect any unauthorized access, unusual behavior, or security breaches. This helps in identifying potential security threats and taking appropriate measures to prevent them. Effective monitoring/asset tracking is essential for maintaining the security of an organization's assets.

The security implications of asset management regarding Disposal/decommissioning focussing on Sanitization

Asset management is a crucial aspect of security management, and it involves the proper disposal or decommissioning of assets. Disposal or decommissioning of assets can pose a significant security risk if not done correctly. Sanitization is a critical process that ensures that all data is removed from the asset before disposal or decommissioning. Sanitization is like cleaning a whiteboard after a presentation. If you don't clean the whiteboard properly, the information on it can be seen by anyone who uses it next. Similarly, if you don't sanitize an asset before disposal or decommissioning, the data on it can be accessed by unauthorized individuals, leading to data breaches and other security incidents. Therefore, it is essential to ensure that all assets are properly sanitized before disposal or decommissioning to prevent unauthorized access to sensitive information.

The security implications of asset management regarding Disposal/decommissioning focussing on Destruction

Asset management is an important aspect of security, and it includes the proper disposal and decommissioning of assets. Destruction is a common method of disposal, and it involves rendering the asset unusable. The security implications of asset management regarding destruction are similar to those of a paper shredder. Just as a paper shredder is used to destroy sensitive documents to prevent unauthorized access, destruction of assets is necessary to prevent unauthorized access to sensitive information. If assets are not properly destroyed, they can be a source of information for attackers, which can lead to data breaches and other security incidents. Therefore, it is important to ensure that assets are properly disposed of and decommissioned to prevent unauthorized access to sensitive information.

The security implications of asset management regarding Disposal/decommissioning focussing on Certification

Asset management is an important aspect of security management. Disposal/decommissioning of assets is a critical component of asset management. Certification is a process that ensures that the disposal/decommissioning of assets is done in a secure manner. It is like a certificate of destruction that is issued when a document is shredded. Just as a certificate of destruction ensures that the document has been destroyed and cannot be reconstructed, certification ensures that the asset has been disposed of in a secure manner and cannot be recovered. The security implications of asset management regarding disposal/decommissioning are significant because if assets are not disposed of securely, they can be recovered and used by unauthorized individuals, which can lead to security breaches. Therefore, certification is an important process that ensures that assets are disposed of securely and cannot be recovered.

The security implications of asset management regarding Disposal/decommissioning focussing on Data retention

Asset management is a crucial aspect of security management, and data retention is an important component of asset management.

Disposal/decommissioning of assets can pose a significant security risk if data is not securely erased. It is like a confidential document that needs to be shredded before disposal to prevent unauthorized access. Data retention involves maintaining important information as long as it is needed and destroying or declassifying it when it is no longer needed. Legal requirements may exist for records retention, and companies must understand these requirements before disposing of assets. Certified data erasure is a process that ensures that data is securely erased and cannot be recovered. It is important to ensure that data is securely erased before disposing of assets to prevent unauthorized access to sensitive information.

Therefore, data retention and certified data erasure are important processes that ensure that assets are disposed of securely and sensitive information is not compromised.

The security implications of asset management regarding Disposal/decommissioning focussing on Inventory

Asset management is an important aspect of security management. Disposal/decommissioning of assets is a critical process that requires proper inventory management. Just like a chef who needs to keep track of the ingredients in their kitchen, an organization needs to keep track of its assets. When an ingredient is past its expiration date, the chef needs to dispose of it to avoid food poisoning. Similarly, when an asset is no longer needed, it needs to be disposed of properly to avoid security risks. If an organization fails to keep track of its assets, it may not know when an asset is no longer needed, and it may not dispose of it properly. This can lead to security risks such as data breaches, theft, or unauthorized access. Therefore, proper inventory management is crucial for the disposal/decommissioning of assets to ensure that they are disposed of securely and in a timely manner.

The security implications of asset management regarding Disposal/decommissioning focussing on Enumeration

Asset management is an important aspect of security management. Disposal/decommissioning of assets is a critical process that requires proper enumeration to ensure that all assets are accounted for and disposed of securely. Enumeration is like taking inventory of all the items in a store before closing it down. Just like how a store owner would want to make sure that all items are accounted for and disposed of properly, an organization needs to ensure that all assets are identified and disposed of securely to prevent unauthorized access to sensitive information. Failure to properly enumerate assets during disposal/decommissioning can lead to security breaches, data loss, and other security incidents. Therefore, it is important to have a proper asset management plan in place that includes enumeration of all assets to ensure that they are disposed of securely.

Identification methods of vulnerability management

Vulnerability management is the process of identifying, assessing, prioritizing, and mitigating security vulnerabilities in systems and applications. Identification methods of vulnerability management include vulnerability scanning, penetration testing, and risk assessments. An analogy to vulnerability management could be a doctor's visit. Just as a doctor performs a check-up to identify any health issues, vulnerability management identifies any security issues in a system. Vulnerability scanning is like a blood test, which can identify any abnormalities in the system. Penetration testing is like a stress test, which can identify how the system responds to an attack. Risk assessments are like a medical history review, which can identify any potential vulnerabilities based on past experiences. By using these identification methods, organizations can proactively address security vulnerabilities before they are exploited by attackers.

The vulnerability management activity, Vulnerability scan

Vulnerability management is a crucial activity in cybersecurity that involves identifying, assessing, and mitigating vulnerabilities in an organization's systems and applications. One of the key activities in vulnerability management is vulnerability scanning, which is the process of using automated tools to identify vulnerabilities in a system or application. This is similar to a doctor performing a routine check-up on a patient to identify any health issues that need to be addressed. Just as a doctor uses various tools and tests to identify potential health problems, vulnerability scanning tools use various techniques to identify potential vulnerabilities in a system or application. Once vulnerabilities are identified, they can be prioritized based on their severity and addressed through various mitigation strategies, such as patching, configuration changes, or other security controls.

The vulnerability management activity, Application security

Vulnerability management is the process of identifying, evaluating, and mitigating vulnerabilities in a system. It involves regularly scanning systems for vulnerabilities, prioritizing them based on their severity, and taking appropriate actions to address them. This process is similar to regularly checking your home for potential security weaknesses, such as unlocked doors or windows, and taking steps to address them before they can be exploited by intruders. Application security, on the other hand, involves ensuring that applications are designed, developed, and deployed securely. This includes identifying and addressing security vulnerabilities in the application code, as well as implementing security controls to protect against attacks. Application security is like building a house with strong foundations, sturdy walls, and secure locks to prevent intruders from entering and stealing your valuables.

The vulnerability management activity, Static analysis

Vulnerability management is the process of identifying, evaluating, and mitigating security vulnerabilities in an organization's systems and applications. Static analysis is a vulnerability management activity that involves analyzing the source code of an application or system to identify potential security vulnerabilities. It is like a doctor examining a patient's medical records to identify any underlying health issues that may be present. Just as a doctor may use various diagnostic tools to identify health issues, static analysis tools use various techniques to identify potential security vulnerabilities in an application's source code. Once identified, these vulnerabilities can be addressed through code changes or other mitigation strategies to reduce the risk of exploitation by attackers.

The vulnerability management activity, Dynamic analysis

Vulnerability management is the process of identifying, evaluating, and mitigating vulnerabilities in an organization's systems and applications. Dynamic analysis is a vulnerability management activity that involves analyzing software or systems while they are running to identify vulnerabilities that may not be apparent during static analysis. An analogy for dynamic analysis in vulnerability management is like a doctor performing a stress test on a patient. During a stress test, the doctor monitors the patient's heart rate and blood pressure while they are exercising to identify any potential issues that may not be apparent during a regular check-up. Similarly, dynamic analysis monitors a system or application while it is running to identify any vulnerabilities that may not be apparent during static analysis. This allows organizations to proactively identify and address vulnerabilities before they can be exploited by attackers.

The vulnerability management activity, Package monitoring

Vulnerability management is the process of identifying, evaluating, and mitigating vulnerabilities in a system. One of the activities involved in vulnerability management is package monitoring. This involves monitoring software packages for vulnerabilities and applying patches or updates as needed to address those vulnerabilities. An analogy for package monitoring in vulnerability management is like regularly checking the expiration dates of food items in your pantry. Just as you would check the expiration dates of food items to ensure they are safe to consume, package monitoring involves regularly checking software packages for vulnerabilities to ensure they are safe to use. If a vulnerability is found, it is like finding an expired food item. You would take action to remove the expired food item from your pantry, just as you would take action to apply a patch or update to address a vulnerability in a software package.

The vulnerability management activity, Package monitoring using Threat feeds

Vulnerability management is a crucial activity in cybersecurity that involves identifying, assessing, and mitigating vulnerabilities in an organization's systems and applications. One aspect of vulnerability management is package monitoring using threat feeds. This involves monitoring software packages and libraries used in an organization's systems and applications for known vulnerabilities by subscribing to threat feeds. Threat feeds are like weather forecasts for cybersecurity, providing information on the latest threats and vulnerabilities that organizations need to be aware of. By monitoring package vulnerabilities using threat feeds, organizations can proactively identify and address vulnerabilities before they can be exploited by attackers, similar to how people prepare for a storm by monitoring weather forecasts and taking appropriate precautions.

The vulnerability management activity package monitoring using, Open-source intelligence (OSINT)

Vulnerability management is a critical activity in cybersecurity that involves identifying, assessing, and mitigating vulnerabilities in an organization's systems and applications. One of the key components of vulnerability management is monitoring, which involves continuously monitoring systems and applications for vulnerabilities. Open-source intelligence (OSINT) is a technique that can be used to support vulnerability management by providing information about potential vulnerabilities that may exist in an organization's systems and applications. OSINT involves gathering information from publicly available sources, such as social media, news articles, and online forums, to identify potential vulnerabilities. This is similar to how a detective might gather information from various sources to solve a case. By using OSINT, organizations can proactively identify potential vulnerabilities and take steps to mitigate them before they can be exploited by attackers.

The vulnerability management activity package monitoring using, Proprietary sources

Vulnerability management is a critical activity in cybersecurity that involves identifying, assessing, and mitigating vulnerabilities in an organization's systems and applications. The vulnerability management activity package includes monitoring the organization's systems and applications for vulnerabilities. This involves using various tools and techniques to scan for vulnerabilities, such as network scanners, vulnerability scanners, and penetration testing. Proprietary sources refer to sources of information that are owned or controlled by the organization, such as internal vulnerability reports, security logs, and threat intelligence feeds. An analogy for this would be a homeowner who regularly inspects their house for vulnerabilities, such as unlocked doors or windows, and uses information from their own security system to monitor for potential threats.

The vulnerability management activity package monitoring using,   third-party sources

Third-party sources are external entities that provide information or services to an organization. They can be compared to a restaurant that provides food to customers. Just as a restaurant sources ingredients from external suppliers to prepare meals, an organization may rely on third-party sources to provide information or services that are necessary for its operations. These sources can include vendors, contractors, or other organizations that provide software, hardware, or other services to the organization. It is important for organizations to manage their relationships with third-party sources to ensure that they are meeting the organization's needs and that any risks associated with these sources are identified and addressed. Vulnerability management is a crucial activity in ensuring the security of an organization's systems and data. One aspect of vulnerability management is monitoring for vulnerabilities using third-party sources. This involves regularly checking external sources such as security bulletins, vendor advisories, and other threat intelligence feeds for information on new vulnerabilities that could affect the organization's systems. It is similar to checking the weather forecast before going on a trip to ensure that you are prepared for any potential weather-related issues that could arise. By monitoring third-party sources for vulnerabilities, organizations can stay informed about potential threats and take proactive measures to mitigate them before they can be exploited by attackers.

The vulnerability management activity package monitoring using,   Information-sharing organization sources

Vulnerability management is a crucial activity in ensuring the security of an organization's systems and data. One aspect of vulnerability management is monitoring, which involves keeping an eye on the organization's systems and networks for any signs of vulnerabilities or attacks. This can be compared to a security guard who patrols a building to detect any suspicious activity. Another important aspect of vulnerability management is information-sharing organization sources, which involves gathering information from external sources such as security vendors, government agencies, and other organizations. This can be compared to a neighborhood watch program, where members share information about suspicious activity in the area to help keep everyone safe. By monitoring and gathering information from various sources, organizations can proactively identify and address vulnerabilities before they can be exploited by attackers. Information-sharing organization sources refer to the process of gathering information from external sources such as security vendors, government agencies, and other organizations to identify potential vulnerabilities and threats. This information can be obtained from public threat intelligence databases, private companies that share information, and organizations that work in the security industry. The Cyber Threat Intelligence (CTA) was created to help members upload the information they have about a particular threat, which is then evaluated and made available to other members of the organization. The biggest challenge in sharing this data is making sure that the information is of the highest quality and can be received quickly. The information gathered from these sources can be compared to a neighborhood watch program, where members share information about suspicious activity in the area to help keep everyone safe. By gathering information from various sources, organizations can proactively identify and address vulnerabilities before they can be exploited by attackers.

The vulnerability management activity package monitoring using, Dark web sources

Vulnerability management is a crucial activity in cybersecurity that involves identifying, assessing, and mitigating vulnerabilities in an organization's systems and applications. One aspect of vulnerability management is monitoring for potential threats and vulnerabilities from external sources, such as the dark web. The dark web is like an underground market where cybercriminals can buy and sell stolen data, malware, and other illegal goods and services. By monitoring the dark web, organizations can proactively identify potential threats and vulnerabilities that could be exploited by cybercriminals. This is similar to a security guard monitoring a building's perimeter for any suspicious activity or individuals who may pose a threat to the building's security. The dark web is a part of the internet that is not indexed by search engines and requires specialized software to access. It is often associated with illegal activities such as the sale of stolen data, malware, and other illegal goods and services. Cybercriminals use the dark web to buy and sell information obtained in data breaches, which can be used to launch cyber attacks. Monitoring the dark web is an important aspect of threat intelligence, as it can help organizations identify potential threats and vulnerabilities that could be exploited by cybercriminals. By understanding the tools and techniques used by cybercriminals, organizations can better protect themselves and their assets.

The vulnerability management activity, Penetration testing

Vulnerability management is the process of identifying, evaluating, and mitigating vulnerabilities in an organization's systems and applications. It involves regularly scanning systems for vulnerabilities, prioritizing them based on their severity, and taking appropriate actions to remediate them. This process is similar to regularly checking your home for potential security weaknesses, such as unlocked doors or windows, and taking steps to address them before a burglar can exploit them. Penetration testing, on the other hand, is a method of testing the effectiveness of an organization's security controls by simulating an attack on its systems and applications. This is similar to hiring a professional burglar to test the security of your home by attempting to break in through various means, such as picking locks or breaking windows. The goal of penetration testing is to identify vulnerabilities that may not have been detected through other means and to provide recommendations for improving the organization's security posture.

The vulnerability management activity, Responsible disclosure programs

Vulnerability management is the process of identifying, assessing, prioritizing, and mitigating vulnerabilities in a system or network. It involves regularly scanning for vulnerabilities, analyzing the results, and taking appropriate actions to address them. It is like regularly checking your car for any issues, such as low tire pressure or worn-out brake pads, and fixing them before they cause an accident. Responsible disclosure programs are policies that encourage individuals who discover vulnerabilities in a system or network to report them to the organization responsible for the system or network, rather than publicly disclosing them or using them for malicious purposes. These programs provide a safe and legal way for security researchers to report vulnerabilities and help organizations improve their security. It is like a lost and found program in a public place, where people can return lost items to the authorities instead of keeping them or selling them on the black market.

The vulnerability management activity, Bug bounty programs

Vulnerability management is the process of identifying, assessing, prioritizing, and mitigating vulnerabilities in a system. It is like a gardener who regularly inspects their garden for pests and weeds, and takes steps to remove or control them before they can cause damage. Vulnerability management involves using tools and techniques to scan for vulnerabilities, analyzing the results, and taking action to address them. This can include applying patches, updating software, or implementing other security controls. Bug bounty programs are a type of vulnerability management activity that involves offering rewards to individuals or groups who find and report vulnerabilities in a system. It is like a company that offers a reward to anyone who finds a lost item, such as a wallet or a phone. Bug bounty programs can help organizations identify and address vulnerabilities that might otherwise go unnoticed, by incentivizing security researchers to actively search for and report them. This can help improve the overall security of a system, by identifying and addressing vulnerabilities before they can be exploited by attackers.

The vulnerability management activity, System/process audit

Vulnerability management is an essential activity in cybersecurity that involves identifying, assessing, and mitigating vulnerabilities in an organization's systems and applications. It is like a regular health check-up for a person to identify any potential health issues and take preventive measures to avoid them. Similarly, vulnerability management helps organizations identify potential security risks and take proactive measures to prevent them from being exploited by attackers. System/process audit is another critical activity in cybersecurity that involves reviewing an organization's systems, processes, and policies to ensure they are compliant with security standards and regulations. It is like a financial audit for a company to ensure that its financial statements are accurate and comply with accounting standards. Similarly, a system/process audit helps organizations ensure that their systems and processes comply with security standards and regulations, and identify any gaps that need to be addressed to improve their security posture.

The vulnerability management activity, Analysis Confirmation

Vulnerability management is a process that involves identifying, assessing, and mitigating vulnerabilities in an organization's systems and applications. One of the key activities in vulnerability management is Analysis Confirmation, which involves verifying the existence and severity of a vulnerability. This is similar to a doctor who performs a diagnosis to confirm the presence and severity of a medical condition before prescribing a treatment. In the same way, security analysts perform Analysis Confirmation to validate the findings of vulnerability scans or assessments and determine the appropriate remediation steps. By confirming the existence and severity of vulnerabilities, organizations can prioritize their remediation efforts and reduce the risk of exploitation by attackers. This process involves verifying the existence and severity of a vulnerability by performing additional testing or analysis. The purpose of Analysis Confirmation is to ensure that the vulnerability is real and that it poses a significant risk to the organization. Once the vulnerability is confirmed, the organization can prioritize its remediation efforts and take appropriate steps to mitigate the risk.

The vulnerability management activity Analysis Confirmation of False positive

Vulnerability management is the process of identifying, evaluating, and mitigating vulnerabilities in an organization's systems and applications. One of the activities in vulnerability management is the analysis confirmation of false positives. This activity involves verifying whether a vulnerability identified by a vulnerability scanner is a true positive or a false positive. A false positive is a vulnerability that is reported by the scanner but does not actually exist. It is like a smoke detector that goes off when there is no fire. Just as you would investigate the cause of a smoke detector alarm before calling the fire department, you would investigate the cause of a vulnerability scanner alert before taking any action to remediate the vulnerability. This helps to avoid wasting resources on fixing non-existent vulnerabilities and ensures that real vulnerabilities are addressed in a timely manner.

The vulnerability management activity Analysis Confirmation of False negative

Vulnerability management is a crucial activity in ensuring the security of an organization's systems. One of the key steps in vulnerability management is the analysis and confirmation of false negatives. This step involves reviewing the results of vulnerability scans to identify any vulnerabilities that were missed or not detected by the scanning tool. It is similar to a doctor reviewing the results of a medical test to ensure that there are no false negatives, which could lead to a misdiagnosis and incorrect treatment. By identifying false negatives, organizations can take steps to address these vulnerabilities and improve their overall security posture.

The vulnerability management activity Analysis Prioritization

Vulnerability management is a crucial activity in cybersecurity that involves identifying, assessing, and mitigating vulnerabilities in an organization's systems and applications. The Analysis and Prioritization phase of vulnerability management involves analyzing the vulnerabilities that have been identified and prioritizing them based on their severity and potential impact on the organization. This is similar to a doctor analyzing the symptoms of a patient and prioritizing them based on their severity and potential impact on the patient's health. Just as a doctor would prioritize a patient's life-threatening symptoms over less severe ones, vulnerability management teams prioritize vulnerabilities that pose the greatest risk to the organization's security and operations. This helps ensure that limited resources are allocated to the most critical vulnerabilities first, reducing the overall risk to the organization.

The vulnerability management activity Analysis using the Common Vulnerability Scoring System (CVSS)

Vulnerability management is the process of identifying, evaluating, and mitigating vulnerabilities in a system. One of the activities involved in vulnerability management is analysis using the Common Vulnerability Scoring System (CVSS). The CVSS is a framework used to assess the severity of vulnerabilities based on their characteristics such as exploitability, impact, and complexity. It assigns a score to each vulnerability, which can be used to prioritize remediation efforts. An analogy for this process could be a doctor assessing a patient's health by evaluating various factors such as symptoms, medical history, and test results to determine the severity of the illness and prioritize treatment.

The vulnerability management activity Analysis using the Common Vulnerability Enumeration (CVE)

Vulnerability management is a critical activity in cybersecurity that involves identifying, assessing, and mitigating vulnerabilities in an organization's systems and applications. One of the key steps in vulnerability management is analysis, which involves examining the vulnerabilities to determine their severity and potential impact on the organization. The Common Vulnerability Enumeration (CVE) is a standardized system for identifying and naming vulnerabilities, which helps to streamline the analysis process. An analogy for this process could be a doctor diagnosing a patient's illness. Just as a doctor uses a standardized system to identify and name diseases, security professionals use CVE to identify and name vulnerabilities. This helps to ensure that vulnerabilities are accurately identified and prioritized for remediation, just as a doctor would prioritize treatment based on the severity of the illness.

The vulnerability management activity Analysis and Vulnerability classification

Vulnerability management is a crucial activity in cybersecurity that involves identifying, analyzing, and mitigating vulnerabilities in an organization's systems and networks. The analysis phase of vulnerability management involves examining the vulnerabilities that have been identified to determine their potential impact on the organization's security posture. This is similar to a doctor examining a patient's symptoms to determine the severity of their illness. Vulnerability classification, on the other hand, involves categorizing vulnerabilities based on their severity and potential impact. This is similar to a triage nurse categorizing patients based on the severity of their injuries or illnesses. By analyzing and classifying vulnerabilities, organizations can prioritize their remediation efforts and allocate resources effectively to address the most critical vulnerabilities first.

The vulnerability management activity Analysis and considering Exposure factors

Vulnerability management is a critical activity in information security that involves identifying, assessing, and mitigating vulnerabilities in an organization's systems and applications. The analysis phase of vulnerability management involves identifying and prioritizing vulnerabilities based on their potential impact on the organization. This is similar to a doctor analyzing a patient's symptoms to determine the severity of their illness and the appropriate treatment. Exposure factors are also considered during the analysis phase, which are factors that increase the likelihood or impact of a vulnerability being exploited. This is similar to a doctor considering a patient's age, medical history, and lifestyle when assessing their risk of developing a particular illness. By analyzing vulnerabilities and exposure factors, organizations can prioritize their remediation efforts and reduce their overall risk of a security breach.

The vulnerability management activity Analysis and considering Environmental variables

Vulnerability management is an essential activity in cybersecurity that involves identifying, assessing, and mitigating vulnerabilities in an organization's systems and applications. The analysis phase of vulnerability management involves identifying and prioritizing vulnerabilities based on their potential impact on the organization's assets and operations. This phase also considers environmental variables such as the organization's business objectives, regulatory requirements, and risk tolerance. An analogy for this process could be a doctor diagnosing a patient's illness. The doctor first analyzes the patient's symptoms and medical history to identify potential health issues. They then prioritize the issues based on their severity and the patient's overall health. Finally, the doctor considers environmental variables such as the patient's lifestyle, occupation, and family history to develop a treatment plan that addresses the patient's specific needs and goals. Similarly, vulnerability management analysts analyze an organization's systems and applications to identify potential vulnerabilities, prioritize them based on their severity and potential impact, and consider environmental variables to develop a mitigation plan that aligns with the organization's business objectives and risk tolerance.

The vulnerability management activity Analysis and considering Industry/organizational impact

Vulnerability management is a critical activity in cybersecurity that involves identifying, assessing, and mitigating vulnerabilities in an organization's systems and applications. The analysis phase of vulnerability management involves identifying and prioritizing vulnerabilities based on their severity and potential impact on the organization. This is similar to a doctor diagnosing a patient's illness and determining the best course of treatment based on the severity of the symptoms and the potential impact on the patient's health. The industry/organizational impact consideration phase involves evaluating the potential impact of a vulnerability on the organization's operations, reputation, and financial stability. This is similar to a business owner assessing the potential impact of a new product or service on their company's bottom line and reputation before deciding whether to invest in it. By conducting a thorough analysis and considering the industry/organizational impact of vulnerabilities, organizations can prioritize their remediation efforts and minimize the risk of a security breach.

The vulnerability management activity Analysis and considering Risk tolerance

Vulnerability management is a crucial activity in cybersecurity that involves identifying, assessing, and mitigating vulnerabilities in an organization's systems and applications. The analysis phase of vulnerability management involves identifying and prioritizing vulnerabilities based on their potential impact on the organization's assets and operations. This is similar to a doctor diagnosing a patient's illness and determining the severity of the condition. Once vulnerabilities are identified and prioritized, the organization must consider its risk tolerance, which is the level of risk it is willing to accept. This is similar to a patient deciding whether to undergo a risky surgery or opt for a less invasive treatment. By considering its risk tolerance, the organization can determine which vulnerabilities to address first and how to allocate its resources to mitigate them.

The vulnerability management activity, Vulnerability response and remediation

Vulnerability management is the process of identifying, assessing, and mitigating vulnerabilities in a system. It involves identifying potential weaknesses in a system, prioritizing them based on their severity, and taking steps to remediate them. Vulnerability response is the process of addressing vulnerabilities once they have been identified. This involves developing a plan to mitigate the vulnerability, testing the plan to ensure it is effective, and implementing the plan to remediate the vulnerability. Remediation is the process of fixing the vulnerability, which can involve patching software, updating configurations, or implementing other security controls. An analogy for vulnerability management could be maintaining a house. Just as a homeowner must identify and prioritize potential security risks, such as broken locks or windows, and take steps to remediate them, such as installing new locks or reinforcing windows, a security professional must identify and prioritize vulnerabilities in a system and take steps to remediate them.

The vulnerability management activity, Patching

Vulnerability management is the process of identifying, assessing, and mitigating vulnerabilities in a system. Patching is a critical activity in vulnerability management that involves applying software updates or patches to fix known vulnerabilities in software or systems. Patching can be compared to fixing a hole in a boat. Just as a hole in a boat can cause it to sink, a vulnerability in a system can be exploited by attackers to gain unauthorized access or cause damage. Patching helps to plug these holes and prevent attackers from exploiting vulnerabilities. It is important to keep systems up-to-date with the latest patches to ensure that they are secure and protected against known vulnerabilities.

The vulnerability management activity, Insurance

Vulnerability management is the process of identifying, assessing, prioritizing, and mitigating vulnerabilities in an organization's systems and applications. It is similar to maintaining a house by regularly checking for and fixing any potential security issues, such as broken locks or windows, to prevent burglars from entering. Insurance, on the other hand, is a risk management strategy that involves transferring the financial risk of a potential loss to an insurance company. In the context of cybersecurity, insurance can be seen as a way to mitigate the financial impact of a security breach. Just as homeowners insurance can help cover the cost of repairs or replacement if a burglary occurs, cybersecurity insurance can help cover the cost of damages and recovery efforts if a data breach occurs. However, insurance should not be seen as a replacement for vulnerability management, as it does not address the root cause of the problem and may not cover all costs associated with a breach.

The vulnerability management activity, Segmentation

Vulnerability management is the process of identifying, assessing, and mitigating vulnerabilities in a system. It involves identifying potential vulnerabilities, assessing their severity, and prioritizing them for remediation. Segmentation is a security technique that involves dividing a network into smaller, isolated segments to limit the spread of threats. An analogy for vulnerability management and segmentation could be a doctor performing a check-up on a patient. The doctor identifies potential health issues, assesses their severity, and prioritizes them for treatment. Similarly, vulnerability management identifies potential security issues, assesses their severity, and prioritizes them for remediation. Segmentation, on the other hand, is like isolating a patient with a contagious disease to prevent it from spreading to others. Similarly, network segmentation isolates different parts of a network to limit the spread of threats. By dividing a network into smaller segments, it becomes easier to manage and secure each segment, reducing the risk of a security breach.

The vulnerability management activity, Compensating controls

Compensating controls are measures taken to address any weaknesses of existing controls or to compensate for the inability to meet specific security requirements due to various different constraints. In the instance of a security vulnerability or threat, compensating controls are typically implemented to mitigate or reduce risk. An analogy for compensating controls could be a car with a faulty brake system. The brake system is the primary control for stopping the car, but if it fails, compensating controls such as the emergency brake or downshifting can be used to slow down or stop the car. Similarly, in cybersecurity, compensating controls are like backup measures that can be used to mitigate the risk of a security vulnerability or threat. They are not meant to be the primary control, but rather a secondary measure to reduce the risk of a cyber incident. By implementing compensating controls, organizations can reduce the impact of a security incident and comply with industry standards.

The vulnerability management activity, Exceptions and exemptions

Vulnerability management is a crucial activity that involves identifying, assessing, and mitigating vulnerabilities in an organization's systems and applications. Exceptions and exemptions are two important aspects of vulnerability management. Exceptions are situations where a vulnerability cannot be remediated due to technical or business reasons, while exemptions are situations where a vulnerability is known but is deemed acceptable due to the low risk it poses to the organization. An analogy for this could be a homeowner who has a small crack in their window that does not pose a significant security risk, but they choose not to fix it due to the cost and inconvenience of repairing it. In both cases, it is important for organizations to document and track exceptions and exemptions to ensure that they are properly managed and reviewed on a regular basis.

The vulnerability management activity, Validation of remediation such as Rescanning

Rescanning is a process that involves scanning systems and applications again to ensure that the vulnerabilities have been properly addressed. This process is a part of the validation of remediation activity in vulnerability management. Rescanning can be compared to a teacher who grades a student's paper and then asks the student to make corrections. After the student makes the corrections, the teacher grades the paper again to ensure that the corrections have been made properly. After vulnerabilities have been identified and remediated, rescanning is done to ensure that the vulnerabilities have been properly mitigated. One of the key activities in vulnerability management is the validation of remediation, which involves verifying that the identified vulnerabilities have been properly addressed and mitigated. This activity can be compared to a doctor who prescribes medication to a patient and then follows up with the patient to ensure that the medication is working and that the patient's condition is improving. In the same way, after vulnerabilities have been identified and remediated, it is important to validate that the remediation has been effective and that the vulnerabilities have been properly mitigated. This can be done through activities such as rescanning, which involves scanning the systems and applications again to ensure that the vulnerabilities have been properly addressed. By validating remediation, organizations can ensure systems and applications are secure and that they are effectively mitigating the risks posed by vulnerabilities.

The vulnerability management activity, Validation of remediation such as Auditing

Vulnerability management is a crucial activity in ensuring the security of an organization's systems and data. One of the key steps in vulnerability management is the validation of remediation, which involves auditing the effectiveness of the remediation measures taken to address identified vulnerabilities. This is similar to a doctor treating a patient's illness. After prescribing a treatment, the doctor would need to monitor the patient's progress and check if the treatment is working effectively. Similarly, in vulnerability management, after identifying and addressing a vulnerability, it is important to validate the remediation measures taken to ensure that the vulnerability has been effectively addressed and the system is secure. Auditing is an important tool in this process, as it helps to identify any gaps or weaknesses in the remediation measures taken and enables organizations to take corrective action to address them. Validation of remediation is a critical step in vulnerability management, which involves auditing the effectiveness of the remediation measures taken to address identified vulnerabilities. The validation process involves testing the remediation measures taken to ensure that they have been implemented correctly and are working as intended. This is similar to a doctor treating a patient's illness. After prescribing a treatment, the doctor would need to monitor the patient's progress and check if the treatment is working effectively. Similarly, in vulnerability management, after identifying and addressing a vulnerability, it is important to validate the remediation measures taken to ensure that the vulnerability has been effectively addressed and the system is secure. Auditing is an important tool in this process, as it helps to identify any gaps or weaknesses in the remediation measures taken and enables organizations to take corrective action to address them.

The vulnerability management activity, Validation of remediation such as Verification

Vulnerability management is a crucial activity in cybersecurity that involves identifying, assessing, and mitigating vulnerabilities in an organization's systems and applications. One of the key steps in vulnerability management is the validation of remediation, which involves verifying that the remediation measures taken to address identified vulnerabilities have been effective in mitigating the risks. This step is analogous to a doctor who prescribes medication to a patient to treat an illness. After the patient has taken the medication, the doctor needs to verify that the medication has been effective in treating the illness by checking the patient's symptoms and conducting tests. Similarly, in vulnerability management, the validation of remediation involves verifying that the remediation measures have been effective in mitigating the identified vulnerabilities by conducting tests and assessments to ensure that the vulnerabilities have been addressed and the risks have been reduced.

The vulnerability management activity, Validation of remediation such as Reporting

Vulnerability management is a process that involves identifying, assessing, and mitigating vulnerabilities in an organization's systems and applications. One of the key activities in vulnerability management is the validation of remediation, which involves verifying that the identified vulnerabilities have been properly addressed and mitigated. This activity is similar to a doctor checking up on a patient after a surgery to ensure that the patient is healing properly and that there are no complications. Once the remediation has been validated, the next step is reporting, which involves documenting the vulnerabilities that were identified, the actions taken to remediate them, and any residual risks that may still exist. This is similar to a doctor's report that summarizes the patient's condition, the surgery that was performed, and any follow-up care that may be required. The reporting phase is important for maintaining an accurate record of vulnerabilities and remediation efforts, and for providing stakeholders with the information they need to make informed decisions about risk management.

Security alerting and monitoring concepts such as, Monitoring computing resources

Security alerting and monitoring concepts are essential in ensuring the security of computing resources. Monitoring computing resources is like having a security guard who keeps watch over a building. Just as a security guard monitors the building for any suspicious activity, monitoring computing resources involves keeping an eye on the system for any unusual behavior or activity that could indicate a security breach. This is done by collecting and analyzing data from various sources, such as logs, metrics, and events, to identify potential security threats. Security alerts are then generated to notify security personnel of any suspicious activity, allowing them to take appropriate action to prevent or mitigate any potential security incidents. In summary, monitoring computing resources is like having a security guard who keeps watch over a building, while security alerts are like alarms that notify security personnel of any suspicious activity.

Monitoring computing resources such as, Systems
Monitoring computing resources refers to the process of keeping track of the usage and performance of computer systems. It involves collecting data on various aspects of the system, such as CPU usage, memory usage, network traffic, and disk usage, among others. This data is then analyzed to identify any issues or anomalies that may indicate a security breach or other problems. An analogy for monitoring computing resources could be monitoring the vital signs of a patient in a hospital. Just as doctors and nurses monitor a patient's heart rate, blood pressure, and other vital signs to ensure that they are healthy and functioning properly, monitoring computing resources involves keeping track of the various metrics that indicate the health and performance of a computer system. By monitoring these metrics, IT professionals can identify any issues or anomalies that may indicate a problem and take appropriate action to address them before they become more serious.

Monitoring computing resources such as, Applications
Monitoring computing resources such as applications is an important aspect of cybersecurity. It involves keeping track of the performance and usage of applications to ensure that they are functioning as intended and to detect any potential security issues. An analogy to understand this concept is to think of a car dashboard. The dashboard provides information about the car's performance, such as speed, fuel level, and engine temperature. Similarly, monitoring computing resources provides information about the performance of applications, such as CPU usage, memory usage, and network traffic. Just as a driver needs to keep an eye on the dashboard to ensure that the car is running smoothly, cybersecurity professionals need to monitor computing resources to ensure that applications are running smoothly and securely. Monitoring computing resources is an essential aspect of cybersecurity, and it involves keeping track of the performance and usage of applications to ensure that they are functioning as intended and to detect any potential security issues.

Monitoring computing resources such as, Infrastructure

Monitoring computing resources such as infrastructure refers to the process of observing and tracking the performance and usage of hardware and software components that make up a computing system. This includes monitoring the health and availability of servers, network devices, storage systems, and applications. An analogy to understand this concept is to think of a car dashboard. Just as a driver monitors the speed, fuel level, and other indicators on the dashboard to ensure the car is running smoothly, monitoring computing resources involves tracking various metrics to ensure that the system is functioning optimally. For example, just as a driver may notice a warning light indicating low fuel and take action to refuel, monitoring computing resources can alert administrators to potential issues such as high CPU usage or low disk space, allowing them to take corrective action before a problem occurs.

Alerting and monitoring activities such as, Log aggregation

Alerting and monitoring activities are crucial components of a security system. Log aggregation is a process of collecting and centralizing logs from various sources in a single location. It is similar to collecting puzzle pieces from different places and putting them together to form a complete picture. Log aggregation helps in identifying security incidents, analyzing system performance, and detecting anomalies. Once the logs are aggregated, they can be monitored and analyzed to identify patterns and trends. Alerting is the process of notifying security personnel when a specific event or condition occurs. It is like a smoke detector that alerts you when there is a fire. Alerting can be triggered by predefined rules or thresholds, and it can be customized to meet specific security requirements. Together, log aggregation and alerting provide a comprehensive security monitoring solution that helps organizations detect and respond to security incidents in a timely manner.

Alerting and monitoring activities such as, Alerting
Alerting and monitoring activities are crucial components of a security system, as they help to detect and respond to security incidents in a timely manner. Monitoring involves the continuous observation of system logs, network traffic, and other security-related events to identify potential security threats. It is similar to a security guard who patrols a building to detect any suspicious activity. Alerting, on the other hand, refers to the process of notifying security personnel or system administrators when a security event occurs. It is similar to a fire alarm that alerts occupants of a building when there is a fire. Alerting can be done through various means such as email, SMS, or phone calls. Once an alert is received, security personnel can take appropriate action to mitigate the risk and prevent further damage. Overall, alerting and monitoring activities are essential for maintaining the security of an organization's systems and data.

Alerting and monitoring activities such as, Scanning
Alerting and monitoring activities are crucial components of a security system. They help to detect and respond to security threats in a timely manner. Scanning is one of the monitoring activities that can be used to identify vulnerabilities in a system. It is similar to a doctor performing a routine check-up on a patient to identify any potential health issues. Just as a doctor uses various tools and techniques to examine a patient's body, a security system can use scanning tools to examine a network or system for vulnerabilities. Scanning can be performed manually or automatically, and can be used to identify open ports, misconfigured systems, and other potential security risks. Once vulnerabilities are identified, appropriate measures can be taken to address them and prevent potential security breaches.

Alerting and monitoring activities such as, Reporting

Alerting and monitoring activities such as reporting are essential components of a security system. Reporting can be compared to a weather forecast, where meteorologists use various tools and techniques to gather data and provide information about potential weather events. Similarly, a security system can use reporting tools to gather data about security events and provide information about potential security threats. Reporting can be performed manually or automatically, and can be used to identify security incidents, track security trends, and provide insights into the overall security posture of an organization. Once security incidents are identified, appropriate measures can be taken to address them and prevent potential security breaches. Automated reporting systems can also be used to generate alerts for technical staff, allowing them to respond to security incidents in a timely manner.

Alerting and monitoring activities such as, Archiving

Alerting and monitoring activities such as archiving are important components of a security system. Archiving can be compared to a library, where books are stored and organized for future reference. Similarly, a security system can use archiving tools to store and organize security-related data for future analysis. Archiving can be performed manually or automatically, and can be used to store logs, network traffic data, and other security-related information. This data can be used to identify security incidents, track security trends, and provide insights into the overall security posture of an organization. Archiving can also be used to comply with legal and regulatory requirements, as it provides a record of security-related activities that can be used for auditing and compliance purposes. Automated archiving systems can also be used to ensure that data is stored securely and is easily accessible when needed.

Alerting and monitoring activities such as, Alert response and remediation/ validation

Alert response and remediation/validation are important components of a security system. Alert response can be compared to a fire alarm, where the alarm is triggered when smoke or fire is detected, and the occupants of the building are alerted to evacuate. Similarly, a security system can use alerting tools to detect and notify security personnel about potential security incidents. Once an alert is triggered, appropriate measures can be taken to investigate and respond to the incident. Remediation/validation can be compared to a firefighter extinguishing a fire and ensuring that the building is safe to re-enter. Similarly, a security system can use remediation/validation tools to address security incidents and ensure that the system is secure and functioning properly. This can involve patching vulnerabilities, removing malware, and restoring data from backups. Validation can also be used to ensure that the system is functioning as expected and that the security incident has been fully resolved. Automated alert response and remediation/validation systems can help to ensure that security incidents are addressed in a timely and effective manner.

Alerting and monitoring activities such as, Quarantine

Alerting and monitoring activities are crucial in maintaining the security of an organization's network. They involve the use of tools and techniques to detect and respond to security incidents. An analogy for this would be a security guard who is constantly monitoring a building for any suspicious activity. If the guard detects any suspicious activity, they will alert the authorities and take appropriate action to prevent any harm. Similarly, in the context of network security, monitoring tools such as intrusion detection systems (IDS) and security information and event management (SIEM) systems are used to detect any suspicious activity on the network. If any suspicious activity is detected, the system will generate an alert, and the security team can take appropriate action, such as quarantining the affected system to prevent further damage. Quarantine is a security measure that isolates a system or network from the rest of the network to prevent the spread of malware or other security threats. It is similar to isolating a sick person to prevent the spread of a contagious disease.

Alerting and monitoring activities such as, Alert tuning

Alert tuning is the process of configuring alerts to ensure that they are triggered only when necessary and not too frequently. It is similar to tuning a musical instrument, where the goal is to adjust the strings to produce the desired sound. In the same way, alert tuning involves adjusting the parameters of alerts to produce the desired outcome. This process involves setting thresholds for alerts, specifying the conditions that trigger alerts, and determining the appropriate response to each alert. Alert tuning helps to reduce the number of false positives and false negatives, ensuring that alerts are triggered only when there is a genuine security threat. Effective alert tuning is essential for efficient incident response and helps to minimize the impact of security incidents.

Alerting and monitoring tools such as, Security Content Automation Protocol (SCAP)

Security Content Automation Protocol (SCAP) is a set of standards and specifications that help organizations automate the process of monitoring and assessing the security of their systems. SCAP is like a toolbox that contains various tools that can be used to check the security of a system. Just as a mechanic uses different tools to diagnose and fix a car, security professionals use different SCAP tools to identify and fix security vulnerabilities. SCAP tools can scan systems for vulnerabilities, check for compliance with security policies, and generate reports on security status. These tools can be used to automate security monitoring and alerting activities, making it easier to detect and respond to security threats. SCAP is an important component of a comprehensive security program and helps organizations to maintain a strong security posture.

Alerting and monitoring tools such as, Benchmarks

Alerting and monitoring tools are essential components of a security system. They help to detect and respond to security incidents in a timely manner. Benchmarks are used to establish a baseline for the performance of a system. They are like a thermometer that measures the temperature of a person. Just as a thermometer helps to identify when a person has a fever, benchmarks help to identify when a system is not performing as expected. Alerting tools are like smoke detectors that alert people when there is a fire. They notify security personnel when a security incident occurs, allowing them to take appropriate action. Monitoring tools are like security cameras that record activity in a building. They provide visibility into the system, allowing security personnel to identify potential security threats and take proactive measures to prevent them. Together, alerting and monitoring tools, along with benchmarks, provide a comprehensive security system that helps to protect against security threats.

Alerting and monitoring tools such as, Agents/agentless

Alerting and monitoring tools such as agents/agentless are used to detect and respond to security incidents in a timely manner. Agents are like security guards that are stationed at specific locations to monitor and report any suspicious activity. They are installed on the system being monitored and collect data on system performance and security events. Agentless monitoring, on the other hand, is like a drone that flies over a large area to monitor and report any suspicious activity. It does not require installation on the system being monitored and collects data remotely. Both agents and agentless monitoring tools collect data from various sources, including network traffic, system event logs, and user activity. They then analyze the data for signs of suspicious or abnormal activity. If a potential security threat is detected, the monitoring tool will generate an alert to take appropriate action. To be effective, monitoring tools must be constantly updated with the latest security intelligence. They must also integrate with other security tools, such as intrusion detection systems (IDS) and firewalls. This allows for a more comprehensive view of an organization's security posture and helps to ensure that potential threats are not missed.

Alerting and monitoring tools such as, Security information and event management (SIEM)

Security information and event management (SIEM) is a type of alerting and monitoring tool that is used to detect and respond to security incidents in a timely manner. SIEM is like a security camera system that records activity in a building and alerts security personnel when there is suspicious activity. SIEM collects data from various sources, including network traffic, system event logs, and user activity. It then analyzes the data for signs of suspicious or abnormal activity. If a potential security threat is detected, the SIEM tool will generate an alert to take appropriate action. SIEM solutions provide real-time analysis and alerts of security events through dashboards that display charts, graphs, and reports in a user-friendly manner. They also provide customizable, real-time alerts. SIEM solutions are equipped to perform forensic analysis, data aggregation, and correlation of events in real-time. Since log data retention is important for analysis, SIEM solutions often employ some form of long-term storage mechanism as well. SIEM is an essential component of a comprehensive security system that helps to protect against security threats.

Alerting and monitoring tools such as, Antivirus

Alerting and monitoring tools are essential components of a security system. They help to detect and respond to security threats in real-time. Antivirus is an example of an alerting and monitoring tool that is used to protect computer systems from malware. It works by scanning files and programs for known patterns of malicious code. If a match is found, the antivirus software will alert the user and take appropriate action to remove the threat. This is similar to how a security guard at a museum would monitor visitors for suspicious behavior. If they notice someone acting suspiciously, they would alert other guards and take appropriate action to prevent any damage to the museum's exhibits. Similarly, antivirus software monitors computer systems for suspicious activity and alerts the user to take appropriate action to prevent any damage to the system.

Alerting and monitoring tools such as, Data loss prevention (DLP)

Alerting and monitoring tools are essential for detecting and responding to security incidents. One such tool is Data Loss Prevention (DLP), which can be compared to a security guard at a museum. Just as a security guard monitors the museum to prevent theft or damage to valuable artifacts, DLP tools monitor an organization's data to prevent unauthorized access, use, or transmission of sensitive information. DLP tools can detect and prevent data breaches by monitoring data in motion, data at rest, and data in use. They can also alert security teams when sensitive data is being accessed or transmitted in an unauthorized manner, allowing them to take immediate action to prevent data loss or theft.

Alerting and monitoring tools such as, Simple network Management Protocol (SNMP) traps

Alerting and monitoring tools are essential for maintaining the security of a network. Simple Network Management Protocol (SNMP) traps are one such tool that can be used to monitor network devices and alert administrators to potential security issues. SNMP traps work by sending notifications to a central management system when certain events occur, such as a device going offline or a security threshold being exceeded. This is similar to a smoke detector in a house, which sends an alert to the homeowner when it detects smoke, allowing them to take action to prevent a fire. Similarly, SNMP traps allow network administrators to quickly identify and respond to potential security threats, helping to keep the network safe and secure.

Alerting and monitoring tools such as, NetFlow

Alerting and monitoring tools are essential for detecting and responding to security incidents. NetFlow is a tool that provides network traffic visibility by capturing and analyzing network packets. It can be compared to a security camera that records and monitors activity in a building. Just as a security camera can help identify intruders or suspicious activity, NetFlow can help identify network anomalies and potential security threats. By analyzing network traffic patterns, NetFlow can provide insights into network performance, identify potential security breaches, and help security teams respond quickly to incidents. Alerting and monitoring tools such as NetFlow are critical components of a comprehensive security strategy.

Alerting and monitoring tools such as, Vulnerability scanners

Alerting and monitoring tools are essential components of a security system. They help to detect and respond to security incidents in real-time. Vulnerability scanners are one such tool that is used to identify vulnerabilities in a system. They work by scanning the system for known vulnerabilities and reporting them to the security team. This is similar to a doctor performing a routine check-up on a patient to identify any health issues. Just as a doctor uses various tools to check the patient's vital signs, a vulnerability scanner uses various techniques to identify vulnerabilities in a system. Once the vulnerabilities are identified, the security team can take appropriate action to mitigate the risk and prevent any potential security incidents.

Enhancing Security with Firewalls

A firewall is a security device that acts as a barrier between a trusted internal network and an untrusted external network, such as the internet. It monitors and controls incoming and outgoing network traffic based on predetermined security rules. Think of a firewall as a security guard at the entrance of a building. The security guard checks the identification of everyone who wants to enter the building and only allows authorized personnel to pass through. Similarly, a firewall checks the source and destination of network traffic and only allows authorized traffic to pass through while blocking unauthorized traffic. Firewalls can be hardware or software-based and are an essential component of network security.

Enhancing Security with Firewall Rules
Firewall rules are used to enhance security by controlling the traffic that enters or leaves a network. Firewall rules are like a security guard at the entrance of a building who checks the identification of people entering and leaving the building. The firewall rules are set up to allow or block traffic based on specific criteria such as IP address, port number, protocol, and application. By using firewall rules, network administrators can prevent unauthorized access to the network and protect against various types of cyber attacks such as malware, viruses, and hacking attempts.

Enhancing Security with Firewall Access lists
Firewall access lists are a security mechanism that can be used to enhance security by filtering network traffic based on a set of predefined rules. Access lists can be thought of as a bouncer at a nightclub who checks the ID of each person trying to enter and only allows those who meet the criteria to enter. Similarly, firewall access lists check the source and destination IP addresses, ports, and protocols of network traffic and only allow traffic that meets the criteria specified in the access list. This helps to prevent unauthorized access to a network and protect against various types of attacks, such as denial-of-service attacks and port scanning.

Enhancing Security with Firewall Ports/protocols

Firewalls are security devices that control access to a network by filtering traffic based on predefined rules. Firewall rules can be configured to allow or block traffic based on the source and destination IP addresses, ports, and protocols. Ports and protocols are like doors and keys, respectively. Just as a door can be locked or unlocked with a key, a port can be open or closed to allow or block traffic. Similarly, protocols define the rules for communication between devices, just as keys define the rules for opening doors. By configuring firewall rules to allow only necessary ports and protocols, organizations can enhance their security posture by reducing the attack surface and preventing unauthorized access to their network.

Enhancing Security with Firewall Screened subnets

A screened subnet is a security architecture that uses a firewall to create a secure zone between two networks. The firewall is configured to allow only authorized traffic to pass through to the internal network, while blocking all other traffic. This creates a buffer zone that acts as a barrier between the internal network and the external network, similar to a security checkpoint at an airport. The screened subnet architecture provides an additional layer of security to the network by isolating critical resources from the public-facing network. This helps to prevent unauthorized access to sensitive data and systems, and reduces the risk of attacks from external threats.

Enhancing Security with IDS/IPS
In computer security, an Intrusion Detection System (IDS) and Intrusion Prevention System (IPS) are security technologies that monitor network traffic for suspicious activity and take action to prevent or block it. An IDS is like a security camera that records and alerts security personnel when it detects suspicious activity, while an IPS is like a security guard who not only detects suspicious activity but also takes action to prevent it. IDS/IPS can help enhance security by detecting and preventing attacks that may bypass other security measures, such as firewalls and antivirus software. They can also provide valuable information for incident response and forensic analysis.

Enhancing Security with IDS/IPS Trends
In the world of cybersecurity, Intrusion Detection Systems (IDS) and Intrusion Prevention Systems (IPS) are like security cameras and security guards in a building. IDS monitors network traffic and alerts security personnel when it detects suspicious activity, while IPS takes action to block or prevent the suspicious activity from happening. The trend in enhancing security with IDS/IPS is to use machine learning and artificial intelligence to improve the accuracy of detecting and preventing attacks. This includes using behavioral analysis to identify patterns of activity that may indicate an attack, and automating the response to quickly and effectively mitigate the threat. Additionally, cloud-based IDS/IPS solutions are becoming more popular, allowing for centralized management and scalability across multiple locations.

Enhancing Security with IDS/IPS Signatures

In computer security, Intrusion Detection Systems (IDS) and Intrusion Prevention Systems (IPS) are used to detect and prevent unauthorized access to computer networks. IDS/IPS signatures are like fingerprints that are used to identify specific types of attacks. Just as a fingerprint can be used to identify a person, an IDS/IPS signature can be used to identify a specific type of attack. By using these signatures, IDS/IPS systems can detect and prevent attacks before they can cause damage to the network, just as a security guard can prevent a person from entering a building if their fingerprint does not match the authorized personnel.

Enhancing Security with Web filters

Enhancing security with web filters is a technique used to protect networks from malicious traffic by filtering out unwanted content. It is similar to a bouncer at a nightclub who checks the IDs of people entering the club to ensure that only authorized individuals are allowed in. Web filters work by examining the content of web traffic and blocking access to websites or content that are deemed harmful or inappropriate. This technique can be used to prevent malware infections, phishing attacks, and other types of cyber threats. By implementing web filters, organizations can reduce the risk of security breaches and protect their sensitive data. Web filters are a security mechanism used to protect networks from malicious traffic by filtering out unwanted content. They work by examining the content of web traffic and blocking access to websites or content that are deemed harmful or inappropriate. Web filters can be used to prevent malware infections, phishing attacks, and other types of cyber threats. They are similar to content filters, which allow or block traffic based on the data that's inside of the packets. Web filters are like a bouncer at a nightclub who checks the IDs of people entering the club to ensure that only authorized individuals are allowed in. By implementing web filters, organizations can reduce the risk of security breaches and protect their sensitive data.

Enhancing Security with Web filter Agent-based
Enhancing security with a web filter agent-based is like
having a security guard at the entrance of a building
who checks everyone's ID before allowing them to
enter. The web filter agent-based acts as a security
guard for a network, filtering out unwanted traffic and
allowing only authorized traffic to pass through. It
monitors and filters web traffic based on predefined
rules and policies, blocking access to malicious
websites and preventing users from downloading
harmful content. This helps to protect the network from
cyber threats and ensures that users are only accessing
safe and appropriate content. Web filter agent-based is
a type of web filtering that uses an agent installed on
the endpoint device to monitor and filter web traffic. The
agent is responsible for enforcing web filtering policies
and blocking access to malicious websites. It can also
prevent users from downloading harmful content and
monitor web traffic based on predefined rules. This type
of web filtering is effective in protecting the network
from cyber threats and ensuring that users are only
accessing safe and appropriate content. It is like having
a security guard at the entrance of a building who
checks everyone's ID before allowing them to enter.
The web filter agent-based acts as a security guard for
a network, filtering out unwanted traffic and allowing
only authorized traffic to pass through.

Enhancing Security with Web filter Centralized proxy

Enhancing security with a web filter centralized proxy is like having a security checkpoint at the entrance of a building where everyone has to go through a metal detector and have their bags checked. The centralized proxy acts as a security checkpoint for a network, filtering out unwanted traffic and allowing only authorized traffic to pass through. It is a type of web filtering that uses a centralized server to monitor and filter web traffic. The server is responsible for enforcing web filtering policies and blocking access to malicious websites. It can also prevent users from downloading harmful content and monitor web traffic based on predefined rules. This type of web filtering is effective in protecting the network from cyber threats and ensuring that users are only accessing safe and appropriate content. It provides centralized management, advanced logging, and analytics capabilities, empowering organizations to protect their networks against cyber threats. Web filter centralized proxy is a type of web filtering that uses a centralized server to monitor and filter web traffic. The server acts as a security checkpoint for a network, filtering out unwanted traffic and allowing only authorized traffic to pass through. It is like having a security checkpoint at the entrance of a building where everyone has to go through a metal detector and have their bags checked. The centralized proxy is responsible for enforcing web filtering policies and blocking access to malicious websites. It can also prevent users from downloading harmful content and monitor web traffic based on predefined rules. This type of web filtering provides centralized management, advanced logging, and analytics capabilities, empowering organizations to protect their networks against cyber threats. It is effective in protecting the network from cyber threats and ensuring that users are only accessing safe and appropriate content.

Enhancing Security with Web filter Universal Resource Locator (URL) scanning

Web filter Universal Resource Locator (URL) scanning is a type of web filtering that scans URLs to determine if they are safe or not. A URL is a web address that precisely displays where a user is on the internet, specifying its location on a computer network. URL filtering is like a bouncer at a nightclub who checks the ID of everyone who wants to enter. The URL scanning feature checks the URL against a database of known malicious ones and blocks access to websites or web pages that are known to contain malware and resort to phishing attempts, thereby greatly reducing the exposure to these infections. It can also be used to block access to websites that are productivity drains, such as gaming and social media sites. URL filtering is a powerful mechanism to block access to malicious websites and is increasingly becoming one of the most preferred tools to leverage and ensure better organizational security. It is an effective way to keep security threats at bay and is among the most common security practices that restrict employees' access to certain websites that can prove to be a major threat to the organization's safety.

Enhancing Security with Web filter Content categorization

Web filter content categorization is a security measure that enhances security by filtering web traffic based on the content of the web pages being accessed. It is similar to a librarian who categorizes books based on their content and allows only authorized users to access certain books. In the same way, web filter content categorization categorizes web pages based on their content and allows only authorized users to access certain web pages. This security measure helps prevent users from accessing malicious or inappropriate content and protects against web-based attacks. Web filter content categorization is a security measure that filters web traffic based on the content of the web pages being accessed. It is used to prevent users from accessing malicious or inappropriate content and protect against web-based attacks. Web filter content categorization can be compared to a librarian who categorizes books based on their content and allows only authorized users to access certain books. Similarly, web filter content categorization categorizes web pages based on their content and allows only authorized users to access certain web pages. This security measure can be implemented using different methods such as URL scanning, content categorization, block rules, and reputation.

Enhancing Security with Web filter Block rules

Web filter block rules are a security measure that can be used to enhance security in an organization. These rules are used to block access to specific websites or web content that may pose a security risk to the organization. It is similar to a bouncer at a club who checks the ID of people trying to enter and denies entry to those who do not meet the criteria. By using web filter block rules, an organization can prevent employees from accessing websites that may contain malware, phishing scams, or other malicious content. This helps to reduce the risk of a security breach and protect sensitive information. Web filter block rules are a security measure used to block access to specific websites or web content that may pose a security risk to an organization. These rules can be implemented using a variety of methods such as URL filtering, content filtering, and reputation-based filtering. URL filtering blocks access to specific websites based on their URL, while content filtering blocks access to specific types of content such as images, videos, or documents. Reputation-based filtering blocks access to websites that have a history of malicious activity. By using web filter block rules, an organization can prevent employees from accessing websites that may contain malware, phishing scams, or other malicious content. This helps to reduce the risk of a security breach and protect sensitive information.

Enhancing Security with Web filter Reputation

Web filter reputation is a security measure that uses website reputation intelligence to block access to websites that have a history of malicious activity. It is similar to a bouncer at a club who checks the reputation of people trying to enter and denies entry to those who have a history of causing trouble. By using web filter reputation, an organization can prevent employees from accessing websites that may contain malware, phishing scams, or other malicious content. This helps to reduce the risk of a security breach and protect sensitive information. Web filtering gateways typically layer multiple security measures, including web reputation, to provide comprehensive protection against web-based threats. Web reputation is a security measure that uses website reputation intelligence to block access to websites that have a history of malicious activity. Web reputation filters provide more granular control for blocking access to websites than reputation filters based merely on domains or IP addresses. By using web reputation, an organization can prevent employees from accessing websites that may contain malware, phishing scams, or other malicious content. This helps to reduce the risk of a security breach and protect sensitive information. Web filtering gateways typically layer multiple security measures, including web reputation, to provide comprehensive protection against web-based threats

---

Enhancing Security with Operating system security
Operating system security is a crucial aspect of enhancing security in an organization. It involves implementing security measures to protect the operating system from unauthorized access, malware, and other threats. Just like a castle with a strong wall and a moat to protect it from invaders, an operating system with strong security measures can protect the organization's data and resources from unauthorized access and malicious attacks. These security measures include access controls, firewalls, antivirus software, intrusion detection and prevention systems, and regular security updates. By implementing these measures, an organization can ensure that its operating system is secure and that its data and resources are protected from potential threats. Operating system security refers to the measures taken to protect the operating system of a computer from unauthorized access, malware, and other threats. It involves implementing security measures such as access controls, firewalls, antivirus software, intrusion detection and prevention systems, and regular security updates. These measures are similar to the locks, alarms, and security cameras used to protect a building from intruders. By implementing these measures, an organization can ensure that its operating system is secure and that its data and resources are protected from potential threats.

Enhancing Security with Operating system security Group Policy

Group Policy is a feature in Windows operating systems that allows administrators to manage and configure security settings for users and computers in a network. It is like a set of rules that govern the behavior of users and computers in a network, similar to how a traffic cop enforces traffic rules on the road. By using Group Policy, administrators can enhance the security of their operating systems by enforcing password policies, restricting access to certain files and folders, and configuring other security settings. This helps to ensure that users and computers in the network are following best security practices and reduces the risk of security breaches. Group Policy is a feature in Microsoft Windows that allows administrators to manage user and computer settings centrally. Group Policy settings are stored in Group Policy Objects (GPOs), which are linked to Active Directory containers, such as domains, sites, and organizational units. Group Policy settings can be used to enforce security policies, such as password complexity requirements, account lockout policies, and software restriction policies. Group Policy can also be used to deploy software, configure network settings, and manage user profiles. By using Group Policy, organizations can ensure that their systems are configured consistently and securely, and that users have access to the resources they need to do their jobs.

Enhancing Security with Operating system security SELinux

SELinux (Security-Enhanced Linux) is a security architecture for Linux systems that allows administrators to have more control over who can access the system. It defines access controls for the applications, processes, and files on a system. SELinux uses security policies, which are a set of rules that tell SELinux what can or can't be accessed, to enforce the access allowed by a policy. SELinux provides an additional layer of security for your system that is built into Linux distributions. It should remain on so that it can protect your system if it is ever compromised. An analogy for SELinux could be a security guard at a building entrance. The security guard checks the identification of people entering the building and only allows authorized personnel to enter. Similarly, SELinux checks the access requests of applications, processes, and files and only allows authorized access based on the security policies.

Enhancing Security with the Implementation of secure protocols

Enhancing security with the implementation of secure protocols is like building a secure tunnel for data transmission. Secure protocols are a set of rules that ensure secure communication between two parties. Just like a tunnel provides a secure path for transportation, secure protocols provide a secure path for data transmission. These protocols use encryption techniques to protect data from unauthorized access and ensure that the data is transmitted securely. Implementing secure protocols such as HTTPS, SSL, and TLS can help prevent data breaches and protect sensitive information from being intercepted by attackers. By using secure protocols, organizations can ensure that their data is transmitted securely and that their systems are protected from cyber threats.

Enhancing Security with the Implementation of secure protocols such as Port selection

Secure protocols are used to ensure secure communication over a network. According to CompTIA Security+ 701, secure protocols are used to secure phone conversations, email, file transfers, directory services, and other types of communication. Some of the most common secure protocols include:
IPsec (Internet Protocol Security): This protocol allows you to send information across a public internet but encrypts the data so that all of that information remains confidential. If you're implementing an IPsec tunnel, you'll be using two main protocols: the Authentication Header (AH), which provides the integrity, and the Encapsulation Security Payload (ESP), which provides the encryption.
SSL/TLS (Secure Sockets Layer/Transport Layer Security): This protocol is used to secure communication between web browsers and servers. SSL/TLS encrypts data in transit to prevent eavesdropping and tampering.
SRTP (Secure Real-time Transport Protocol): This protocol is used to secure phone calls and video calls over a network. SRTP adds encryption using AES to make sure that all the video and audio is confidential as it goes through the network. SRTP also includes authentication, integrity, and replay protection by including HMAC-SHA1 as a hashing function. It is

important to use secure protocols to protect sensitive information from unauthorized access.

Enhancing Security with the Implementation of secure protocols such as the Transport method

Secure protocols are an essential part of enhancing security in a network. They are like a secret code that only the sender and receiver can understand, ensuring that the information transmitted is confidential. For example, imagine that you are sending a message to your friend, but you don't want anyone else to read it. You could use a secure protocol to encrypt the message, making it unreadable to anyone who intercepts it. Only your friend, who has the key to decrypt the message, can read it. Implementing secure protocols such as the Transport method can help protect sensitive information from unauthorized access and ensure that communication remains confidential.

Enhancing Security with DNS filtering

DNS filtering is a security mechanism that helps to protect against malicious activities by blocking access to known malicious domains. It works by filtering out unwanted traffic based on domain names. It is similar to a bouncer at a nightclub who checks the ID of each person before allowing them to enter. The bouncer only allows people who are on the guest list and denies entry to those who are not. Similarly, DNS filtering checks the domain name of each incoming traffic and only allows access to domains that are on the whitelist while blocking access to domains that are on the blacklist. This helps to prevent malware, phishing, and other cyber attacks that rely on communication with malicious domains. By enhancing security with DNS filtering, organizations can reduce the risk of cyber attacks and protect their sensitive data.

Enhancing Email Security security through Domain-based Message Authentication Reporting and Conformance (DMARC)

Domain-based Message Authentication Reporting and Conformance (DMARC) is an email authentication protocol that enhances email security by validating the sender's identity and preventing email fraud and phishing attacks. DMARC combines Sender Policy Framework (SPF) and DomainKeys Identified Mail (DKIM) authentication methods to verify email alignment and specify how incoming email should be authenticated and handled by the recipient's email servers. DMARC allows domain owners to gain control over the emails being sent on their behalf and safeguard their domains against email spoofing and phishing attacks. DMARC enhances email security by providing reporting and enabling organizations to enforce policies that protect against phishing and spoofing. An analogy for DMARC is a bouncer at a club who checks the ID of each person before allowing them to enter. Similarly, DMARC checks the identity of each incoming email and only allows legitimate emails to enter while blocking fraudulent ones. Domain-based Message Authentication Reporting and Conformance (DMARC) is an email authentication protocol designed to protect email domains from unauthorized use, commonly known as email spoofing. DMARC extends two existing email authentication mechanisms, Sender Policy Framework (SPF) and DomainKeys Identified Mail (DKIM), by allowing the administrative owner of a domain to publish a policy in their DNS records to specify how to check the From: field presented to end-users and how the receiver should deal with failures. DMARC also provides a reporting mechanism for actions performed under those policies. DMARC is defined in the Internet Engineering Task Force's published document RFC 7489, dated March 2015, as "Informational." By implementing DMARC, organizations can protect their email domains from being used in business email compromise attacks, phishing email, email scams, and other cyber threat activities. DMARC is an important component of email security and helps to prevent email spoofing and phishing attacks.

Enhancing Email Security security through DomainKeys Identified Mail (DKIM)

DomainKeys Identified Mail (DKIM) is an email authentication protocol that enhances email security by verifying the authenticity of the sender's domain name and preventing email spoofing and phishing attacks. DKIM works by adding a digital signature to the email header that verifies the message's integrity and authenticity. The signature is generated using a private key that is stored on the sender's mail server and can be verified using a public key that is published in the sender's DNS record. DKIM enhances email security by providing a mechanism for email recipients to verify that the email was sent by the domain owner and has not been tampered with during transmission. An analogy for DKIM is a wax seal on a letter that ensures the letter has not been opened or tampered with during transit.

Enhancing Email Security security through Sender Policy Framework (SPF)

Sender Policy Framework (SPF) is an email authentication protocol that enhances email security by verifying the sender's identity and preventing email spoofing and phishing attacks. SPF works by allowing domain owners to publish a list of authorized mail servers in their DNS records. When an email is received, the recipient's email server checks the SPF record of the sender's domain to verify that the email was sent from an authorized mail server. If the email was sent from an unauthorized mail server, it is likely to be fraudulent and can be rejected or marked as spam. An analogy for SPF is a bouncer at a club who checks the ID of each person before allowing them to enter. Similarly, SPF checks the identity of each incoming email and only allows legitimate emails to enter while blocking fraudulent ones.

Enhancing Email Security security through Gateway

An email gateway is a type of email server that acts as a gateway through which every incoming and outgoing email passes through. It is designed to prevent unwanted email and deliver good email. Email gateway protection helps to block malware, phishing attacks, spam emails, and a host of other unwanted email-borne threats from reaching recipients and compromising their devices, user credentials, email systems, or sensitive data. An analogy for an email gateway is a security checkpoint at an airport that checks every passenger and their luggage before allowing them to board the plane. Similarly, an email gateway checks every incoming and outgoing email and only allows legitimate emails to pass while blocking fraudulent ones. By using a secure email gateway, organizations can enhance their security posture with greater control, policy management, and customized protection. A gateway is a device or software that acts as an entry point between two networks, allowing traffic to flow between them. A gateway can be a hardware device, such as a router or firewall, or a software application, such as a proxy server. The primary function of a gateway is to provide security by filtering traffic and enforcing access controls. Gateways can also provide other security features, such as intrusion detection and prevention, antivirus and antimalware protection, and content filtering. By using gateways, organizations can protect their networks from unauthorized access, data breaches, and other security incidents.

Enhancing Security with File integrity monitoring

File integrity monitoring (FIM) is a security mechanism that enhances security by monitoring and verifying the integrity of critical files and directories. FIM works by continuously scanning and monitoring files for any unauthorized changes or modifications that could lead to data loss, business disruptions, or security breaches. FIM provides an essential layer of protection for sensitive files, data, applications, and devices by detecting and alerting security teams to any unauthorized changes. An analogy for FIM is a security guard who patrols a building and checks every door and window to ensure that they are locked and secure. Similarly, FIM checks every file and directory to ensure that they are secure and have not been tampered with. By investing in the right FIM tools and following best practices, organizations can instantly flag changes, determine whether they are authorized, and take action to prevent a security incident.

Enhancing Security with Data loss Prevention (DLP)

Data loss prevention (DLP) is a security mechanism that enhances security by preventing sensitive data from being accessed, misused, or lost by unauthorized users. DLP works by monitoring and controlling data in motion, data at rest, and data in use. It uses a combination of content inspection and contextual analysis to detect and prevent data breaches. DLP provides an essential layer of protection for sensitive data by identifying, classifying, and protecting it from unauthorized access, sharing, or theft. An analogy for DLP is a security guard who patrols a building and checks every door and window to ensure that they are locked and secure. Similarly, DLP checks every data access point to ensure that sensitive data is secure and has not been tampered with. By investing in the right DLP tools and following best practices, organizations can instantly flag unauthorized access, determine whether it is authorized, and take action to prevent a security incident.

Enhancing Security with Network access control (NAC)

Network access control (NAC) is a security mechanism that enhances security by controlling access to a network and enforcing security policies. NAC works by verifying the identity of devices and users that are trying to access the network and ensuring that they comply with a defined security policy. NAC provides an essential layer of protection for networks by preventing unauthorized access, reducing the risk of malware infections, and enforcing compliance with security policies. An analogy for NAC is a security guard who checks the ID of each person before allowing them to enter a building. Similarly, NAC checks the identity of each device and user that is trying to access the network and only allows legitimate ones to enter while blocking unauthorized ones. By investing in the right NAC tools and following best practices, organizations can instantly flag unauthorized access, determine whether it is authorized, and take action to prevent a security incident.

Enhancing Security with Endpoint detection and response

Endpoint detection and response (EDR) is a security mechanism that enhances security by providing real-time monitoring and advanced analytics to detect and respond to threats at the endpoint level. EDR works by continuously monitoring endpoints such as laptops, desktops, and mobile devices for suspicious activities and potential security incidents. It provides an essential layer of protection for endpoints by detecting and responding to threats in real-time, minimizing their impact, and preventing data loss. An analogy for EDR is a security camera that continuously monitors a building for any suspicious activities and alerts security personnel in real-time. Similarly, EDR continuously monitors endpoints for any suspicious activities and alerts security teams in real-time, enabling them to take immediate action to prevent a security incident. By investing in the right EDR tools and following best practices, organizations can enhance their security posture with greater visibility, context, and early threat detection capabilities.

Enhancing Security with Endpoint detection and response (EDR)/extended detection and response (XDR)

Endpoint detection and response (EDR) and extended detection and response (XDR) are security solutions that provide advanced threat detection and response capabilities. EDR is like a security camera that monitors and records activity on a computer or device, while XDR is like a network of security cameras that monitor and record activity across multiple devices and networks. These solutions use advanced analytics and machine learning to detect and respond to threats in real-time, providing organizations with greater visibility and control over their security posture. By enhancing security with EDR/XDR, organizations can better protect their assets and data from cyber threats.

Enhancing Security with User behavior analytics

User behavior analytics (UBA) is a security solution that focuses on monitoring and analyzing user behavior to detect and prevent potential security incidents. UBA is like a security guard who monitors and analyzes the behavior of people entering and exiting a building to identify any suspicious activity. By establishing baselines of normal user behavior and identifying deviations from these baselines, UBA can quickly flag any suspicious activities, such as unauthorized data access or unusual data transfers, helping organizations prevent potential insider threats. UBA can adapt to evolving threats and changing patterns of behavior, allowing security systems to stay up to date and respond effectively to emerging risks. By enhancing security with UBA, organizations can improve threat detection capabilities, enhance incident response, and strengthen their overall security posture.

Enforcing identity and access management with Provisioning/de-provisioning useraccounts

Enforcing identity and access management with provisioning/de-provisioning user accounts is a critical security measure that helps organizations manage user access to resources and data. Provisioning is like issuing a badge to an employee that grants them access to certain areas of a building, while de-provisioning is like revoking that badge when the employee no longer needs access. By automating the provisioning and de-provisioning of user accounts, organizations can ensure that users have access to the resources they need to do their jobs, while also preventing unauthorized access. This process helps to maintain consistency across digital identities and ensures that access is granted based on specific conditions. Additionally, privileged identity management (PIM) provides time-based and approval-based role activation to mitigate the risks of excessive, unnecessary, or misused access permissions on resources that organizations care about. By implementing these measures, organizations can improve their security posture and reduce the risk of data breaches and other security incidents.

Enforcing identity and access management with Permission assignments and implications

Enforcing identity and access management with permission assignments is a crucial security measure that helps organizations manage user access to resources and data. Permission assignments are like a bouncer at a nightclub who checks IDs and only allows people with the right credentials to enter. By assigning permissions based on specific roles, organizations can ensure that users have access to the resources they need to do their jobs, while also preventing unauthorized access. Organizations can also leverage attribute-based access control to further define the permissions necessary across different departments. However, it is important to regularly audit usage, reduce unnecessary standing permissions, and grant system function permissions to limit capabilities wherever possible. Additionally, it is essential to limit administrative and change capabilities to ensure single admins don't have excessive permissions they don't need. By implementing these measures, organizations can improve their security posture and reduce the risk of data breaches and other security incidents.

Enforcing identity and access management with Identity proofing

Enforcing identity and access management with identity proofing is a security measure that helps organizations verify the identities of users before granting them access to resources and data. Identity proofing is like a bouncer at a club who checks IDs to ensure that only authorized individuals are allowed to enter. By verifying the identity of users, organizations can ensure that only legitimate users have access to sensitive data and resources. Identity proofing can be done through various methods, including biometric authentication, multi-factor authentication, and digital certificates. It is important to ensure that the identity proofing process is secure and reliable, and that it is regularly updated to keep up with evolving threats. By implementing these measures, organizations can improve their security posture and reduce the risk of data breaches and other security incidents. Identity proofing is the process of verifying the identity of an individual before granting them access to a system or resource. This process involves collecting and verifying personal information, such as name, date of birth, and social security number, and comparing it to trusted sources, such as government-issued identification documents. Identity proofing is an important component of identity and access management (IAM) and is used to prevent unauthorized access to sensitive data and systems. By verifying the identity of users, organizations can ensure that only authorized individuals have access to resources and that access is granted based on the principle of least privilege. This helps to prevent data breaches and other security incidents.

Enforcing identity and access management with

Federation
Enforcing identity and access management with
Federation is a way to provide secure access to
resources across different systems and organizations. It
allows users to access resources using a single set of
credentials, which are authenticated by a trusted third-
party identity provider. This is similar to using a
passport to travel to different countries. Just as a
passport is a trusted document that verifies a person's
identity and allows them to travel across borders,
Federation allows users to access resources across
different systems and organizations using a single set
of credentials that are verified by a trusted identity
provider. This helps to simplify the management of user
identities and access, while also improving security by
reducing the need for users to remember multiple sets
of credentials.

**Enforcing identity and access management with
Single sign-on (SSO)**
Enforcing identity and access management with Single
sign-on (SSO) is a security mechanism that allows
users to authenticate once and access multiple
applications or systems without having to re-enter their
credentials. It is like having a master key that unlocks
multiple doors instead of having to carry a separate key
for each door. SSO simplifies the authentication
process and reduces the risk of password fatigue,
where users tend to use the same password across
multiple systems, making them vulnerable to cyber
attacks. By enforcing identity and access management
with SSO, organizations can ensure that only
authorized users have access to sensitive data and
resources, while also improving user experience and
productivity.

**Enforcing identity and access management with
Lightweight Directory Access Protocol (LDAP)**
Enforcing identity and access management with
Lightweight Directory Access Protocol (LDAP) involves
using a centralized directory service to manage user
identities and access permissions. LDAP is like a phone
book that contains information about users and their
access rights. It allows administrators to create and
manage user accounts, assign roles and permissions,
and control access to resources. By enforcing identity
and access management with LDAP, organizations can
ensure that only authorized users have access to

sensitive data and systems, and that access is granted based on the principle of least privilege. This helps to prevent unauthorized access, data breaches, and other security incidents. LDAP, which stands for Lightweight Directory Access Protocol, is a protocol used to access directories that contain information about users, such as their names, email addresses, and access rights. LDAP is a standardized protocol that uses a specification called X.500, which was written by the International Telecommunications Union. LDAP works through the TCP/IP protocol stack and sits at layer seven, the application layer. LDAP is vendor-neutral, meaning it can be used with different operating systems, such as Windows, Apple, or Linux. LDAP can be secured using a security layer called LDAPS, which stands for LDAP over SSL. LDAPS incorporates encryption and works over port 636. By using LDAP, organizations can manage user identities and access permissions in a centralized manner, which helps to prevent unauthorized access and data breaches.

Enforcing identity and access management with Open authorization (OAuth)

Enforcing identity and access management with Open Authorization (OAuth) involves using an authentication standard that allows a resource owner logged into one application or system to authorize third-party applications or systems to gain limited access to user data, without sharing authentication information. OAuth is like a valet key that allows a valet to temporarily drive and park a car, but it doesn't allow the holder full, unlimited access like a regular key. OAuth essentially allows the user, via an authentication provider that they have previously successfully authenticated with, to give another website/service a limited access authentication token for authorization to additional resources. By enforcing identity and access management with OAuth, organizations can ensure that only authorized users have access to sensitive data and systems, and that access is granted based on the principle of least privilege. This helps to prevent unauthorized access, data breaches, and other security incidents.

Enforcing identity and access management with Security Assertions Markup Language (SAML)

Enforcing identity and access management with Security Assertions Markup Language (SAML) is a way to provide secure access to resources by verifying the identity of users. SAML is like a bouncer at a club who checks your ID before letting you in. In this case, the bouncer is the SAML identity provider (IdP) that authenticates the user's identity and issues a SAML assertion, which is like a stamp on the user's hand that grants access to the club. The SAML assertion contains information about the user's identity and access privileges, which is used by the service provider (SP) to grant or deny access to resources. This helps to enforce access control policies and prevent unauthorized access to sensitive information.

Enforcing identity and access management with Interoperability
Enforcing identity and access management with interoperability refers to the ability of different identity and access management systems to work together seamlessly. Interoperability is like a universal remote control that can operate different devices from different manufacturers. In this case, the universal remote control is the interoperability standard that enables different identity and access management systems to communicate with each other. This helps to ensure that users can access resources across different systems without having to log in multiple times or remember different credentials. Interoperability also helps to simplify the management of access control policies and reduce the risk of errors or inconsistencies. However, achieving interoperability can be challenging due to the diversity of standards and protocols used by different systems. Organizations need to adopt a holistic approach that integrates diverse protocols, maintains data privacy, minimizes fragmentation, and balances scalability, usability, and security to achieve interoperability. Interoperability refers to the ability of different identity and access management systems to work together seamlessly. It is like a universal remote control that can operate different devices from different manufacturers. Interoperability agreements such as service level agreements, business partner agreements, and more are important when working with third parties or outsource services. In this case, interoperability agreements are like legal agreements that ensure that the connection that's being built between your part of the organization and the third party will have the proper security controls in place to make sure that all of that information will stay secure. Achieving interoperability can be challenging due to the

diversity of standards and protocols used by different systems. Organizations need to adopt a holistic approach that integrates diverse protocols, maintains data privacy, minimizes fragmentation, and balances scalability, usability, and security to achieve interoperability.

Enforcing identity and access management with Attestation

Enforcing identity and access management with attestation is a process that verifies that access to information, data, and resources is limited to authorized users. Attestation is like a security guard who checks your ID before allowing you to enter a restricted area. In this case, the security guard is the attestation process that verifies the user's identity and access privileges. The attestation process ensures that access is granted only to those who should have access and revoked from those who are unauthorized. It is a central component of identity governance that helps organizations reduce risk by granting users the right access to systems and applications, evaluating the risk associated with that access, and reviewing access deemed as risky or inappropriate. Automating attestation processes eliminates the need for IT intervention as all verifications and access validation is carried out automatically, based on specific elements previously designated. This helps to increase data security and reduce human errors caused by manual tasks. With attestation being a key component of identity governance, organizations are better able to monitor the access of their data and resources, ensuring that it is done only by authorized users

Enforcing identity and access management with Access controls

Enforcing identity and access management with access controls is a process that restricts access to information, data, and resources to authorized users only. Access controls are like a security checkpoint at an airport that verifies your identity and ensures that you have the right to board the plane. In this case, access controls are the security measures that verify the user's identity and grant access privileges based on their role, job function, or other criteria. Access controls can be implemented at different levels, such as physical, logical, or administrative, and can include measures such as biometric authentication, passwords, smart cards, and firewalls. Access controls help organizations to enforce security policies, prevent unauthorized access, and reduce the risk of data breaches. They are a critical component of identity and access management that helps organizations to protect their sensitive information and resources from unauthorized access

Enforcing identity and access management with Mandatory Access controls

Enforcing identity and access management with Mandatory Access Controls (MAC) is a process that restricts access to information, data, and resources to only those who have been granted permission by system administrators. MAC is like a security guard who only allows authorized personnel to enter a restricted area. In this case, the security guard is the MAC system that verifies the user's identity and grants access privileges based on the user's profile. The MAC system uses variable tags linked to a profile describing what access level the user has. MAC is often used in the most confidential and sensitive systems. MAC is a type of access control that is used to enforce strict security policies and prevent unauthorized access to sensitive information. It is a critical component of identity and access management that helps organizations to protect their sensitive information and resources from unauthorized access.

Enforcing identity and access management with Discretionary Access controls

Enforcing identity and access management with Discretionary Access Controls (DAC) is a process that restricts access to information, data, and resources based on the identity of subjects and groups to which they belong. DAC is like a lock on a door that can be opened with a key that only the owner has. In this case, the lock is the DAC system that verifies the user's identity and grants access privileges based on the owner's settings. The owner initially has total control over which other users gain access, but they can also give other officials this ability. An IAM system with discretionary access control regulates access based on the owner's settings. DAC is a type of access control that is used to enforce security policies and prevent unauthorized access to sensitive information. It is a critical component of identity and access management that helps organizations to protect their sensitive information and resources from unauthorized access.

Enforcing identity and access management with Role-based Access controls

Enforcing identity and access management with Role-Based Access Controls (RBAC) is a process that restricts access to information, data, and resources based on the user's role within the organization. RBAC is like a backstage pass at a concert that grants access to specific areas based on the user's role, such as performer, crew, or security. In this case, the backstage pass is the RBAC system that grants access privileges based on the user's role within the organization. RBAC allows organizations to define roles and assign permissions to those roles, which simplifies the management of access control policies and reduces the risk of errors or inconsistencies. Users are then assigned roles, and the RBAC system grants access based on the user's role. This schema disassociates the need for continual changes directly to user permissions, thus supporting a more robust way to manage the security and permissions for the organization. RBAC is a type of access control that is used to enforce security policies and prevent unauthorized access to sensitive information. It is a critical component of identity and access management that helps organizations to protect their sensitive information and resources from unauthorized access.

Enforcing identity and access management with Rule-based Access controls

Enforcing identity and access management with Rule-Based Access Controls (RBAC) is a process that restricts access to information, data, and resources based on predefined rules and permissions. RBAC is like a traffic light that regulates the flow of traffic based on the rules of the road. In this case, the traffic light is the RBAC system that grants access privileges based on the predefined rules and permissions. RBAC allows organizations to define roles and assign permissions to those roles, which simplifies the management of access control policies and reduces the risk of errors or inconsistencies. Users are then assigned roles, and the RBAC system grants access based on the user's role. This schema disassociates the need for continual changes directly to user permissions, thus supporting a more robust way to manage the security and permissions for the organization. RBAC is a type of access control that is used to enforce security policies and prevent unauthorized access to sensitive information. It is a critical component of identity and access management that helps organizations to protect their sensitive information and resources from unauthorized access.

Enforcing identity and access management with Attribute-based Access controls

Enforcing identity and access management with Attribute-Based Access Controls (ABAC) is a process that restricts access to information, data, and resources based on the attributes of the user, the resource, and the environment. ABAC is like a bouncer at a club who checks your ID, dress code, and age before letting you in. In this case, the bouncer is the ABAC system that verifies the user's identity, attributes, and context, and grants access privileges based on the policies and rules defined by the organization. ABAC allows organizations to define complex rules and policies that take into account multiple attributes, such as user roles, job functions, location, time of day, and device type. This helps to enforce fine-grained access control policies and prevent unauthorized access to sensitive information. ABAC is a type of access control that is used to enforce security policies and prevent unauthorized access to sensitive information. It is a critical component of identity and access management that helps organizations to protect their sensitive information and resources from unauthorized access.

Enforcing identity and access management with Access controls using Time-of-day restrictions

Enforcing identity and access management with Time-of-day restrictions is a process that restricts access to information, data, and resources based on specific time parameters. Time-of-day restrictions are like a curfew that limits the time when people can be outside. In this case, the curfew is the time-of-day restriction that limits access privileges based on the time of day or day of the week. Time-of-day restrictions can be implemented at different levels, such as physical, logical, or administrative, and can include measures such as biometric authentication, passwords, smart cards, and firewalls. Time-of-day restrictions help organizations to enforce security policies, prevent unauthorized access, and reduce the risk of data breaches. They are a critical component of identity and access management that helps organizations to protect their sensitive information and resources from unauthorized access.

Enforcing identity and access management with Access controls through the principle of Least privilege

Enforcing identity and access management with Access controls through the principle of Least Privilege is a process that restricts access to information, data, and resources based on the minimum level of access required to perform a specific task. The principle of least privilege is like a key that only opens the door to the room you need to enter, and not the entire building. In this case, the key is the access control system that grants access privileges based on the minimum level of access required to perform a specific task. The principle of least privilege ensures that users are granted only the access rights necessary to fulfill their work duties, and no more. This helps to reduce the risk of unauthorized access, modification, or misuse of sensitive information. The principle of least privilege applies to Authorization in the AAA identity and access management model. Access Authorization Process... When someone's access is beyond that person's required access to perform their job duties, then that access is considered to be beyond the principle of least privilege. The principle of least privilege can be implemented in many ways, such as Role-based access control (RBAC), Access control lists (ACLs), and Discretionary access control (DAC). In summary, the principle of least privilege is a concept in cybersecurity that is closely tied to identity and access management. When access to resources is limited, the risk of unauthorized access, modification, or misuse of sensitive information is reduced.

Enforcing identity and access management with Multifactor authentication using Biometrics

Enforcing identity and access management with Multifactor Authentication using Biometrics is a process that requires users to provide two or more forms of authentication to access information, data, and resources. Biometric authentication is one of the most common forms of multifactor authentication, which uses unique physical characteristics such as fingerprints, facial recognition, or iris scans to verify the user's identity. Multifactor authentication using biometrics is like a combination lock that requires two or more numbers to be entered to open the lock. In this case, the combination lock is the multifactor authentication system that requires the user to provide two or more forms of authentication to access the resource. Multifactor authentication using biometrics helps organizations to enforce security policies, prevent unauthorized access, and reduce the risk of data breaches. It is a critical component of identity and access management that helps organizations to protect their sensitive information and resources from unauthorized access.

Enforcing identity and access management with Multifactor authentication using hard authentication tokens

Enforcing identity and access management with Multifactor Authentication using Hard Authentication Tokens is a process that requires users to provide two or more forms of authentication to access information, data, and resources. Hard authentication tokens are one of the most common forms of multifactor authentication, which uses a physical device such as a smart card or USB token to verify the user's identity. Multifactor authentication using hard authentication tokens is like a bank vault that requires two keys to open, one of which is a physical key that only the owner has. In this case, the bank vault is the multifactor authentication system that requires the user to provide two or more forms of authentication to access the resource. Multifactor authentication using hard authentication tokens helps organizations to enforce security policies, prevent unauthorized access, and reduce the risk of data breaches. It is a critical component of identity and access management that helps organizations to protect their sensitive information and resources from unauthorized access.

Enforcing identity and access management with Multifactor authentication using soft authentication tokens

Enforcing identity and access management with Multifactor Authentication using Soft Authentication Tokens is a process that requires users to provide two or more forms of authentication to access information, data, and resources. Soft authentication tokens are one of the most common forms of multifactor authentication, which uses a software application on a mobile device or computer to generate a one-time password (OTP) that verifies the user's identity. Multifactor authentication using soft authentication tokens is like a password manager that generates a unique password for each login attempt. In this case, the password manager is the multifactor authentication system that requires the user to provide two or more forms of authentication to access the resource. Multifactor authentication using soft authentication tokens helps organizations to enforce security policies, prevent unauthorized access, and reduce the risk of data breaches. It is a critical component of identity and access management that helps organizations to protect their sensitive information and resources from unauthorized access.

Enforcing identity and access management with Multifactor authentication using Security keys

Enforcing identity and access management with Multifactor Authentication using Security Keys is a process that requires users to provide two or more forms of authentication to access information, data, and resources. Security keys are one of the most common forms of multifactor authentication, which uses a physical device that plugs into a USB port or connects wirelessly to a device to verify the user's identity. Multifactor authentication using security keys is like a car that requires both a key and a remote to start the engine. In this case, the car is the multifactor authentication system that requires the user to provide two or more forms of authentication to access the resource. Multifactor authentication using security keys helps organizations to enforce security policies, prevent unauthorized access, and reduce the risk of data breaches. It is a critical component of identity and access management that helps organizations to protect their sensitive information and resources from unauthorized access.

Enforcing identity and access management with Multifactor authentication using the security key factor "Something you know"

Enforcing identity and access management with Multifactor Authentication using the security key factor "Something you know" is a process that requires users to provide two or more forms of authentication to access information, data, and resources. The "Something you know" factor is typically a password or a PIN that the user must enter to verify their identity. Multifactor authentication using the "Something you know" factor is like a combination lock that requires a specific sequence of numbers to be entered to open the lock. In this case, the combination lock is the multifactor authentication system that requires the user to provide two or more forms of authentication to access the resource. Multifactor authentication using the "Something you know" factor helps organizations to enforce security policies, prevent unauthorized access, and reduce the risk of data breaches. It is a critical component of identity and access management that helps organizations to protect their sensitive information and resources from unauthorized access.

Enforcing identity and access management with Multifactor authentication using the security key factor "Something you have"

Multifactor authentication (MFA) is a security mechanism that requires users to provide two or more forms of authentication before accessing a system or application. One of the factors used in MFA is the "something you have" factor, which refers to a physical object that only the user possesses, such as a security key. This factor is used to enforce identity and access management by ensuring that only authorized users can access the system or application. An analogy for this would be a key to a lock. Just as a key is required to unlock a door, a security key is required to access a system or application. Without the key, the door remains locked, and without the security key, access to the system or application is denied.

Enforcing identity and access management with Multifactor authentication using the security key factor "Something you are"
Multifactor authentication (MFA) is a security mechanism that requires users to provide two or more forms of authentication before accessing a system or application. One of the factors used in MFA is the "something you are" factor, which refers to biometric authentication, such as a fingerprint or facial recognition. This factor is used to enforce identity and access management by ensuring that only authorized users can access the system or application. An analogy for this would be a fingerprint scanner to unlock a door. Just as a fingerprint scanner is required to unlock a door, biometric authentication is required to access a system or application. Without the correct fingerprint, the door remains locked, and without the correct biometric authentication, access to the system or application is denied.

Enforcing identity and access management with Multifactor authentication using the security key factor "Somewhere you are"
Multifactor authentication (MFA) is a security mechanism that requires users to provide two or more forms of authentication to access a system or application. One of the factors used in MFA is the "Somewhere you are" factor, which refers to the user's physical location. This factor can be enforced by requiring users to use a security key that is tied to a specific location, such as a USB key that must be plugged into a specific computer. This ensures that the user is physically present in the location where access is being requested, adding an extra layer of security to the authentication process. An analogy for this could be a physical key that unlocks a door. Just as a key is required to physically unlock a door, a security key is required to access a system or application, and the key must be in the right place to grant access.

Enforcing identity and access management with Password concepts

Password concepts are an essential part of identity and access management (IAM) policies. Passwords are a form of authentication that requires users to provide a unique combination of characters to access a system or application. Passwords can be strengthened by enforcing password complexity requirements, such as requiring a minimum length, a combination of upper and lower case letters, numbers, and special characters. An analogy for this could be a lock on a door. Just as a lock requires a unique combination of keys to open a door, a password requires a unique combination of characters to access a system or application. However, passwords can be vulnerable to cyber attacks, such as brute force attacks, where an attacker tries to guess the password by trying different combinations of characters. To mitigate this risk, IAM policies can enforce password expiration and require users to change their passwords regularly. Additionally, multi-factor authentication (MFA) can be used in conjunction with passwords to add an extra layer of security to the authentication process.

Enforcing identity and access management with Password best practices such as password Length

Password length is an essential aspect of password best practices in identity and access management (IAM). Passwords should be long enough to make them difficult to guess or crack. A good analogy for this is a combination lock. Just as a combination lock requires a long and unique combination of numbers to open, a password should be long and unique to provide adequate security. The National Institute of Standards and Technology (NIST) recommends a minimum password length of eight characters, but longer passwords are generally more secure. Passwords should also be complex, including a combination of upper and lower case letters, numbers, and special characters. Additionally, password policies should require users to change their passwords regularly to prevent unauthorized access. By enforcing password length and complexity requirements, IAM policies can help prevent cyber attacks that exploit weak passwords.

Enforcing identity and access management with Password best practices such as password Complexity

Enforcing identity and access management with password best practices such as password complexity is an important aspect of securing systems and data. Password complexity refers to the use of strong passwords that are difficult to guess or crack. It involves using a combination of uppercase and lowercase letters, numbers, and special characters to create a password that is unique and difficult to guess.

Password complexity can be compared to building a strong fortress around a castle. Just as a strong fortress is difficult to penetrate, a complex password is difficult to guess or crack, making it more secure. By enforcing password complexity, organizations can reduce the risk of unauthorized access to their systems and data, and ensure that only authorized users have access to sensitive information.

Enforcing identity and access management with Password best practices such as password Reuse

Enforcing identity and access management with password best practices such as password reuse is an important aspect of securing systems and data. Password reuse is like using the same key to lock multiple doors. If someone gains access to the key, they can unlock all the doors. Similarly, if a user's password is compromised and they use the same password for multiple accounts, an attacker can gain access to all those accounts. To prevent this, users should be encouraged to use unique, complex passwords for each account and to change them regularly. Additionally, organizations should implement password policies that require strong passwords, limit password reuse, and enforce password expiration. This can help prevent unauthorized access and protect sensitive information.

Enforcing identity and access management with Password best practices such as password Expiration

Enforcing identity and access management with password best practices such as password expiration is an important aspect of securing systems and data. Password expiration is like changing the lock on your front door periodically to prevent someone who has a copy of the key from accessing your home. By requiring users to change their passwords regularly, organizations can reduce the risk of unauthorized access to their systems and data. This practice ensures that passwords are not used indefinitely and that users are prompted to create new, strong passwords that are less likely to be guessed or cracked by attackers. Additionally, organizations can enforce password complexity requirements, such as minimum length and the use of special characters, to further strengthen password security.

Enforcing identity and access management with Password best practices such as password Age

Enforcing identity and access management with password best practices such as password age is an important aspect of securing systems. Password age refers to the length of time a password can be used before it must be changed. This practice helps to ensure that passwords are not used indefinitely, which can increase the risk of unauthorized access. Password age can be compared to the expiration date on food products. Just as food products have an expiration date to ensure that they are not consumed after they have gone bad, passwords have an expiration date to ensure that they are not used after they have become compromised. By enforcing password age, organizations can help to ensure that passwords are regularly updated and that systems remain secure.

Enforcing identity and access management with Password managers

Enforcing identity and access management with password managers is a security measure that helps to protect sensitive information by ensuring that only authorized individuals have access to it. Password managers act as a digital vault that stores all of a user's login credentials in one place. This allows users to create strong, unique passwords for each account without having to remember them all. It's like having a keychain that holds all your keys in one place, so you don't have to carry them all around with you. By enforcing the use of password managers, organizations can ensure that employees are using strong passwords and not reusing them across multiple accounts, which can help prevent unauthorized access to sensitive information. Additionally, password managers can help organizations enforce password policies, such as requiring regular password changes, to further enhance security.

Enforcing identity and access management with Passwordless Passwords

Enforcing identity and access management with Passwordless Passwords is a security measure that eliminates the need for passwords and instead uses other forms of authentication such as biometrics, smart cards, or tokens. This approach enhances security by reducing the risk of password-related attacks such as phishing, brute force attacks, and password reuse. It is similar to using a fingerprint to unlock a phone instead of a password. Just as a fingerprint is unique to an individual and cannot be easily replicated, biometrics and other forms of authentication provide a more secure and reliable way to verify a user's identity. By enforcing identity and access management with Passwordless Passwords, organizations can better protect their sensitive data and systems from unauthorized access.

Enforcing identity and access management with Privileged access management tools such as Just-in-time permissions

Enforcing identity and access management with privileged access management (PAM) tools such as Just-in-time (JIT) permissions is a security measure that restricts access to sensitive resources to only authorized personnel. JIT permissions provide temporary access to users for a specific period of time, after which the access is revoked. This is similar to a hotel room key that is issued to a guest for a limited time and is deactivated after the guest checks out. JIT permissions help to reduce the attack surface by limiting the time frame in which an attacker can exploit a vulnerability. PAM tools also provide additional security features such as multi-factor authentication, session recording, and auditing to ensure that access to sensitive resources is monitored and controlled.

Enforcing identity and access management with Privileged access management tools such as Password vaulting

Enforcing identity and access management with privileged access management (PAM) tools such as password vaulting is an important aspect of securing an organization's assets. PAM tools act as a gatekeeper, allowing only authorized users to access sensitive information. Password vaulting is like a safe deposit box at a bank, where only authorized individuals have access to the contents. In the same way, password vaulting stores sensitive information such as passwords, encryption keys, and other credentials in a secure location, accessible only to authorized users. This helps prevent unauthorized access to sensitive information and reduces the risk of data breaches. By enforcing identity and access management with PAM tools such as password vaulting, organizations can ensure that only authorized users have access to sensitive information, thereby reducing the risk of data breaches and other security incidents.

Enforcing identity and access management with Privileged access management tools such as Ephemeral credentials

Enforcing identity and access management with privileged access management tools such as ephemeral credentials is like using a temporary key to open a locked door. Ephemeral credentials are short-lived access tokens that are generated on-demand and used for a specific purpose. They provide a secure way to grant temporary access to privileged accounts without exposing the actual credentials. This helps to reduce the risk of unauthorized access and limit the scope of potential damage in case of a security breach. By enforcing identity and access management with privileged access management tools, organizations can ensure that only authorized users have access to sensitive data and systems, and that their actions are monitored and audited.

The Use cases of automation and scripting to acomplish User provisioning

Automation and scripting can be used to accomplish user provisioning in a more efficient and accurate manner. User provisioning involves creating, modifying, and deleting user accounts and their associated permissions. Just like a chef who uses a recipe to prepare a dish, automation and scripting can be thought of as a recipe for user provisioning. By automating the process, the system can create user accounts and assign permissions automatically, without the need for manual intervention. This can save time and reduce the risk of errors that can occur when provisioning users manually. Scripting can also be used to customize the user provisioning process to meet specific business needs. For example, a script can be created to automatically assign specific permissions to users based on their job roles. Overall, automation and scripting can help organizations streamline their user provisioning process and improve their security posture.

The Use cases of automation and scripting to acomplish Resource provisioning

Automation and scripting can be used to accomplish resource provisioning in a more efficient and reliable manner. Resource provisioning involves allocating and configuring resources such as servers, storage, and network devices to meet the needs of an organization. Just like a chef who uses a recipe to prepare a meal, automation and scripting can be used to create a recipe for resource provisioning. This recipe can be used repeatedly to provision resources in a consistent and repeatable manner, reducing the risk of errors and saving time. For example, a script can be created to automatically provision a virtual machine with the necessary software and configurations, eliminating the need for manual intervention. This can be especially useful in large-scale environments where multiple resources need to be provisioned quickly and accurately.

The Use cases of automation and scripting to acomplish Guard rails

Automation and scripting can be used to implement guardrails in a security environment. Guardrails are like the bumpers on a bowling alley that keep the ball from going into the gutter. Similarly, guardrails in security help to prevent security incidents by guiding users towards secure practices and preventing them from making mistakes. Automation and scripting can be used to enforce these guardrails by automatically performing security tasks, such as scanning for vulnerabilities or enforcing password policies. This reduces the risk of human error and ensures that security policies are consistently applied across the organization. Additionally, automation and scripting can help to detect and respond to security incidents more quickly, reducing the impact of a potential breach. Overall, automation and scripting are powerful tools that can help organizations to implement effective guardrails and improve their security posture.

The Use cases of automation and scripting to acomplish Security groups

Automation and scripting can be used to accomplish security groups in a manner similar to how a chef prepares a meal. Just as a chef uses a recipe to prepare a meal, automation and scripting use a set of instructions to create and manage security groups. These instructions can be used to automate the process of creating and managing security groups, which can save time and reduce the risk of human error. For example, a script can be used to automatically create a security group and add users to it based on certain criteria, such as their job role or department. This can help ensure that the right people have access to the right resources, while also reducing the risk of unauthorized access. Additionally, automation and scripting can help ensure that security groups are consistent and up-to-date, which can help improve overall security posture.

The Use cases of automation and scripting to acomplish Ticket creation

Automation and scripting can be used to accomplish ticket creation in a security operations center (SOC) in a similar way to how a chef uses a recipe to prepare a meal. Just as a recipe provides a set of instructions for preparing a meal, automation and scripting provide a set of instructions for performing a task. By automating the ticket creation process, SOC analysts can save time and reduce the risk of errors. For example, a script could be used to automatically create a ticket when a security event is detected, such as a failed login attempt or a malware infection. This can help ensure that all security events are properly documented and addressed in a timely manner. Additionally, automation and scripting can help improve consistency and reduce variability in the ticket creation process, which can help improve the overall effectiveness of the SOC.

The Use cases of automation and scripting to acomplish Escalation

Automation and scripting can be used to accomplish escalation in a similar way to how a chef might use a recipe to prepare a meal. Just as a recipe provides a set of instructions for a chef to follow, automation and scripting provide a set of instructions for a computer to follow. By automating repetitive tasks and scripting complex processes, security professionals can save time and reduce the risk of human error. This can be particularly useful when it comes to escalation, which involves increasing the severity of a security incident and involving higher-level personnel. By automating the initial steps of an escalation process, such as gathering information and notifying the appropriate parties, security professionals can ensure that the process is initiated quickly and consistently. This can help to minimize the impact of a security incident and ensure that it is resolved as efficiently as possible. Escalation refers to the process of increasing the severity of a security incident and involving higher-level personnel. This can be necessary when a security incident is beyond the scope of the initial responders or requires additional resources to resolve. Escalation can involve notifying management, involving specialized teams, or even contacting law enforcement. Privilege escalation is a specific type of escalation that involves gaining higher-level access to a system than what is allowed by the user's authentication. This is often done through the exploitation of vulnerabilities or weaknesses in the system. Security professionals can use automation and scripting to initiate the escalation process quickly and consistently, which can help to minimize the impact of a security incident and ensure that it is resolved as efficiently as possible.

The Use cases of automation and scripting to acomplish Enabling/disabling services

Automation and scripting can be used to enable or disable services on a system. This can be compared to a chef in a restaurant who uses a recipe to prepare a dish. The recipe provides a set of instructions that the chef follows to ensure that the dish is prepared correctly. Similarly, automation and scripting provide a set of instructions that a system follows to enable or disable services. This can be useful in situations where multiple systems need to be configured in the same way, as it allows for consistent and efficient configuration across all systems. Additionally, automation and scripting can help to reduce the risk of human error, as the instructions are executed in a consistent and repeatable manner. Overall, the use of automation and scripting can help to streamline the process of enabling or disabling services on a system, making it more efficient and reliable.

The many benefits of automation such as Efficiency/time saving

Automation offers many benefits, including efficiency and time-saving. This can be compared to a factory that uses machines to automate the production process. The machines perform repetitive tasks quickly and accurately, allowing the factory to produce goods more efficiently and at a faster rate. Similarly, automation can help to streamline processes and reduce the time and effort required to complete tasks. This is particularly useful in situations where tasks are repetitive or require a high degree of accuracy, as automation can help to reduce the risk of human error. Additionally, automation can help to free up time for employees to focus on more complex tasks that require human input. Overall, the use of automation can help to improve efficiency and productivity, allowing organizations to achieve more in less time.

The many benefits of automation such as Enforcing baselines

Automation offers many benefits, including the ability to enforce baselines. This can be compared to a teacher who sets a standard for their students to follow. The teacher provides a set of guidelines that the students must adhere to in order to meet the standard. Similarly, automation can help to enforce baselines by providing a set of guidelines that a system must follow in order to meet a certain standard. This can be useful in situations where multiple systems need to be configured in the same way, as it allows for consistent and efficient configuration across all systems. Additionally, automation can help to reduce the risk of human error, as the guidelines are executed in a consistent and repeatable manner. Overall, the use of automation can help to improve the security posture of an organization by ensuring that all systems are configured to meet a certain standard.

The many benefits of automation such as Standard infrastructure configurations

Automation has many benefits, including standardization of infrastructure configurations. Standardization is like baking a cake using a recipe. The recipe provides a set of instructions that must be followed to produce a consistent and high-quality cake. Similarly, standardization in infrastructure configurations ensures that all systems are configured in the same way, which reduces the risk of errors and inconsistencies. Automation can help achieve this standardization by automating the process of configuring systems, which ensures that all systems are configured in the same way every time. This reduces the time and effort required to configure systems manually and ensures that the configurations are consistent and accurate. Additionally, automation can help reduce the risk of human error, which can lead to security vulnerabilities and other issues. Overall, automation can help organizations achieve greater efficiency, consistency, and security in their operations.

The many benefits of automation such as Scaling in a secure manner

Automation has many benefits in the context of security, including the ability to scale in a secure manner. Scaling refers to the ability to increase or decrease the size of a system or application based on demand. Automation can help with scaling by allowing for the creation of repeatable processes that can be easily replicated across multiple systems. This can be compared to a chef who uses a recipe to create a dish. Once the recipe has been perfected, the chef can easily make the same dish in large quantities without having to worry about making mistakes or variations. Similarly, automation can help ensure that security processes are consistently applied across all systems, reducing the risk of errors or inconsistencies. Additionally, automation can help reduce the time and effort required to perform security tasks, allowing security teams to focus on more complex or high-priority tasks. Overall, automation can help organizations improve their security posture by making it easier to scale and manage security processes in a consistent and efficient manner.

The many benefits of automation such as Employee retention

Automation has many benefits in the context of employee retention. Automation can help reduce the workload of employees by automating repetitive and mundane tasks, allowing them to focus on more complex and high-priority tasks. This can be compared to a personal assistant who helps their boss manage their schedule and tasks. By taking care of the routine tasks, the assistant frees up the boss's time to focus on more important tasks. Similarly, automation can help reduce the workload of employees, allowing them to focus on tasks that require their expertise and creativity. This can help improve employee satisfaction and retention by reducing burnout and increasing job satisfaction. Additionally, automation can help reduce the risk of errors and inconsistencies, which can help improve the quality of work and reduce the need for rework. Overall, automation can help organizations improve employee retention by reducing workload, improving job satisfaction, and reducing the risk of errors and inconsistencies.

The many benefits of automation such as Reaction time

Automation has many benefits, including faster reaction time. To understand this benefit, consider the analogy of a person driving a car versus a self-driving car. A person driving a car has to react to changes in the road, such as traffic, roadblocks, or pedestrians. This reaction time can vary depending on the person's attention, experience, and other factors. On the other hand, a self-driving car can react much faster to changes in the road because it is programmed to do so. Similarly, automation in security can help detect and respond to security threats faster than a human could. Automated security systems can monitor networks, detect anomalies, and respond to threats in real-time, reducing the time it takes to identify and mitigate security incidents. This faster reaction time can help prevent or minimize the impact of security breaches, which can be critical in today's fast-paced and interconnected world.

Using automation to accomplish Workforce multiplier and access

Using automation to accomplish workforce multiplier and access can be compared to using a machine to lift heavy objects. Just as a machine can lift heavy objects that would be difficult or impossible for a person to lift alone, automation can help accomplish tasks that would be difficult or impossible for a single person or team to complete alone. By automating certain tasks, such as security monitoring or incident response, organizations can increase their efficiency and productivity, allowing them to accomplish more with fewer resources. Additionally, automation can help ensure consistent and accurate results, reducing the risk of errors or oversights that could compromise security. Overall, using automation to accomplish workforce multiplier and access can help organizations achieve their security goals more effectively and efficiently.

The many benefits of automation such as Continuous integration and testing

Continuous integration and testing are essential components of the software development process that offer many benefits. Continuous integration involves automatically building and testing code changes as soon as they are committed to the code repository. This process helps to identify issues early in the development cycle, making it easier and less expensive to fix them. Continuous testing, on the other hand, involves running automated tests every time there is a code check-in or a code change that is integrated into the codebase. This process ensures that the code is reliable and consistent, accelerating the testing process and boosting efficiency. An analogy to understand the benefits of automation in continuous integration and testing is to think of a car assembly line. Just as each part of the car is assembled and tested before moving to the next stage, continuous integration and testing ensure that each code change is built and tested before moving to the next stage of development. This process helps to identify issues early in the development cycle, making it easier and less expensive to fix them, just as identifying a faulty part early in the assembly line can save time and money. Overall, automation in continuous integration and testing reduces the chances of human error, ensures that only high-quality code is released, and helps developers to iterate faster, delivering better software products to users.

The many benefits of automation such as Integrations and Application programming interfaces (APIs)

Automation has many benefits, including integrations and application programming interfaces (APIs). Integrations allow different systems to work together seamlessly, much like how different parts of a car work together to make it run smoothly. APIs provide a standardized way for different applications to communicate with each other, much like how a universal remote control can communicate with different devices. By automating security tasks, organizations can reduce the risk of procedural errors and ensure that all processes are followed. Automation can also improve incident response by allowing faster threat detection and eliminating alert fatigue. Additionally, automation can reduce manual tasks, improve efficiency, reduce human error, and provide threat intelligence and analysis. Overall, automation can help organizations improve their security posture and stay ahead of cyber threats

The automation consideration of Complexity

In the context of security automation, complexity refers to the number of different systems, tools, and processes that need to be integrated and managed. The more complex the automation process, the more difficult it is to maintain and secure. It is like a puzzle with many pieces that need to be put together. The more pieces there are, the more difficult it is to assemble and the more likely it is that some pieces will be lost or misplaced. Therefore, it is important to consider the complexity of an automation process when designing and implementing security solutions to ensure that they are manageable and secure.

The automation consideration of Cost

In the context of security automation, the consideration of cost refers to the financial resources required to implement and maintain automated security solutions. Just as a car owner must consider the cost of fuel, maintenance, and repairs when deciding whether to purchase a car, an organization must consider the cost of implementing and maintaining automated security solutions when deciding whether to adopt them. The cost of automation can include the initial investment in hardware, software, and personnel, as well as ongoing costs such as licensing fees, maintenance, and upgrades. Therefore, just as a car owner must weigh the benefits of owning a car against the costs, an organization must weigh the benefits of implementing automated security solutions against the costs to determine whether it is a worthwhile investment.

The automation consideration of Single points of failure

In the context of security automation, the consideration of single points of failure (SPOF) refers to the potential risk posed by a flaw in the design, implementation, or configuration of a system. Just as a human body can be vulnerable to a single point of failure, such as a heart attack, a system can also be vulnerable to a single point of failure, such as a hardware or software failure. A single point of failure can cause an entire system to stop operating, leading to downtime, data loss, and other negative consequences. Therefore, when implementing automated security solutions, it is important to identify and mitigate single points of failure to ensure the reliability and availability of the system. This can be achieved through redundancy, backups, and failover mechanisms that provide alternative paths for interconnected systems if the original path should fail. By doing so, the system can continue to operate even if a single component fails, reducing the risk of downtime and data loss.

The automation consideration of Technical debt
In the context of security automation, the consideration of technical debt refers to the long-term costs associated with implementing and maintaining automated security solutions. Just as a person can accumulate debt by borrowing money and paying interest over time, an organization can accumulate technical debt by implementing automated security solutions that require ongoing maintenance, upgrades, and support. Technical debt can result from using outdated or unsupported software, failing to implement proper security controls, or neglecting to address vulnerabilities and other security issues. Therefore, when implementing automated security solutions, it is important to consider the long-term costs and benefits to ensure that the organization does not accumulate technical debt that could lead to security breaches or other negative consequences. This can be achieved by regularly assessing and updating the organization's security posture, implementing best practices for security automation, and investing in ongoing training and education for personnel to ensure that they have the skills and knowledge necessary to maintain and support the automated security solutions.

The automation consideration of Ongoing supportability
Ongoing supportability in automation refers to the ability to maintain and update automated systems over time. It is important to ensure that automated systems can be easily modified and updated as needed to keep up with changing requirements and technologies. This is similar to maintaining a car - just as a car requires regular maintenance and updates to keep it running smoothly, automated systems require ongoing support to ensure they continue to function effectively. Without ongoing support, automated systems can become outdated and ineffective, leading to potential security vulnerabilities and other issues.

The incident response Process of Preparation
The incident response process of preparation is the first step in responding to a security incident. It involves identifying potential security incidents and developing a plan to respond to them. This process is similar to preparing for a natural disaster, such as a hurricane. Just as you would prepare for a hurricane by identifying potential risks and developing a plan to protect yourself and your property, you would prepare for a security incident by identifying potential risks to your organization and developing a plan to respond to them. This plan should include procedures for detecting and reporting security incidents, as well as steps for containing and mitigating the damage caused by the incident. By preparing for security incidents in advance, organizations can minimize the impact of security breaches and respond more effectively to security incidents when they occur.

The incident response Process of Detection
The incident response process of detection is the first step in identifying a security incident. It involves monitoring and analyzing system logs, network traffic, and other data sources to identify any unusual or suspicious activity. This process can be compared to a security guard who patrols a building, looking for any signs of a break-in or other security breach. Just as a security guard must be vigilant and observant to detect any potential threats, the incident response team must be diligent in monitoring and analyzing data to identify any signs of a security incident. Once a potential incident has been detected, the incident response team can move on to the next step in the incident response process, which is containment.

The incident response Process of Analysis

The incident response process of analysis is the second step in the incident response process. It involves collecting and analyzing information about the incident to determine the scope, impact, and root cause of the incident. This process is similar to a detective investigating a crime scene. The detective collects evidence, interviews witnesses, and analyzes the evidence to determine what happened, who was involved, and why it happened. Similarly, in the incident response process of analysis, the incident response team collects data from various sources, such as system logs, network traffic, and user interviews, to determine the nature and scope of the incident. The team then analyzes the data to identify the root cause of the incident and develop a plan to contain and remediate the incident.

The incident response Process of Containment

The incident response process of containment is the second step in the incident response process. It involves isolating the affected systems and preventing further damage to the network. This is similar to a firefighter containing a fire by putting up barriers to prevent it from spreading to other areas. The goal of containment is to limit the scope of the incident and prevent it from causing further damage. This is achieved by disconnecting affected systems from the network, disabling user accounts, and blocking network traffic to and from the affected systems. Once the incident has been contained, the incident response team can move on to the next step, which is eradication.

The incident response Process of Eradication
The incident response process of Eradication is the stage where the security team takes action to remove the threat from the system. This is similar to a doctor treating a patient with an infection. Once the doctor has identified the type of infection, they will prescribe medication to eradicate the infection from the patient's body. Similarly, in the Eradication stage, the security team will use the information gathered in the previous stages to identify the type of threat and take action to remove it from the system. This may involve removing malicious files, disabling user accounts, or blocking network traffic associated with the threat. The goal of the Eradication stage is to completely remove the threat from the system and prevent it from causing further damage.

The incident response Process of Recovery
The incident response process of recovery is the phase where the organization attempts to restore normal operations after an incident has occurred. This phase is similar to a hospital patient recovering from an illness or injury. Just as a patient may need to undergo physical therapy or take medication to recover, an organization may need to restore data from backups, repair or replace damaged equipment, or implement new security measures to prevent future incidents. The goal of the recovery phase is to return the organization to a state of normalcy as quickly as possible while minimizing the impact of the incident.

The incident response Process of Lessons learned

The incident response process of lessons learned is a crucial step in improving an organization's security posture. It involves analyzing the incident and identifying what went wrong, what worked well, and what could be improved. This process is similar to a sports team reviewing game footage to identify areas for improvement. By learning from past incidents, an organization can better prepare for future incidents and reduce the likelihood of similar incidents occurring. The lessons learned can also be used to update policies, procedures, and training programs to ensure that the organization is better equipped to handle future incidents.

Incident response Training activities

Incident response training activities are designed to prepare individuals and organizations to respond effectively to security incidents. These activities can be compared to fire drills in a building. Just as fire drills help people to know what to do in case of a fire, incident response training activities help people to know what to do in case of a security incident. These activities may include tabletop exercises, simulations, and other training exercises that simulate real-world scenarios. By participating in these activities, individuals and organizations can identify weaknesses in their incident response plans and improve their ability to respond to security incidents.

The incident response Testing activity Tabletop exercises

Tabletop exercises are a type of incident response testing activity that simulates a security incident in a controlled environment. It involves a group of stakeholders, including IT staff, management, and other relevant personnel, who gather to discuss and analyze a hypothetical security breach scenario. The participants then work together to identify the potential impact of the incident, assess the effectiveness of the existing security controls, and develop a response plan to mitigate the risks. Tabletop exercises are similar to a fire drill, where everyone practices what to do in case of a fire, but in this case, it is a simulated security incident.

The incident response Testing activity of aSimulation

The incident response testing activity of a simulation is a process of testing the effectiveness of an organization's incident response plan. It involves simulating a real-world security incident and evaluating the organization's response to it. This activity is similar to a fire drill in a building. Just as a fire drill tests the effectiveness of a building's evacuation plan, an incident response simulation tests the effectiveness of an organization's incident response plan. The simulation helps identify gaps in the plan and provides an opportunity to improve the plan before a real incident occurs. The incident response testing activity of a simulation is an important part of an organization's overall security strategy and helps ensure that the organization is prepared to respond to security incidents effectively.

The incident response activity of Root cause analysis

Root cause analysis is an incident response activity that involves identifying the underlying cause of a security incident. It is like investigating a car accident to determine the cause of the crash. Just as a car accident can have multiple contributing factors, a security incident can have multiple root causes. Root cause analysis helps organizations to identify and address the underlying issues that led to the incident, rather than just treating the symptoms. By addressing the root cause, organizations can prevent similar incidents from occurring in the future.

The incident response activity of Threat hunting

Threat hunting is an incident response activity that involves proactively searching for threats that may have gone undetected by traditional security measures. It is like a detective searching for clues to solve a crime before it happens. Threat hunters use a variety of techniques, such as analyzing network traffic and logs, to identify suspicious activity and potential threats. By identifying and addressing these threats early, organizations can prevent or minimize the impact of a security breach.

The incident response activity of Digital forensics

Digital forensics is an incident response activity that

involves the collection, preservation, analysis, and presentation of digital evidence in a manner that is admissible in a court of law. It is similar to a detective investigating a crime scene, where they collect and analyze physical evidence to determine what happened and who was involved. In digital forensics, investigators use specialized tools and techniques to collect and analyze digital evidence from computers, networks, and other digital devices to determine the cause of a security incident, identify the attacker, and gather evidence for legal proceedings. The goal of digital forensics is to provide a clear and accurate picture of what happened during a security incident, and to help organizations improve their security posture to prevent future incidents.

The Digital forensics incident response activity of a Legal hold

The legal hold is a digital forensics incident response activity that involves preserving evidence related to a legal matter. It is similar to putting a book on a shelf and not allowing anyone to touch it until it is needed for a legal case. In the same way, a legal hold preserves digital evidence, such as emails, documents, and other data, so that it can be used as evidence in a legal case. This activity is important to ensure that the evidence is not tampered with or destroyed, and it helps to maintain the integrity of the evidence.

The Digital forensics incident response activity of Chain of custody

The Chain of Custody is a critical aspect of Digital Forensics Incident Response activity. It refers to the process of maintaining the integrity of evidence collected during an investigation. It involves documenting the collection, handling, and storage of evidence to ensure that it is not tampered with or altered in any way. An analogy for the Chain of Custody is a relay race where the baton is passed from one runner to another. Each runner must ensure that the baton is not dropped or altered in any way before passing it on to the next runner. Similarly, in digital forensics, each person who handles the evidence must ensure that it is not tampered with or altered before passing it on to the next person in the chain. This ensures that the evidence is admissible in court and can be used to support the investigation.

The Digital forensics incident response activity of Acquisition

Digital forensics incident response (DFIR) is a specialized field focused on identifying, remediating, and investigating cybersecurity incidents. DFIR consists of two components: digital forensics and incident response. Digital forensics involves collecting, preserving, and analyzing forensic evidence, while incident response involves containing, stopping, and preventing a cyberattack. The digital forensic process is the accepted method investigators follow to gather and preserve digital evidence, with the express intent of maintaining a chain of custody. The process consists of three key steps: Acquisition, Analysis, and Reporting. In the Acquisition phase, investigators create an exact duplicate of the media in question, usually using a hard drive duplicator or specialized software tools. An analogy for the Acquisition phase is taking a photograph of a crime scene to preserve the evidence.

The Digital forensics incident response activity of Reporting

Reporting is a crucial activity in digital forensics incident response. It involves documenting the findings of an investigation and presenting them to relevant stakeholders. Reporting can be compared to a detective's report on a crime scene. Just as a detective gathers evidence and presents it to a judge and jury, a digital forensics investigator gathers evidence and presents it to management, law enforcement, or other relevant parties. The report should be clear, concise, and accurate, and should include details such as the scope of the investigation, the methods used, and the findings. The report should also provide recommendations for preventing similar incidents in the future.

The Digital forensics incident response activity of Preservation

Digital forensics incident response activity of Preservation is a process in which investigators create an exact duplicate of the media in question, usually using a hard drive duplicator or specialized software tools. The original media is secured to prevent any tampering. The purpose of this step is to maintain a chain of custody and ensure that the original evidence is not altered or destroyed. An analogy for this process is making a copy of a key to a house before giving it to someone else. The original key is preserved, and the copy is used to access the house. Similarly, in digital forensics, the original media is preserved, and the duplicate is used for analysis.

The Digital forensics incident response activity of E-discovery

Digital forensics incident response activity of E-discovery is a process that involves collecting, examining, and analyzing data from compromised computer systems and storage devices to identify, investigate, and contain a security incident. It is a specialized form of eDiscovery that aims to find specific elements of personal identifiable information (PII) data contained within data sets that may have been compromised, copied, or downloaded during a cyber breach, for subsequent illegal distribution. In simpler terms, it is like a detective investigating a crime scene to collect evidence that can be presented in court. The evidence collected through digital forensics can be used to file lawsuits against identified attackers, and it can also be used by law enforcement as evidence in court proceedings against cybercriminals.

Supporting an investigation with Log data

Supporting an investigation with log data involves analyzing and interpreting log files to identify potential security incidents. Log data is like a trail of breadcrumbs that can be used to retrace the steps of an attacker or to identify suspicious activity. Just as a detective might use footprints or fingerprints to solve a crime, a security analyst can use log data to piece together the sequence of events leading up to a security incident. By analyzing log data, security analysts can identify patterns of behavior, detect anomalies, and uncover evidence of malicious activity. This information can then be used to support an investigation and to take appropriate action to mitigate the threat.

Supporting an investigation with Firewall logs

Firewall logs can be used to support an investigation by providing a record of network traffic and identifying potential security incidents. Firewall logs are like a security camera that captures all the traffic that passes through the network. Just as a security camera can be used to identify individuals involved in a crime, firewall logs can be used to identify the source and destination of network traffic, as well as the type of traffic and any attempts to bypass security measures. By analyzing firewall logs, investigators can identify patterns of behavior, detect anomalies, and determine the scope and impact of a security incident. This information can be used to identify the source of an attack, assess the damage, and take steps to prevent future incidents.

Supporting an investigation with Application logs

Application logs can be used to support an investigation by providing a record of events that have occurred within an application. These logs can be compared to other logs or data sources to identify patterns or anomalies that may indicate suspicious activity. In a way, application logs are like a diary that records everything that happens within an application. Just as a detective might use a diary to piece together events leading up to a crime, an investigator can use application logs to reconstruct events leading up to a security incident. By analyzing application logs, investigators can identify the source of an attack, determine the extent of the damage, and take steps to prevent similar incidents from occurring in the future.

Supporting an investigation with Endpoint logs

Endpoint logs are records of activities that occur on a computer or device. They can be compared to a security camera that captures footage of people entering and exiting a building. Endpoint logs can provide valuable information during an investigation, such as when a user logged in, what files were accessed, and what programs were run. By analyzing endpoint logs, investigators can identify potential security incidents, track the movement of attackers, and determine the scope of a breach. Just as a security camera can help identify a suspect in a crime, endpoint logs can help identify the source of a security incident and provide evidence to support an investigation.

Supporting an investigation with OS-specific security logs

Supporting an investigation with OS-specific security logs involves analyzing the logs generated by the operating system to identify any security-related events that may have occurred. These logs can provide valuable information about user activity, system events, and network traffic, which can be used to identify potential security breaches or other suspicious activity. Think of these logs as a security camera that captures everything that happens on a computer system. By reviewing these logs, investigators can piece together a timeline of events and identify any anomalies or patterns that may indicate a security incident. Just as a security camera can provide valuable evidence in a criminal investigation, OS-specific security logs can provide valuable evidence in a security investigation.

Supporting an investigation with data sources such as Vulnerability scans

Supporting an investigation with data sources such as vulnerability scans is like using a magnifying glass to examine a crime scene. Vulnerability scans provide a detailed view of the security posture of a system or network by identifying potential weaknesses that could be exploited by attackers. This information can be used to support an investigation by providing insights into how an attacker may have gained access to a system or network. Just as a magnifying glass can reveal small details that may have been missed by the naked eye, vulnerability scans can reveal vulnerabilities that may have been overlooked during routine security assessments. By analyzing the data collected from vulnerability scans, investigators can piece together a more complete picture of the attack and identify the root cause of the security breach.

Supporting an investigation with data sources such as Automated reports

Supporting an investigation with data sources such as automated reports is like using a magnifying glass to examine a crime scene. The data sources provide a detailed view of the events that occurred, allowing investigators to identify patterns and anomalies that may have gone unnoticed otherwise. Automated reports can be generated from various sources, such as security logs, network traffic, and system activity, and can provide valuable insights into the incident being investigated. By analyzing the data provided by these reports, investigators can piece together the sequence of events leading up to the incident and identify the root cause of the problem. This information can then be used to develop a remediation plan to prevent similar incidents from occurring in the future.

Supporting an investigation with data sources such as Dashboards

Supporting an investigation with data sources such as dashboards is like using a map to navigate through a city. Just as a map provides a visual representation of the city's streets and landmarks, a dashboard provides a visual representation of data that can help investigators identify patterns and trends. Dashboards can display data from multiple sources, such as logs, network traffic, and user activity, in a single location, making it easier to analyze and interpret the data. By using dashboards, investigators can quickly identify anomalies and suspicious activity, which can help them to focus their investigation and make more informed decisions.

Supporting an investigation with data sources such as Packet captures

Supporting an investigation with data sources such as packet captures is like having a recording of a conversation. Just as a recording can be played back to determine what was said and by whom, packet captures can be analyzed to determine what data was transmitted and by whom. Packet captures can provide valuable information for investigating security incidents, such as identifying the source of an attack or determining what data was exfiltrated. By analyzing packet captures, investigators can reconstruct the sequence of events leading up to an incident and identify any malicious activity that occurred.

Supporting an investigation with data sources such as IPS/IDS logs

Supporting an investigation with data sources such as IPS/IDS logs is like using a surveillance camera to investigate a crime. Just as a surveillance camera records all the activities happening in a particular area, an IPS/IDS system records all the network traffic and events happening in a network. These logs can be used to identify the source and nature of an attack, the time of the attack, and the extent of the damage caused. By analyzing the IPS/IDS logs, security analysts can determine the type of attack, the vulnerabilities exploited, and the methods used by the attacker. This information can be used to prevent future attacks and improve the security posture of the organization.

Supporting an investigation with data sources such as Network logs

Supporting an investigation with data sources such as network logs is like using a trail of breadcrumbs to track someone's path. Network logs are records of network activity that can provide valuable information about who accessed a network, when they accessed it, and what they did while they were there. Just as breadcrumbs can help you retrace your steps through a forest, network logs can help investigators retrace the steps of a cybercriminal through a network. By analyzing network logs, investigators can identify patterns of behavior, detect anomalies, and piece together a timeline of events. This information can be used to identify the source of an attack, determine the extent of the damage, and develop strategies to prevent future attacks.

Supporting an investigation with data sources such as Metadata

Metadata is data that describes other data. It provides information about the characteristics of data, such as when it was created, modified, or accessed. In an investigation, metadata can be used as a source of information to support the investigation. It can provide valuable insights into the activities of a user or system, such as when a file was created, who created it, and when it was last accessed. Metadata can be compared to the information on a shipping label of a package. Just as a shipping label provides information about the sender, recipient, and contents of a package, metadata provides information about the data it describes. By analyzing metadata, investigators can gain a better understanding of the data and its context, which can help them to identify patterns, relationships, and anomalies that may be relevant to the investigation.

The effective security governance element called, Guidelines

Guidelines are an important element of effective security governance, as they provide a framework for making decisions and taking actions that align with security objectives. Guidelines can be thought of as a set of rules or best practices that help to guide behavior and ensure that security policies are followed consistently. Just as a set of traffic rules helps to ensure that drivers operate their vehicles safely and efficiently, guidelines help to ensure that security measures are implemented in a way that is effective and consistent with organizational goals. By providing clear guidance on how to implement security policies and procedures, guidelines can help to reduce the risk of security breaches and ensure that security measures are aligned with business objectives.

The effective security governance element called, Policies

Policies are a crucial element of effective security governance, as they provide a set of rules and guidelines that help to ensure that security objectives are met. Policies can be thought of as a set of instructions that dictate how security measures should be implemented and enforced. Just as a set of house rules helps to ensure that everyone in a household behaves in a way that is consistent with the values and goals of the family, policies help to ensure that security measures are implemented in a way that is consistent with the goals and objectives of the organization. By providing clear guidance on how to implement security measures, policies can help to reduce the risk of security breaches and ensure that security measures are aligned with business objectives. Policies should be developed based on the results of a risk assessment and should be clear, concise, and easy to understand. They should also be reviewed and updated regularly to ensure that they remain relevant and effective in the face of changing security threats and IT infrastructure.

Creating Effective security through Acceptable use policy (AUP) policies

An Acceptable Use Policy (AUP) is a set of rules and guidelines that define how an organization's computer network and resources can be used. It is similar to a set of traffic rules that govern how drivers should behave on the road. Just as traffic rules help ensure the safety of drivers and passengers, an AUP helps ensure the security of an organization's network and resources. A well-crafted AUP should clearly define what is and is not allowed on the network, and should be communicated to all users. It should also outline the consequences of violating the policy, which could include disciplinary action or legal consequences. By creating and enforcing an effective AUP, an organization can help prevent security breaches and protect sensitive data.

Creating Effective security through Information security policies

Creating effective security through information security policies is like building a strong foundation for a house. Just as a house needs a solid foundation to withstand external forces, an organization needs a strong information security policy to protect its assets from external and internal threats. Information security policies provide a framework for implementing security controls and procedures that protect an organization's information assets. They define the roles and responsibilities of employees, establish guidelines for access control, and outline procedures for incident response and disaster recovery. By creating and enforcing effective information security policies, an organization can ensure that its information assets are protected from unauthorized access, theft, and misuse.

Creating Effective security through Business continuity policies

Creating effective security through business continuity policies is like building a strong foundation for a house. Just as a house needs a solid foundation to withstand natural disasters, a business needs a strong security foundation to withstand cyber threats. Business continuity policies are designed to ensure that a business can continue to operate in the event of a disruption, such as a cyber attack or natural disaster. These policies include procedures for data backup and recovery, incident response, and disaster recovery. By implementing these policies, a business can minimize the impact of a disruption and quickly resume normal operations. Just as a strong foundation is essential for a house, effective security through business continuity policies is essential for a business to protect its assets and maintain its operations.

Creating Effective security through Disaster recovery policies

Creating effective security through disaster recovery policies is like having a backup plan in case of a fire. Just as a fire can destroy a building and its contents, a security breach can compromise sensitive data and systems. Disaster recovery policies help to ensure that critical data and systems can be restored in the event of a security breach or other disaster. These policies should include procedures for backing up data, testing backups, and restoring data and systems. By having a disaster recovery plan in place, organizations can minimize the impact of a security breach and quickly resume normal operations.

Creating Effective security through Incident response policies

Creating effective security through incident response policies is like having a fire evacuation plan in place. Just as a fire evacuation plan outlines the steps to take in case of a fire, an incident response policy outlines the steps to take in case of a security incident. The policy should include procedures for identifying, containing, and mitigating the incident, as well as for reporting and documenting it. By having a well-defined incident response policy, an organization can minimize the damage caused by a security incident and quickly return to normal operations. The policy should be regularly reviewed and updated to ensure that it remains effective and relevant to the organization's needs.

Creating Effective security through Software development lifecycle (SDLC) policies

Creating effective security through Software Development Lifecycle (SDLC) policies is a crucial aspect of securing software systems. It is like building a house with a strong foundation. Just as a house needs a strong foundation to withstand natural disasters, software systems need a strong SDLC policy to withstand cyber threats. The SDLC policy should be integrated into the software development process from the beginning to the end. It should include security requirements, design, coding, testing, and deployment. The policy should also ensure that security is tested and validated at every stage of the SDLC. By doing so, the software system will be more secure, and the risk of cyber threats will be minimized.

Creating Effective security through Change management policies

Creating effective security through change management policies is like building a strong foundation for a house. Just as a house needs a solid foundation to withstand the test of time, an organization needs a strong change management policy to ensure that changes to the IT infrastructure are made in a controlled and secure manner. Change management policies help to ensure that changes are properly planned, tested, and implemented, and that any potential risks are identified and mitigated. By implementing effective change management policies, an organization can reduce the risk of security breaches and ensure that its IT infrastructure remains secure and stable over time.

Creating Effective security through Password Standards

Creating effective security through password standards is an essential aspect of securing systems and data. Password standards are like the locks on the doors of a house. Just as locks prevent unauthorized access to a house, password standards prevent unauthorized access to systems and data. Password standards should be designed to ensure that passwords are strong, unique, and difficult to guess. This can be achieved by requiring passwords to be a certain length, including a mix of uppercase and lowercase letters, numbers, and special characters. Passwords should also be changed regularly to prevent them from being compromised. By implementing strong password standards, organizations can significantly reduce the risk of unauthorized access to their systems and data.

Creating Effective security through Access control Standards

Access control is a security mechanism that restricts access to resources based on policies and rules. It is like a bouncer at a club who checks your ID before allowing you to enter. Access control standards are a set of guidelines and procedures that define how access control should be implemented in an organization. These standards help create effective security by ensuring that only authorized users have access to resources and that access is granted based on the principle of least privilege. This means that users are only given the minimum level of access required to perform their job functions. By implementing access control standards, organizations can prevent unauthorized access, reduce the risk of data breaches, and protect sensitive information.

Creating Effective security through Physical security Standards

Creating effective security through physical security standards is an important aspect of securing an organization's assets. Physical security standards refer to the policies and procedures that are put in place to protect an organization's physical assets, such as buildings, equipment, and people. Just as a castle has walls, gates, and guards to protect its inhabitants and treasures, an organization should have physical security measures in place to protect its assets. These measures may include access control systems, surveillance cameras, security personnel, and environmental controls. By implementing physical security standards, an organization can deter potential threats, detect and respond to security incidents, and minimize the impact of security breaches.

Creating Effective security through Encryption Standards

Encryption is a security technique that involves converting plain text into a coded message to prevent unauthorized access. It is like locking a message in a safe that can only be opened with a key. Creating effective security through encryption standards involves using strong encryption algorithms and keys to protect sensitive data. Just like a strong lock and key system, strong encryption standards ensure that only authorized individuals can access the data. This helps to prevent data breaches and unauthorized access to sensitive information. Encryption standards are important for several reasons. Firstly, encryption helps to protect sensitive data from unauthorized access by converting it into ciphertext, which is unreadable without an encryption key. This makes it nearly impossible for cybercriminals or other unauthorized parties to steal and misuse the data. Secondly, encryption can enhance the security of communication between client apps and servers, protecting private information and sensitive data. Thirdly, encryption standards can protect data in transit, ensuring that only the intended recipient can read the data. Fourthly, encryption standards can protect against data breaches, reducing the risk of a data breach. Finally, data encryption standards can help organizations comply with data privacy regulations, ensuring that they are compliant with these regulations. Despite the benefits of encryption, there are also some challenges associated with it, such as the resource-intensive nature of encrypting data and the need to regularly monitor the encryption system.

Creating Effective security through Change management Procedures

Creating effective security through change management procedures is like building a strong foundation for a house. Just as a house needs a solid foundation to withstand the test of time, an organization needs a well-defined change management process to ensure that changes to the IT environment are made in a controlled and secure manner. Change management procedures help to minimize the risk of security breaches and ensure that changes are made in a way that does not negatively impact the organization's security posture. By implementing a change management process, an organization can ensure that all changes are properly documented, tested, and approved before they are implemented. This helps to prevent unauthorized changes and ensures that any changes that are made are done so in a way that is consistent with the organization's security policies and procedures.

Creating Effective security through Onboarding/offboarding Procedures

Creating effective security through onboarding/offboarding procedures is like building a strong and secure house. Just as a house needs a solid foundation to support the structure, an organization needs a well-defined and comprehensive onboarding/offboarding process to ensure that employees have the necessary access to perform their job duties and that access is revoked when they leave the organization. This process should include steps such as background checks, security awareness training, and access control measures to ensure that only authorized personnel have access to sensitive information. By implementing a strong onboarding/offboarding process, an organization can reduce the risk of insider threats and ensure that its sensitive data remains secure.

Creating Effective security through Playbook Procedures

Creating effective security through playbook procedures is like following a recipe to cook a meal. Just as a recipe provides a step-by-step guide to cooking a meal, a playbook provides a step-by-step guide to implementing security procedures. Playbooks are a set of procedures that define how to respond to security incidents, and they can be used to automate security tasks. By following a playbook, security teams can ensure that they are responding to incidents in a consistent and effective manner. Playbooks can also be used to train new security team members, ensuring that they are following the same procedures as the rest of the team. Overall, creating effective security through playbook procedures involves defining a set of procedures that can be followed consistently and automating security tasks to ensure that they are performed correctly every time.

Creating Effective security through Regulatory considerations

Creating effective security through regulatory considerations is like building a house with a strong foundation. Just as a house needs a solid foundation to withstand external forces, an organization needs a strong regulatory framework to ensure that its security measures are effective and sustainable. Regulatory considerations provide a framework for establishing security policies, procedures, and controls that are aligned with industry standards and best practices. This framework helps organizations to identify and mitigate risks, protect sensitive data, and ensure compliance with legal and regulatory requirements. By building a strong regulatory foundation, organizations can create a culture of security that promotes accountability, transparency, and continuous improvement.

Creating Effective security through Legal considerations

Creating effective security through legal considerations involves understanding the laws and regulations that apply to the organization and its operations. It is similar to building a house with a strong foundation and sturdy walls to protect it from external threats. Just as a house needs to comply with building codes and regulations to ensure its safety, an organization needs to comply with legal requirements to ensure its security. This includes understanding the legal framework that governs data protection, privacy, and cybersecurity, and implementing appropriate policies and procedures to comply with these laws. Failure to comply with legal requirements can result in legal and financial consequences, just as a house that does not comply with building codes can be unsafe and subject to penalties. Therefore, creating effective security through legal considerations is essential for protecting the organization and its assets from external threats.

Creating Effective security through Industry considerations

Creating effective security through industry considerations involves implementing security measures that are tailored to the specific needs of an organization. Just as a tailor would create a suit that fits perfectly for a specific individual, security measures must be customized to fit the unique needs of an organization. This involves taking into account the industry in which the organization operates, as well as the specific threats and risks that are associated with that industry. For example, a bank would have different security needs than a retail store, as the risks associated with each industry are different. By taking into account these industry considerations, organizations can create effective security measures that are tailored to their specific needs, and that provide the necessary protection against the threats and risks that they face.

Creating Effective security through Local/regional considerations

Creating effective security through local/regional considerations means taking into account the specific security needs of a particular area or region. Just as a tailor would create a suit that fits perfectly for a specific individual, security measures should be tailored to fit the specific needs of a particular area. For example, a city with a high crime rate may require more surveillance cameras and police patrols than a small town with a low crime rate. Similarly, a company that operates in a region with a high risk of cyber attacks may need to invest more in cybersecurity measures than a company that operates in a region with a lower risk. By taking into account the local/regional considerations, security measures can be more effective and better suited to the specific needs of the area or region.

Creating Effective security through National considerations

Creating effective security through national considerations involves taking into account the unique security needs of a country and implementing measures to address those needs. This can be compared to building a house. Just as a house needs to be built with the specific climate and weather conditions of the area in mind, security measures need to be tailored to the specific threats and risks faced by a country. For example, a country with a high risk of cyber attacks may need to invest in advanced cybersecurity measures, while a country with a high risk of terrorism may need to focus on physical security measures such as border control and surveillance. By taking into account national considerations and implementing appropriate security measures, a country can create a strong and effective security posture that protects its citizens and assets.

Creating Effective security through Global considerations

Creating effective security through global considerations involves taking into account the various factors that can impact security across different regions and cultures. Just as a building's foundation must be strong enough to withstand different weather conditions, security measures must be designed to address the unique challenges and threats that exist in different parts of the world. For example, a security system that works well in one country may not be effective in another due to differences in laws, regulations, and cultural norms. Therefore, it is important to consider these factors when designing security measures to ensure that they are effective and can be implemented globally. Just as a building's foundation must be strong enough to withstand different weather conditions, security measures must be designed to address the unique challenges and threats that exist in different parts of the world.

Creating effective security governance through Monitoring and revision

Creating effective security governance through monitoring and revision is like maintaining a garden. Just as a gardener must regularly monitor the plants for pests and diseases, and revise their care plan as needed to ensure the health and growth of the garden, an organization must regularly monitor their security measures and revise their security policies as needed to ensure the safety and growth of their business. This involves implementing security controls, monitoring their effectiveness, and revising them as needed to address new threats and vulnerabilities. It also involves regularly reviewing and updating security policies and procedures to ensure they are up-to-date and effective. By doing so, an organization can create a strong security governance framework that protects their assets and helps them grow and thrive.

Creating Effective security through Types of governance structures such as, Boards

Governance structures are important for creating effective security in an organization. One type of governance structure is a board, which is responsible for setting policies and making decisions that affect the organization's security posture. A board can be thought of as the captain of a ship, responsible for steering the ship in the right direction and making sure it stays on course. The board sets the overall direction for the organization's security program, and ensures that the organization is complying with relevant laws and regulations. The board also provides oversight and guidance to the security team, ensuring that they have the resources they need to carry out their duties effectively. By establishing a strong governance structure, organizations can ensure that their security program is effective and aligned with their overall business objectives.

Creating Effective security through Types of governance structures such as, Committees

Governance structures are important for creating effective security in an organization. One type of governance structure is committees. Committees are like a team of experts who work together to achieve a common goal. In the context of security, committees can be formed to oversee different aspects of security such as risk management, compliance, and incident response. Each committee can have its own set of responsibilities and members with specific expertise. By having committees, an organization can ensure that security is being managed effectively and efficiently. Committees can also provide a forum for discussion and decision-making, which can help to identify and address security issues before they become major problems. Overall, committees are an important part of a governance structure that can help to create effective security in an organization.

Creating Effective security through Types of governance structures such as, Government entities

Governance structures are essential in creating effective security. Government entities are one type of governance structure that can be used to establish security policies and regulations. Just like a city government that creates laws and regulations to ensure the safety and well-being of its citizens, government entities can create policies and regulations to ensure the security of their organizations. These policies and regulations can include security standards, guidelines, and procedures that must be followed by all employees and contractors. By having a strong governance structure in place, organizations can ensure that security is a top priority and that everyone is working towards the same goal of protecting the organization's assets and data.

Creating Effective security through Types of governance structures such as, Centralized/decentralized

Governance structures are important for creating effective security in an organization. Centralized governance is like a monarchy where all the power is concentrated in one central authority. In this structure, decisions are made by a single entity, which can be efficient but can also lead to a lack of flexibility and responsiveness. Decentralized governance, on the other hand, is like a democracy where power is distributed among multiple entities. In this structure, decisions are made by a group of people, which can be slower but can also lead to more collaboration and innovation. Both centralized and decentralized governance structures have their advantages and disadvantages, and the choice of which one to use depends on the specific needs and goals of the organization.

Creating effective security governance through Roles and responsibilities for systems and data Owners

Creating effective security governance through roles and responsibilities for systems and data owners is like building a house. The security governance framework is the foundation of the house, and the roles and responsibilities of systems and data owners are the walls and roof. Just as the foundation of a house must be strong and stable to support the weight of the walls and roof, the security governance framework must be well-defined and comprehensive to support the roles and responsibilities of systems and data owners. The walls and roof of a house protect the interior from external threats such as weather and intruders, and the roles and responsibilities of systems and data owners protect the organization's assets from internal and external threats. By defining clear roles and responsibilities for systems and data owners, the organization can ensure that everyone understands their role in maintaining security and can work together to create a secure environment.

Creating effective security governance through Roles and responsibilities for systems and data Controllers

Creating effective security governance through roles and responsibilities for systems and data controllers is like building a house. Just as a house needs a strong foundation to support the structure, an organization needs a strong security governance framework to support its security posture. The roles and responsibilities of systems and data controllers are like the walls and roof of the house, providing protection and security for the organization's assets. Without these roles and responsibilities, the organization's security posture would be weak and vulnerable to attack. By defining clear roles and responsibilities for systems and data controllers, the organization can ensure that everyone knows what is expected of them and can work together to build a strong security governance framework. This framework will help to protect the organization's assets and ensure that it can continue to operate effectively and securely.

Creating effective security governance through Roles and responsibilities for systems and data Processors

Creating effective security governance through roles and responsibilities for systems and data processors is like building a house. Just as a house needs a strong foundation to support the structure, an organization needs a strong security governance framework to support its security posture. The roles and responsibilities of systems and data processors are like the walls and roof of the house, providing protection and security for the organization's assets. Without these roles and responsibilities, the organization's security posture would be weak and vulnerable to attacks. By defining clear roles and responsibilities for systems and data processors, the organization can ensure that everyone is working together towards a common goal of protecting the organization's assets. This creates a culture of security and helps to ensure that security is a top priority for everyone in the organization.

Creating effective security governance through Roles and responsibilities for systems and data Custodians/stewards

Creating effective security governance through roles and responsibilities for systems and data custodians/stewards is like building a house. The custodians/stewards are like the builders who are responsible for constructing the house and ensuring that it is built according to the blueprint. They are responsible for maintaining the integrity, confidentiality, and availability of the data and systems they are entrusted with. The security governance framework is like the blueprint that outlines the roles and responsibilities of the custodians/stewards and provides guidance on how to build a secure and resilient system. Just as a house needs a solid foundation to withstand external forces, a security governance framework needs to be built on a solid foundation of policies, procedures, and standards to ensure that the system is secure and resilient. By following the security governance framework, custodians/stewards can ensure that the system is built to withstand external threats and protect the data and systems from unauthorized access, modification, or destruction.

Cyber Risk identification

Cyber risk identification is the process of identifying potential threats and vulnerabilities that could lead to a cyber attack. It involves analyzing the organization's assets, such as hardware, software, and data, to determine their value and the potential impact of a security breach. This process is similar to a security guard who patrols a building to identify potential security risks, such as unlocked doors or windows, and takes steps to mitigate those risks. By identifying potential cyber risks, an organization can take proactive measures to prevent security breaches and protect its assets.

Apsects of Risk assessment such as, Ad hoc Risk assessment

Risk assessment is a process of identifying, analyzing, and evaluating potential risks to an organization's assets, operations, and individuals. Ad hoc risk assessment is a type of risk assessment that is done on an as-needed basis, without a formal structure or methodology. It is similar to a doctor diagnosing a patient's illness based on symptoms and experience, rather than following a specific protocol. While ad hoc risk assessment can be useful in identifying immediate risks, it may not provide a comprehensive view of all potential risks and may not be repeatable or consistent. Therefore, it is important to have a formal risk assessment process in place to ensure that all risks are identified and addressed appropriately.

Apsects of Risk assessment such as, Recurring Risk assessment

Risk assessment is an important aspect of security management. It involves identifying, analyzing, and evaluating potential risks to an organization's assets, including information, personnel, and physical infrastructure. Recurring risk assessment is a process of regularly reviewing and updating the risk assessment to ensure that it remains relevant and effective. It is similar to maintaining a car, where regular check-ups and maintenance are necessary to ensure that the car is running smoothly and to prevent any potential issues from becoming major problems. By conducting recurring risk assessments, organizations can identify new risks, assess the effectiveness of existing controls, and make informed decisions about risk mitigation strategies.

Apsects of Risk assessment such as, One-time Risk assessment

Risk assessment is a process of identifying, analyzing, and evaluating potential risks to an organization's assets, operations, and individuals. One-time risk assessment is a type of risk assessment that is conducted only once, usually at the beginning of a project or when a new system is implemented. It is like a snapshot of the risks at a particular point in time. Just like taking a picture, a one-time risk assessment captures the risks that exist at a specific moment, but it does not account for changes that may occur over time. Therefore, it is important to conduct regular risk assessments to ensure that the organization's risk management strategies remain effective and up-to-date.

Apsects of Risk assessment such as, Continuous Risk assessment

Risk assessment is a crucial aspect of security management. It involves identifying, analyzing, and evaluating potential risks to an organization's assets, including people, information, and technology. Continuous risk assessment is a process of regularly monitoring and evaluating risks to ensure that security measures remain effective. It is like regularly checking the tire pressure of a car to ensure that it is safe to drive. Just as tire pressure can change over time due to various factors, such as temperature and wear and tear, the risk landscape of an organization can also change due to various factors, such as new threats and vulnerabilities. Therefore, continuous risk assessment is necessary to ensure that security measures are up-to-date and effective in mitigating potential risks.

Apsects of cyber Risk analysis such as, Qualitative Risk analysis

Qualitative risk analysis is a method of assessing the likelihood and impact of a cybersecurity threat based on subjective criteria such as expert judgment, experience, and intuition. It involves identifying and prioritizing risks based on their potential impact on an organization's assets, operations, and reputation. An analogy for qualitative risk analysis is a chef tasting a dish and assessing its quality based on their experience and expertise. The chef may not be able to quantify the exact amount of salt or spices used, but they can provide a subjective assessment of the dish's overall taste and quality. Similarly, qualitative risk analysis relies on the expertise and judgment of cybersecurity professionals to assess the potential impact of a threat based on subjective criteria.

Apsects of cyber Risk analysis such as, Quantitative Risk analysis

Quantitative risk analysis is a method of cyber risk analysis that involves assigning numerical values to the likelihood and impact of a risk. This approach is similar to calculating the probability of winning a game of dice. Just as the probability of rolling a six on a single die is 1/6, the probability of a particular risk occurring can be calculated based on historical data, expert opinions, and other factors. The impact of a risk can also be quantified in terms of financial loss, reputational damage, or other measurable factors. By combining the likelihood and impact of a risk, a quantitative risk analysis can provide a numerical estimate of the overall risk level, which can be used to prioritize risk mitigation efforts.

Apsects of cyber Risk analysis such as, Single loss expectancy (SLE)

Single loss expectancy (SLE) is a term used in cyber risk analysis to estimate the monetary value of a single loss that could occur from a security incident. It is calculated by multiplying the asset value (AV) by the exposure factor (EF). The asset value is the estimated value of the asset that could be lost or damaged in a security incident, while the exposure factor is the percentage of the asset value that could be lost or damaged in a security incident. An analogy to understand SLE is to think of a car accident. The asset value is the value of the car, while the exposure factor is the percentage of the car that could be damaged in an accident. The SLE is the estimated monetary value of the damage that could occur in a single car accident.

Apsects of cyber Risk analysis such as, Annualized loss expectancy (ALE)

Annualized Loss Expectancy (ALE) is a metric used in cyber risk analysis to estimate the expected monetary loss from a security incident over a one-year period. It is calculated by multiplying the Single Loss Expectancy (SLE) by the Annual Rate of Occurrence (ARO). The SLE is the expected monetary loss from a single security incident, while the ARO is the estimated frequency of such incidents occurring in a year. ALE is similar to an insurance premium, where the premium is the expected loss and the probability of the loss occurring is the ARO. For example, if a company estimates that the SLE of a data breach is $10,000 and the ARO is 2, then the ALE would be $20,000. This means that the company can expect to lose $20,000 per year due to data breaches. ALE is a useful metric for organizations to prioritize their security investments and determine the cost-effectiveness of security controls.

Apsects of cyber Risk analysis such as, Annualized rate of occurrence (ARO)

Annualized Rate of Occurrence (ARO) is a metric used in cyber risk analysis to estimate the frequency of a specific threat occurring within a year. It is calculated by dividing the total number of incidents that occurred in a year by the total number of opportunities for the incident to occur. ARO is similar to the probability of an event occurring in a given time period. For example, if a company experiences 10 cyber attacks in a year and has 1000 opportunities for an attack to occur, then the ARO would be 0.01 or 1%. This means that the company can expect to experience one cyber attack every 100 years, assuming the same conditions remain constant. ARO is an important metric in cyber risk analysis as it helps organizations to prioritize their security efforts and allocate resources effectively.

Apsects of cyber Risk analysis such as, Probability Risk analysis

Cyber risk analysis is the process of identifying, assessing, and prioritizing risks to an organization's information assets. Probability risk analysis is a method of assessing the likelihood of a risk occurring and the potential impact it could have on the organization. This is similar to a weather forecast, where meteorologists use data and models to predict the likelihood of a storm occurring and the potential impact it could have on the area. By using probability risk analysis, organizations can prioritize their resources and focus on the risks that are most likely to occur and have the greatest impact. This helps them to make informed decisions about how to manage their cyber risks and protect their information assets.

Apsects of cyber Risk analysis such as, Likelihood Risk analysis

Cyber risk analysis is the process of identifying, assessing, and prioritizing risks to an organization's information assets. One aspect of cyber risk analysis is likelihood risk analysis, which involves estimating the probability of a risk occurring. This can be compared to predicting the likelihood of rain based on the weather forecast. Just as a weather forecast can predict the likelihood of rain based on factors such as temperature, humidity, and atmospheric pressure, likelihood risk analysis can estimate the probability of a cyber attack based on factors such as the organization's security posture, threat intelligence, and historical attack data. By understanding the likelihood of a risk occurring, organizations can prioritize their resources and focus on the most critical risks.

Apsects of cyber Risk analysis such as, Exposure factor Risk analysis

Cyber risk analysis is the process of identifying, assessing, and prioritizing risks associated with the use of technology. Exposure factor is a measure of the extent to which an asset is exposed to a particular threat. It is expressed as a percentage of the asset's value. For example, if a company's server is worth $10,000 and it is exposed to a threat that has a 50% exposure factor, the potential loss from that threat is $5,000. Risk analysis involves identifying the potential threats to an asset, estimating the likelihood of those threats occurring, and determining the potential impact of those threats. Exposure factor is an important component of risk analysis because it helps to quantify the potential loss from a particular threat. By understanding the exposure factor for each asset, organizations can prioritize their risk management efforts and allocate resources more effectively.

Apsects of cyber Risk analysis such as, Impact Risk analysis

Cyber risk analysis is the process of identifying, assessing, and prioritizing risks associated with the use of technology. Impact risk analysis is a critical aspect of cyber risk analysis that involves evaluating the potential consequences of a security incident. It helps organizations to understand the potential impact of a security breach on their operations, reputation, and financial stability. An analogy to understand impact risk analysis is to think of a game of chess. Just as a chess player considers the potential consequences of each move before making it, an organization must consider the potential impact of a security incident before taking any action. By analyzing the potential impact of a security breach, an organization can make informed decisions about how to allocate resources to prevent, detect, and respond to cyber threats.

managing risks though a Risk register such as, Key risk indicators

A risk register is a document used in risk management to identify potential risks that could affect the execution of a project plan. It is a tool that helps to collectively identify, analyze, and solve risks before they become problems. The purpose of a risk register is to log the information of potential risks, so that the team members can be informed and prepared to respond quickly before project risks become real problems that could impact the project. A risk register is essentially a table of project risks that allows you to track each identified risk and any vital information about it. It is like a spreadsheet or database document that lists the risks you face, along with a variety of relevant factors for each one. The risk register is the first step in project risk management, and it's an important part of any risk management framework. It helps project managers list risks, their priority level, mitigation strategies, and the risk owner so everybody on the project team knows how to respond to project risk. The key objective of a risk register is to identify, log, and track potential project risks. It is important to note that the risk register should be updated regularly as risks change over time and new risks can arise.

managing risks though a Risk register such as, Risk owners

A risk register is a document that is used as a risk management tool to identify potential setbacks within a project. It is essentially a table of project risks that allows you to track each identified risk and any vital information about it. A risk register is the first step in project risk management, and it's an important part of any risk management framework. It helps project managers list risks, their priority level, mitigation strategies, and the risk owner so everybody on the project team knows how to respond to project risk. The risk owner is the person responsible for managing the risk and ensuring that the mitigation strategies are implemented. The risk register is like a map that helps the project team navigate through the potential risks and challenges that may arise during the project. It is important to note that the risk register is not a one-time activity, but rather a continuous process that should be updated regularly to ensure that the project team is aware of any new risks that may arise.

managing risks though a Risk register such as, Risk threshold

A risk register is a document used in risk management to identify potential risks that could affect the execution of a project plan. It is like a table that lists the risks you face, along with a variety of relevant factors for each one. The purpose of a risk register is to record the details of all risks that have been identified along with their analysis and plans for how those risks will be treated. The risk register is the first step in project risk management, and it's an important part of any risk management framework. It helps project managers list risks, their priority level, mitigation strategies, and the risk owner so everybody on the project team knows how to respond to project risk. The risk register can be viewed by project managers as a management tool for monitoring the risk management processes within the project. The risk threshold is the level of risk that an organization is willing to accept before taking action to reduce it. An analogy for a risk register could be a medical chart that lists a patient's medical history, including any allergies, medications, and previous illnesses. Just as a medical chart helps doctors identify potential health risks and develop a treatment plan, a risk register helps project managers identify potential risks and develop a risk management plan.

Risk tolerance

Risk tolerance refers to the level of risk that an organization is willing to accept or tolerate. It is similar to a person's tolerance for risk in their personal life. Just as some people are willing to take more risks than others, some organizations are willing to accept more risk than others. For example, a person who enjoys extreme sports may be willing to take more risks than someone who prefers more sedentary activities. Similarly, an organization that operates in a high-risk industry, such as finance or healthcare, may be willing to accept more risk than an organization that operates in a low-risk industry, such as retail. The level of risk tolerance is determined by a variety of factors, including the organization's goals, resources, and regulatory requirements.

Risk tolerance elements such as, Expansionary

Risk tolerance refers to the level of risk that an organization is willing to accept in order to achieve its objectives. Expansionary risk tolerance is a type of risk tolerance where an organization is willing to take on more risk in order to achieve greater rewards. This can be compared to a person who is willing to invest in a high-risk, high-reward stock in order to potentially earn a larger return on their investment. While this approach can lead to greater success, it also carries a higher risk of failure. Therefore, organizations must carefully consider their risk tolerance and weigh the potential benefits against the potential risks before making any decisions.

Risk tolerance elements such as, Conservative
Risk tolerance refers to the level of risk that an organization is willing to accept in order to achieve its objectives. Conservative risk tolerance is a low-risk approach where an organization is willing to accept only a minimal level of risk. This approach is similar to a person who is very cautious and avoids taking risks. For example, a person who is conservative may choose to invest their money in a savings account rather than in the stock market, which is considered a higher-risk investment. Similarly, an organization with a conservative risk tolerance may choose to implement strict security measures to minimize the risk of a security breach, even if it means sacrificing some level of convenience or efficiency.

Risk tolerance elements such as, Neutral
Risk tolerance refers to the level of risk that an organization is willing to accept in order to achieve its objectives. Neutral risk tolerance is a state where an organization is neither risk-averse nor risk-seeking. It is similar to driving a car at a moderate speed on a straight road. The driver is not taking unnecessary risks by driving too fast or too slow, but is also not being overly cautious. In the same way, an organization with a neutral risk tolerance is not taking unnecessary risks, but is also not being overly cautious and is willing to accept a moderate level of risk to achieve its objectives.

Risk management strategies such as, Transfer
Risk management is a crucial process for organizations to identify, assess, and control threats to their capital, earnings, and operations. One of the strategies used in risk management is transfer, which is similar to buying insurance to transfer the risk of loss to another party. For instance, when a person buys car insurance, they transfer the risk of financial loss from an accident to the insurance company. Similarly, a company can transfer the risk of loss from a cyber attack to a cybersecurity insurance company. By transferring the risk, the organization can reduce the impact of the risk on its operations and financial stability. However, it is important to note that transferring the risk does not eliminate it completely, and the organization still needs to have a plan in place to manage the residual risk.

Risk management strategies such as, Accept
Risk management is the process of identifying, assessing, and controlling threats to an organization's capital, earnings, and operations. One of the risk management strategies is to accept the risk. This means that the organization acknowledges the risk and decides not to take any action to mitigate it. It is similar to accepting the risk of driving a car, knowing that there is a risk of getting into an accident. The organization may decide to accept the risk if the cost of mitigating the risk is higher than the potential loss from the risk itself. However, accepting the risk does not mean that the organization should ignore it. The organization should still monitor the risk and be prepared to take action if the risk materializes.

Risk management strategies, Accepting Risk Exemptions

Risk management strategies are used to identify, assess, and prioritize risks to an organization's assets, operations, and reputation. One of the strategies is accepting risk exemptions. This means that the organization acknowledges the risk but decides not to take any action to mitigate it. It is similar to a person who decides to drive a car despite knowing the risks associated with driving, such as the possibility of getting into an accident. The person accepts the risk and decides not to take any action to mitigate it, such as not driving at all or taking public transportation. Similarly, an organization may decide to accept a risk exemption if the cost of mitigating the risk is too high or if the risk is deemed acceptable based on the organization's risk appetite. However, it is important to note that accepting a risk exemption does not mean that the organization is ignoring the risk. Rather, it is a conscious decision to accept the risk and its potential consequences.

Risk management strategies, Accepting Risk Exception

Risk management strategies are used to identify, assess, and prioritize risks to an organization's assets, operations, and reputation. One of the strategies is accepting risk, which means acknowledging the potential impact of a risk and deciding to live with it. This strategy is like driving a car on a rainy day. You know that there is a risk of an accident due to slippery roads, but you accept the risk and continue driving. However, you may take some measures to reduce the risk, such as driving slower, keeping a safe distance from other vehicles, and using headlights. Similarly, in risk management, accepting risk does not mean ignoring it completely, but rather acknowledging it and taking measures to minimize its impact. An exception to accepting risk is when the risk is too high and the potential impact is severe, in which case the organization may need to implement other risk management strategies such as transferring, mitigating, or avoiding the risk.

Risk management strategies, Avoiding risk
Risk management strategies are essential for organizations to identify, assess, and mitigate risks that could impact their operations. One of the risk management strategies is avoiding risk. Avoiding risk means taking steps to eliminate the risk altogether. It is like avoiding a pothole on the road by taking a different route. If you know that a particular road has a pothole that could damage your car, you would avoid that road and take a different route. Similarly, if an organization identifies a risk that could have severe consequences, it may choose to avoid that risk altogether by not engaging in the activity that poses the risk. Avoiding risk is an effective strategy for risks that are too severe or costly to mitigate. However, it may not always be possible to avoid risks, and in such cases, organizations may need to implement other risk management strategies such as transferring, mitigating, or accepting the risk.

Risk management strategies, Mitigateing risk
Risk management strategies are used to identify, assess, and prioritize risks to an organization's assets, operations, and reputation. Mitigating risk involves taking steps to reduce the likelihood or impact of a risk. This can be compared to driving a car. When driving, you identify potential risks such as other cars, pedestrians, or road hazards. You assess the likelihood and potential impact of these risks and prioritize them based on their severity. To mitigate the risk of an accident, you take steps such as wearing a seatbelt, obeying traffic laws, and maintaining your vehicle. Similarly, in risk management, you identify potential risks, assess their likelihood and impact, and prioritize them based on their severity. To mitigate the risk, you take steps such as implementing security controls, training employees, and developing incident response plans. By taking these steps, you can reduce the likelihood or impact of a risk, just as wearing a seatbelt can reduce the likelihood or impact of an accident.

Risk management strategies, Risk reporting
Risk management strategies are the methods used to identify, assess, and mitigate risks to an organization. These strategies include risk avoidance, risk acceptance, risk transfer, and risk mitigation. Risk avoidance is like avoiding a pothole on the road by taking a different route. Risk acceptance is like driving over the pothole because it is too expensive or impractical to avoid it. Risk transfer is like buying insurance to transfer the risk to an insurance company. Risk mitigation is like filling the pothole to reduce the risk of damage to the vehicle. Risk reporting is the process of communicating risk information to stakeholders. It involves identifying the risks, assessing their likelihood and impact, and reporting the results to the appropriate stakeholders. Risk reporting is like a weather forecast that provides information about the likelihood and severity of a storm, allowing people to take appropriate action to protect themselves and their property.

Risk management strategies, Business impact analysis
Risk management strategies are the processes and methods used to identify, assess, and mitigate risks to an organization. It involves identifying potential risks, analyzing their likelihood and impact, and developing strategies to manage or mitigate them. An analogy for risk management strategies is a game of chess. Just as a chess player must anticipate their opponent's moves and plan their own moves accordingly, an organization must anticipate potential risks and plan strategies to mitigate them. Business impact analysis (BIA) is the process of identifying and evaluating the potential impact of a disruption to an organization's critical business functions. It involves identifying critical business processes, determining the potential impact of a disruption to those processes, and developing strategies to minimize the impact. An analogy for BIA is a fire drill. Just as a fire drill helps people prepare for a potential fire and evacuate a building safely, a BIA helps an organization prepare for a potential disruption and minimize the impact on critical business functions.

Managing risks utalizing business impact analysis such as, Recovery time objective (RTO)
Managing risks involves identifying potential threats and vulnerabilities, assessing the likelihood and impact of those risks, and implementing measures to mitigate them. Business impact analysis (BIA) is a key component of risk management that helps organizations understand the potential impact of a disruption to their operations. Recovery time objective (RTO) is a metric used in BIA to determine the maximum amount of time that a business process can be down before it starts to have a significant impact on the organization. An analogy to understand RTO is to think of a car that has run out of gas. The RTO is the amount of time it takes to refill the gas tank and get the car back on the road. In the same way, RTO helps organizations determine how quickly they need to recover from a disruption to their operations to minimize the impact on their business.

Managing risks utalizing business impact analysis such as, Recovery point objective (RPO)
Managing risks involves identifying potential threats and vulnerabilities, and taking steps to mitigate them. One way to do this is by conducting a business impact analysis (BIA), which helps to identify critical business functions and the potential impact of disruptions to those functions. Recovery point objective (RPO) is a key component of BIA, which refers to the maximum amount of data loss that an organization can tolerate. It is like a safety net that catches a trapeze artist if they fall. In the same way, RPO helps to ensure that an organization can recover from a disaster by setting a limit on the amount of data that can be lost. By utilizing RPO, an organization can ensure that it has the necessary backups and recovery procedures in place to minimize the impact of a disaster and quickly resume normal operations.

Managing risks utalizing business impact analysis such as, Mean time to repair (MTTR)

Managing risks is an essential part of any organization's security strategy. One way to manage risks is by utilizing business impact analysis, which involves identifying critical business functions and the potential impact of a disruption to those functions. Mean time to repair (MTTR) is a metric used to measure the average time it takes to repair a system after a failure. It is an important metric to consider when conducting a business impact analysis because it helps organizations understand how long it will take to recover from a disruption. An analogy to understand MTTR is to think of a car that breaks down on the side of the road. The MTTR would be the average time it takes for a mechanic to repair the car and get it back on the road. Similarly, in an organization, the MTTR would be the average time it takes to repair a system and get it back up and running after a disruption. By understanding the MTTR, organizations can better plan for and manage risks to their critical business functions.

Managing risks utalizing business impact analysis such as, Mean time between failures (MTBF)

Managing risks utilizing business impact analysis involves identifying potential risks and assessing their potential impact on the organization. One way to measure the impact of a risk is by calculating the Mean Time Between Failures (MTBF). MTBF is a measure of the average time between failures of a system or component. It is similar to the concept of a car's reliability - the longer a car can go without breaking down, the more reliable it is. Similarly, the longer the MTBF of a system or component, the more reliable it is. By calculating the MTBF, organizations can determine the likelihood of a failure occurring and the potential impact it could have on the business. This information can then be used to prioritize risk mitigation efforts and allocate resources accordingly.

Third-party risk assessment through, Vendor assessment

Third-party risk assessment is the process of evaluating the security risks associated with vendors, suppliers, and other third-party entities that have access to an organization's sensitive data or systems. It is similar to a homeowner evaluating the security risks associated with hiring a contractor to work on their home. Just as a homeowner would want to ensure that the contractor is trustworthy and has a good reputation before allowing them access to their home, an organization should evaluate the security risks associated with third-party entities before granting them access to their sensitive data or systems. Vendor assessment is a key component of third-party risk assessment and involves evaluating the security controls and practices of vendors to ensure that they meet the organization's security requirements. This is similar to a homeowner evaluating the quality of work and safety practices of a contractor before hiring them to work on their home. By conducting third-party risk assessments and vendor assessments, organizations can help mitigate the risk of data breaches and other security incidents caused by third-party entities.

Third-party risk Vendor assessment through, Penetration testing

A third-party risk assessment is a process of evaluating the security posture of vendors and suppliers that have access to an organization's sensitive data. It is preferred over an internal vendor assessment because it provides an objective, comprehensive, and cost-effective evaluation of the vendor's security posture. A third-party risk assessment is conducted by security experts who have experience in identifying and mitigating security risks. It evaluates the vendor's security posture from multiple angles, including compliance, operational, financial, and reputational risks. This provides a more comprehensive evaluation of the vendor's security posture than an internal vendor assessment. Third-party risk vendor assessment is the process of evaluating the security posture of vendors and suppliers that have access to an organization's sensitive data. This is done to ensure that the third-party is not a security risk to the organization. Penetration testing is a type of security testing that simulates an attack on a system to identify vulnerabilities that could be exploited by an attacker. It is like a burglar trying to break into a house to identify weaknesses in the security system. In the context of third-party risk vendor assessment, penetration testing is used to identify vulnerabilities in the vendor's systems that could be exploited by an attacker to gain access to the organization's sensitive data. By conducting penetration testing, the organization can identify and remediate vulnerabilities before they are exploited by an attacker.

Third-party risk Vendor assessment through, Right-to-audit clause

Third-party risk vendor assessment is a process of evaluating the security posture of vendors and suppliers who have access to an organization's sensitive data or systems. The right-to-audit clause is a contractual agreement that allows an organization to conduct an audit of a vendor's security controls and processes. The clause is important because it gives the organization the ability to verify that the vendor is meeting its contractual obligations and is taking appropriate measures to protect the organization's sensitive data or systems. However, the right-to-audit clause can pose several challenges for organizations, such as ensuring that third-party vendors are willing to agree to such a provision in their contracts. The parameters of the audit vary, so it is important to determine whether the objective of the audit is achievable under the parameters that are set forth. Selective and well-documented use of the right-to-audit clause can provide companies with an effective tool in mitigating third-party risks. Third-party risk vendor assessment is a process of evaluating the security posture of vendors and suppliers who have access to an organization's sensitive data or systems. The right-to-audit clause is a contractual agreement that allows an organization to conduct an audit of a vendor's security controls and processes. This clause is similar to a landlord inspecting a rental property before renting it out to a tenant. Just as a landlord wants to ensure that the property is in good condition and meets certain standards, an organization wants to ensure that a vendor's security controls and processes meet its security requirements. The right-to-audit clause gives the organization the ability to verify that the vendor is meeting its contractual obligations and is taking appropriate measures to protect the organization's sensitive data or systems.

Third-party risk Vendor assessment through, Evidence of internal audits

Third-party risk vendor assessment is a process of evaluating the security posture of vendors and suppliers who have access to an organization's sensitive data or systems. The right-to-audit clause is a contractual agreement that allows an organization to conduct an audit of a vendor's security controls and processes. This clause is similar to a landlord inspecting a rental property before renting it out to a tenant. Just as a landlord wants to ensure that the property is in good condition and meets certain standards, an organization wants to ensure that a vendor's security controls and processes meet its security requirements. The right-to-audit clause gives the organization the ability to verify that the vendor is meeting its contractual obligations and is taking appropriate measures to protect the organization's sensitive data or systems.

Third-party risk Vendor assessment through, Independent assessments

Third-party risk refers to the potential risks that arise when an organization engages with external vendors or partners. Vendor assessment is the process of evaluating the security posture of these third-party vendors to ensure that they meet the organization's security requirements. Independent assessments are evaluations conducted by a third-party organization that is not affiliated with the vendor or the organization. These assessments provide an unbiased view of the vendor's security posture. An analogy for this process could be a home inspection before purchasing a house. Just as a home inspection provides an independent assessment of the condition of a house, a vendor assessment provides an independent evaluation of a vendor's security posture.

Third-party risk Vendor assessment through, Supply chain analysis

Third-party risk refers to the potential risks that arise when an organization engages with external parties such as vendors, suppliers, or contractors. Vendor assessment is a process of evaluating the security posture of third-party vendors to ensure that they meet the organization's security requirements. Supply chain analysis is a process of identifying and assessing the risks associated with the products and services provided by third-party vendors. An analogy to explain this concept is to think of a chain where each link represents a vendor or supplier. If one link in the chain is weak, it can compromise the entire chain's strength. Similarly, if a third-party vendor has weak security measures, it can pose a significant risk to the organization's security posture. Therefore, it is essential to conduct vendor assessments and supply chain analysis to identify and mitigate potential risks.

Third-party risk management through, Vendor selection

Third-party risk management is an important aspect of cybersecurity. It involves assessing and managing the risks associated with vendors and other third-party service providers that have access to an organization's sensitive data. Vendor selection is a key part of third-party risk management, as it involves choosing vendors that have a proven track record of security and reliability. This is similar to choosing a babysitter for your child. You want to choose someone who has a good reputation, is trustworthy, and has experience taking care of children. Similarly, when selecting a vendor, you want to choose a company that has a good reputation, is trustworthy, and has experience providing secure and reliable services. By selecting the right vendors and managing third-party risks, organizations can help protect their sensitive data and reduce the risk of data breaches.

Third-party risk management through, Due diligence

Third-party risk management is the process of identifying, assessing, and mitigating risks associated with the use of third-party vendors. Due diligence is a critical component of third-party risk management, as it involves conducting a thorough investigation of a vendor's security posture before engaging in business with them. This investigation should include a review of the vendor's security policies, procedures, and controls, as well as an assessment of their security practices. An analogy for due diligence in third-party risk management is like checking the credentials of a babysitter before leaving your child in their care. Just as you would want to ensure that the babysitter is trustworthy and capable of providing a safe environment for your child, due diligence helps ensure that third-party vendors are capable of protecting your organization's sensitive information and assets.

Third-party risk management through, Conflict of interest

Third-party risk management is the process of identifying, assessing, and mitigating risks associated with third-party vendors. It involves evaluating the security posture of third-party vendors and ensuring that they comply with security policies and standards. Conflict of interest, on the other hand, refers to a situation where an individual or organization has competing interests that could influence their decision-making. In the context of third-party risk management, conflict of interest could arise when a vendor has a financial interest in the outcome of a security assessment. This could lead to biased assessments and a lack of objectivity. An analogy for this could be a student who is grading their own exam. The student may be tempted to give themselves a higher grade than they deserve, leading to an inaccurate assessment of their performance. Similarly, a vendor with a conflict of interest may be tempted to give themselves a higher security rating than they deserve, leading to an inaccurate assessment of their security posture. Therefore, it is important to identify and manage conflicts of interest when conducting third-party risk assessments to ensure that they are objective and unbiased.

Third-party risk management through, Service-level agreement (SLA)

Third-party risk management is the process of identifying, assessing, and mitigating risks associated with the use of third-party vendors. Service-level agreements (SLAs) are a key component of third-party risk management. An SLA is like a contract between a customer and a vendor that outlines the level of service that the vendor will provide. It sets expectations for the quality of service, the availability of the service, and the vendor's responsibilities in the event of a service outage. Just like a contract, an SLA should be carefully reviewed and negotiated to ensure that it meets the needs of both parties. By using SLAs, organizations can manage the risks associated with third-party vendors and ensure that they are getting the level of service they need to operate their business effectively.

Third-party risk management through, Memorandum of agreement (MOA)

Third-party risk management is an important aspect of cybersecurity. It involves assessing and managing the risks associated with third-party vendors and service providers that have access to an organization's sensitive data. One way to manage these risks is through a Memorandum of Agreement (MOA). An MOA is like a prenuptial agreement between two parties. Just as a prenuptial agreement outlines the terms and conditions of a marriage, an MOA outlines the terms and conditions of a business relationship between two parties. It establishes the expectations, responsibilities, and liabilities of each party, and helps to ensure that both parties are on the same page. In the context of third-party risk management, an MOA can help to ensure that vendors and service providers are aware of their responsibilities and obligations with respect to cybersecurity, and can help to mitigate the risks associated with third-party access to sensitive data.

Third-party risk management through, Memorandum of understanding (MOU)

Third-party risk management is a crucial aspect of cybersecurity. It involves assessing and managing the risks associated with third-party vendors, suppliers, and partners who have access to an organization's sensitive data. One way to manage third-party risks is through a Memorandum of Understanding (MOU). An MOU is a formal agreement between two or more parties that outlines the terms and conditions of their relationship. In cybersecurity, an MOU can be compared to a prenuptial agreement between two people getting married. Just as a prenuptial agreement outlines the terms and conditions of a marriage, an MOU outlines the terms and conditions of a business relationship. It helps to establish clear expectations and responsibilities for both parties, and it can be used to hold third-party vendors accountable for their actions. By using an MOU, organizations can reduce the risks associated with third-party vendors and ensure that their sensitive data is protected.

Third-party risk management through, Master service agreement (MSA)

Third-party risk management is the process of identifying, assessing, and mitigating risks associated with third-party vendors. A Master Service Agreement (MSA) is a contract between a company and a vendor that outlines the terms and conditions of their business relationship. It is similar to a prenuptial agreement between two people who are about to get married. Just as a prenuptial agreement outlines the terms and conditions of a marriage, an MSA outlines the terms and conditions of a business relationship. It specifies the services to be provided, the payment terms, and the responsibilities of each party. By having an MSA in place, companies can reduce the risks associated with third-party vendors by ensuring that both parties understand their obligations and responsibilities.

Third-party risk management through, Work order (WO)/statement of work (SOW)

Third-party risk management is a crucial aspect of general risk management, which involves policies and systems to ensure third parties comply with regulations, avoid unethical practices, protect confidential information, and strengthen business processes. Work orders (WO) and statements of work (SOW) are essential components of third-party risk management. A WO/SOW is like a contract between a company and a third-party vendor, outlining the work to be done, the timeline, and the payment terms. It is a critical part of the third-party risk management program, providing the information needed to create a program suitable to the organization's specific risks, standards, and compliance requirements. In other words, a WO/SOW is like a blueprint that outlines the expectations and responsibilities of both parties, ensuring that the third-party vendor complies with the organization's policies and standards.

Third-party risk management through, Non-disclosure agreement (NDA)

Third-party risk management is a crucial aspect of cybersecurity. It involves assessing and mitigating the risks associated with third-party vendors and service providers that have access to an organization's sensitive data. One way to manage third-party risks is through the use of Non-disclosure agreements (NDAs). An NDA is a legal contract that prohibits the disclosure of confidential information to unauthorized parties. It is like a lock on a door that prevents unauthorized access to a room. Just as a lock provides security to a room, an NDA provides security to confidential information by preventing third-party vendors from disclosing it to unauthorized parties. By using NDAs, organizations can ensure that their sensitive data is protected from unauthorized access and disclosure by third-party vendors.

Third-party risk management through, Business partners agreement (BPA)

Third-party risk management is an important aspect of cybersecurity that involves managing the risks associated with third-party vendors and partners. One way to manage these risks is through Business Partner Agreements (BPA). A BPA is like a prenuptial agreement between two parties that outlines the terms and conditions of their relationship. In the context of third-party risk management, a BPA is a legal agreement between a company and its business partners that outlines the security requirements and expectations for the handling of sensitive data. This agreement helps to ensure that both parties understand their responsibilities and obligations when it comes to protecting sensitive information. By establishing clear guidelines and expectations, a BPA can help to mitigate the risks associated with third-party vendors and partners.

Third-party risk management through, Vendor monitoring

Third-party risk management is the process of identifying, assessing, and mitigating risks associated with third-party vendors. Vendor monitoring is a key component of third-party risk management, which involves ongoing monitoring of vendors to ensure they continue to meet security requirements. This can be compared to a homeowner who hires a contractor to build an addition to their house. The homeowner would want to ensure that the contractor is licensed, insured, and has a good reputation before hiring them. Once the contractor is hired, the homeowner would want to monitor their progress to ensure they are building the addition to code and within budget. Similarly, organizations need to ensure that their vendors are meeting security requirements and are not introducing new risks into their environment. Ongoing monitoring of vendors can help organizations identify and address security issues before they become major problems.

Third-party risk management through, Questionnaires

Third-party risk management is a crucial aspect of cybersecurity. It involves assessing and managing the risks associated with third-party vendors and suppliers that have access to an organization's sensitive data. One way to manage third-party risks is through the use of questionnaires. Questionnaires are like a survey that is used to gather information about the third-party vendor's security practices, policies, and procedures. It is like a checklist that helps organizations to identify potential risks and vulnerabilities that may exist in the vendor's environment. By using questionnaires, organizations can evaluate the security posture of their third-party vendors and suppliers and take appropriate measures to mitigate any risks that may be identified.

Third-party risk management through, Rules of engagement

Third-party risk management is the process of identifying, assessing, and mitigating risks associated with third-party vendors. It involves establishing rules of engagement that outline the expectations and responsibilities of both parties. This can be compared to a game of chess, where each player has their own set of pieces and moves, but must also anticipate and respond to the moves of their opponent. Similarly, third-party risk management requires both parties to understand their own strengths and weaknesses, as well as those of their counterpart, in order to effectively manage risks and achieve their objectives. Rules of engagement serve as a framework for this process, providing guidelines for communication, collaboration, and conflict resolution. By following these rules, both parties can work together to achieve their goals while minimizing the risks associated with third-party relationships.

Compliance reporting

Compliance reporting refers to the process of documenting and reporting on an organization's adherence to relevant laws, regulations, and industry standards. It involves collecting and analyzing data to ensure that the organization is meeting its compliance obligations and identifying areas where improvements can be made. Compliance reporting can be compared to a report card for a student, where the student's grades reflect their performance in different subjects. Similarly, compliance reporting provides a snapshot of an organization's compliance posture and helps stakeholders understand how well the organization is meeting its obligations.

Internal Compliance reporting

Internal compliance reporting is the process of providing reports about corporate compliance to ensure that an organization is meeting its regulatory obligations. Compliance reports come in different shapes and sizes, depending on the subject matter, and can take any form and structure that makes the most sense for the organization's needs. An analogy for internal compliance reporting is a health check-up. Just as a health check-up provides a report on an individual's health status, internal compliance reporting provides a report on an organization's compliance status. The report should be concise, use clear language and sentence structure, include an executive summary, list action items or timelines for improvement, and state any necessary action from executives or the board. The report should also anticipate the reality of the organization's compliance status and be written in such a way that its readers can put the report to good use.

External Compliance reporting

External compliance reporting refers to the process of reporting an organization's compliance with external regulations, standards, and laws to external entities such as regulatory bodies, auditors, or customers. It is similar to a student submitting a report card to their parents or a company submitting a financial report to its shareholders. Just as a report card shows a student's academic performance, external compliance reporting shows an organization's adherence to external regulations and standards. This process helps to ensure that the organization is operating within legal and ethical boundaries and can help to build trust with external stakeholders.

Consequences of non-compliance such as, Fines

Non-compliance with security regulations can have serious consequences, including fines. Fines are like speeding tickets - if you break the rules, you have to pay a penalty. In the case of non-compliance with security regulations, the penalty can be a significant amount of money. For example, if a company fails to comply with the General Data Protection Regulation (GDPR), they can be fined up to 4% of their annual global revenue or $22.3 million, whichever is greater. This is a substantial amount of money that can have a significant impact on a company's finances. Therefore, it is important for organizations to take security compliance seriously and ensure that they are following all relevant regulations to avoid these fines.

Consequences of non-compliance such as, Sanctions

Non-compliance with security regulations can have serious consequences, including sanctions. Sanctions can be thought of as penalties or punishments for failing to comply with regulations. Just as a driver who fails to follow traffic laws may receive a ticket or have their license suspended, an organization that fails to comply with security regulations may face fines, legal action, or other penalties. These sanctions can have significant financial and reputational impacts on the organization, just as a traffic ticket can have financial and legal consequences for a driver. Therefore, it is important for organizations to take security compliance seriously and ensure that they are following all relevant regulations to avoid these potential consequences.

Consequences of non-compliance such as, Reputational damage

Non-compliance with security policies and regulations can have serious consequences, including reputational damage. This can be compared to a person who has a reputation for being trustworthy and reliable suddenly being caught in a lie or breaking a promise. The damage to their reputation can be long-lasting and difficult to repair. Similarly, if an organization is known for being secure and trustworthy with sensitive information, a breach or violation of security policies can cause significant reputational damage. This can lead to a loss of trust from customers, partners, and stakeholders, which can have a negative impact on the organization's bottom line.

Consequences of non-compliance such as, Loss of license

Non-compliance with security regulations can have serious consequences, including the loss of license. This is similar to a driver's license being revoked for repeatedly breaking traffic laws. Just as a driver who ignores traffic laws puts themselves and others at risk, an organization that fails to comply with security regulations puts sensitive information and systems at risk. The loss of license can be a severe penalty, and it can have long-lasting effects on an organization's reputation and ability to operate effectively. Therefore, it is essential for organizations to take compliance seriously and ensure that they are following all relevant regulations and guidelines.

Consequences of non-compliance such as, Contractual impacts

Non-compliance with security regulations can have serious consequences, including contractual impacts. This means that if an organization fails to comply with security requirements, it may be in breach of contract with its customers or partners. This can be compared to a driver who fails to follow traffic laws and causes an accident. Just as the driver may be held liable for damages resulting from the accident, an organization that fails to comply with security regulations may be held liable for any damages or losses suffered by its customers or partners as a result of a security breach. Therefore, it is important for organizations to take security compliance seriously and ensure that they are meeting all relevant requirements.

Compliance monitoring through, Due diligence/care

Compliance monitoring is the process of ensuring that an organization is following the relevant laws, regulations, and policies. Due diligence/care is the process of taking reasonable steps to avoid harm to others. An analogy for compliance monitoring through due diligence/care is a driver who follows traffic laws and takes reasonable precautions to avoid accidents. The driver is monitoring their compliance with traffic laws and taking due diligence/care to avoid causing harm to others. Similarly, an organization can monitor its compliance with laws and regulations and take due diligence/care to avoid causing harm to its customers, employees, and other stakeholders.

Compliance monitoring through, Attestation and acknowledgement

Compliance monitoring is the process of ensuring that an organization is following the relevant laws, regulations, and policies. Attestation is a form of compliance monitoring where an individual or organization confirms that they are following the required policies and procedures. It is similar to a student signing an attendance sheet to confirm that they were present in class. Acknowledgement is another form of compliance monitoring where an individual or organization acknowledges that they have received and understood the relevant policies and procedures. It is similar to signing a contract to confirm that you have read and understood the terms and conditions. Both attestation and acknowledgement are important in ensuring that an organization is compliant with the relevant laws, regulations, and policies.

Compliance monitoring through, Internal and external

Compliance monitoring is the process of ensuring that an organization is following the relevant laws, regulations, and policies. Internal compliance monitoring involves monitoring the organization's own policies and procedures to ensure that they are being followed. This is similar to a teacher monitoring their own classroom to ensure that their students are following the rules. External compliance monitoring involves monitoring the organization's compliance with external laws and regulations. This is similar to a school principal monitoring the teacher's classroom to ensure that they are following the school's policies and procedures.

Compliance monitoring through, Automation
Compliance monitoring is the process of ensuring that an organization is following the relevant laws, regulations, and policies. It involves monitoring and analyzing the organization's activities to identify any non-compliance issues and taking corrective actions to address them. Compliance monitoring can be compared to a traffic cop who ensures that drivers follow the rules of the road. Automation, on the other hand, is the use of technology to perform tasks that would otherwise be done manually. In the context of compliance monitoring, automation can be used to streamline the process of monitoring and analyzing an organization's activities. It can be compared to a self-driving car that uses sensors and algorithms to navigate the road without human intervention. By automating compliance monitoring, organizations can reduce the risk of human error and ensure that they are always in compliance with the relevant laws, regulations, and policies.

Cyber Compliance and Privacy
Cyber compliance and privacy refer to the measures taken to ensure that organizations comply with laws, regulations, and industry standards related to cybersecurity and data privacy. It is similar to following traffic rules while driving a car. Just as traffic rules are in place to ensure the safety of drivers and passengers, cyber compliance and privacy regulations are in place to protect sensitive information and prevent cyber attacks. Organizations must implement security controls, such as firewalls and encryption, to safeguard data and ensure that they are in compliance with relevant laws and regulations. Failure to comply with these regulations can result in legal and financial consequences, just as breaking traffic rules can result in fines or even accidents.

Cyber Compliance surrounding privacy and Legal implications

Cybersecurity professionals must be aware of applicable laws and policies, including principles of governance, risk, and compliance. Compliance regulations and security concerns are wrapped around compliance in almost every part of every organization. Failure to comply with these regulations can result in fines, civil penalties, and even jail time. The General Data Protection Regulation (GDPR) is a set of rules and regulations that allows someone in the EU to control what happens with their private information. The new CompTIA Security+ emphasizes hands-on practical skills, ensuring IT pros are prepared to solve a wider variety of cybersecurity issues and to proactively prevent the next cyberattack. Cyber compliance is like following traffic laws while driving. Just as traffic laws are in place to ensure the safety of drivers and pedestrians, cyber compliance regulations are in place to ensure the safety and privacy of individuals' data. Failure to comply with these regulations can result in legal implications, just as breaking traffic laws can result in legal consequences. Therefore, it is important for organizations to understand and comply with these regulations to avoid legal issues and protect the privacy of their customers' data.

Cyber Compliance surrounding privacy and Legal implications at the Local/regional level

The legal implications at the local/regional level refer to the laws and regulations that are specific to a particular area or region. These laws may differ from one region to another, just as the rules of a game may differ depending on where it is played. For example, just as a basketball game may have different rules in the United States compared to Europe, the laws governing data privacy and security may differ between different regions. It is important for organizations to be aware of these differences and ensure that they comply with the relevant laws and regulations in each region where they operate, just as basketball players must follow the rules of the game in each country where they play.

Children's Online Privacy Protection Act (COPPA)

The Children's Online Privacy Protection Act (COPPA) is a law that governs the collection of personal information from children under the age of 13 by online services and websites designed for students under the age of 13 where personal information is collected. COPPA's intent is to safeguard a student's personal information while accessing online services and websites designed for students under the age of 13 where personal information is collected. CompTIA uses a variety of applications and web-based tools to facilitate student learning, and the use of these tools by students under the age of 13 years is governed by COPPA. The notice provided by CompTIA describes how they collect, use, and disclose personal information from their students under the age of 13 in compliance with COPPA.

Payment Card Industry Data Security Standard (PCI DSS)

The Payment Card Industry Data Security Standard (PCI DSS) is a set of security policies and procedures designed to protect credit and payment card data and transactions. It was created in 2004 by five major credit card companies: Visa, Mastercard, Discover, JCB, and American Express, and is administered by the Payment Card Industry Security Standards Council (PCI SSC). The primary goal of PCI DSS is to safeguard and optimize the security of sensitive cardholder data, such as credit card numbers, expiration dates, and security codes. The standard's security controls help businesses minimize the risk of data breaches, fraud, and identity theft. Compliance with PCI DSS also ensures that businesses adhere to industry best practices when processing, storing, and transmitting credit card data, which fosters trust among customers and stakeholders. All merchants and service providers that process, transmit, or store cardholder data must comply with the PCI DSS. The standard provides specific, actionable guidance on protecting payment card data, which can be applied to organizations of any size or type that use any method of processing or storing data. PCI DSS is not a law, and it is enforced through contracts between merchants, acquiring banks that process payment card transactions, and the payment brands.

Health Insurance Portability and Accountability Act (HIPAA)

The Health Insurance Portability and Accountability Act (HIPAA) is a federal law that was enacted in 1996 to establish national standards for protecting individuals' medical records and other personal health information. The HIPAA Privacy Rule sets standards for safeguarding protected health information (PHI) and gives individuals rights over their health information, such as the right to access and correct their records. The rule applies to three types of HIPAA covered entities: health plans, health care clearinghouses, and health care providers that conduct certain health care transactions electronically. HIPAA also includes a Security Rule that protects a subset of information covered by the Privacy Rule. HIPAA-covered entities must comply with the Privacy and Security Rules to protect sensitive patient health information from being disclosed without the patient's consent or knowledge. HIPAA-covered entities include health, dental, vision, and prescription drug insurers, health maintenance organizations (HMOs), Medicare, Medicaid, Medicare+Choice, and Medicare supplement insurers, long-term care insurers (excluding nursing home fixed-indemnity policies), and employer-sponsored group health plans. HIPAA also allows for certain uses and disclosures of PHI without an individual's authorization, such as for public health activities, victims of abuse or neglect or domestic violence, health oversight activities, judicial and administrative proceedings, law enforcement, and research under certain conditions.

Federal Information Security Management Act (FISMA)

The Federal Information Security Management Act (FISMA) is a federal legislation that defines a framework of guidelines and security standards to protect government information and operations. The act was signed into law as part of the Electronic Government Act of 2002 and later updated and amended. FISMA's scope has widened to apply to state agencies that administer federal programs or private businesses and service providers that hold a contract with the U.S. government. FISMA requires federal agencies and others it applies to, to develop, document, and implement agency-wide information security programs that can protect sensitive data. The act assigns responsibilities to various agencies to ensure the security of data. FISMA defines a framework for managing information security that must be followed for all information systems used or operated by a U.S. federal government agency in the executive or legislative branches, or by a contractor or other organization on behalf of a federal agency in those branches. The act requires each federal agency in the US government to develop, document, and implement an agency-wide information security program to protect sensitive data and information systems that support the operations and assets of the agency, including those provided or managed by another agency, third-party vendor, or service provider. FISMA assigns specific responsibilities to federal agencies, the National Institute of Standards and Technology (NIST), and the Office of Management and Budget (OMB) to strengthen information security systems.

General Data Protection Regulation (GDPR)
The General Data Protection Regulation (GDPR) is a policy created by the European Union to address the issue of private information being available on many different websites across the internet. The GDPR is a set of rules and regulations that allows someone in the EU to control what happens with their private information. The regulation allows individuals to understand where their information is stored and it prevents this information from being exported outside of the European Union. It also puts the control of this data back into the hands of individuals. The GDPR requires every website to provide detailed information about their privacy policy. The GDPR regulations are extensive and complex, and it is important to understand the scope of those if you are planning to collect this type of data on your network. The GDPR applies to all organizations that collect and store data on EU citizens. The GDPR specifies that if data is collected on EU citizens, that data must be stored in the European Union. The GDPR regulations are enforced by the EU and can result in significant fines for non-compliance.

Financial Information
Financial information refers to data related to an organization's financial transactions, such as revenue, expenses, and profits. In the context of cybersecurity, financial information is considered sensitive data that requires protection from unauthorized access, disclosure, and modification. Financial information can be used by attackers to commit fraud, identity theft, or other financial crimes. Therefore, it is essential to implement security controls to protect financial information from unauthorized access, such as access controls, encryption, and monitoring. Organizations should also ensure that their employees are trained to handle financial information securely and that they follow best practices for data protection

Personally Identifiable Information (PII)

Personally Identifiable Information (PII) refers to any data that can be linked to an individual or person. This information includes name, address, telephone number, biometric information, credit card number, social security number, and health records. PII is highly sensitive and must be protected by any organization that holds it. Protected Health Information (PHI) is a type of PII that has a very high level of privacy associated with it, especially in healthcare. One way to protect the privacy of individuals is to obfuscate PII, which limits the exposure of designated PII. PII can be obfuscated by either nullifying or masking. Nullifying PII means returning its value as null, while masking PII means returning a portion of its value with placeholder characters. Organizations should apply appropriate safeguards to protect the confidentiality of PII based on the PII confidentiality impact level. Some PII does not require the same level of protection as others. PII encryption is a crucial aspect of data protection strategy, which involves securing PII data using novel security practices, tools, and methodologies.

Protected Health Information (PHI)

Protected Health Information (PHI) is a term used in the healthcare industry to refer to any information that can be used to identify an individual and is related to their past, present, or future physical or mental health condition, the provision of healthcare to the individual, or the payment for that healthcare. PHI includes information such as a person's name, address, date of birth, social security number, medical history, test results, and insurance information. PHI is subject to strict privacy and security regulations under the Health Insurance Portability and Accountability Act (HIPAA) in the United States. HIPAA requires healthcare providers, health plans, and healthcare clearinghouses to implement administrative, physical, and technical safeguards to protect the confidentiality, integrity, and availability of PHI. In summary, PHI is any information that can be used to identify an individual and is related to their health condition, healthcare provision, or payment for healthcare. It is subject to strict privacy and security regulations under HIPAA.

Cyber Compliance surrounding privacy and Legal implications at the National level

Legal implications at the national level refer to the laws and regulations that govern the use and protection of information and technology assets within a country. These laws are put in place to ensure that individuals and organizations are held accountable for any illegal activities that may occur in the digital space. An analogy to understand this concept is to think of a country as a house, and the laws and regulations as the locks and security systems that protect the house from intruders. Just as locks and security systems are put in place to protect a house, laws and regulations are put in place to protect a country's information and technology assets.

Cyber Compliance surrounding privacy and Legal implications at the Global level

Legal implications at the global level refer to the laws and regulations that govern the use and protection of information and technology across different countries and regions. It is similar to how different countries have different traffic laws that drivers must follow when driving in those countries. Failure to comply with these laws can result in legal consequences, just as violating traffic laws can result in fines or other penalties. In the context of information security, legal implications at the global level can include issues such as data privacy, intellectual property rights, and cybercrime laws. It is important for organizations to understand and comply with these laws to avoid legal and financial repercussions.

Cyber Compliance surrounding the Data subject
Cyber compliance surrounding the data subject refers to the measures taken to ensure that personal data is collected, processed, and stored in accordance with applicable laws and regulations. It involves implementing policies and procedures that protect the confidentiality, integrity, and availability of personal data. An analogy for cyber compliance surrounding the data subject is a bank vault. Just as a bank vault is designed to protect valuable assets, cyber compliance measures are designed to protect personal data. The vault has multiple layers of security, such as locks, alarms, and security cameras, to prevent unauthorized access. Similarly, cyber compliance measures include access controls, encryption, and monitoring to prevent unauthorized access to personal data.

Cyber Compliance surrounding the Controller vs. the processor
In cybersecurity, the controller is the entity that determines the purposes, conditions, and means of the processing of personal data, while the processor is the entity that processes personal data on behalf of the controller. An analogy to understand this relationship is that of a chef and a sous chef. The chef is the controller who decides what dish to prepare, what ingredients to use, and how to cook the dish. The sous chef is the processor who follows the chef's instructions to prepare the dish. In terms of cyber compliance, the controller is responsible for ensuring that the processor complies with data protection regulations and that appropriate security measures are in place to protect personal data. The processor, on the other hand, is responsible for processing personal data only as instructed by the controller and implementing appropriate security measures to protect personal data.

Cyber Compliance surrounding data Ownership
According to the CompTIA Security+ SY0-701 Exam
Objectives document, cyber compliance surrounding
data ownership refers to the policies and procedures
that organizations must follow to ensure that data is
collected, stored, and used in a manner that is
consistent with legal and ethical standards. This
includes ensuring that data is only accessed by
authorized personnel, that it is protected from
unauthorized access or theft, and that it is properly
disposed of when it is no longer needed. An analogy for
data ownership could be a safe deposit box at a bank.
Just as a bank customer owns the contents of their safe
deposit box and the bank is responsible for keeping it
secure, an organization owns its data and is
responsible for keeping it secure and ensuring that it is
used appropriately.

**Cyber Compliance surrounding Data inventory and
retention**
Cyber compliance surrounding data inventory and
retention refers to the policies and procedures that
organizations must follow to ensure that they are
properly managing their data. This includes identifying
all data that is collected, stored, and processed, as well
as determining how long that data should be retained.
An analogy for this process could be organizing a
closet. Just as you would sort through your clothes,
shoes, and accessories to determine what you want to
keep and what you want to get rid of, organizations
must sort through their data to determine what is
necessary to keep and what can be deleted. Once the
data has been sorted, it must be properly labeled and
stored in a way that makes it easy to find and access
when needed. Finally, organizations must determine
how long each type of data should be retained, just as
you might decide to keep your winter coat for several
years but get rid of a shirt that no longer fits. By
following these policies and procedures, organizations
can ensure that they are in compliance with regulations
and best practices for data management.

Cyber Compliance surrounding the Right to be forgotten

The right to be forgotten is a concept that allows individuals to request the removal of their personal data from online platforms. Cyber compliance surrounding the right to be forgotten requires organizations to have policies and procedures in place to ensure that they can comply with such requests. This includes having a process for identifying and removing personal data, as well as ensuring that the data is not stored or shared with third parties. An analogy for this would be a library that has a process for removing books from its shelves upon request. The library must ensure that the book is removed from its catalog and that it is not shared with other libraries or individuals. Similarly, organizations must ensure that personal data is removed from their systems and that it is not shared with other organizations or individuals.

Attestation cyber audits and assessments

Attestation, cyber audits, and assessments are all methods used to evaluate the security posture of an organization. An analogy to understand these methods is to think of them as a health check-up for an individual. Just as a doctor performs a check-up to assess the overall health of a patient, an organization can undergo an attestation, cyber audit, or assessment to evaluate its security posture. Attestation is like a self-assessment where the organization evaluates its own security controls and provides a report to a third-party. A cyber audit is like an external audit where an independent auditor evaluates the organization's security controls and provides a report. An assessment is like a comprehensive health check-up where the organization undergoes a thorough evaluation of its security posture, including its policies, procedures, and technical controls. These methods help organizations identify vulnerabilities and weaknesses in their security posture and provide recommendations for improvement.

Internal cyber audits and assessments and Compliance

Internal cyber audits and assessments are processes that organizations use to evaluate their cybersecurity posture and identify potential vulnerabilities. These assessments are similar to a health checkup that a person undergoes to identify any health issues and take corrective measures. Similarly, internal cyber audits and assessments help organizations identify any weaknesses in their cybersecurity defenses and take corrective measures to address them. Compliance, on the other hand, refers to the process of ensuring that an organization adheres to relevant laws, regulations, and industry standards. Compliance is similar to following traffic rules while driving a car. Just as following traffic rules helps ensure the safety of drivers and passengers, compliance helps ensure that organizations operate within legal and ethical boundaries. Internal cyber audits and assessments and compliance are critical components of an organization's cybersecurity strategy and help ensure that the organization is adequately protected against cyber threats.

Internal cyber audits and assessments and an Audit committee

Internal cyber audits and assessments are important for organizations to identify and manage cyber risks. They provide a holistic approach to identifying where an organization may be vulnerable to cyber threats and help in assessing the organization's capabilities in managing the associated risks. An analogy to this could be a regular health check-up that helps in identifying potential health risks and taking preventive measures to manage them. Similarly, internal cyber audits and assessments help organizations to identify potential cyber risks and take preventive measures to manage them. An Audit committee is a group of individuals responsible for overseeing an organization's financial reporting and disclosure processes. They are responsible for ensuring that the organization's financial statements are accurate and complete and that the organization is complying with relevant laws and regulations. An analogy to this could be a group of referees in a sports game who ensure that the game is played fairly and according to the rules. Similarly, an Audit committee ensures that the organization is following the rules and regulations and that the financial statements are accurate and complete.

Internal cyber audits and assessments using Self-assessments

Self-assessments are a type of internal cyber audit and assessment that organizations can use to evaluate their cybersecurity posture. A self-assessment is a management tool that evaluates the overall performance of a company and helps to identify areas that need improvement. An analogy to this could be a self-checkup that individuals do to evaluate their health and identify areas that need improvement. Similarly, self-assessments help organizations to evaluate their cybersecurity posture and identify areas that need improvement. Self-assessments can be less formal than third-party assessments, but they can still add considerable value, particularly if an organization has never done any form of audit before. Self-assessments can help organizations to identify gaps in their cybersecurity framework and policies and develop a better picture of their security posture and its overall effectiveness.

External cyber audits and assessments

External cyber audits and assessments are processes that evaluate an organization's cybersecurity posture from an external perspective. It is similar to a health checkup where a doctor examines a patient to identify any health issues. In the same way, external cyber audits and assessments are conducted by third-party cybersecurity experts to identify vulnerabilities and weaknesses in an organization's security systems. These audits and assessments can help organizations identify areas where they need to improve their security posture and take corrective actions to mitigate risks. Just as a doctor's checkup can help prevent future health problems, external cyber audits and assessments can help prevent future cyber attacks.

Regulatory External cyber audits and assessments

Regulatory external cyber audits and assessments refer to the process of evaluating an organization's cybersecurity measures by an external entity to ensure compliance with regulatory requirements. This process is similar to a health inspection at a restaurant, where an external inspector evaluates the restaurant's compliance with health and safety regulations. The inspector checks for any potential violations and provides recommendations for improvement. Similarly, external cyber audits and assessments evaluate an organization's cybersecurity posture, identify potential vulnerabilities, and provide recommendations for improvement to ensure compliance with regulatory requirements.

Examinations External cyber audits and assessments

Examinations, external cyber audits, and assessments are all methods used to evaluate the security posture of an organization's information systems. These evaluations are conducted by external entities, such as third-party auditors, to identify vulnerabilities and potential threats to the organization's information systems. An analogy for this process could be a home security system. Just as a homeowner may hire a security company to evaluate their home's security system and identify potential vulnerabilities, an organization may hire an external entity to evaluate their information systems and identify potential security risks. The results of these evaluations can then be used to improve the organization's security posture and reduce the risk of a cyber attack.

External cyber audits and assessments Assessment

External cyber audits and assessments are a way to evaluate the security posture of an organization by an external entity. It is similar to a health check-up that a person undergoes to assess their overall health and identify any potential health issues. In the same way, an external cyber audit and assessment evaluates an organization's security controls, policies, and procedures to identify any vulnerabilities or weaknesses that could be exploited by attackers. The assessment is conducted by an external entity, such as a third-party auditor, to provide an unbiased evaluation of the organization's security posture. The results of the assessment can be used to identify areas that need improvement and to develop a plan to address any identified weaknesses.

Independent third-party audit through External cyber audits and assessments

An independent third-party audit is a process of evaluating an organization's cybersecurity posture by an external entity. This audit is conducted by a third-party that is not affiliated with the organization being audited. It is similar to a homeowner hiring a professional home inspector to evaluate the condition of their home. The inspector will evaluate the home's structure, electrical, plumbing, and other systems to identify any issues that need to be addressed. Similarly, an external cyber audit evaluates an organization's cybersecurity systems, policies, and procedures to identify any vulnerabilities or weaknesses that could be exploited by attackers. The audit provides an objective assessment of the organization's cybersecurity posture and helps identify areas that need improvement.

Penetration testing

Penetration testing is a security assessment technique that involves simulating an attack on a computer system or network to identify vulnerabilities that could be exploited by attackers. It is like a burglar attempting to break into a house to find weaknesses in the security system. The goal of penetration testing is to identify security weaknesses before they can be exploited by attackers, and to provide recommendations for improving the security of the system or network. Penetration testing can be performed manually or using automated tools, and can be conducted internally or externally. It is an important part of a comprehensive security program and helps organizations to identify and mitigate security risks.

Physical Penetration testing

Physical penetration testing is a type of security testing that aims to validate physical security controls and provide recommendations for areas of improvement. It involves an ethical hacker or social engineer attempting to gain entry to a physical location, such as an office building, warehouse, storage facility, or data center, without causing actual damage to the location. An analogy for physical penetration testing is a burglar attempting to break into a house to test its security measures. The goal is to identify weaknesses in the physical security controls and raise awareness among staff around the risks of social engineering and potential physical attack vectors. The pen tester may use techniques such as social engineering, tailgating, or deception to gain access to sensitive areas. The results of the test are recorded with hidden cameras and shared in a report with remediation recommendations to improve security.

Offensive Penetration testing
Offensive penetration testing is a proactive approach to cybersecurity that involves simulating an attack on a system or network to identify vulnerabilities and weaknesses before they can be exploited by real attackers. It is like a security drill where the security team tries to break into their own system to see how well it is protected and to identify any weaknesses that need to be addressed. The goal of offensive penetration testing is to find and fix vulnerabilities before they can be exploited by attackers, thereby improving the overall security posture of the system or network.

Defensive Penetration testing
Defensive Penetration Testing is a security testing technique that involves simulating an attack on a system or network to identify vulnerabilities and weaknesses that could be exploited by attackers. It is like a fire drill for a building, where the security team tests the security measures in place to identify any gaps or weaknesses that could be exploited by attackers. Defensive Penetration Testing is conducted by security professionals who use the same tools and techniques as attackers to identify vulnerabilities and weaknesses in the system or network. The goal is to identify these vulnerabilities before attackers can exploit them and to implement measures to mitigate the risks.

Integrated Penetration testing
Integrated Penetration Testing is a security testing methodology that involves simulating a real-world attack on a system or network to identify vulnerabilities and weaknesses. It is like a burglar trying to break into a house to find the weak points in the security system. The goal of Integrated Penetration Testing is to identify and exploit vulnerabilities before attackers can do so, and to provide recommendations for improving the security of the system or network. This methodology involves a combination of automated and manual testing techniques, and it is typically performed by a team of security professionals who have expertise in different areas of security. The results of the testing are used to improve the security posture of the system or network and to ensure that it is protected against real-world attacks.

Known environment Penetration testing

Known environment penetration testing is a type of penetration testing where the tester has prior knowledge of the target system's environment. It is like a burglar who has already been inside a house and knows the layout and security measures. The tester uses this knowledge to simulate an attack on the system and identify vulnerabilities that could be exploited by an attacker. The goal of known environment penetration testing is to identify weaknesses in the system's security measures and provide recommendations for improving them. This type of testing is often used to assess the effectiveness of security controls and to ensure that they are properly configured and functioning as intended.

Partially known environment Penetration testing

Penetration testing is a process of testing the security of a system by simulating an attack on it. In a partially known environment, the tester has some knowledge of the system, but not all of it. This is similar to a burglar who has some information about a house, such as the location of the doors and windows, but not the security system or the layout of the interior. The tester uses this partial knowledge to try to gain access to the system and identify vulnerabilities that could be exploited by an attacker. The goal of penetration testing is to identify weaknesses in the system before they can be exploited by malicious actors.

Unknown environment Penetration testing

Unknown environment penetration testing is a type of penetration testing that is conducted in an environment where the tester has little or no knowledge of the target system. It is similar to exploring a new city without a map or any prior knowledge of the area. The tester must use their skills and experience to identify vulnerabilities and potential attack vectors in the target system. This type of testing is particularly useful for simulating real-world scenarios where an attacker may have limited knowledge of the target system. The goal of unknown environment penetration testing is to identify vulnerabilities and provide recommendations for improving the security posture of the target system.

Reconnaissance Penetration testing

Reconnaissance is the first phase of penetration testing, where the tester gathers information about the target system or network. This information can be used to identify vulnerabilities and potential attack vectors. An analogy for reconnaissance in penetration testing is like a burglar casing a house before attempting to break in. The burglar may observe the house from the outside, look for security cameras, check for unlocked doors or windows, and gather information about the occupants' schedules. Similarly, a penetration tester may use various tools and techniques to gather information about the target system or network, such as scanning for open ports, identifying the operating system and software versions, and searching for publicly available information about the organization. This information can then be used to plan and execute further attacks.

Passive Reconnaissance Penetration testing

Passive reconnaissance is a type of information-gathering technique used in penetration testing. It is like a spy who observes and collects information about a target without being detected. In passive reconnaissance, the attacker tries to gain information about targeted computers and networks without actively engaging with the systems. The purpose is simply to obtain information, rather than to actively exploit the target. The attacker can use various techniques such as observing network traffic, analyzing publicly available information, and social engineering to gather information about the target. Passive reconnaissance is commonly used when preparing for an attack against a target system. It is also used by ethical hackers to carry out attacks against a system to determine its vulnerabilities. The main idea behind passive reconnaissance is to discover as much relevant information as possible about the target organization and its infrastructure without being detected.

Active Reconnaissance Penetration testing

Active reconnaissance is a type of penetration testing that involves actively probing a target system to gather information about it. This can be compared to a burglar who is casing a house before attempting to break in. The goal of active reconnaissance is to identify vulnerabilities in the target system that can be exploited to gain unauthorized access. This can include scanning for open ports, identifying the operating system and software versions running on the target system, and probing for weaknesses in the network infrastructure. The information gathered during active reconnaissance can be used to plan and execute further attacks on the target system.

Implementing security awareness practices with Phishing

Implementing security awareness practices with phishing is like teaching people how to recognize and avoid scams. Just like how people can be tricked into giving away their personal information or money through scams, phishing attacks can trick people into giving away sensitive information or access to their accounts. By implementing security awareness practices, people can learn how to identify phishing emails and avoid falling for them. This can include training on how to spot suspicious emails, how to verify the authenticity of emails, and how to report phishing attempts. Just like how people can learn to recognize and avoid scams, they can also learn to recognize and avoid phishing attacks through security awareness practices.

Implementing security awareness practices with Phishing Campaigns

Implementing security awareness practices with phishing campaigns involves educating employees on how to identify and avoid phishing attacks. This can be compared to teaching people how to recognize counterfeit money. Just as people need to be trained to identify the security features of genuine currency to avoid being scammed, employees need to be trained to recognize the signs of phishing emails to avoid falling victim to cybercriminals. Phishing campaigns can be used to simulate real-world attacks and test employees' ability to identify and report them. By regularly conducting phishing campaigns and providing feedback to employees, organizations can improve their security posture and reduce the risk of successful attacks.

Implementing security awareness practices with Phishing Recognizing a phishing attempt

Phishing is a type of social engineering attack that aims to trick people into revealing sensitive information such as usernames, passwords, and credit card details. It is like a fisherman who uses bait to lure fish into biting the hook. In a phishing attack, the attacker sends an email or message that appears to be from a legitimate source, such as a bank or a social media site, and asks the recipient to click on a link or provide personal information. To recognize a phishing attempt, one should look out for signs such as suspicious URLs, spelling and grammar errors, urgent or threatening language, and requests for personal information. For example, an email that claims to be from a bank but has a URL that does not match the bank's official website is likely a phishing attempt. Similarly, an email that contains spelling and grammar errors or uses urgent or threatening language to pressure the recipient into taking immediate action is also likely a phishing attempt. It is important to be vigilant and cautious when receiving unsolicited emails or messages and to verify the authenticity of the sender and the message before taking any action.

Implementing security awareness practices with Phishing Responding to reported suspicious messages

When responding to reported suspicious messages, it is important to follow a systematic approach to ensure that the threat is properly contained and mitigated. Just like a firefighter responding to a fire, the first step is to assess the situation and determine the extent of the damage. This involves analyzing the message and identifying any potential indicators of compromise. Once the threat has been identified, the next step is to contain it by isolating the affected system or network. This is similar to containing a fire by preventing it from spreading to other areas. Finally, the threat must be eradicated by removing any malicious code or files and restoring the system to a secure state. This is like extinguishing a fire and ensuring that all embers have been put out to prevent it from reigniting.

Implementing security awareness practices to identify Risky Anomalous behavior recognition

Risky anomalous behavior recognition refers to the ability to identify unusual or suspicious behavior that may indicate a security threat. This can be compared to a security guard who is trained to recognize when someone is acting suspiciously in a store or other public place. Just as a security guard may notice someone who is wandering aimlessly, looking around nervously, or acting in an unusual manner, security systems can be designed to recognize patterns of behavior that are out of the ordinary. By identifying these anomalies, security systems can alert administrators to potential security threats and allow them to take action to prevent them.

Implementing security awareness practices to identify Unexpected Anomalous behavior recognition

Unexpected anomalous behavior recognition refers to the ability to detect unusual or abnormal behavior that deviates from the expected or normal behavior. It involves identifying patterns of behavior that are outside the norm and may indicate a security threat. An analogy for this could be a security guard who is trained to recognize suspicious behavior in a shopping mall. The guard is familiar with the normal behavior of shoppers and can quickly identify any behavior that deviates from the norm, such as someone carrying a large bag or acting nervously. Similarly, security systems can be trained to recognize anomalous behavior in computer networks, such as unusual traffic patterns or attempts to access restricted areas. By detecting and responding to anomalous behavior, security systems can help prevent security breaches and protect sensitive data.

Implementing security awareness practices to identify Unintentional Anomalous behavior recognition

Unexpected anomalous behavior recognition is the process of identifying unusual or abnormal behavior that may indicate a security breach or attack. It involves monitoring systems and networks for patterns of activity that deviate from normal behavior and may indicate a security threat. This can be compared to a security guard who is trained to recognize suspicious behavior in a crowded area. For example, if someone is walking around aimlessly, looking nervous, and carrying a large bag, the security guard may become suspicious and investigate further. Similarly, in a computer system, unexpected behavior such as a user logging in from an unusual location, accessing files they don't normally access, or attempting to run unauthorized commands may indicate a security threat and should be investigated further. By identifying and responding to unexpected anomalous behavior, security professionals can help prevent security breaches and protect sensitive data.

Implementing security awareness practices with User guidance and training

Implementing security awareness practices with user guidance and training is an essential aspect of cybersecurity. It involves educating users on how to identify and respond to security threats, such as phishing attacks, malware, and social engineering. This can be compared to teaching someone how to drive a car. Just as a driver needs to be aware of the rules of the road, traffic signals, and potential hazards, users need to be aware of the risks associated with using technology and how to avoid them. By providing users with the necessary knowledge and skills, they can become more proactive in protecting themselves and their organization from cyber threats. This can include training on password management, safe browsing practices, and how to report suspicious activity. Ultimately, implementing security awareness practices with user guidance and training can help to create a culture of security within an organization, where everyone is responsible for protecting sensitive information and preventing cyber attacks.

Implementing security awareness User guidance and training with Policy/handbooks

Implementing security awareness user guidance and training with policy/handbooks is an important aspect of cybersecurity. It is like providing a map and a set of rules to people who are new to a city. Just like a map helps people navigate through the city and avoid getting lost, security policies and handbooks help users navigate through the organization's security protocols and avoid making mistakes that could lead to security breaches. Similarly, just like a set of rules helps people understand what is expected of them and what they should avoid doing, security training and awareness programs help users understand the organization's security policies and procedures and how to follow them. By providing clear guidance and training, organizations can help their users become more aware of security risks and better equipped to protect sensitive information.

Implementing security awareness User guidance and training with Situational awareness

Implementing security awareness user guidance and training with situational awareness involves educating users on how to identify and respond to security threats. It is like teaching someone how to drive a car. Just as a driver needs to be aware of their surroundings and potential hazards on the road, users need to be aware of potential security threats and how to respond to them. This includes training on how to identify phishing emails, how to create strong passwords, and how to report suspicious activity. By providing users with the knowledge and tools to identify and respond to security threats, organizations can reduce the risk of security breaches and protect sensitive information.

Implementing security awareness User guidance and training with Insider threat

Implementing security awareness user guidance and training with insider threat involves educating employees on how to identify and prevent security breaches caused by insiders. This can be compared to teaching people how to identify and prevent theft in their homes. Just as people can install locks, alarms, and cameras to protect their homes from burglars, organizations can implement security measures such as access controls, monitoring, and incident response plans to protect their data from insider threats. However, just as people need to be aware of the signs of suspicious activity and take precautions to prevent theft, employees need to be trained to recognize the signs of insider threats and take appropriate action to prevent data breaches. This can include reporting suspicious behavior, following security policies and procedures, and participating in security awareness training programs.

Implementing security awareness User guidance and training with Password management

Implementing security awareness user guidance and training with password management involves educating users on how to create and manage strong passwords, as well as how to recognize and avoid common password-related attacks such as phishing and brute-force attacks. This can be compared to teaching someone how to lock their front door and keep their key safe. Just as a person would be taught to use a strong lock and key to protect their home, users must be taught to use strong passwords and keep them safe to protect their digital assets. Additionally, users must be trained to recognize and avoid common password-related attacks, just as they would be taught to recognize and avoid common burglary tactics. By implementing security awareness user guidance and training with password management, organizations can help ensure that their users are equipped with the knowledge and skills necessary to protect their digital assets from unauthorized access.

Implementing security awareness User guidance and training with Removable media and cables

Implementing security awareness user guidance and training with removable media and cables involves educating users on how to properly handle and secure removable media and cables to prevent security breaches. This can be compared to teaching someone how to properly handle a sharp knife in the kitchen. Just as a sharp knife can be dangerous if not handled properly, removable media and cables can pose a security risk if not used correctly. Users should be trained on how to properly store and transport removable media, such as USB drives, and how to securely dispose of them when they are no longer needed. They should also be taught how to identify and report suspicious cables or devices that may be used for unauthorized access or data theft. By providing security awareness training and guidance, organizations can help prevent security incidents and protect sensitive information.

Implementing security awareness User guidance and training with Social engineering

Implementing security awareness user guidance and training with social engineering involves educating users on how to identify and avoid social engineering attacks. Social engineering is like a con artist who tricks people into giving them sensitive information or access to secure systems. Just as a person can learn to recognize a con artist's tactics and avoid being scammed, users can be trained to recognize social engineering attacks and avoid falling victim to them. This involves providing users with guidance on how to identify suspicious emails, phone calls, or other forms of communication, as well as training on how to respond to these situations. By implementing security awareness user guidance and training with social engineering, organizations can help prevent security breaches and protect sensitive information.

Implementing security awareness User guidance and training with Operational security

Implementing security awareness user guidance and training with operational security is an essential aspect of securing an organization's information systems. It involves educating employees on security policies, procedures, and best practices to ensure that they understand their roles and responsibilities in maintaining the security of the organization's assets. This can be compared to teaching someone how to drive a car. Just as a driver needs to be aware of traffic rules, road signs, and safe driving practices to avoid accidents, employees need to be aware of security policies, procedures, and best practices to avoid security incidents. By providing security awareness training, employees can learn how to identify and report security incidents, protect sensitive information, and prevent security breaches. This, in turn, helps to create a culture of security within the organization and reduces the risk of security incidents.

Implementing security awareness User guidance and training with Hybrid/remote work environments

Implementing security awareness user guidance and training with hybrid/remote work environments involves educating employees on the best practices for maintaining security while working remotely. This can be compared to teaching someone how to drive a car. Just as a driver needs to be aware of the rules of the road and how to operate a vehicle safely, remote workers need to be aware of the risks associated with working outside of a traditional office environment and how to protect sensitive information. Security awareness training can include topics such as password management, phishing scams, and the use of secure networks and devices. By providing employees with the knowledge and tools they need to work securely, organizations can reduce the risk of data breaches and other security incidents.

Implementing security awareness practices with Reporting and monitoring

Implementing security awareness practices with reporting and monitoring is like having a neighborhood watch program. Just as a neighborhood watch program involves community members looking out for each other and reporting any suspicious activity to the authorities, implementing security awareness practices involves educating employees about security risks and encouraging them to report any suspicious activity to the IT department. Monitoring the network for unusual activity is like having security cameras installed in the neighborhood to detect any unusual activity. By implementing security awareness practices with reporting and monitoring, organizations can create a culture of security where everyone is responsible for keeping the network safe and secure.

Implementing security awareness Reporting and monitoring with Initial training

Implementing security awareness, reporting, and monitoring with initial training is like building a security system for a house. The initial training is like installing locks on the doors and windows, and teaching the family members how to use them. Security awareness is like reminding the family members to lock the doors and windows when they leave the house. Reporting is like having a security camera that records any suspicious activity, and monitoring is like having a security guard who watches the camera footage and alerts the family members if there is any potential threat. By implementing security awareness, reporting, and monitoring with initial training, an organization can create a culture of security where employees are aware of potential threats and know how to respond to them, and the organization can detect and respond to security incidents in a timely manner.

Implementing security awareness Reporting and monitoring with Recurring training

Implementing security awareness, reporting, and monitoring with recurring training is like building a strong immune system for an organization. Just as a healthy immune system can detect and fight off harmful viruses and bacteria, a well-implemented security awareness program can help an organization detect and prevent security threats. Regular training and awareness programs can help employees recognize and report suspicious activities, while monitoring and reporting mechanisms can help identify and respond to security incidents. By implementing these measures, an organization can build a strong defense against potential security threats and minimize the impact of any incidents that do occur.

Development security awareness practices
Development security awareness practices refer to the measures taken to ensure that security is integrated into the software development process from the beginning. It involves creating a culture of security awareness among developers and other stakeholders involved in the software development process. This can be compared to building a house with a strong foundation. Just as a house with a strong foundation is less likely to collapse, software developed with security in mind from the beginning is less likely to be vulnerable to attacks. Development security awareness practices include training developers on secure coding practices, conducting security reviews of code, and implementing security testing throughout the development process. By integrating security into the development process, organizations can reduce the risk of security breaches and ensure that their software is secure from the ground up.

Execution of security awareness practices
Security awareness practices are the measures taken to educate and train individuals on how to identify and respond to security threats. It involves creating a culture of security awareness in an organization by providing regular training and awareness programs to employees. This is similar to teaching people how to drive a car. Just as driving requires knowledge of traffic rules, road signs, and safe driving practices, security awareness requires knowledge of security policies, procedures, and best practices. Just as a driver must be aware of their surroundings and anticipate potential hazards, security awareness requires individuals to be vigilant and identify potential security threats. By implementing security awareness practices, organizations can reduce the risk of security incidents and protect their assets.

Ports and Protocols You'll Encounter

Well-known/System Ports are a range of port numbers from 0 to 1023 that are reserved for specific applications or services. These ports are also known as system ports because they are used by system processes that provide widely used types of network services. Examples of well-known ports include port 21 for FTP, port 22 for SSH, port 23 for Telnet, port 25 for SMTP, port 53 for DNS, port 80 for HTTP, and port 443 for HTTPS. These ports are assigned by the Internet Assigned Numbers Authority (IANA) and are used by transport protocols (TCP, UDP, DCCP, SCTP) to identify an application or service. Well-known ports are different from registered ports (1024-49151) and dynamic or private ports (49152-65535), which are used for user applications and temporary or private ports, respectively. On Unix-like operating systems, a process must execute with superuser privileges to be able to bind a network socket to an IP address using one of the well-known ports.

Port number	Service name	Transport protocol	Description
7	Echo	TCP, UDP	Echo service
19	CHARGEN	TCP, UDP	Character Generator Protocol, has severe vulnerabilities and thus is rarely used nowadays
20	FTP-data	TCP, SCTP	File Transfer Protocol data transfer
21	FTP	TCP, UDP, SCTP	File Transfer Protocol command control
22	SSH/SCP /SFTP	TCP, UDP, SCTP	Secure Shell, secure logins, file transfers (scp, sftp), and port forwarding
23	Telnet	TCP	Telnet protocol, for unencrypted text communications

25	SMTP	TCP	Simple Mail Transfer Protocol, used for email routing between mail servers
42	WINS Replicatio n	TCP, UDP	Microsoft Windows Internet Name Service, vulnerable to attacks on a local network
43	WHOIS	TCP, UDP	Whois service, provides domain-level information
49	TACACS	UDP; can also use TCP but not necessarily on port 49	Terminal Access Controller Access-Control System, provides remote authentication and related services for network access
53	DNS	TCP, UDP	Domain Name System name resolver
67	DHCP/B OOTP	UDP	Dynamic Host Configuration Protocol and its predecessor Bootstrap Protocol Server; server port
68	DHCP/B OOTP	UDP	Dynamic Host Configuration Protocol and its predecessor Bootstrap Protocol Server; client port
69	TFTP	UDP	Trivial File Transfer Protocol

70	Gopher	TCP	Gopher is a communication protocol for distributing, searching, and retrieving documents in Internet Protocol (IP) networks
79	Finger	TCP	Name/Finger protocol and Finger user information protocol, for retrieving and manipulating user information
80	HTTP	TCP, UDP, SCTP	Hypertext Transfer Protocol (HTTP) uses TCP in versions 1.x and 2. HTTP/3 uses QUIC, a transport protocol on top of UDP
88	Kerberos	TCP, UDP	Network authentication system
102	Microsoft Exchange ISO-TSAP	TCP	Microsoft Exchange ISO Transport Service Access Point (TSAP) Class 0 protocol
110	POP3	TCP	Post Office Protocol, version 3 (POP3)
113	Ident	TCP	Identification Protocol, for identifying the user of a particular TCP connection
119	NNTP (Usenet)	TCP	Network News Transfer Protocol

123	NTP	UDP	Network Time Protocol
135	Microsoft RPC EPMAP	TCP, UDP	Microsoft Remote Procedure Call (RPC) Endpoint Mapper (EPMAP) service, for remote system access and management
137	NetBIOS-ns	TCP, UDP	NetBIOS Name Service, used for name registration and resolution
138	NetBIOS-dgm	TCP, UDP	NetBIOS Datagram Service, used for providing access to shared resources
139	NetBIOS-ssn	TCP, UDP	NetBIOS Session Service
143	IMAP	TCP, UDP	Internet Message Access Protocol (IMAP), management of electronic mail messages on a server
161	SNMP-agents (unencrypted)	UDP	Simple network management protocol; agents communicate on this port
162	SNMP-trap (unencrypted)	UDP	Simple network management protocol; listens for asynchronous traps
177	XDMCP	UDP	X Display Manager Control Protocol
179	BGP	TCP	Border Gateway Protocol

194	IRC	UDP	Internet Relay Chat
201	AppleTalk	TCP, UDP	AppleTalk Routing Maintenance. Trojan horses and computer viruses have used UDP port 201.
264	BGMP	TCP, UDP	Border Gateway Multicast Protocol
318	TSP	TCP, UDP	Time Stamp Protocol
381	HP Openview	TCP, UDP	HP performance data collector
383	HP Openview	TCP, UDP	HP data alarm manager
389	LDAP	TCP, UDP	Lightweight directory access protocol
411	(Multiple uses)	TCP, UDP	Direct Connect Hub, Remote MT Protocol
412	(Multiple uses)	TCP, UDP	Direct Connect Client-to-Client, Trap Convention Port
427	SLP	TCP	Service Location Protocol
443	HTTPS (HTTP over SSL)	TCP, UDP, SCTP	Hypertext Transfer Protocol Secure (HTTPS) uses TCP in versions 1.x and 2. HTTP/3 uses QUIC, a transport protocol on top of UDP.
445	Microsoft DS SMB	TCP, UDP	Microsoft Directory Services: TCP for Active Directory, Windows shares; UDP for

			Server Message Block (SMB) file-sharing
464	Kerberos	TCP, UDP	For password settings on Kerberos
465	SMTP over TLS/SSL, SSM	TCP	Authenticated SMTP over TLS/SSL (SMTPS), URL Rendezvous Directory for Cisco's Source Specific Multicast protocol (SSM)
497	Dantz Retrospect	TCP, UDP	A software suite for backing up operating systems
500	IPSec / ISAKMP / IKE	UDP	Internet Protocol Security / Internet Security Association and Key Management Protocol / Internet Key Exchange
512	rexec	TCP	Remote Process Execution
513	rlogin	TCP	The Unix program rlogin allows users to log in on another host using a network.
514	syslog	UDP	Syslog Protocol, for collecting and organizing all of the log files sent from the various devices on a network

515	LPD/LPR	TCP	Line Printer Daemon protocol, or Line Printer Remote protocol
520	RIP	UDP	Routing Information Protocol, used to find the optimal path between source and destination networks
521	RIPng (IPv6)	UDP	Routing Information Protocol next generation, the IPv6 compatible version of RIP
540	UUCP	TCP	Unix-to-Unix Copy Protocol
548	AFP	TCP	Apple Filing Protocol
554	RTSP	TCP, UDP	Real Time Streaming Protocol
546	DHCPv6	TCP, UDP	Dynamic Host Configuration Protocol version 6. DHCPv6 Clients listen for DHCPv6 messages on UDP port 546.
547	DHCPv6	TCP, UDP	DHCPv6 Servers and DHCPv6 Relay Agents listen for DHCPv6 messages on UDP port 547.
560	rmonitor	UDP	Remote Monitor
563	NNTP over TLS/SSL	TCP, UDP	Network News Transfer Protocol with encryption and verification
587	SMTP	TCP	For email message submission via

			SMTP
591	FileMaker	TCP	FileMaker Web Companion, the web publishing technology available in FileMaker versions 4-6
593	Microsoft DCOM	TCP, UDP	Distributed Component Object Model (DCOM)
596	SMSD	TCP, UDP	SysMan Station daemon
631	IPP	TCP	Internet Printing Protocol
636	LDAP over TLS/SSL	TCP, UDP	Lightweight Directory Access Protocol over TLS/SSL
639	MSDP (PIM)	TCP	Multicast Source Discovery Protocol, which is part of the Protocol Independent Multicast (PIM) family
646	LDP (MPLS)	TCP, UDP	Label Distribution Protocol, applies to routers capable of Multiprotocol Label Switching (MPLS)
691	Microsoft Exchange	TCP	Microsoft Exchange Routing
860	iSCSI	TCP	Internet Small Computer Systems Interface

873	rsync	TCP	The rsync file synchronization protocol efficiently transfers and synchronizes files between devices and networked computers.
902	VMware Server	TCP, UDP	VMware ESXi, a hypervisor
989	FTPS	TCP	File Transfer Protocol (data) over TLS/SSL
990	FTPS	TCP	File Transfer Protocol (control) over TLS/SSL
993	IMAP over SSL (IMAPS)	TCP	Internet Message Access Protocol over TLS/SSL
995	POP3 over SSL (POP3S)	TCP, UDP	Post Office Protocol 3 over TLS/SSL

Registered Ports are a range of port numbers from 1024 to 49151 that are assigned by the Internet Assigned Numbers Authority (IANA) to specific applications or services. These ports are used by transport protocols (TCP, UDP, DCCP, SCTP) to identify an application or service. Registered ports are also known as user ports because they are assigned to user applications. They are used by applications that are mostly vendor-specific, such as Skype and BitTorrent. Well-known ports (0-1023) are reserved for specific applications or services, while dynamic or private ports (49152-65535) are used for temporary or private ports. The range of registered ports is managed by the IANA, and the registration procedure is defined in document RFC4340, section 19.9. The assignment of a port number does not imply an endorsement of an application or product, and the fact that network traffic is flowing to or from a registered port does not mean that it is "good" traffic. Firewall and system administrators should choose how to configure their systems based on their knowledge of the traffic in question, not whether there is a port number registered or not.

1025	Microsoft RPC	TCP	Microsoft Remote Procedure Call
1026-1029	Windows Messenger	UDP	Windows Messenger popup spam
1080	SOCKS proxy	TCP (or UDP since SOCKS5)	SOCKS stands for Socket Secure. This protocol exchanges network packets between a client and server through a proxy server.
1080	MyDoom	TCP	Computer virus
1194	OpenVPN	TCP, UDP	OpenVPN
1214	KAZAA	TCP	A peer-to-peer file-sharing protocol
1241	Nessus	TCP, UDP	Nessus Security Scanner
1311	Dell OpenMa	TCP	Dell EMC OpenManage

	nage		Server Administrator Web GUI
1337	WASTE	TCP	WASTE peer-to-peer encrypted file-sharing Program
1589	Cisco VQP	TCP, UDP	Cisco VLAN Query Protocol (VQP)
1701	L2TP VPN	TCP	Layer Two Tunneling Protocol Virtual Private Networking
1720	H.323	TCP	H.323 Call Control Signaling, a VoIP call control protocol
1723	Microsoft PPTP	TCP, UDP	Point-to-Point Tunneling Protocol Virtual Private Networking
1725	Steam	UDP	Valve Steam Client uses port 1725
1741	CiscoWorks SNMS 2000	TCP	CiscoWorks Small Network Management Solution web server
1755	MMS	TCP, UDP	Microsoft Media Server
1812	RADIUS	UDP	RADIUS server authentication and authorization
1813	RADIUS	UDP	RADIUS server accounting
1863	(Multiple uses)	TCP, UDP	MSN Messenger, Xbox Live 360
1900	UPnP	UDP	Universal Plug and Play
1985	Cisco HSRP	UDP	Hot Standby Router Protocol
2000	Cisco SCCP	TCP	Skinny Client Control Protocol

2002	Cisco ACS	TCP	Access Control Server
2049	NFS	UDP	Network File Sharing
2082	cPanel	TCP, UDP	cPanel default
2083	radsec, cPanel	TCP, UDP	Secure RADIUS Service (radsec), cPanel default SSL
2100	amiganet fs	TCP	Amiga Network Filesystem
2222	DirectAd min	TCP	Graphical web hosting control panel
2302	Gaming	UDP	The game HALO uses this port extensively
2483	Oracle	TCP, UDP	Oracle database listening for insecure client connections to the listener, replaces port 1521
2484	Oracle	TCP, UDP	Oracle database listening for SSL client connections to the listener
2745	Bagle.C – Bagle.H	TCP	Computer worms
2967	Symante c AV	TCP, UDP	Symantec System Center agent (SSC-AGENT)
3050	Interbase DB	TCP, UDP	Borland Interbase database
3074	XBOX Live	TCP, UDP	Gaming: Xbox LIVE and Games for Windows – Live
3127	MyDoom	TCP	Computer worm
3128	HTTP Proxy	TCP	Common web proxy server ports: 80, 8080, 3128, 6588

3222	GLBP	TCP, UDP	Gateway Load Balancing Protocol
3260	iSCSI Target	TCP, UDP	Microsoft iSCSI Target Server
3306	MySQL	TCP	MySQL database system
3389	RDP	TCP	Windows Remote Desktop Protocol (Microsoft Terminal Server)
3689	DAAP	TCP	Digital Audio Access Protocol, used by Apple's iTunes and AirPort Express
3690	SVN	TCP, UDP	Apache Subversion, a version control system
3724	World of Warcraft	TCP, UDP	Some Blizzard games, Unofficial Club Penguin Disney online game for kids
3784-3785	Ventrilo VoIP	TCP, UDP	Ventrilo's Voice over Internet Protocol program
4333	mSQL	TCP	Mini SQL server
4444	Blaster	TCP, UDP	Computer worm
4500	IPSec NAT Traversal	UDP	Internet Protocol Security Network Address Translation (NAT) Traversal
4664	Google Desktop	TCP	Google Desktop's built-in HTTP server and indexing software

4672	eMule	UDP	Peer-to-peer file-sharing software
4899	Radmin	TCP	Remote computer control software
5000	UPnP	TCP	Universal Plug and Play
5001	iperf	TCP	Tool for measuring TCP and UDP bandwidth performance
5004-5005	RTP, RTSP	UDP	Real-time Transport Protocol, Real Time Streaming Protocol
5050	Yahoo! Messenger	TCP	Instant messaging service from Yahoo
5060	SIP	TCP, UDP	Session Initiation Protocol
5061	SIP-TLS	TCP	Session Initiation Protocol over TLS
5190	(Multiple uses)	TCP, UDP	ICQ, AIM (AOL Instant Messenger), Apple iChat
5222-5223	XMPP	TCP, UDP	Extensible Messaging and Presence Protocol Client Connection; also used in Google Talk, Jabber, Apple iChat, WhatsApp, etc.
5353	MDNS	UDP	Multicast DNS
5432	PostgreSQL	TCP	PostgreSQL database system
5554	Sasser	TCP	Computer worm
5631-	pcAnywh	UDP	Symantec

5632	ere		pcAnywhere
5800	VNC over HTTP	TCP	Virtual Network Computing (VNC)
5900-5999	RFB/VNC Server	TCP, UDP	VNC Remote Frame Buffer RFB protocol
6000	X11	TCP	X Window System protocol for delivering payloads between X clients and servers
6001	X11	UDP	X Window System protocol for delivering payloads between X clients and servers
6112	Diablo	TCP, UDP	Gaming
6129	DameWare	TCP	Remote access software developed by SolarWinds
6257	WinMX	UDP	Windows Music Exchange, peer-to-peer file-sharing freeware
6346-6347	Gnutella2	TCP, UDP	Peer-to-peer network protocol
6379	Redis	TCP	Popular non-relational database management system (NoSql)
6500	GameSpy	TCP, UDP	Gaming
6566	SANE	TCP, UDP	Scanner Access Now Easy
6588	AnalogX	TCP	AnalogX proxy server
6588	HTTP Proxy	TCP	Common web proxy server ports: 80, 8080, 3128, 6588
6665-	IRC	TCP	Internet Relay

6669			Chat
6679, 6697	IRC over SSL	TCP	Internet Relay Chat
6699	Napster	TCP	Peer-to-peer file-sharing application
6881- 6999	BitTorren t	TCP, UDP	BitTorrent uses this range of ports the most often
6891- 6901	Windows Live Messeng er	TCP, UDP	Alternatively: MSN Messenger
6970	Quicktim e	TCP, UDP	QuickTime streaming server
7000	Cassandr a	TCP	Inter-node communication within the cluster on Apache Cassandra
7001	Cassandr a	TCP	SSL-enabled inter-node communication within the cluster on Apache Cassandra
7199	Cassandr a JMX	TCP	Java Management Extensions on Apache Cassandra
7648- 7649	CU- SeeMe	TCP, UDP	Internet video conferencing client made by Cornell University
8000	Internet Radio	TCP	Commonly choice of alternate HTTP port for web applications
8080	HTTP Proxy	TCP	Common web proxy server ports: 80, 8080, 3128, 6588

8086	Kaspersky AV	TCP	Kaspersky AV Control Center
8087	Kaspersky AV	UDP	Kaspersky AV Control Center
8118	Privoxy	TCP	Advertisement-filtering Web proxy
8200	VMware Server	TCP, UDP	VMware vSphere Fault Tolerance
8222	VMware Server	TCP, UDP	VMware Server Management User Interface (insecure Web interface).
8500	(Multiple uses)	TCP, UDP	Adobe ColdFusion, Flight Message Transfer Protocol
8767	Teamspeak	UDP	VoIP communication system for online gaming
8866	Bagle.B	TCP	Computer worm
9042	Cassandra	TCP	Apache Cassandra, a NoSql database
9100	PDL	TCP	PDL Data Stream, used for printing to certain network printers
9101-9103	Bacula	TCP, UDP	For automating backup tasks
9119	MXit	TCP, UDP	MXit Instant Messaging (deprecated)
9800	WebDAV	TCP, UDP	Web-based Distributed Authoring and Versioning, an extension of HTTP
9898	Dabber	TCP	Computer worm (Sasser)
9999	Urchin	TCP, UDP	Urchin Web Analytics

10000	(Multiple uses)	TCP, UDP	Network Data Management Protocol; applications: Webmin, BackupExec, Viatalk; gaming: The Matrix Online, Dungeon Fighter
10161	SNMP-agents (encrypted)	TCP	Simple network management protocol; agents communicate on this port
10162	SNMP-trap (encrypted)	TCP	Simple network management protocol; listens for asynchronous traps
10113	NetIQ	TCP, UDP	NetIQ Endpoint
10114	NetIQ	TCP, UDP	NetIQ Qcheck
10115	NetIQ	TCP, UDP	NetIQ Endpoint
10116	NetIQ	TCP, UDP	NetIQ VoIP Assessor
11371	OpenPGP	TCP, UDP	OpenPGP HTTP Keyserver
12345	NetBus	TCP	NetBus remote administration tool (Trojan horse)
13720-13721	NetBackup	TCP, UDP	NetBackup request daemon
14567	Battlefield	UDP	Gaming
15118	Dipnet/Oddbob	TCP	Trojan horse
19226	AdminSecure	TCP	Panda Software AdminSecure Communication Agent
19638	Ensim	TCP	Ensim Control Panel
20000	Usermin	TCP, UDP	Web email interface for regular non-root

			users
24800	Synergy	TCP, UDP	Keyboard/mouse sharing software
25999	Xfire	TCP	Communication tool for gamers (deprecated)
27015	Half-Life	UDP	Gaming
27017	MongoDB	TCP	NoSql database
27374	Sub7	TCP, UDP	Trojan horse
28960	Call of Duty	TCP, UDP	Gaming
31337	Back Orifice	TCP, UDP	Remote administration tool used for Trojan horses
33434+	traceroute	UDP	Utility for displaying paths and measuring transit delays of packets across a network

Dynamic/Private Ports are a range of port numbers from 49152 to 65535 that are not assigned, controlled, or registered. They are used for temporary or private ports and are also known as private or ephemeral ports. These ports are used by clients and not servers. When a client initiates a connection with a server, it chooses a random port number from this range as the source port. This port number is used to direct traffic back to the client. Dynamic ports are assigned to a process or service at the time the port is needed, usually when the process or service is started. Once the process or service is stopped, the port becomes available again for other processes or services to use. Dynamic ports are different from well-known ports (0-1023) and registered ports (1024-49151), which are reserved for specific applications or services.

Summary List of Ports that are the most likely to appear on any Cyber Certification Exam

Author's Note: *When preparing for a cybersecurity certification exam, it is important to understand commonly used ports and protocols, but it is not necessary to memorize them all. Instead, focus on reviewing and understanding them, and remember that in real-world production environments, you can look up port numbers. It is more likely that you will be given a scenario that describes another aspect of cybersecurity using a port or protocol, and you'll be expected to understand what port or protocol is in the question so that you can answer the underlying scenario question about another security topic. Therefore, it is recommended to focus on ports and protocols as only 10% of your study time while preparing for the exam.*

7	Echo	TCP, UDP	Echo service
20	FTP-data	TCP, SCTP	File Transfer Protocol data transfer
21	FTP	TCP, UDP, SCTP	File Transfer Protocol command control
22	SSH/SCP/SFTP	TCP, UDP, SCTP	Secure Shell, secure logins, file transfers (scp, sftp), and port forwarding

23	Telnet	TCP	Telnet protocol, for unencrypted text communications
25	SMTP	TCP	Simple Mail Transfer Protocol, used for email routing between mail servers
53	DNS	TCP, UDP	Domain Name System name resolver
67	DHCP/BOOTP	UDP	Dynamic Host Configuration Protocol and its predecessor Bootstrap Protocol Server; server port
68	DHCP/BOOTP	UDP	Dynamic Host Configuration Protocol and its predecessor Bootstrap Protocol Server; client port
69	TFTP	UDP	Trivial File Transfer Protocol
80	HTTP	TCP, UDP, SCTP	Hypertext Transfer Protocol (HTTP) uses TCP in versions 1.x and 2. HTTP/3 uses QUIC, a transport protocol on top of UDP
88	Kerberos	TCP, UDP	Network authentication system
110	POP3	TCP	Post Office Protocol, version 3 (POP3)
123	NTP	UDP	Network Time

			Protocol
137	NetBIOS-ns	TCP, UDP	NetBIOS Name Service, used for name registration and resolution
143	IMAP	TCP, UDP	Internet Message Access Protocol (IMAP), management of electronic mail messages on a server
161	SNMP-agents (unencrypted)	UDP	Simple network management protocol; agents communicate on this port
194	IRC	UDP	Internet Relay Chat
389	LDAP	TCP, UDP	Lightweight directory access protocol
443	HTTPS (HTTP over SSL)	TCP, UDP, SCTP	Hypertext Transfer Protocol Secure (HTTPS) uses TCP in versions 1.x and 2. HTTP/3 uses QUIC, a transport protocol on top of UDP.
445	Microsoft DS SMB	TCP, UDP	Microsoft Directory Services: TCP for Active Directory, Windows shares; UDP for Server Message Block (SMB) file-sharing
464	Kerberos	TCP, UDP	For password settings on Kerberos

547	DHCPv6	TCP, UDP	DHCPv6 Servers and DHCPv6 Relay Agents listen for DHCPv6 messages on UDP port 547.
596	SMSD	TCP, UDP	SysMan Station daemon
636	LDAP over TLS/SSL	TCP, UDP	Lightweight Directory Access Protocol over TLS/SSL
1720	H.323	TCP	H.323 Call Control Signaling, a VoIP call control protocol
3389	RDP	TCP	Windows Remote Desktop Protocol (Microsoft Terminal Server)
5060	SIP	TCP, UDP	Session Initiation Protocol
5061	SIP-TLS	TCP	Session Initiation Protocol over TLS

About the Author:

Kie Yavorsky who goes by the name "Yavo" is the creator of Yavoz.tech. He is a cyber security specialist with 14 years of IT experience who served as a Sergeant in the United States Marine Corps from 2009 to 2017, filling cyber security roles including Cyber Chief, Firewall Admin, Network Engineer, Server Admin, Satcom Admin, Radio Admin, Crypto Electronic Key Management System (EKMS) Manager, SharePoint Webmaster, IT Project Manager and Cyber Security Expert. He has been recognized for leading the communication plan of 266th Pope, Pope Francis to the National Capital Region and the 2011 Presidential State of the Union Address, while stationed at Chemical Biological Incident Response force (CBIRF) in Washington DC. Yavo was also recognized during

Operation Key Resolve, Cobra Gold, and other operations in the Asia-Pacific region supporting tens of thousands of users while serving in Okinawa Japan. Yavo then became the Cyber Chief of the infantry battalion 3rd Battalion, 4th Marines. The unit holds the nicknames "Thundering Third"and "Darkside". After the Marine Corps Yavo has received multiple innovation and performance awards in his civilian career serving in roles to include Network Operations Lead in Iwakuni Japan, Lead Network Engineer for Defense Information Systems Agency (DISA), Information System Security Officer (ISSO) for the Nuclear Intercontinental Ballistic Missile (ICBM) Minute Man III program In Ogden Utah, Risk Management Framework (RMF) Security Control Assessor (SCA) for AFRICOM, and Information System Security Officer (ISSO) for EUCOM in Stuttgart Germany. His education includes a Master's Degree in Cybersecurity and Information Assurance from Western Governors University and a Bachelor's Degree in Cyber Security with two concentrations, the first concentration in Information Warfare, and the second concentration in Cyber Connections Management from Norwich University. His industry certifications include the Certified Information Systems Security Professional (CISSP), Certified Ethical Hacker (CEH), CompTIA Cybersecurity Analyst (CySA+), CompTIA Security+, Cisco Certified Network Professional Enterprise (CCNP - Enterprise), Cisco Certified Specialist - Enterprise Core, Cisco Certified Specialist - Enterprise Advanced Infrastructure Implementation, Cisco Certified Network Associate (CCNA) and 44 other IT cyber security training certifications. Yavo is continuously innovating and very passionate about cyber security, leading others, and working as a mentor to aspiring IT professionals.

Made in the USA
Las Vegas, NV
02 December 2023

81966637R00252